THE BEST TEST PREPARATION FOR THE
ADVANCED PLACEMENT EXAMINATION

STATISTICS

Jack J. Berger, M.A.
Adjunct Statistics Professor
Fashion Institute of Technology, New York, NY

Mel H. Friedman, M.S.
Mathematics Consultant
Plainsboro, NJ

Marilyn Greenberger, M.B.A.
Acturial Analyst
The Equitable Life Assurance Society of the U.S.,
New York, NY

George C. Oluikpe, M.A., M.Ed.
Assistant Professor of Mathematics Education
Florida Memorial College, Miami, FL

Michael W. Lanstrum
Mathematics Instructor
Kent State University—Geauga, Burton, OH

Melissa L. Allen
Research Assistant
Department of Experimental Psychology
New York University, New York, NY

Mark Shapiro, M.A.
Adjunct Mathematics Instructor
Capital Community-Technical College, Hartford, CT

Research and Education Association
61 Ethel Road West
Piscataway, New Jersey 08854

The Best Test Preparation for the
ADVANCED PLACEMENT EXAMINATION
IN STATISTICS

Printed in the United States of America

Library of Congress Catalog Card Number 97-65092

International Standard Book Number 0-87891-082-4

Research & Education Association
61 Ethel Road West
Piscataway, New Jersey 08854

REA supports the effort to conserve and
protect environmental resources by
printing on recycled papers.

CONTENTS

About Research & Education Association

Research and Education Association (REA) is an organization of educators, scientists, and engineers specializing in various academic fields. Founded in 1959 with the purpose of disseminating the most recently developed scientific information to groups in industry, government, and universities, REA has since become a successful and highly respected publisher of study aids, test preps, handbooks, and reference works.

REA's Test Preparation series includes study guides for all academic levels in almost all disciplines. Research and Education Association publishes test preps for students who have not yet completed high school, as well as high school students preparing to enter college. Students from countries around the world seeking to attend college in the United States will find the assistance they need in REA's publications. For college students seeking advanced degrees, REA publishes test preps for many major graduate school admission examinations in a wide variety of disciplines, including engineering, law, and medical schools. Students at every level, in every field, with every ambition can find what they are looking for among REA's publications.

Unlike most Test Preparation books that present only a few practice tests which bear little resemblance to the actual exams, REA's series presents tests which accurately depict the official exams in both degree of difficulty and types of questions. REA's practice tests are always based upon the most recently administered exams, and include every type of question that can be expected on the actual exams.

REA's publications and educational materials are highly regarded and continually receive an unprecedented amount of praise from professionals, instructors, librarians, parents, and students. Our authors are as diverse as the subjects and fields represented in the books we publish. They are well-known in their respective fields and serve on the faculties of prestigious universities throughout the United States.

Acknowledgments

In addition to our authors, we would like to thank Dr. Max Fogiel, President, for his overall guidance which has brought this publication to its completion; Stacey A. Daly, Managing Editor, for directing the editorial staff throughout each phase of the project; Nicole Mimnaugh, Project Editor, for coordinating the development of the book; L. Charles Biehl and Diane Yurek for their editorial contributions; and Marty Perzan and Wende Solano for typesetting the book.

INDEPENDENT STUDY SCHEDULE

INDEPENDENT STUDY SCHEDULE FOR THE AP EXAM IN STATISTICS

The following study schedule will help you become thoroughly prepared for the Statistics exam. Although the schedule is designed as a six-week study program, it can be condensed into three weeks if less time is available by combining two weeks into one. Be sure to set aside enough time each day for studying purposes. If you choose the six-week program, you should plan to study for at least one hour per day. If you choose the three-week program, you should plan to study for at least two hours per day. Keep in mind that the more time you devote to studying for the Statistics exam, the more prepared and confident you will be on the day of the exam.

Week	Activity
1	Read and study Chapter 1, which will introduce you to the AP Statistics exam. Then, take and score the practice AP Examination in Statistics Test 1 to determine your strengths and weaknesses. You should have someone with knowledge of statistics score your free response questions. When you grade your exam, you should determine what types of questions cause you the most difficulty, as this will help you determine what review areas to study most thoroughly. For example, if you answer incorrectly a number of questions dealing with hypothesis testing, you should carefully study the chapter five, Statistical Inferences. Begin studying the AP Statistics Review starting with Chapter Two, Exploring Data.
2	Begin carefully reading and studying the review sections in Chapter 3, Planning a Study and Chapter 4, Anticipating Patterns. Make sure to answer all of the drill questions.
3	Begin carefully reading and studying the review section in Chapter 5, Statistical Inferences. Make sure to answer all of the drill questions.
4	Take Practice Tests 2 and 3, and after scoring your exam, review carefully all incorrect answer explanations. If there are any type of questions or particular subjects that seem difficult to you, review those subjects by studying again the appropriate sections of the review chapters.

Week	Activity
5	Take Practice Tests 4 and 5, and after scoring your exam, review carefully all incorrect answer explanations. If there are any type of questions or particular subjects that seem difficult to you, review those subjects by studying again the appropriate sections of the review chapters.
6	Take Practice Test 6, and after scoring your exam, review carefully all incorrect answer explanations. Restudy the section(s) of the review for any area(s) in which you are still weak.

CHAPTER 1
SUCCEEDING IN AP STATISTICS

Chapter 1

SUCCEEDING IN AP STATISTICS

The objective of the book is to prepare you for the Advanced Placement Examination in Statistics by providing you with an accurate representation of the test. To help you prepare for this, we give you reviews and practice tests for the AP Statistics exam.

The book is designed to thoroughly prepare you for this test. Presented is a complete review of the topics covered in the course that cover what you need to know to score well on the test. Six-full length, practice Statistics exams are provided.

Following each practice exam is an answer key and detailed explanations to every question. The explanations not only provide the correct response, but also explain why the remaining answers are not the best choice.

By studying the appropriate review sections, taking the corresponding exams, and studying the answer explanations, you can discover your strengths and weaknesses, and prepare yourself to score well on the AP in Statistics examination.

ABOUT THE ADVANCED PLACEMENT PROGRAM

The Advanced Placement program consists of two components: an AP course and an AP exam. Advanced Placement examinations are offered each May at participating schools and multischool centers throughout the world. The Advanced Placement program is designed to provide high school students with the opportunity to pursue college-level studies while still attending high school. The participating colleges, in turn, grant credit and/or advanced placement to students who do well on the examinaion.

The AP Statistics course is designed to represent the content of a typical, introductory college course in statistics. The full-year course covers the skills and knowledge expected of students in the field of introductory statistics. The course is intended for high school students who wish to complete studies equivalent to a one-semester, non-calculus based college course in statistics.

THE AP STATISTICS EXAM

The AP Statistics Exam is 180 minutes and is divided into two sections:

I.   Multiple Choice (50% of your grade): This 90-minute section is composed of 35 questions designed to test your proficiency in a wide variety of topics. The distribution of topics

II. Free-Response (a combined 50% of your grade): This 90-minute section requires the student to answer five open-ended questions and to complete one investigative task question involving more extended reasoning. Each open-ended question has been created to be answered in approximately 10 minutes. The longer investigative task question has been created to be answered in approximately 30 minutes. The questions require students to relate different content areas as they plan an extensive solution to a statistics or probability problem. Students are expected to use their analytical and organizational skills to formulate cogent answers in writing their responses. It will be expected that the student will show enough of their work that the reader will be able to follow their line of reasoning.

Note that it is not necessary to write out routine statistical calculations that can be done on a calculator. Each student is expected to bring a calculator with statistical capabilities to the examination. The computational capabilities of the calculator should include common univariate and bivariate summaries through linear regression. The graphical capabilities of the calculator should include common univariate and bivariate displays such as boxplots, histograms, and scatterplots. Most graphing calculators on the market are acceptable; non-graphing calculators are only allowed if they have the computational capabilities described previously. The following, however, is not allowed: powerbooks and portable computers, pocket organizers, electronic writing pads, pen input devices, or devices with typewriter-style (QWERTY) keyboards.

ABOUT THE REVIEW SECTIONS

As mentioned earlier, this book has a review chapter for each of the four topics covered on the exam. The following are the four review chapters in this book that cover the topics on the AP Statistics:

- Exploring Data

- Planning a Study

- Anticipating Patterns

- Statistical Inferences

The review chapters provide a thorough discussion of the material tested on the exam. By studying the review chapters and by taking the practice test(s), you can prepare yourself to score high on the AP in Statistics exam.

SCORING THE EXAM

After the May AP administration, a group of college and secondary teachers are brought together in June to grade the exams. These readers are chosen from around the country for their familiarity with the AP program.

The multiple-choice section of the exam is scored by crediting each correct answer with one point and deducting one-fourth of a point for each incorrect answer. Unanswered questions receive neither credit or deduction.

The free-response questions are graded by readers chosen from around the country for their familiarity with the AP Program. Each free-response question is read and scored with the reader providing the score between 0 and 4 (with 0 being the lowest and 4 being the highest). The free-reponse questions are scored based on the statistical knowledge and communication the student used to answer the question . The statistical knowledge criteria includes identifying the important concepts of the problem and demonstrating statistical concepts and techniques that result in a correct solution of the problem. The communication criteria includes an explanation of what was done and why, along with a statement of conclusions drawn. When the free-response questions have been graded by all of the readers, the scores are then converted. The open-ended questions count as 75% of the free-response score; the investigative task question counts as 25%.

SCORING THE MULTIPLE-CHOICE SECTION

For the multiple choice section, use this formula to calculate your raw score:

number   number   raw score
right   wrong   (round to the nearest whole #)

Note: Do not include unanswered questions in the formula.

SCORING THE FREE-RESPONSE QUESTIONS

For the free response section, use this formula to calculate your raw score:

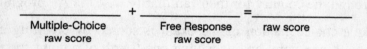

5 open-ended   1 investigative task   raw score
questions (75%)   question (25%)

THE COMPOSITE SCORE

To obtain your composite score, use the following method:

_____ + _____ = _____

Multiple-Choice   Free Response   raw score
raw score   raw score

AP grades are interpreted as follows: 5-extremely well qualified, 4-well qualified, 3-qualified, 2-possibly qualified, and 1-no recommendation.

SCORES THAT RECEIVE COLLEGE CREDIT AND/OR ADVANCED PLACEMENT

Most colleges grant students who earn a 3 or above college credit and/or advanced placement. You should check with your school guidance office about specific college requirements.

STUDYING FOR YOUR AP EXAMINATION

It is never too early to start studying. The earlier you begin, the more time you will have to sharpen your skills. Do not procrastinate! Last-minute studying and cramming is not an effective way to study, since it does *not* allow you the time needed to learn the test material.

It is very important for you to choose the time and place for studying that works best for you. Some students may set aside a certain number of hours every morning to study, while others may choose to study at night before going to sleep. Other students may study during the day, while waiting on a line, or even while eating lunch. Only you can determine when and where your study time will be most effective. However, be consistent and use your time wisely. Work out a study routine and stick to it!

When you take the practice exam(s), try to make your testing conditions as much like the actual test as possible. Turn your television and radio off, and sit down at a quiet table free from distraction. Make sure to time yourself.

Complete the practice test(s), score your test(s) and thoroughly review the explanations to the questions you answered incorrectly. However, do not review too much during any one sitting. Concentrate on one problem area at a time by reviewing the question and explanation, and by studying our review(s) until you are confident that you completely understand the material.

Since you will be allowed to write in your test booklet during the actual exam, you may want to write in the margins and spaces of this book when practicing. However, do not make miscellaneous notes on your answer sheet. Mark your answers clearly and make sure the answer you have chosen corresponds to the question you are answering.

Keep track of your scores! By doing so, you will be able to gauge your progress and discover general weaknesses in particular sections. You should carefully study the reviews that cover the topics causing you difficulty, as this will build your skills in those areas.

To get the most out of your studying time, we recommend that you follow the Study Schedule. It details how you can best budget your time.

TEST-TAKING TIPS

Although you may be unfamiliar with tests such as the Advanced Placement exams, there are many ways to acquaint yourself with this type of examination and help alleviate your test-taking anxieties. Listed below are ways to help yourself become accustomed to the AP exam, some of which may also be applied to other standardized tests.

Become comfortable with the format of the AP Examination in Statistics that you are taking. When you are practicing to take the exam(s), simulate the conditions under which you will be taking the actual test(s). You should practice under the same time constraints as well. Stay calm and pace yourself. After simulating the test only a couple of times, you will boost your chances of doing well, and you will be able to sit down for the actual test much more confidently.

Know the directions and format for each section of the exam. Familiarizing yourself with the directions and format of the different test sections will not only save you time, but will also ensure that you are familiar enough with the AP exam to avoid nervousness (and the mistakes caused by being nervous).

Work on the easier questions first If you find yourself working too long on one question, make a mark next to it in your test booklet and continue. After you have answered all of the questions that you can, go back to the ones you have skipped.

Use the process of elimination when you are unsure of an answer. If you can eliminate three of the answer choices, you have given yourself a fifty-fifty chance of getting the item correct since there will only be two choices left from which to make a guess. If you cannot eliminate at least three of the answer choices, you may choose not to guess, as you will be penalized one-quarter of a point for every incorrect answer. Questions not answered will not be counted.

Be sure that you are marking your answer in the circle that corresponds to the number of the question in the test booklet. Since the multiple-choice section is graded by machine, marking the wrong answer will throw off your score.

CHAPTER 2
EXPLORING DATA

Chapter 2

EXPLORING DATA

EXPLORING UNIVARIATE DATA

Univariate (or one-variable) data are measurements of one quantity, called a variable. The data could be the heights in feet of 15 mountains in North America, or it could be the prices of a white silk blouse in 12 stores in Manhattan. In any case, the data can be presented by listing the observed values of the variable in a column of a chart. It can be displayed graphically by plotting the observed values of the variable in a scatter plot, also known as a dotplot or scatter diagram. Additional forms of graphical displays that involve grouping the data are stemplots and histograms, both of which will be discussed later.

EXAMPLE OF UNIVARIATE DATA, AND ANALYSIS

For example, if the measured quantities for the 37 campgrounds in Long Island and the Hudson Valley of New York State are the basic rates (in dollars), the data would be displayed as the second column in the following chart:

Campground Community	Basic Rate
Brookhaven	14
East Hampton	14
East Islip	11
Fire Island	5
Greenport	20

Greenport Village	12
Hampton Bays	15
Montauk	11
Old Bethpage	9
Riverhead	14
Shirley	14
Smithtown	15
Wading River	10
Ancram	9.5
Austerlitz	15
Bear Mountain	9.5
Carmel	10
Copake Falls	8
Croton	10
Cuddebackville	17
Elizaville	14
Fishkill	12
Florida	18
Ghent	12
Godeffroy	19
Hopewell Junction	11
Middletown	15
Millerton	10.5
Montgomery	9
Otisville	15
Rhinebeck - (1 of 3)	16
Rhinebeck - (2 of 3)	19
Rhinebeck - (3 of 3)	16
Spencertown	20
Staatsburg	10
Stanfordville	9.5
West Copake	15

DISTRIBUTIONS

The distribution of a variable is found by noting for each value the variable takes on, how many times the value occurs. The number of times each value occurs is called the frequency of that value in the distribution. For example, the frequency of the basic rate of 14 is five, because five campgrounds have that basic rate. The frequency of the basic rate of 10.5 is one. A chart of the distribution of basic rates follows:

Basic Rate	Frequency
5	1
8	1
9	2
9.5	3
10	4
10.5	1
11	3
12	3
14	5
15	6
16	2
17	1
18	1
19	2
20	2

This distribution can be displayed graphically in a dotplot (or scatter plot). The x axis (horizontal axis) represents the basic rates and the y axis (vertical axis) represents the frequency. The scatter plot of the distribution of basic rates follows:

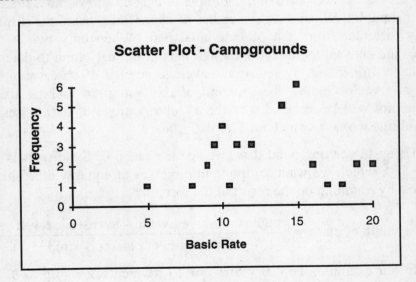

The above scatter plot shows the individual observations graphically. A graphical display allows a distribution to be described in terms of having a center, spread, clusters, gaps, outliers and even an overall shape. Often, these characteristics become clearer when the individual data is grouped into classes and displayed graphically.

A simple method to do this is called a **stemplot**. Each observation is broken up into two pieces called a "stem" for the piece on the left and a "leaf" for the piece on the right. Using the basic rates observations, the first digit is used as the "stem" and the second digit and decimal as the "leaf". The stemplot would be the following:

stem I leaves

0 I 5.0 8.0 9.0 9.0 9.5 9.5 9.5

1 I 0.0 0.0 0.0 0.0 0.5 1.0 1.0 1.0 2.0 2.0 2.0 4.0 4.0 4.0 4.0 4.0 5.0 5.0 5.0
5.0 5.0 5.0 6.0 6.0 7.0 8.0 9.0 9.0

2 I 0.0 0.0

The stemplot allows a quick description of the shape. The above stemplot broke the basic rates data into three classes. It shows that the majority of the basic rates are between 10.0 and 19.9 dollars.

A bar graph made to graphically display the distribution using the breakdown of the data into classes is called a **histogram**. In order to have a histogram that can be useful in determining the shape and other characteristics of a distribution, it is important to choose not too few and not too many classes. This control of the number of classes allows more flexibility than a stemplot. When a large number of classes is chosen, the display is hardly different from that of individual data. When only two or three classes are chosen, there aren't enough bars in the bar graph to determine the shape. In general, by setting the average number of observations in a class at five (or more), the problem of the histogram looking like the scatter plot will be avoided. For the 37 observations of basic rates, this general rule would mean about 37/5 or 7 classes.

Using the campground data, we see the range of basic rates is from $5 to $20, which we want to divide into classes of equal width. This can be done by rounding up the result of the formula:

$$\text{width of class} = \frac{\text{highest observed value} - \text{lowest observed value}}{\text{number of classes desired}}$$

In our example, the $(20 - 5) / 7 = 2^1/_7$, which rounds up to 3. Note that the width for six desired intervals is $(20 - 5) / 6 = 2^1/_2$, which also rounds up to 3. The first class will start with the smallest observed value 5, and since the width is three the next classes will start with 8, 11, 14, and so on. The seventh class starts with 23, which is bigger than any of the observed values. This class will be omitted, leaving six classes. The chart of each class with the frequency or number of observations follows. Note that the observation of 10.5 falls between classes 2 and 3. In this case, observations from 10 to 10.5 count in class 2 and observations from 10.5 to 11 count in class 3. An observation of 10.5 exactly is rounded up and is counted in class 3.

Class	Basic Rates	Frequency
1	5–7	1
2	8–10	10
3	11–13	7
4	14–16	13
5	17–19	4
6	20–22	2

A histogram is a bar graph of the data grouped by class where the classes are along the x axis and height of the bars are frequencies on the y axis. The corresponding histogram would be:

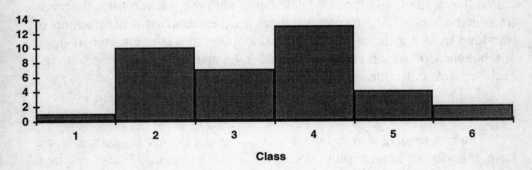

The histogram allows a description of the shape of the distribution. If the left half of the histogram above can be folded vertically to almost overlap over the right half of the histogram, the distribution is **symmetric**. Distributions with a shape like a bell are called bell shaped. Distributions with a long tail to one side only, the left or the right, are called **skewed** to the left or right, respectively. The distribution of basic rates does not appear to fit any of these shapes.

We can see from the histogram the **spread** of the distribution, where the bulk of the distribution is concentrated, is in classes 2, 3 and 4. The spread is at most the **range** of the distribution. The range is defined as the difference of the largest and smallest observations. The concept of range was introduced earlier in the formula for finding the width of an interval in a histogram. To find the width, the range was divided by the number of intervals desired.

The one value in class 1 is an **outlier**, or an observation which does not fit the overall shape of the distribution. The basic rate corresponding to this outlier is five dollars. It is interesting to note that if the outlier 5 is excluded entirely from the data, the histogram would start with class 2. The histogram would then appear skewed to the right, with the bulk of the observations in classes 2, 3, and 4, and a tail in classes 5 and 6 to the right. However, exclusion of an outlier can only be justified when there is reason to believe that it is an erroneous observation. It is necessary to have additional information about the data and how it was gathered in order to be able to determine it is erroneous. In this case, it is not an error, because it is the actual basic rate of a campground in Long Island which can be verified. We can conclude that, when appropriate to do so, the exclusion of an outlier can change the shape of a distribution.

From the histogram, the **center** of the distribution appears to be between classes 3 and 4, which would correspond to basic rates of 13 or 14. This is because half of the distribution appears to be to the left and the other half to the right of this center. The center defined in this way is called the median, and it can be calculated with the median formula given in a later chapter. A different approach to the center of a distribution is provided by using the mean formula, also given in a later chapter. If there are bunches of observations separated by **gaps** with few observations, each separate concentration of observations is called a **cluster**.

SUMMARY—UNIVARIATE DATA

Univariate data can be displayed using the forms of dataplots we have introduced: scatter plots, stemplots and histograms. These displays allow a description of the shape of the distribution. Some examples of shapes to look for are symmetric, skewed, and bell shaped. The center is the x axis value where it appears that half of the observations are to the left and half to the right. The spread is the x axis values, which have the bulk of the observations concentrated in it. A group of observations with similar values is called a cluster. An observation which does not appear to fit the shape of the distribution is called an outlier. Further understanding of the data can help add insight into why the outlier is an important part of the data which cannot be excluded. If the outlier is determined to be the result of an error, it should be excluded, as should other observations which are determined to be erroneous whether it is an outlier or not. Excluding an outlier will have a greater effect on the shape of the distribution than excluding an observation in a cluster for example.

STANDARDIZED SCORES (Z-SCORES)

When observations are given, the mean and standard deviation can be determined using the appropriate formulas in a previous chapter. Consider the following observations of cargo volume for ten 1996 models made by one U.S. manufacturer, given in cubic feet and cubic decimeters with the means and population standard deviations (division by n in the standard deviation formula):

Model	Cargo Volume (cubic feet)	Cargo Volume (cubic decimeters)
A 2 door notchback coupe	13.1	371
C 4 door van std wheelbase	146.2	4,140
C 4 door van long wheelbase	172.3	4,879
I 4 door notchback sedan	16.7	473
N 2 door notchback subcompact	11.8	334
N 2 door notchback subcompact	11.8	334
S 3 door hatchback coupe	11.1	314
S 4 door notchback sedan	15.7	445
V 2 door convertible coupe	11.8	334
V 3 door hatchback coupe	19.0	538
Mean (nearest whole number)	43.0	1,216
Population SD (nearest whole number)	58.0	1,656

We are using the same vehicles, but the results show the means and standard deviations are different. This can be explained by the difference in units. The conversion rate is one cubic foot equals 28.317 cubic decimeters.

A standardized cargo volume can be introduced for each vehicle so that the distribution of cargo volumes will have the same mean and standard deviation no matter which unit is used. The standard that is agreed upon for statistical analysis is a distribution with mean 0 and standard deviation 1. To convert an observation to this standard distribution, its *z-score* is calculated. The formula is:

$$z\text{-score} = \frac{(\text{observation} - \text{mean})}{\text{standard deviation}}$$

For example, for the convertible the z-score calculated from the data in cubic feet is:

$$\frac{11.8 - 43}{58} = -0.54$$

and the z-score calculated from the data in cubic decimeters is:

$$\frac{334 - 1,216}{1,656} = -0.53$$

These z-scores are the same except for rounding errors, which will become apparent when looking at both z-scores for all the observations in the following chart.

Model	Z-score (from cubic feet data)	Z-score (from cubic decimeters data)
A 2 door notchback coupe	−0.52	−0.51
C 4 door van std wheelbase	1.78	1.77
C 4 door van long wheelbase	2.23	2.21
I 4 door notchback sedan	−0.45	−0.45
N 2 door notchback subcompact	−0.54	−0.53
N 2 door notchback subcompact	−0.54	−0.53
S 3 door hatchback coupe	−0.55	−0.54
S 4 door notchback sedan	−0.47	−0.47
V 2 door convertible coupe	−0.54	−0.53
V 3 door hatchback coupe	−0.41	−0.41
Mean (nearest whole number)	0.00	0.00

This chart illustrates that observations will have the same standardized z-scores regardless of the units used in measurement.

The z-score corresponding to the mean by the formula is zero by the z-score formula because the numerator in the formula would be the mean minus the mean or zero. This is confirmed in the chart above.

The z-score can be interpreted as the number of standard deviations away from the mean an individual observation lies. For example, a long wheelbase van will have more cargo space than average. The z-score for a long wheelbase van shows that it is over two standard deviations greater than the mean. A convertible, as expected, has a z-score indicating that its cargo space is over 1/2 standard deviation less than the mean.

CONVERTING FROM Z-SCORES BACK TO THE ORIGINAL UNITS

Given a particular z-score, the corresponding value in the original units can be calculated by using the standardized z-score formula backwards as follows:

x = mean + (z) (standard deviations)

where x is the value in original units, the mean and standard deviation are in the original units, and z is the z-score in standardized units.

For example, the z-score of 1.1 would indicate a vehicle whose cargo volume was 1.1 standard deviations more than the mean.

Using cubic feet the cargo volume would be

$43 + (1.1) (58) = 106.8$ cubic feet.

Using cubic decimeters the cargo volume would be

$1,216 + (1.1) (1,656) = 3,037.6$ cubic decimeters.

SUMMARY—USING Z-SCORES

Z-scores enable the statistician to describe data in terms of how many standard deviations each observation is from the mean of the distribution. Such a description is independent of the unit used to measure the data.

An example of the usefulness of standardized z-scores is the following. Two different students taking different standardized tests like the SAT and ACT are being compared. Such comparisons are made by university admission offices. A direct comparison would be misleading, because the tests are scored on different scales (i.e. the units are different). However, if the mean and standard deviation of the scores for each test were known, the scores could be standardized and compared. For example, if it was known that the mean of the SAT math scores was 500 with a standard deviation of 100, a score of 590 would have a 0.9 standardized z-score. A similar calculation could be performed with the ACT score and information about the ACT

mean and standard deviation. Then, the two standardized z-scores could be compared directly.

ADDITIONAL CONSIDERATIONS IN THE USE OF Z-SCORES

We have just seen that the z-score is independent of the unit used to measure the data. However, there still are situations where z-scores are not appropriate for comparison. Consider high school average as a factor in the admissions decision. Admission offices know that it is important to know a student gets good grades in classroom situations, in addition to their national test scores. Different high schools across the country have different grading systems and offer different qualities of education to different pools of students entering the high schools. These differences make it difficult to compare high school averages for students from different high schools. Use of z-scores will not solve this. Use of z-scores will allow different grading systems, for example 0–100 and 0.0–4.0, to be compared. However, the differences in the qualities of education and student pools between different high schools will make comparing the z-scores like "comparing apples and oranges".

Returning to the SAT/ACT example, before a comparison of z-scores is made, it needs to be determined if the exams test basically the same knowledge and if the pools of students taking each exam are basically the same. If a determination is made that they are basically the same, the z-scores can be compared. Otherwise, once again we will have "apples and oranges".

EXPLORING BIVARIATE DATA

EXAMPLE OF BIVARIATE DATA AND ANALYSIS

Bivariate data, or two-variable data, are measurements of two quantities, each called a variable. A graphical method of displaying these quantities is called a scatter plot or a scatter diagram.

This graphical display of the two variables may resemble a straight line. This is called a linear relationship. The scatter plot is the first step in determining such a relationship. Further development of the linear relationship between the two variables is called linear regression analysis. Regression will be discussed in a later section.

As an example of bivariate data, if the two measured quantities for the 15 hitters on a baseball team are home runs (HR) and stolen bases (SB), the bivariate data would be displayed as:

Player No.	HR	SB
25	0	11
13	5	12
20	5	30
12	2	21
18	5	3
45	30	2
26	2	9
2	7	9
14	0	0
24	18	2
21	13	0
31	2	6
39	8	5
51	22	12
29	5	7

The player number is listed above in addition to the home runs and stolen bases for each hitter on the team. This is done as a convenience. However, these player numbers are just as much a variable as the home runs or stolen bases.

EXAMPLES OF SCATTER PLOTS

The scatter plot below is a graphical presentation of the home runs and stolen bases variables. The home runs are on the horizontal *x*-axis of the graph and the stolen bases are on the vertical *y*-axis of the graph. The variable on the *x*-axis is called the **independent variable**, and the variable on the *y*-axis is called the **dependent variable**. In this case home runs are the independent variable and stolen bases are the dependent variable.

A different scatter plot for the same data can be made with the stolen bases on the *x*-axis and the home runs on the *y*-axis. In that case, stolen

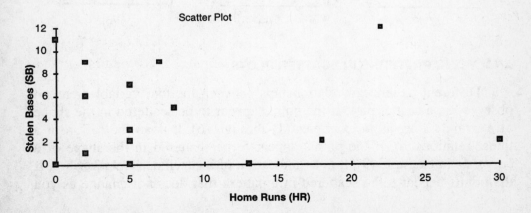

Scatter Plot

bases would be the independent variable and home runs would be the dependent variable.

The terms "independent" and "dependent" come from studies where one variable is set independently and the measurement of the other variable depends on the setting of the first. For example, in a study of the relation between eating chocolate and getting acne, the amount of chocolate served to an individual would be set by the researcher and the amount of acne would be measured. In this example, it is clear that chocolate is the independent variable and would be on the x-axis of a scatter plot. Acne is the dependent variable and would be on the y-axis. The independent and dependent variables are also known by the terminology explanatory and response variables, respectively. In the chocolate/acne example, the source of this terminology is that the amount of chocolate eaten is being used to explain the amount of acne measured as a response to that chocolate being eaten.

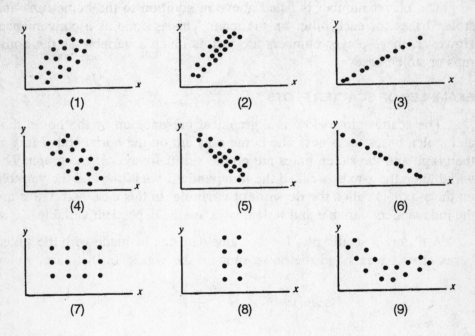

ANALYZING PATTERNS IN SCATTER PLOTS

Different patterns or relationships between the two variables can be observed in a scatter plot. If the points appear to be scattered in the shape of a straight line, as in examples (1) through (6), it is an indication of a linear relationship. If the points appear to be scattered in the shape of a curve, as in example (9), it is an indication of a curvilinear relationship. If the points appear to be scattered in a pattern that does not change as you go from left to right, as in examples (7) and (8) and also in the home runs and stolen bases scatter plot above, it is an indication of no relationship or a weak relationship.

LEAST SQUARES REGRESSION LINE

In the cases where we are satisfied that there is a linear relationship between two variables as shown in examples (1) through (6) above, a straight line can be drawn which will pass "close" to the points on the scatter plot. This closeness can be defined or measured in several ways, for example, total distance, total horizontal distance, total vertical distance, or the squares of those distances between the points and the line. In practice, one uses the square of the vertical distances from the line to the points in the scatter plot as the definition of closeness. These squares are then summed and minimized, which is the source of the term "least squares" for the least squares regression line.

This line, called the regression line for short, is used to predict the value of one variable (the dependent variable x) from the value of the other variable (the independent variable y). This prediction is applicable when the value of the dependent variable is within the range of actual x values in the scatter plot.

The least squares regression line is given by the equation $y = a + bx$ or equivalently and alternatively $y = b_0 + (b_1) x$,

where x represents the independent variable (shown on x-axis on scatter plot);

y represents the dependent variable (shown on y-axis on scatter plot);

a or b_0 represents the y intercept of the least squares regression line;

b or b_1 represents the slope of the least squares regression line.

a and b (or b_0 and b_1) are called the regression coefficients. The y intercept is known as the constant of the regression line.

To calculate the regression line from the x and y data, a calculation of the coefficients a and b is carried out as follows.

CALCULATING THE REGRESSION LINE IN SEVEN STEPS

It is suggested that as you read through the steps the first time you follow each step on the example which follows so that the steps will have meaning.

The first step in calculating the coefficients a and b is to count the number of observations, that is. the number of points in the scatter plot. This number will be referred to as n.

The second step in calculating the coefficients a and b is to build a table with five columns and n rows, one for each observation in the data, that is each point in the scatter plot. For each row, the first two columns will be the x and y values from the data. The two columns can be titled x and y.

The third step is to calculate the next three columns from the first two columns. The three calculations are x^2, y^2, and xy and the three columns can be titled x^2, y^2, and xy.

The fourth step is to sum each of the five columns. The notation for the five sums is:

Σx, the sum of the x column

Σy, the sum of the y column

Σx^2, the sum of the x^2 column

Σy^2, the sum of the y^2 column

Σxy, the sum of the xy column

The fifth step is to calculate the mean of x by dividing the sum of the x column by n and the mean of y by dividing the sum of the y column by n. The notation and formula for the means is:

$x = \Sigma x / n$

$y = \Sigma y / n$

The sixth step is to calulate b using the formula

$$b = \frac{n(\Sigma xy) - (\Sigma x)(\Sigma y)}{n(\Sigma x^2) - (\Sigma x)^2}$$

The seventh step is to calculate a using the formula

$a = \bar{y} - b(\bar{x})$

The calculation of a and b completes the calculation of the regression line. The regression line is $y = a + bx$

Note the y^2 column was not used in calculating the regression line. It is recommended to calculate this column at this time anyway to save time later. In a later section, the correlation coefficient r formula will be shown which requires Σy^2. The calculation of r is a part of many regression problems.

We now have the regression line equation $y = a + bx$.

EXAMPLE

The speed of the earth's rotation is measured at points in the northern hemisphere 10 degrees latitude apart from the equator ($0°$ latitude) to the north pole ($90°$N latitude). Find the equation of the least squares regression line $y = a + bx$ for the following data:

Latitude (Degrees N)	Speed (Miles per hour)
0	1,000
10	985
20	940
30	865
40	770
50	640
60	500
70	340
80	175
90	0

The scatter plot for the data is shown below.

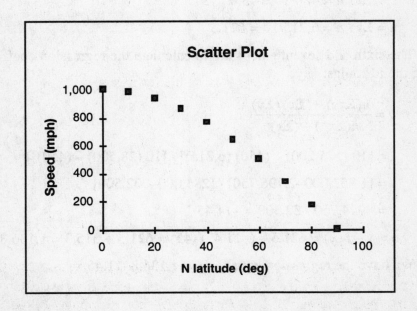

SOLUTION

Since the latitude is determined by picking points on earth 10° apart, and the speed at those points is measured, the independent variable, x, is latitude, and the dependent variable, y, is speed.

The first step is to count the observations to determine n. We have $n = 10$.

The second, third, and fourth steps are to build a five column chart. Do the x^2, y^2, and xy calculations and sum the columns. We have:

	x	y	x^2	y^2	xy
	0	1,000	0	1,000,000	0
	10	985	100	970,225	9,850
	20	940	400	883,600	18,800
	30	865	900	748,225	25,950
	40	770	1,600	592,900	30,800
	50	640	2,500	409,600	32,000
	60	500	3,600	250,000	30,000
	70	340	4,900	115,600	23,800
	80	175	6,400	30,625	14,000
	90	0	8,100	0	0
Sum	450	6,215	28,500	5,000,775	185,200

The fifth step is to calculate the mean of x and the mean of y.

$\bar{x} = \Sigma x / n = 450/10 = 45.0$

$\bar{y} = \Sigma y / n = 6{,}215/10 = 621.5$

The sixth and seventh steps are to calculate the regression coefficient using the formulas:

$$b = \frac{n(\Sigma xy) - (\Sigma x)(\Sigma y)}{n(\Sigma x^2) - (\Sigma x)^2}$$

$$= [10\,(185{,}200) - (450)\,(6{,}215)] / [10\,(28{,}500) - (450)^2]$$

$$= [1{,}852{,}000 - 2{,}796{,}750] / [285{,}000 - 202{,}500]$$

$$= -944{,}750 / 82{,}500 = -11.45$$

$$a = y - b(\bar{x}) = 621.5 - (-11.45)\,(45) = 621.5 + 515.3 = 1{,}136.8$$

We have the regression equation $y = 1{,}136.8 - 11.45\,x$

EXAMPLE

Graph a scatter plot of the observed and predicted points from the regression line $y = 1136.8 - 11.45 x$

SOLUTION

Predicted y values

The predicted values for the observed x values only are plotted on the scatter plot shown on the following page. For any value x, a corresponding y on the regression line can be calculated using the regression equation

$$y = a + bx.$$

This y value is called the predicted y.

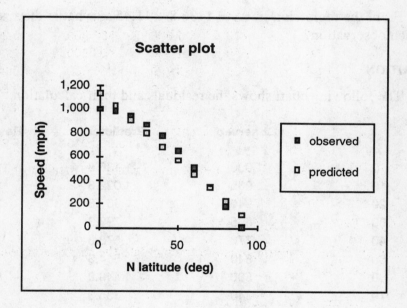

EXAMPLE

From the regression line $y = 1,136.8 - 11.45 x$, what is the predicted speed at a latitude of 42°N.

SOLUTION

It is appropriate to predict a value of speed for 42°N, because 42 is in the range of observed x values from 0° N to 90°N. (See note 3 on page 32). The prediction is $1,136.8 - 11.45 (42) = 1,136.8 - 480.9 = 655.9$ mph.

RESIDUALS

Each observed value x may be used to calculate a corresponding predicted value. The predicted value will be close to the observed value of y because the regression line is close to the observed value. The difference is called the **residual** or error. The notation is e. Graphically the residual is vertical distance between each point on the scatter plot and the regression line.

For each observation:

residual = observed y – predicted y.

or $e = y - (a + bx)$

EXAMPLE

From the regression line $y = 1136.8 - 11.45\ x$, what is the residual e at each observation?

SOLUTION

The following chart shows the residuals and their calculation.

x	Observed y	Predicted y	Residual e
0	1,000	1,136.8	−136.8
10	985	1,022.3	−37.3
20	940	907.8	32.2
30	865	793.3	71.7
40	770	678.8	91.2
50	640	564.3	75.7
60	500	449.8	50.2
70	340	335.3	4.7
80	175	220.8	−45.8
90	0	106.3	−106.3

The slope of the line connecting the predicted points is −11.45, even though it appears to be much less steep in the graph due to the scales used on the axes.

RESIDUAL PLOTS

A scatter plot of the independent variable x and the residuals as the dependent variable is called a **residual plot**. It can be analyzed for a pattern among the residuals. Mathematically, it can be shown that the sum of the residuals is zero, so the scatter plot will be centered around the horizontal *x*-axis.

EXAMPLE

From the regression line y = 1,136.8–11.45 *x*, what is the residual plot?

SOLUTION

The following chart is a residual plot for the latitude–speed of rotation example.

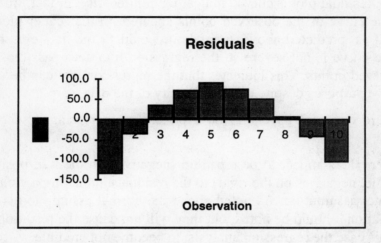

INDICATIONS FROM RESIDUAL PLOTS

A curved pattern for the residual plot is an indicator of nonlinearity. A pattern of increasing spread (i.e. the residuals are further above and below the *x* axis as you scan the plot from left to right) indicates predicted values of *y* are less reliable as *x* increases. They are less reliable because the increased spread indicates larger errors. Similarly, a pattern of decreasing spread indicates the predicted values of *y* are less reliable as *x* decreases.

The pattern of the residuals is an indicator of the normality of the data. Normally distributed data is an underlying assumption of regression analysis. If the residuals are randomly scattered about the *x*-axis, this would be a confirmation of the underlying normal assumption. If there is a pattern which is not random, for example, if going from left to right the first half of the residuals are negative and the second half are positive, this would put into question the underlying normality assumption. When the normality assumption is in doubt, the regression model is still used because, it is **robust** regarding the normality assumption. This means the violations of the normality assumption will not cause big swings in the numerical values of a and b, so that the analysis will still be credible.

EXAMPLE

What are the indications from the residual plot above for the latitude–speed of rotation example? Are these indications apparent on the scatter plot of the original data?

SOLUTION

The residual plot is curved indicating nonlinearity. In fact, from looking at the curve of the observed points apparent in the scatter plot of the observed vs. predicted above, a parabola would fit the data closer than a line. The curve is not severe so the regression line does pass close to all the observed points. This indicates that the regression line can be used for predictive purposes despite the nonlinearity of the data.

There does not appear to be a pattern of increasing or decreasing speed.

There does appear to be a pattern (negatives on the left, positives in the middle, negatives on the right) to the residuals indicating a violation of the normal assumption. As noted above the normal assumption is robust. The violations should be noted, but they will *not* cause the resulting analysis, in this case the regression analysis, to become not credible.

OUTLIERS

It is possible that the scatter plot shows that one point does not belong with the other points. For example, it might be easy to visualize a regression line close to all the points in the scatter plot except this one point which would be far from the visualized line. This point is called an **outlier**. It is possible for there to be more than one outlier where those points would not fit with the rest of the data. An outlier cannot fit the data, because it is different in terms of its horizontal x value or in terms of its vertical y value or both.

An outlier, particularly in the vertical direction, can also be determined from a residual plot. An outlier would have a residual much larger than the other points.

INFLUENTIAL POINTS

An **influential point** shifts the whole regression line towards it. If an influential point is excluded, the regression line would be much different (much different slope and/or intercept). It is interesting to note that an outlier in terms of its x value is more influential than an outlier in terms of its y value.

In the case of an outlier in the x direction, it would be way to the right or way to the left of the rest of the points. If the regression line when it is excluded from the data misses it, its inclusion will cause the slope of the new regression line to shift towards it, so its vertical distance to the line is minimized. The vertical distance of the line to the other points will not be changed relatively as much, despite the shift in the slope.

In the case of an outlier in the y direction, it would be way above or way below the rest of the points. The shift of the regression line would be a shift up and down (in y intercept), not a shift in slope. Shifting the line up or down to minimize its vertical distance from the line would increase just as much the vertical distance from all the other points. The other points serve as an "anchor," and the regression line would not change very much.

Influential points present a dilemma as to which regression line is correct, the one including or excluding the point. An obvious solution would be to exclude the influential outlier. The resulting regression line would fit the data better and be of great predictive value. Getting neater results is not reason enough to exclude an outlier. If the outlier is an actual observation, it does add information to the data and cannot be excluded. The fact that it does not fit the data is itself valuable information about the data. If further investigation determines that a mistake was made in collecting the data for this observation, then it should be excluded.

NOTES ON EXPLORING BIVARIATE DATA

(1) The choice of which of the two variables in the bivariate data is the dependent variable and the independent variable will affect the least squares regression line. This is because the regression line is a result of minimizing vertical distances and by switching the independent and dependent variables, x and y are switched. As a result, vertical distances become horizontal distances and vice versa. With the independent and dependent variables switched, minimizing the vertical distances equates to minimizing the horizontal distances before the switch. Since the horizontal and vertical distances are generally not the same, switching the x and y

would result in a different regression line. A different regression line would result in different predictive values.

(2) In terms of residuals, the least squares regression line minimizes the sum of the squares of the residuals.

(3) The reason why it was noted above that y predictions should only be made for x close to or within the range of x in the data, is because to extrapolate far outside the range of x would involve an assumption that the same linear model would continue where we have no data.

CORRELATION AND LINEARITY

We have mentioned how we can recognize visually if a relationship is linear or not from the pattern on a scatter plot. We need to quantify the amount of linearity to decide whether or not to a line is appropriate as a model to predict y values from x values by quantifying the amount of linearity. The amount of linearity is referred to as **linear correlation**.

A linear relationship is **positively correlated** when the relationship between x and y are directly proportional so that when one increases the other increases. Graphically, the y values of the observations rise as the graph is scanned from left to right, indicating that the line that best fits the points would have a positive slope.

A linear relationship is **negatively correlated** when the relationship between x and y are inversely proportional so that when one increases, the other decreases. Graphically, the y values of the observations drop as the graph is scanned from left to right, indicating that the line that best fits the points would have a negative slope.

A linear relationship (positive or negative) is **perfect** when the regression line goes through all the observed points.

The scatter plots shown on the following page illustrate common patterns and a description of the correlation for each.

We can quantify the linear correlation in a relationship between x and y by calculating the **Pearson linear correlation coefficient**. This coefficient, identified with the letter r, equals 1 when there is a perfect positively correlated linear relationship. When r equals -1, there is a perfect negatively correlated linear relationship. When r equals 0, there is no linear relationship. In most cases, r is not $-1,0$ nor 1 exactly, but somewhere in between (mathematically, r cannot possibly take on values greater than 1 or less than -1). The closer the absolute value of r is to 1, the more comfortable we would be approximating the data with a linear model

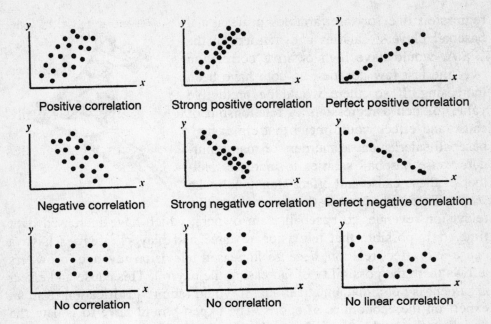

because the linear association is relatively stronger. The closer the absolute value of r is to 0, the weaker the linear association.

In summary, we have:

value of r	regression line
$r > 0$	positive slope
$r < 0$	negative slope
$r = 0$	no linear relationship, line would be horizontal if drawn
$r = -1$ or $r = 1$	passes exactly through all observed points.
$r > 1$ or $r < -1$	mathematically impossible

CAUSE AND EFFECT AS A CONCLUSION OF HIGHLY CORRELATED DATA

When a regression line is used for prediction of one variable y from a second variable x and the Pearson linear correlation coefficient between the two variables has absolute value near one, it would be concluded that the regression line is an excellent predictive model. Such a conclusion is appropriate, but it is sometimes confused with a conclusion of cause and effect, that is to conclude x causes y. **It is wrong to conclude based only on high correlation that a relationship is one of cause and effect**. The reason is that cause and effect is not a mathematical concept.

There may be other different variables which are important to the relationship. These important variables, which are not among the regression variables, are called **lurking variables**. For example, it is likely that a regression line for the variables professional baseball players' salaries and murders in the U.S.A. would have high positive correlation over the last few decades, as both have been increasing. If so, there would be predictive value to such a regression. A relationship of cause and effect would mean that either high baseball salaries cause murders or many murders cause baseball salaries to increase. Neither of these cause and effect situations make sense. There are other lurking variables like

television revenues to baseball team owners, which have increased over time. It is possible that television revenue and players' salaries have a cause and effect relation, because increased television revenue to owners allows them the possibility of increasing the payroll. This cause and effect argument is not a mathematical one. It would require justification from an expert on the economics of sports. The expert would have to isolate the variables from other variables so the possibility of cause and effect could be analyzed.

CALCULATING THE CORRELATION COEFFICIENT IN FIVE STEPS

It is suggested that as you read through the steps the first time you follow each step on the example which follows so that the steps will have meaning.

The first four steps in calculating the correlation coefficient r from the observed values of x and y are the same four steps shown earlier to calculate the linear regression coefficients a and b from the observed values. You may pick up the steps from the fifth step if you have read the chapter in order.

The first step in calculating the correlation coefficient r is to count the number of observations, that is, the number of points in the scatter plot. This number will be referred to as n.

The second step in calculating the correlation coefficient r is to build a table with five columns and n rows, one for each observation in the data, that is, each point in the scatter plot. For each row, the first two columns will be the x and y values from the data. The two columns can be titled x and y.

The third step is to calculate the next three columns from the first two columns. The three calculations are x^2, y^2, and xy and the three columns can be titled x^2, y^2, and xy.

The fourth step is to sum each of the five columns. The notation for the five sums is:

Σx, the sum of the x column

Σy, the sum of the y column

Σx^2, the sum of the x^2 column

Σy^2, the sum of the y^2 column

Σxy, the sum of the xy column

The fifth step is to calculate r using the formula

$$r = \frac{m(\Sigma xy) - (\Sigma x)(\Sigma y)}{\sqrt{[n(\Sigma x^2) - (\Sigma x)^2]}\sqrt{[n(\Sigma y^2) - (\Sigma y)^2]}}$$

EXAMPLE

Once again, we look at the latitude/rotation speed example. The speed of the earth's rotation is measured at points in the northern hemisphere 10 degrees latitude apart from the equator ($0°$ latitude) to the north pole ($90°N$ latitude). Find the correlation coefficient r for the following data:

Latitude (Degrees N)	Speed (Miles per hour)
0	1,000
10	985
20	940
30	865
40	770
50	640
60	500
70	340
80	175
90	0

SOLUTION

The first step is to count the observations to determine n. We have $n = 10$.

The second, third, and fourth steps are to build a five column chart, do the x^2, y^2, and xy calculations and sum the columns. We have:

x	y	x^2	y^2	xy
0	1,000	0	1,000,000	0
10	985	100	970,225	9,850
20	940	400	883,600	18,800
30	865	900	748,225	25,950
40	770	1,600	592,900	30,800
50	640	2,500	409,600	32,000
60	500	3,600	250,000	30,000
70	340	4,900	115,600	23,800
80	175	6,400	30,625	14,000
90	0	8,100	0	0
Sum 450	6,215	28,500	5,000,775	185,200

The fifth step is to calculate the correlation coefficient using the formula:

$$r = \frac{m(\Sigma xy) - (\Sigma x)(\Sigma y)}{\sqrt{[n(\Sigma x^2) - (\Sigma x)^2]}\sqrt{[n(\Sigma y^2) - (\Sigma y)^2]}}$$

$$= [10\,(185{,}200) - (450)\,(6{,}215)]\,/([10\,(28{,}500) - (450)^2]$$

$$[10\,(5{,}000{,}775) - (6{,}215)^2]\,)$$

$$= [1{,}852{,}000 - 2{,}796{,}750]\,/(\,[285{,}000 - 202{,}500]$$

$$[50{,}007{,}750 - 38{,}626{,}225]\,)$$

$$= -944{,}750\,/\,(\,82{,}500 \quad 11{,}381{,}525)$$

$$= -944{,}750\,/\,(\,[287.23]\,[3373.65]$$

$$= -944{,}750\,/\,969{,}013.48 = -0.97$$

EXAMPLE

How would you describe a correlation of –0.97?

SOLUTION

0.97 is very close to –1, indicating strong negative correlation. The conclusion is to use the regression line as a predictive model.

NOTES ON LINEAR RELATIONSHIPS

(1) By no linear relationship it is meant that the best fitting least squares regression line would be simply a horizontal line at the height of the mean of the y values. For any value of x, the predicted value of y from this regression line with slope 0 would be simply the mean of the y values.

With no regression analysis at all, the mean of the y values would have been suggested as a reasonable predicted value for any x. The regression analysis does not improve this prediction in this case.

(2) The statement $b = 0$ made about the slope of the regression line has an interpretation similar to the statement $r = 0$ about the correlation coefficient, except for the trivial cases below. $b = 0$ means the slope of the regression line is zero which graphically means the regression line is horizontal. This would mean as you go from left to right, there is no difference in the y value, indicating no linear relationship meaning r equals 0. Conversely, $r = 0$ means no linear relationship, which from note 1 means that the regression line is horizontal. This would mean b, the slope of the regression line equals 0. Mathematically, this can be illustrated by the formulas for b and r. They have identical numerators, so that one numerator is zero if, and only if, the other numerator is zero. Therefore $r = 0$ if, and only if, $b = 0$ except in the trivial cases where one or both of the denominators is zero. These trivial cases are specified below: (This may be omitted. However, trivial cases allow deeper understanding of a concept).

Trivial case of identical observed y values for different independent x values: In this case, a horizontal line goes through all the observed points. In this case, b, the slope of the horizontal line will be 0, but r will be undefined 0/0. In this trivial case, there is a perfect linear relationship because the regression line goes through all the observed points, even though $b = 0$ and r is undefined.

Trivial case of identical independent x values being chosen with different y values: In this case, a vertical line goes through all the observed points. In this case, b the slope of the vertical line will be undefined 0/0, and r will be undefined 0/0. In this trivial case, there is a perfect linear relationship because the regression line goes through all the observed points, even though b and r are undefined.

There are also the trivial cases of no observed point, one observed point, or several identical observed points, which are even more trivial than the trivial cases above. They are so trivial because it takes two different points to determine a line, in particular a regression line.

(3) The choice of which of the two variables in the bivariate data is the dependent variable and the independent variable will NOT affect the value of r, and whether we decide if the relationship is linear or not. This is shown by the mathematical formula for r, which is symmetric with respect to x and y.

(4) The choice of units used in the data will not affect the value of

the coefficient *r*. Mathematically, the units all cancel out in the formula leaving *r* as a quantity without units.

For example, if the lengths of vehicles were used to predict the cargo space of vehicles and the regression lines and correlations were calculated, the correlation coefficients would be identical whether the data was in meters and cubic decimeters or in yards and cubic feet.

As for the slope of the regression line *b*, that would vary depending on the units used. That is because slope is a mathematical concept that involves units. Slope equals change in *y* (measured in units of *y*) / change in *x* (measured in units of *x*).

(5) Our determination of linear correlation as strong or weak has been based on how close the absolute value of *r* was to 1, or on interpretation of the scatter plot and residual plot. The terms strong and weak are subjective. A researcher would describe the correlation using the statistical terms **significant** or insignificant. In practice, when a decision is made by a researcher to use the linear model for predictions, it is done after it is determined that the correlation is statistically significant A significant result means the probability that it really isn't so is less than a predetermined amount, for example 5%. Such a method in general is called hypothesis testing. In this case, the hypothesis to be tested is whether $r = 0$ (no linear correlation) or not. Hypothesis testing in general and testing of the hypothesis $r = 0$ in particular are discussed in the section on statistical inference.

(6) When no linear relationship is apparent, that is it is concluded *r* is close to 0, there could still be a relationship that is nonlinear. Such a relationship can be analyzed using nonlinear techniques, which is a complex undertaking. There is also the possibility of adapting the data so a regression model will be appropriate as in the two ways suggested below to deal with the following example:

We look at the two variables: the speed at which one can throw a baseball and age of the person throwing. As a child grows older, he or she can probably throw a baseball faster each year. When an adult ages, he or she can probably throw a baseball slower each year. This relationship is clearly not linear. It may be curvilinear. One way to adapt the data for linear regression is to find an appropriate transformation to transform the data so that it becomes linear. Then, regression can be performed on the transformed data. This is discussed in the next section.

Another way to adapt the data would be to look for cut-off ages which separate the data into sets of data, each of which might be appropriate for a linear predictive model. If we notice the speed of hurling a baseball increases up to a certain age, for example age 25, and then starts decreasing, we can use 25 as the cut-off age. The data can be separated into two data sets. For the data set of younger people, there may be a positive linear correlation. For the data set of older people, there may be a negative linear correlation. This is known as **piece-wise** linear regression and would involve two (or more) separate regression lines.

TRANSFORMATIONS TO ACHIEVE LINEARITY: LOGARITHMIC AND POWER TRANSFORMATIONS

We have seen the linear regression method of fitting a straight line to data. We have seen cases where we could tell from the scatterplot that a straight line will not fit the data. We have also seen cases of poor linear correlation which would make use of a straight line not credible. Instead of coming up with a nonlinear curve to fit the data, a transformation can be carried out on one or both variables in the data so that the transformed data will be approximately linear. Regression can be carried out on the transformed data, predictions made, and the prediction transformed back to terms of the original data.

Finding transformation(s) that will result in the desired linear relationship is done on a trial and error basis with the guidance of general statistical procedures. An example of a statistical procedure is that a logarithmic transformation would generally apply to positive curvilinearly related data to result in linearly related data. Two of the most useful linear functions that have been obtained by means of a transformation on x and/or on y are exponential and power. For an exponential function relationship, only y is transformed. For a power function relationship, both x and y are transformed.

Reciprocals, square roots, powers, exponentials, arcsines and other functions may be tried as transformations when defined. An example of a transformation not being defined is when square root is applied to a variable that takes on some or all negative values.

EXAMPLE

A butcher in 1985 is curious about the relation between how much meat is consumed by a family and the family's annual income. The researcher chooses 10 families who are regular customers. The families are chosen so that they are similar in total weight.

Annual meat expenses ($)	Annual salary ($)
400	10,000
800	12,000
1,000	14,000
1,200	16,000
1,400	20,000
1,600	24,000
1,800	30,000
2,000	40,000
2,200	60,000
2,400	80,000

A scatter plot of the data is made. It does not appear that a linear model would be appropriate to predict the salary of a family given its meat expenses.

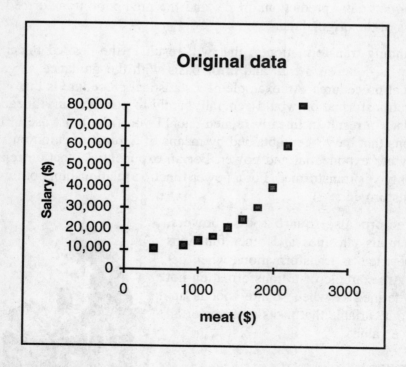

The dependent variable y is transformed by taking the logarithm (base 10) of each salary.

Annual meat expenses ($)	Log (salary ($))
400	4.00
800	4.08
1,000	4.15
1,200	4.20
1,400	4.30
1,600	4.38
1,800	4.48
2,000	4.60
2,200	4.78
2,400	4.90

A scatter plot (shown below) is made for the transformed data with the meat expenses remaining the independent variable on the x axis and with the log of salary on the y axis as the new dependent variable.

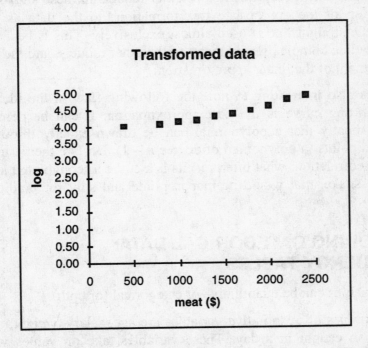

The relationship now is much closer to linear. We end the trial and error process to find an appropriate transformation with the selection of $\log_{10}$. Regression is carried out The resulting regression coefficients a and b will provide the regression equation

$$\log y = a + bx$$

where y is salary and x is meat expenses.

Solving for y explicitly we have:

$$y = 10^{(a + bx)}$$

$$y = 10^a 10^{bx}$$

This is the predictive model for y based on the log transformation of the salary variable and linear regression.

NOTE ON USING NONLINEAR MODELS

In the cases where a nonlinear relationship is apparent, a straight line would not be appropriate for the original not transformed data. In the cases where a curvilinear relationship is apparent, a polynomial as a model would better approximate the relationship. In the cases where a different pattern is apparent, an approximation based on that pattern would be appropriate as a representation of the relationship.

Despite the appropriateness of other models in these situations, after application of the appropriate transformations to the data as discussed above, the straight line is used almost exclusively. This is because of the mathematical complexities in many of the other models, and the extensive development of the linear approximation.

It is also interesting to note the following flaw in the idea that the closest fitting curve is the best approximation. It can be demonstrated mathematically that a polynomial can be drawn exactly through any n observed points (a polynomial of degree $n - 1$). Despite the perfect "polynomial" correlation, what often results is a curve as convoluted and squiggly as a snake, that would be inappropriate and silly for predictive purposes.

EXPLORING CATEGORICAL DATA: FREQUENCY TABLES

Variables can be quantitative or categorical (or both).

Examples of quantitative variables are age, salary, weight, and number of fish caught in a day. These variables take on values which are numbers in the appropriate units used to measure each. Examples of values would be 22 years, $22,000, 220 pounds, and 2 fish, respectively.

Examples of categorical variables would be sex, race, occupation, and political party. These variables take on values which are categories. Examples of values would be female, other, bus driver, and communist, respectively.

A quantitative variable like age could also be a categorical variable when data is collected or presented, so that the value of the variable would be a particular age group. Ages 20-29 would be an example of a category appropriate to classify a 22 year-old.

A categorical variable can technically be a quantitative variable if numbers are assigned to each category. For example, the sex categorical variable can take on values of 0 for male and 1 for female. It is still a categorical variable in many ways because all observations in an entire category will have the same value and the choice of 0 and 1 as the two values is arbitrary. However, researchers do use this, for example, to include a categorical variable as an independent variable in a regression model.

TWO-WAY TABLES

Consider the following table of data about wage and salary workers (not including self-employed) from 1988. There are two categorical variables. They are occupation, broken up into six categories, and union affiliation, broken up into two categories. The choice of the six categories that comprise the occupation variable was done by the source of the data, the U.S. Bureau of Labor Statistics. The two categories of the union affiliation variable are union represented and not union represented. The value 4,470,000 in the upper left cell indicates that there were 4,470,000 wage and salary workers in the United States in 1988 whose occupation was managerial and professional specialty and who were represented by a union.

Two-Way Table—Wage and Salary Workers by Occupation and Union Affiliation

Occupation	Union	Not union	Total
Managerial and professional specialty	4,470,000	19,899,000	24,369,000
Technical, Sales, Administrative Support	3,976,000	28,295,000	32,271,000
Service occupations	2,225,000	11,953,000	14,178,000
Precision production, craft and repair	3,374,000	8,392,000	11,766,000
Operators, fabricators and laborers	5,105,000	11,905,000	17,010,000
Farming, forestry and fishing	91,000	1,722,000	1,813,000
Total	19,241,000	82,166,000	101,407,000

A table which presents data for two categorical variables is called a two-way table. It is also known as a frequency table, contingency table, crosstabulations, or crosstabs. In the above two-way table, union affiliation is the column variable and occupation is the row variable.

JOINT AND MARGINAL DISTRIBUTION

The cells in the heart of the two-way table, like the 4,470,000 whose occupation was managerial and professional specialty and who were represented by a union, make up the **joint** distribution of the row and column variables. The reason for the use of the term "joint" is that these 4,470,000 wage and salary workers are jointly in the managerial and professional specialty **and** are represented by a union.

The row totals in the two-way table involve only the row variable and are found in the rightmost column (margin). For example, the 24,369,000 in the top row indicates there were 24,369,000 wage and salary workers in the managerial and professional specialty occupation with no regard to the column variable union affiliation, that is whether union represented or not The row totals make up the **marginal** distribution of the row variable, in this case occupation.

The column totals in the two-way table involve only the column variable and are found in the bottom row (margin). For example, the 19,241,000 in the union column indicates there were 19,241,000 wage and salary workers represented by a union with no regard to the row variable occupation, that is whether a manager, salesperson, etc. The column totals make up the **marginal** distribution of the column variable, in this case union affiliation.

The 101,407,000 in the lower right corner is the grand total. In this case it represents all the wage and salary workers in the United States in 1988. It is the sum of the row totals for each of the six occupation categories. It is the sum of the column totals for each of the two union affiliation categories. It is also the sum of the cells making up the joint distribution.

JOINT, MARGINAL AND CONDITIONAL PROBABILITIES

Joint and marginal probabilities are used to express the category variables as a part of the whole.

The joint probability of wage and salary workers who are Technical, Sales and Administrative Support **and** are represented by a union as a part of all wage and salary workers is:

Joint probability = (3,976,000 / 101,407,000) = 0.039

In the case of the column variable union affiliation, the marginal probabilities of wage and salary workers who are and are not represented by a union as a part of all wage and salary workers are:

Marginal probability represented by a union

$$= (19{,}241{,}000 / 101{,}407{,}000) = 0.190$$

Marginal probability not represented by a union

$$= (82{,}166{,}000 / 101{,}407{,}000) = 0.810$$

The marginal probabilities of the two categories add to 1.000 because every wage and salary worker is either represented by a union or is not represented by a union.

In the case of the row variable occupation, the marginal probabilities of wage and salary workers who are in each of the six occupation categories as a part of all wage and salary workers are:

Marginal probability Managerial and professional specialty

$$= (24{,}369{,}000 / 101{,}407{,}000) = 0.240$$

Marginal probability Technical, Sales, Administrative Support

$$= (32{,}271{,}000 / 101{,}407{,}000) = 0.318$$

Marginal probability Service occupations

$$= (14{,}178{,}000 / 101{,}407{,}000) = 0.140$$

Marginal probability Precision production, craft and repair

$$= (11{,}766{,}000 / 101{,}407{,}000) = 0.116$$

Marginal probability Operators, fabricators and laborers

$$= (17{,}010{,}000 / 101{,}407{,}000) = 0.168$$

Marginal probability Farming, forestry and fishing

$$= (1{,}813{,}000 / 101{,}407{,}000) = 0.018$$

The marginal probabilities of the six categories add to 1.000 because every wage and salary worker is classified into one of the six occupation categories.

CONDITIONAL PROBABILITIES

Conditional probabilities are not used to express the category variables as a part of the whole. Instead, conditional probabilities are expressed as part of the row totals or column totals.

The conditional probabilities of union affiliation given that a wage and salary worker is in the Service occupations are:

Conditional probability Union given Service occupations

= (2,225,000 / 14,178,000) = 0.157

Conditional probability Not union given Service occupations

= (11,953,000 / 14,178,000) = 0.843

The conditional probabilities of the two categories add to 1.000 because every wage and salary worker in the Service occupations is either represented by a union or is not represented by a union. Since the sum is unity, the probabilities can be referred to as a **conditional distribution**.

The reason 15.7% and 84.3% are called "conditional" probabilities is that they refer to wage and salary workers who satisfy the condition that they are in the Service occupations occupation category.

The same concept expressed as frequencies is known as **conditional relative frequencies**. For example, there is the conditional relative frequency of wage and salary workers who are Union represented on the condition that they are in the Service Occupations. That conditional relative frequency would be 2,225,000 union represented out of 14,178,000 in the Service Occupations.

The conditional probabilities of occupation given that a wage and salary worker is represented by a union are:

Conditional probability Managerial and professional specialty given Union

= (4,470,000 / 19,241,000) = 0.232

Conditional probability Technical, Sales, Administrative Support given Union

= (3,976,000 / 19,241,000) = 0.207

Conditional probability Service occupations given Union

= (2,225,000 / 19,241,000) = 0.116

Conditional probability Precision production, craft and repair given Union

= (3,374,000 / 19,241,000) = 0.175

Conditional probability Operators, fabricators and laborers given Union

$= (5,105,000 / 19,241,000) = 0.265$

Conditional probability Farming, forestry and fishing given Union

$= (91,000 / 19,241,000) = 0.005$

The conditional probabilities of the six categories add to 1.000 because every wage and salary worker represented by a union is in one of the six wage and salary earner occupation categories.

EXAMPLE

Consider two film developing enterprises.

The FilmFast Chain Branch #34 provides the following data. It had 10,000 orders in 1994. Due to customer complaints, 2,000 orders had to be redone. Of the 1,000 orders from professional photographers, 700 had to be redone due to customer complaints.

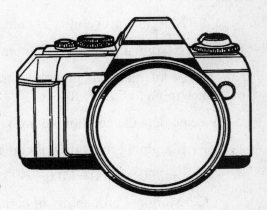

The CreativeCorner provides the following data. It had 5,000 orders in 1994. Due to customer complaints, 2,000 had to be redone. Out of the orders from 4,000 professional photographers, 1,900 had to be redone due to customer complaints.

Where would you go to develop your film if you did not want to complain? Would it matter if you were an artist or not?

At first glance it appears the answer is FilmFast because it redid the same amount of orders but had twice as many orders. We will now analyze the data using marginal and conditional probabilities.

Each film place gets its own two-way table as follows:

FilmFast Chain Branch # 34

Customer	Redone- Customer complaint	Customer satisfied	Total
Professionals	700	300	1,000
Amateurs	1,300	7,700	9,000
Total	2,000	8,000	10,000

CreativeCorner

Customer	Redone-Customer complaint	Customer satisfied	Total
Professionals	1,900	2,100	4,000
Amateurs	100	900	1,000
Total	2,000	3,000	5,000

We calculate the marginal probabilities for FilmFast (FF) and CreativeCorner (CC) as follows:

FF Marginal probability of complaints = 2,000 / 10,000 = 20%

CC Marginal probability of complaints = 2,000 / 5,000 = 40%

The use of marginal probabilities confirms the conclusion made at first glance to go to FilmFast.

We calculate the conditional probabilities as follows:

FF Marginal probability of complaints given professional

= 700 / 1,000 = 70.0%

CC Marginal probability of complaints given professional

= 1,900 / 4,000 = 47.5%

The use of conditional probabilities would have professional photographers make a different decision and go to CreativeCorner.

FF Marginal probability of complaints given amateur

= 7,700 / 9,000 = 85.6%

CC Marginal probability of complaints given amateur

= 900 / 1,000 = 90.0%

The use of conditional probabilities would have amateur photographers make a different decision and go to CreativeCorner.

SIMPSON'S PARADOX

The apparent paradox in the above example is known as Simpson's paradox.

FilmFast had better success overall in customer satisfaction than CreativeCorner. However, CreativeCorner had better success with professional photographers and with amateur photographers. There is no other category of customers, so why is this?

This can be explained by the fact that 80% of CreativeCorner's customers are professional photographers (marginal probability = 4,000 / 5,000). Only 10% of FilmFast's customers are pros (marginal probability = 1,000 / 10,000). The pros at both stores have a greater percentage of complaints (see conditional probabilities above). Whichever store ends up with more professional photographers will have a larger number of complaints from them going into their overall numbers.

Both stores of course will claim to be the best. FilmFast will base that claim on the marginal probabilities and CreativeCorner will use the conditional probabilities. Neither is falsely advertising, but FilmFast is not telling the complete story.

The numbers don't "lie". CreativeCorner has better numbers, but that is not apparent at first glance because they have many professional photographers for customers.

ASSOCIATION

Consider the conditional probabilities of union affiliation given that a wage and salary worker is in the service occupations as calculated above and the same conditional probabilities given the wage and salary worker is in the Farming, forestry and fishing occupation category.

Conditional probability Union given Service occupations = 0.157

Conditional probability Not union given Service occupations = 0.843

Conditional probability Union given Farming, forestry and fishing

= (91,000 / 1,813,000) = 0.050

Conditional probability Not union given Farming, forestry and fishing

= (1,722,000 / 1,813,000) = 0.950

There appears to be **association** between occupation and union affiliation. Given a change in occupation from service to farming, forestry and fishing there is a change in union representation from 15.7% to 5%. If there was no association between the two variables, then union affiliation would not vary so greatly from one occupation category to another.

When two categorical variables are determined not to be associated that is also known as the two variables being **independent**. Similarly, association corresponds to dependence.

CAUSE AND EFFECT AS A CONCLUSION OF AN ASSOCIATION

When it is concluded that there is association or dependence between two variables based on categorical data, it is sometimes confused with a conclusion of cause and effect, that is to conclude the row variable causes the column variable or vice versa. **It is wrong to conclude based only on categorical data that an association is one of cause and effect**. Similar to correlation, the determining factors of cause and effect are not mathematical, and involve isolation of the variables from other variables and may involve lurking variables (see the *Cause and Effect as a Conclusion of Highly Correlated Data* section earlier in this chapter).

For example, to conclude from the association between occupation and union affiliation that union representation causes a certain occupation or belonging to a certain occupation category causes union representation would require more economical not mathematical research. Such a conclusion is called one of cause and effect.

NOTES ON ASSOCIATION

Our determination of association has been based on the subjective decision of whether or not the conditional distribution of one variable is the same no matter what category of the other variable is given. A researcher would describe the association in the statistical terms **significant** or insignificant. In practice, when a decision is made by a researcher that there is association, it is done after it is determined that the correlation is statistically significant A significant result means the probability that it really isn't so is less than a predetermined amount, for example 5%. Such a method in general is called hypothesis testing. In this case the hypothesis to be tested is whether the row and column variables are independent (no association) or not. Hypothesis testing in general is discussed in the section on statistical inference.

CONTINGENCY PROBABILITY TABLES

The data in the two-way table can also be presented as a table of probabilities or percentages of the grand total when each cell is divided by the grand total. Such a presentation of the data is known as a **contingency probability table**. In the example above, each cell would be

divided by 101,407,000. The contingency probability table for the above data would be the following:

Contingency Probability Table—Wage and Salary Workers by Occupation and Union Affiliation

Occupation	Union	Not union	Total
Managerial and professional specialty	0.044	0.196	0.240
Technical, Sales, Administrative Support	0.039	0.279	0.318
Service occupations	0.022	0.118	0.140
Precision production, craft and repair	0.033	0.083	0.116
Operators, fabricators and laborers	0.050	0.117	0.168
Farming, forestry and fishing	0.001	0.017	0.018
Total	0.190	0.810	1.000

The sum of the row totals and column totals should each be 1.00 or 100%. The sum of the columns and rows should be the column and row totals.

There is a rounding error in the Operators, fabricators and laborers row, which sums to 0.167 instead of the 0.168 in total column. There is also a rounding error in the Union column which sums to 0.189 instead of the 0.190 in the bottom row.

We make a minor adjustment to the cell in the Operators, fabricators and laborers row and the Union column to 0.051 instead of 0.050 to take care of rounding errors so that the rows and columns sum properly. The adjusted contingency probability table would be as follows:

Adjusted Contingency Probability Table—Wage and Salary Workers by Occupation and Union Affiliation

Occupation	Union	Not union	Total
Managerial and professional specialty	0.044	0.196	0.240
Technical, Sales, Administrative Support	0.039	0.279	0.318
Service occupations	0.022	0.118	0.140
Precision production, craft and repair	0.033	0.083	0.116
Operators, fabricators and laborers	0.051	0.117	0.168
Farming, forestry and fishing	0.001	0.017	0.018
Total	0.190	0.810	1.000

JOINT AND MARGINAL PROBABILITIES IN PROBABILITY CONTINGENCY TABLE

The probabilities in a contingency probability table are joint and marginal probabilities. The joint probabilities are in the heart of the table and the marginal probabilities are in the total column for the row variable and the total row for the column variable.

For example, the 0.022 (or 2.2%) in the Service occupations row and the Union column indicates the joint probability of wage and salary workers who are in the Service occupations and who are represented by a union. The 0.140 (or 14.0%) in the Service occupations row and the Total column indicates the marginal probability of wage and salary workers who are in the Service occupations. The 0.190 (or 19.0%) in the Union column and the Total row indicates the marginal probability of wage and salary workers who are represented by a union.

FORMULA CONNECTING CONDITIONAL, JOINT AND MARGINAL PROBABILITIES

In probability theory, the conditional probability of A given B is defined by the formula:

Probability (A given B) = Probability (A and B) / Probability (B)

where

Probability (A given B)	refers to a conditional probability
Probability (A and B)	refers to a joint probability
and Probability (B)	refers to a marginal probability.

The formula is expressed more succinctly as:

Probability ($A \mid B$) = Probability ($A \cap B$) / Probability (B).

This formula can be applied to categorical data.

For example, we calculate the conditional probability Not union represented given Service occupations from the formula as follows:

The joint probability of wage and salary workers who are Not union represented **and** in the Service occupations is

$(11,953,000 / 101,407,000) = 0.118$

(This can also be found on the probability contingency table.)

In this case, *B* is Service occupations. The marginal probability of the service occupations is

(14,178,000 / 101,407,000) = 0.140

(This can also be found on the probability contingency table.)

The conditional probability from the formula is

0.118 / 0.140 = 0.843

The conditional probability earlier was calculated as

(11,953,000 / 14,178,000) = 0.843

These calculations will give the same results except for possible roundoff errors.

MEASURES OF CENTRAL TENDENCY

A measure of central tendency is an average. The purpose of an average is to reduce a quantity of data to a single typical figure.

ARITHMETIC MEAN

The **arithmetic mean** (usually referred to as simply the "mean") is the most commonly used average and is calculated by summing all data values and dividing by the number of points summed.

The formula is:

$$\mu = \frac{\Sigma X}{N}$$

where:

μ = notation for the population mean

Σ = (sigma) = sum of

X = data values

N = number of items in population

or $\overline{X} = \frac{\Sigma X}{n}$

X = the notation for the sample mean

X = data values

n = number of items in sample

EXAMPLE

Histogram of the Number of Phone Calls
Received per Day During April 1990

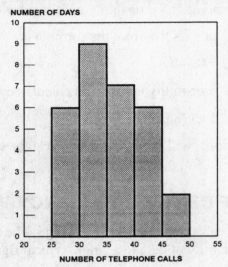

Assume the 30 phone calls made in April represent sample data. What is the arithmetic mean?

SOLUTION

$$\overline{X} = \frac{1,048}{30} = 34.93 \text{ phone calls per day.}$$

WEIGHTED MEAN

The **weighted mean** is used to average data when all data values do not count (weigh) equally.

The formula is:

$$\overline{X}_w = \frac{\Sigma wx}{\Sigma w}$$

where W = Weight assigned to each data value.

EXAMPLE

Four exams are given during a semester. The grades made by a student along with the assigned weights are shown below. What is the average grade for the course?

Grade	% Weight	WX
	(X)	(W)
86	50	4,300
75	30	2,250
60	10	600
90	10	900
Total	100	8,050

SOLUTION

$$\overline{X}_w = \frac{8,050}{100} = 80.5 \text{ average grade for course}$$

MEDIAN

The **median**, symbolized by *Md*, is the middle value in an array (ordered either from smallest to largest or vice versa) of data. When there is an odd number of observations, the median is equal to the central value in the array; when there is an even number of observations, the two middle values in the array are averaged to determine the median.

EXAMPLE

Using the information below, what is the median number of phone calls per day?

Array of Number of Phone Calls Received per Day in April 1990

25	29	33	35	38	41
25	30	34	35	39	42
27	30	34	36	40	42
28	31	34	36	40	45
28	32	34	37	40	48

SOLUTION

$$Md = \frac{34+35}{2} = 34.5 \text{ phone calls per day}$$

MODE

The **mode**, symbolized by *Mo*, is the value that occurs most often. It is possible for a set of data to have two modes (bimodal) or more (multimodal).

EXAMPLE

Using the data from the previous example, what is the mode?

SOLUTION

Mo = 34 phone calls per day, because the value 34 occurs four times.

RANGE AND PERCENTILES

The degree to which numerical data tend to spread about an average value is called the variation or dispersion of the data. We shall define various measures of dispersion.

The simplest measure of data variation is the range.

DEFINITION OF RANGE

The range of a set of numbers is defined to be the difference between the largest and the smallest number of the set.

EXAMPLE

The range of the numbers 3, 6, 21, 24, 38 is $38 - 3 = 35$.

For grouped data the range is the difference between the upper limit of the last interval and the lower limit of the first interval.

Next we shall define percentiles.

DEFINITION OF PERCENTILES

The nth percentile of a set of numbers arranged in order of magnitude is that value which has $n\%$ of the numbers below it and $(100 - n)\%$ above it.

EXAMPLE

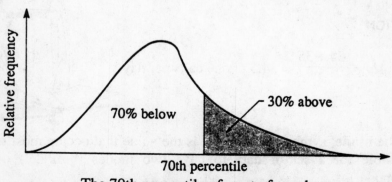

The 70th percentile of a set of numbers.

Percentiles are often used to describe the results of achievement tests. For example, someone graduates in the top 10% of his class. Frequently used percentiles are the 25th, 50th, and 75th percentiles, which are called the lower quartile, the middle quartile (median), and the upper quartile, respectively.

DEFINITION OF INTERQUARTILE RANGE

The interquartile range, denoted IQR, of a set of numbers is the difference between the upper and lower quartiles.

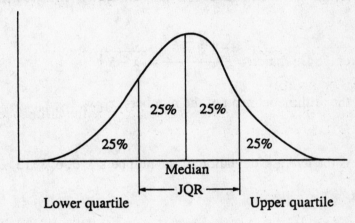

Now we shall introduce an important concept of deviation.

The deviation of a number x from its mean $\overline{x}$ is defined to be

$$x - \overline{x}$$

Using deviations we can construct many different measures of variability.

Observe that the mean deviation for any set of measurements is always zero. Indeed, let $x_1, x_2, \ldots, x_n$ be measurements. Their mean is given by

$$\overline{x} = \frac{\Sigma x_i}{n}$$

The deviations are

$$x_1 - \overline{x}, x_2 - \overline{x}, \ldots, x_n - \overline{x}$$

and their mean is equal to

$$\frac{\sum_{i=1}^{n}(x_i - \bar{x})}{n} = \frac{\sum x_i}{n} - \bar{x} = 0$$

MEASURES OF DISPERSION

DEFINITION OF AVERAGE DEVIATION

The average deviation of a set of n numbers $x_1, x_2, ..., x_n$ is defined by

$$\text{Average Deviation} = \frac{\sum_{i=1}^{n} |x_i - \bar{x}|}{n} = \overline{|x - \bar{x}|}$$

where $\bar{x}$ is the arithmetic mean of the numbers $x_1, x_2, ..., x_n$.

EXAMPLE

What is the average deviation of the numbers 3, 5, 6, 8, 13, 21?

SOLUTION

$$\bar{x} = \frac{3+5+6+8+13+21}{6} = 9.33$$

$$\text{Average Deviation} = \frac{6.33 + 4.33 + 3.33 + 1.33 + 4.33 + 12.33}{6}$$

$$= 5.33$$

If the frequencies of the numbers $x_1, x_2, ..., x_n$ are $f_1, f_2, ..., f_n$ respectively, then the average deviation becomes

$$\text{Average Deviation} = \frac{\sum_i f_i |x_i - \bar{x}|}{\sum f_i}$$

We will be using this formula for grouped data where x_i's represent class marks and f_i represents class frequencies.

The sum

$$\sum_{i=1}^{n} |x_i - a|$$

is the maximum when a is the median.

DEFINITION OF STANDARD DEVIATION

The standard deviation of a set $x_1, x_2, ..., x_n$ of n numbers is defined by

$$s = \sqrt{\frac{\sum_{i=1}^{n}(x_1 - \bar{x})^2}{n}} = \sqrt{\overline{(x - \bar{x})^2}}$$

The sample standard deviation is denoted by s, while the corresponding population standard deviation is denoted by σ.

For grouped data, we use the modified formula for standard deviation. Let the frequencies of the numbers $x_1, x_2, ..., x_n$ be $f_1, f_2, ..., f_n$ respectively. Then

$$s = \sqrt{\frac{\Sigma f_i \, (x_i - \bar{x})^2}{\Sigma f_i}} = \sqrt{\frac{\Sigma f \, (x - \bar{x})^2}{\Sigma f}}$$

Often, in the definition of the standard deviation the denominator is not n but $n - 1$. For large values of n, the difference between the two definitions is negligible.

DEFINITION OF VARIANCE

The variance of a set of measurements is defined as the square of the standard deviation. Thus

$$s^2 = \frac{\sum_{i=1}^{n}(x_i - \bar{x})^2}{n}$$

or

$$s^2 = \frac{\sum_{i=1}^{n} f_i \, (x_i - \bar{x})^2}{\sum_{i=1}^{n} f_i}$$

Usually, the variance of the sample is denoted by s^2 and the corresponding population variance is denoted by σ^2.

EXAMPLE

A simple manual task was given to six children and the time each child took to complete the task was measured. Results are shown in the table. What is the standard deviation and variance?

x_i	$x_i - \bar{x}$	$(x_i - \bar{x})^2$
12	2.5	6.25
9	−0.5	0.25
11	1.5	2.25
6	−3.5	12.25
10	0.5	0.25
9	−0 +	0.25
Total 57	0	21.5

SOLUTION

For this sample, we shall find the standard deviation and variance.

The average $\bar{x}$ is 9.5.

$$\bar{x} = 9.5$$

The standard deviation is

$$s = \sqrt{\frac{21.5}{6}} = 1.893$$

and the variance is

$$s^2 = 3.583$$

SIMPLIFIED METHODS FOR COMPUTING THE STANDARD DEVIATION AND VARIANCE

By definition

$$s^2 = \frac{\sum_{i=1}^{n}(x_i - \bar{x})^2}{n}$$

Hence

$$s^2 = \frac{\Sigma(x - \bar{x})^2}{n} = \frac{\Sigma(x^2 - 2x\bar{x} - \bar{x}^2)}{n}$$

$$= \frac{\Sigma x^2}{n} - 2\bar{x} \frac{\Sigma x}{n} + \frac{n\bar{x}^2}{n} = \frac{\Sigma x^2}{n} - 2\bar{x}^2 + \bar{x}^2$$

$$= \overline{x^2} - \bar{x}^2 = \frac{\Sigma x_i^2}{n} - \left(\frac{\Sigma x_i}{n}\right)^2$$

and $\quad s = \sqrt{\overline{x^2} - \bar{x}^2} = \sqrt{\frac{\Sigma x_i^2}{n} - \left(\frac{\Sigma x_i}{n}\right)^2}$

Similarly for

$$s^2 = \frac{\sum_{i=1}^{n} f_i(x_i - \bar{x})^2}{\Sigma f_i}$$

We find

$$s^2 = \frac{\Sigma f(x - \bar{x})^2}{\Sigma f} = \frac{\Sigma fx^2 - 2\bar{x} \Sigma fx + \bar{x}^2 \Sigma f}{\Sigma f}$$

$$= \frac{\Sigma fx^2}{\Sigma f} - \bar{x}^2 = \frac{\Sigma fx^2}{\Sigma f} - \left(\frac{\Sigma fx}{\Sigma f}\right)^2$$

EXAMPLE

Consider the example on the previous page. We shall use the formula

$$s^2 = \overline{x^2} - \bar{x}^2$$

to compute the value of s^2.

$$s^2 = \frac{563}{6} - (9.5)^2 = 3.583$$

and $\quad s = 1.893$

Remember that $\overline{x^2}$ denotes the mean of the squares of all values of x and $\bar{x}^2$ denotes the square of the mean of all x's.

Let D be an arbitrary constant and

$$d_i = x_i - D$$

be the deviations of x_i from D. Then

$$x_i = d_i + D$$

and $\quad \overline{x} = \overline{d} + D$

Hence

$$s^2 = \overline{(x - \overline{x})^2} = \overline{(d - \overline{d})^2} = \overline{d^2 - 2\overline{d}d + \overline{d}^2}$$

$$= \overline{d^2} - \overline{d}^2 = \frac{\Sigma \, fd^2}{\Sigma \, f} - \left(\frac{\Sigma \, fd}{\Sigma \, f} \right)^2$$

EXAMPLE

We find the standard deviation for the data shown below. The height of 100 students was measured and recorded.

Height (inches)	Class Mark x	x^2	Frequency f	fx^2	fx
60 – 62	61	3,721	7	26,047	427
63 – 65	64	4,096	21	86,016	1,344
66 – 68	67	4,489	37	166,093	2,479
69 – 71	70	4,900	26	127,400	1,820
72 – 74	73	5,329	9	47,961	657
			Σf =100	Σfx^2= 453,517	Σfx= 6,727

We apply the formula

$$s = \sqrt{\frac{\Sigma \, fx^2}{\Sigma \, f} = \left(\frac{\Sigma \, fx}{\Sigma \, f} \right)^2}$$

Hence

$$s = \sqrt{4,535 - 4,525} = 3.16$$

Using the empirical rule we can interpret the standard deviation of a set of measurements.

EMPIRICAL RULE

If a set of measurements has a bell-shaped histogram, then:

1. the interval $\bar{x} \pm s$ contains approximately 68% of the measurements.

2. $\bar{x} \pm 2s$ contains approximately 95% of the measurements.

3. $\bar{x} \pm 3s$ contains approximately all the measurements.

Note that from the empirical rule we can find the approximate value of the sample standard deviation s. Approximately 95% of all the measurements are located in the interval $\bar{x} \pm 2s$. The length of this interval is $4s$. Hence the range of the measurements is equal to approximately $4s$.

$$\text{Approximate Value of } s = \frac{\text{range}}{4}$$

For normal (bell-shaped) distributions we have

Empirical Rule

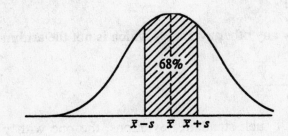

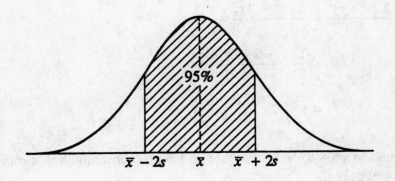

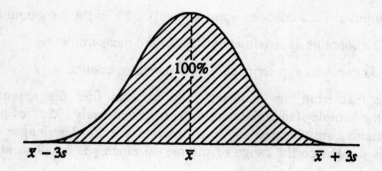

We shall discuss some properties of the standard deviation.

In the definition of the standard deviation

$$s = \sqrt{\frac{\sum\limits_{i=1}^{n}(x_i - \bar{x})^2}{n}}$$

we can replace $\bar{x}$ by any other average y which is not the arithmetic mean

$$s = \sqrt{\frac{\sum (x_i - y)^2}{n}}$$

Note that of all such standard deviations, the one with $y = \bar{x}$ is the minimum. Indeed

$$\frac{\sum (x - y)^2}{n} = \frac{\sum (x^2 - 2xy + y^2)}{n}$$

$$= \frac{\sum x^2 - 2y \sum x + ny^2}{n}$$

$$= y^2 - 2y\frac{\sum x}{n} + \frac{\sum x^2}{n}$$

Equation $y^2 + ay + b$, where a and b are constants, has a minimum value if and only if

$$y = -\frac{1}{2}a.$$

Hence

$$y = \frac{\Sigma x}{n} = \bar{x}$$

Consider two sets consisting of N_1 and N_2 measurements or two frequency distributions with total frequencies N_1 and N_2. The variances are s_1^2 and s_2^2 respectively.

If both sets have the same mean $\bar{x}$, then the combined (or pooled) variance of both sets or both frequency distributions is given by

$$s^2 = \frac{N_1 s_1^2 + N_2 s_2^2}{N_1 + N_2}$$

SAMPLING ERROR

When a sample is selected for an investigation instead of taking a census, it is expected that some difference will exist between the results provided by the sample and the results that would have been provided if a complete census had been taken. This difference is referred to as **sampling error**, and the size of this error will differ from sample to sample. In other words, every sample of a certain size does not yield identical results for a particular estimate, such as the mean. In fact, the results may be substantially different from sample to sample.

If samples are selected using a random technique, the amount of this error may be mathematically calculated, which is another important reason for selecting a probability selection technique, as opposed to one of the non-probability techniques. If we can determine the amount of error that exists in our results, we can also determine the degree of precision or accuracy of the population estimates which are being made from the sample. Sampling error is basically a function of three factors: (1) the size of the sample being used to make the population estimates; (2) the dispersion or scatter of the data points within the population and; consequently, the sample, and (3) the degree of confidence one may place on the accuracy of the results.

☞ Drill: Exploring Data

DIRECTIONS: Choose the best answer choice.

1. The mean salary for four company employees who make $5/hr., $8/hr., $12/hr., and $15/hr. is

   (A) $9/hr.   (C) $10/hr,

   (B) $11/hr.   (D) $12/hr.

2. The mean length of five fish with lengths of 7.5 in., 7.75 in., 8.5 in., 8.5 in., and 8.25 in. is

   (A) 8.0 in.   (C) 8.2 in.

   (B) 8.1 in.   (D) 8.3 in.

3. The median of the sample 34, 29, 26, 37, and 31 is

   (A) 31.   (C) 35.

   (B) 26.   (D) 29.

4. The median of the sample 34, 29, 26, 37, 31 and 34 is

   (A) 26.   (C) 32.5.

   (B) 37.   (D) 33.5.

5. The median age in a sample of 6 children with ages 3, 6, 4, 7, 9, 8 is

   (A) 5.5.   (C) 6.0.

   (B) 7.5.   (D) 6.5.

6. A family had eight children. The ages were 9, 11, 8, 15, 14, 12, 17, and 14. The range of the data is

   (A) 10.   (C) 15.

   (B) 9.   (D) 14.

7. The variance of the sample of observations 2, 5, 7, 9, and 12 is

   (A) 11.0.   (C) 11.5.

   (B) 11.2.   (D) 11.6.

8. From the sample of data 5, 8, 2, 1, the standard deviation of the sample is

(A) 2.7. (C) 2.74.

(B) 3.0. (D) 2.75.

DIRECTIONS: Draw a histogram for questions 9 and 10.

---

9. Twenty students are enrolled in the foreign language department, and their major fields are as follows: Spanish, Spanish, French, Italian, French, Spanish, German, German, Russian, Russian, French, German, German, German, Spanish, Russian, German, Italian, German, Spanish.

Make a frequency histogram.

10. The following data is a sample of the accounts receivable of a small merchandising firm.

37	42	44	47	46	50	48	52	90
54	56	55	53	58	59	60	62	92
60	61	62	63	67	64	64	68	
67	65	66	68	69	66	70	72	
73	75	74	72	71	76	81	80	
79	80	78	82	83	85	86	88	

Using a class interval of 5, i.e. 35–39, construct a histogram.

Answers to Drill Questions

1. The correct answer is (C). The mean salary is the average.

$$\overline{X} = \frac{\Sigma x_i}{n}$$

$$= \frac{\$5 + \$8 + \$12 + \$15}{4}$$

$$= \frac{\$40}{4}$$

$$= \$10/\text{hr}.$$

2. The correct answer is (B). The mean length is the average length.

$$\overline{X} = \frac{\Sigma x_i}{n}$$
$$= \frac{7.5 + 7.75 + 8.5 + 8.5 + 8.25}{5}$$
$$= \frac{40.5}{5}$$
$$= 8.1 \text{ in.}$$

3. The correct answer is (A). The median, a measure of central tendency, is the middle number. The number of observations that lie above the median is the same as the number of observations that lie below it.

Arranged in order we have 26, 29, 31, 34 and 37. The number of observations is odd and thus the median is 31. Note that there are two numbers in the sample above 31 and two below 31.

4. The correct answer is (C). The sample arranged in order is 26, 29, 31, 34, 34, and 37. The number of observations is even and thus the median, or middle number is chosen halfway between the third and fourth number. In this case the median is

$$\frac{21 + 34}{2} = 32.5.$$

5. The correct answer is (D). Arranging the observations in order, we have 3, 4, 6, 7, 8, 9. There are six observations in the sample so the median will be the average of the third and fourth observations, 6 and 7. The median is

$$\frac{6 + 7}{2} = 6.5.$$

6. The correct answer is (B). Often we want to know how spread out the observations of data were. The range of the sample is a quantity which measures dispersion. We define the range to be the difference between the largest and smallest observations in our sample. In this case,

$$R = 17 - 8 = 9.$$

7.   The correct answer is (D). The variance of the sample is defined as

$$s^2 = \frac{\Sigma(X_i - \overline{X})^2}{n}.$$

This is an average of the squared deviations from the sample mean, $\overline{X}$.

$$\overline{X} = \frac{\Sigma X_i}{n}$$
$$= \frac{2+5+7+9+12}{5}$$
$$= \frac{35}{5}$$
$$= 7$$

and $$s^2 = \frac{(2-7)^2 + (5-7)^2 + (7-7)^2 + (9-7)^2 + (12-7)^2}{5}$$
$$= \frac{25+4+0+4+25}{5}$$
$$= \frac{58}{5}$$
$$= 11.6.$$

8.   The correct answer is (C). The degree to which numerical data tends to spread about an average value is usually called dispersion or variation of the data. One way to measure the degree of dispersion is with the standard deviation. We define it as

$$s = \sqrt{\frac{\sum\limits_{i}(X_i - \overline{X})^2}{n}}.$$

It gives a feeling for how far away from the mean we can expect an observation to be. Sometimes the standard deviation for the data of a sample is defined with $n - 1$ replacing n in the denominator of our expression. The resulting value represents a "better" estimate of the true standard deviation of the entire population. For large n ($n > 30$) there is practically no difference between the 2 values. Let us find the mean for our sample.

$$\overline{X} = \frac{\Sigma X_i}{n}$$

$$= \frac{5+8+2+1}{n}$$

$$= \frac{16}{4}$$

$$= 4.$$

X_i	$X_i - \overline{X}$	$(X_i - \overline{X})^2$
5	$5 - 4 = 1$	$1^2 = 1$
8	$8 - 4 = 4$	$4^2 = 16$
2	$2 - 4 = -2$	$(-2)^2 = 4$
1	$1 - 4 = -3$	$(-3)^2 = 9$

$$\Sigma (X_i - X)^2 = 1 + 16 + 4 + 9 = 30$$

$$n = 4$$

$$s = \sqrt{\frac{\Sigma(X_i - \overline{X})^2}{n}}$$

$$= \sqrt{\frac{30}{4}}$$

$$= \sqrt{\frac{15}{2}}$$

$$= \sqrt{7.5}$$

$$= 2.74.$$

9.   The frequency distribution table is constructed by writing down the major field and next to it the number of students

Major Field	Number of Students
German	7
Russian	3
Spanish	5
French	3
Italian	2
Total	20

A histogram follows:

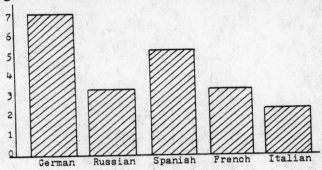

In the histogram, the fields are listed and spaced evenly along the horizontal axis. Each specific field is represented by a rectangle, and all have the same width. The height of each, identified by a number on the vertical axis, corresponds to the frequency of that field.

10.

Class Interval	Class Boundaries	Tally	Interval Median	Frequency
35 – 39	34.5 – 39.5	/	37	1
40 – 44	39.5 – 44.5	//	42	2
45 – 49	44.5 – 49.5	///	47	3
50 – 54	49.5 – 54.5	////	52	4
55 – 59	54.5 – 59.6	////	57	4
60 – 64	59.5 – 64.5	///// ///	62	8
65 – 69	64.5 – 69.5	///// ///	67	8
70 – 74	69.5 – 74.5	///// /	72	6
75 – 79	74.5 – 79.5	////	77	4
80 – 84	79.5 – 84.5	/////	82	5
85 – 89	84.5 – 89.5	///	87	3
90 – 94	89.5 – 94.5	//	92	2

We use fractional class boundaries. One reason for this is that we cannot break up the horizontal axis of the histogram into only integral values. We must do something with the fractional parts. The usual thing to do is to assign all values to the closest integer. Hence our above class boundaries. The appropriate histogram follows.

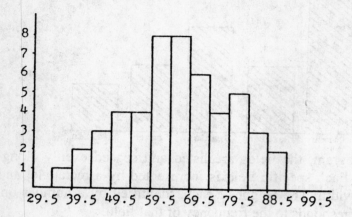

CHAPTER 3
PLANNING A STUDY

Chapter 3

PLANNING A STUDY

METHODS OF DATA COLLECTION

CENSUS

A census is an official, usually periodic, inventory of a population, often including a collection of related demographic information. Usually taken every five or ten years, the census contains a description of persons and their life conditions and of national resources, thus providing vital statistical information for social scientists and government planners. Information collected by a census is useful in describing the health and well-being of a society because it includes data regarding variables, such as race, age, average life span, occupations and social strata of people from a particular city, state, region or country. If a researcher wishes to know, for example, whether a New Yorker or a Californian is more likely to be an engineer, such statistical information can be extracted from the census database. The researcher is free to choose any demographic variables of interest for comparison, and can perform appropriate statistical comparisons once this data is obtained from the census.

SAMPLE SURVEY

A survey uses self report measures to question people about themselves. Questionnaires and interviews are used to gain knowledge about people's attitudes, demographics and behaviors. A small sample of individuals are given surveys; the results are then generalized to a large population. The population consists of all the individuals of interest to the researcher (for example, the entire voting population of the United States). The sample consists of a much smaller number of the people representative of the population (for example, ten citizens from every U.S. state). In this way, the researcher can generalize the results of sampling this small group to explain the attitudes and desired behavior of the larger population.

The survey is used most frequently to study human behavior at one particular point in time. However, the same survey can be presented at many different points in time, and the results can then be compared to discover the possible changes of a particular behavior or dimension under question.

EXPERIMENT

An **experiment** involves the manipulation of variables. In describing an experiment, the variable that is hypothesized to cause some effect on another variable is called the independent variable, and the variable that is hypothesized to be affected is called the dependent variable. An experimenter systematically manipulates one or more independent variables, and measures a dependent variable. For example, if the experimenter wishes to study whether exercise reduces stress, exercise would be manipulated and anxiety would then be measured. Such a manipulation could involve one group of subjects exercising one hour a day for a month, while a second group of subjects abstains from exercising. In this case, exercise is the independent variable, and anxiety, the variable we wish to measure, is the dependent variable.

The researcher is free to choose any manipulation which is hypothesized to have an effect on the dependent variable. The experiment allows the researcher to formulate an idea (hypothesis), set up a manipulation or several manipulations, and study the dependent variable to determine if the manipulations produce any significant effects. An experiment allows the researcher to determine a cause-and-effect relationship between variables. Suppose an experimenter wanted to find out whether the amount of studying has an effect on teenagers' performance on a mathematical examination. In this case, the independent variable would be the amount of studying done by each subject and the dependent variable would be the performance on the mathematical examination. Ideally, the experimenter would randomly assign teenagers to different groups; one group would abstain from studying and another group would study for one hour per night for two weeks. (Note: The experimenter can set any conditions for the experiment—the study can contain three groups, the amount of studying can be two hours a night). After a two-week period, the students are given a math exam. The scores on the exam (the dependent variable) are compared between the two groups. If the group that studied one hour each night scores significantly higher on the exam, and all other variables are constant, we can conclude that the studying caused the higher scores.

OBSERVATIONAL STUDY

An **observational study** allows the researcher to directly observe the behavior of interest rather than rely on subjects' self-descriptions. The observational method allows the researcher to study the subject in its natural environment. Jane Goodall practiced this method when she lived in the jungles for many years studying chimps; she was able to observe the natural, uninterrupted daily behaviors of the animals. As a part of the environment, the researcher can remove the potentially biased effect of the unnatural laboratory setting on a subjects' performance. However, it is important that the observer attempt to stay out of the way and not influence the subjects' normal activities. The subjects are left in their natural environment so as to eliminate any artificial influence that may be caused by taking them out of their natural habitat.

In a field observation study, observations are made in a particular natural setting over an extended period of time. The researcher must be immersed in the situation, observing the setting, behaviors of its inhabitants and relationship between inhabitants. This type of observation is performed when a researcher wishes to understand and describe how people in a particular social setting live, work and experience the setting.

Systematic observation refers to the observation of one or more particular behaviors in a specific setting. This type of research is much less global than a field observational study; the observations are quantifiable and hypotheses are generally predetermined by the experimenter before the observations begin.

☞ Drill: Methods of Data Collection

DIRECTIONS: Select the best answer.

1. When conducting a well-constructed survey, a researcher should use

   (A) open-ended questions.

   (B) questionnaires only.

   (C) non-randomized presentation of questions.

   (D) closed-ended questions.

2. The best method of obtaining reliable research data is a(n)

   (A) experiment.

   (B) observational study.

   (C) survey.

   (D) none of the above.

3. Bias in an experiment can be caused by

   (A) stratification of variation.

   (B) small sample size.

   (C) manipulation of an independent variable.

   (D) blocking.

4. The manipulation of variables is necessary in

   (A) the survey.

   (B) the experiment.

   (C) the census.

   (D) the observational study.

5. If you want to study the behavior of children at play, which is the best method for collecting data?

   (A) Presenting questionnaires to the children

   (B) Conducting one-on-one interviews with the children's parents

(C)   Observing the children's behavior in a playground

(D)   Simulating a playground in the laboratory and setting up an experiment to examine the effects of the playground on the behavior of children

---

DIRECTIONS: Determine the correct responses from the information provided in questions 6 and 7.

---

6.   Describe how you would set up a method of data collection given the following situation. Include why you selected such a method, and stress the main advantages and disadvantages of your method.

Situation: You wish to study whether pets have an effect on the stress level of humans.

7.   You wish to study the behavior of chimps, including foraging patterns, sexual behaviors, and interaction between members of a society. Describe how you would perform an observational study to collect relevant data. State the advantages and disadvantages of the observational method.

Answers to Drill Questions

1.   **(D)**   The correct answer is (D). Open-ended questions are difficult to code and can promote non-specific responses from the subject. Questionnaires and interviews are both useful in obtaining reliable information; it is up to the experimenter to choose the method most appropriate for the study. Questions should be presented randomly in order to reduce possible bias. Closed-ended questions force the subject to choose a specific answer; these types of questions also allow the researcher to code the answers before the study, thus allowing for ease in the interpretation of data.

2.   **(D)**   The correct answer is (D). There is no singular "best" overall method of data collection. Each type of data collection has individual pros and cons, and the type of method used will depend on what questions the researcher wishes to answer, and what types of manipulations are to be performed on the data. It is up to the researcher to determine the best type of data collection method by determining what is to be studied and who the subjects will be.

3.   **(B)**   The correct answer is (B). Stratifying to reduce variance helps to reduce bias in an experiment; the manipulation of an independent vari-

able is essential in an experiment and should not add any additional bias to the study design. Blocking also helps to reduce bias in an experiment by preventing any effect by the order of question presentation. A small sample size may introduce bias into the experiment because the sample may not be representative of the population: the larger the sample size, the more representative the sample will be of the population at large.

4. **(B)** The correct answer is (B). The only research method in which variables are manipulated by the researcher is the experiment. A survey involves questionnaires or interviews which possess pre-determined questions selected by the researcher. The census provides a database of demographic data, again without any manipulations. The observational study is used precisely when the experimenter wishes to refrain from manipulations, observing the natural behavior of the subjects without interfering in such daily behaviors.

5. **(C)** The correct answer is (C). In this case, the best way to collect data regarding play behavior of children is to actually observe the children in a playground. A questionnaire presented to the children could have many potential problems, including possible lack of comprehension by the children, and it would be difficult to find out information about playing. Although an interview with the children's parents could potentially provide an abundance of information about the child's individual behavior, the parent's answers and descriptions could be biased because of omission of aggressive tendencies. An experiment would also not be useful given this situation; since play behavior occurs in natural, real-life settings, we could not safely generalize the behavior in a laboratory to behavior outside of the laboratory.

6. This is one possible answer to the question.

An experiment would be useful to collect information about the effect of pets on the human stress level. The independent variables would be: presence of pets, number of pets in household, and daily time spent with pet(s). The dependent variable would be the stress level of the individual (quantified before initiating the experiment).

The experiment is useful here because we can examine any possible cause-and-effect relationship between the variables. An advantage to this method is that we can control the number of pets in the household, and control the amount of time each person spends with each animal, thereby manipulating the independent variables. If the experiment is designed in a way where extraneous variables are controlled for, any differences in the level of stress can be attributed to the presence of pets in the household.

A disadvantage of experimentation is the inconvenience and time needed to perform the study. The experimental procedure generally is quite costly, and it requires much work on the part of the experimenter to set up the study, perform it, and analyze the outcome. The results often can not be generalized from the experimental condition to the outside population because of the difference in conditions.

7.   This is a possible answer to the question.

In order to perform an observational study on chimps, it is necessary for the researcher to be immersed with the chimps in their natural environment. The researcher should record all daily activities of the members in the society, preferably remaining out of sight of the animals as not to influence their behavior. Advantages of this method include the gathering of data of naturally occurring events; behavior observed in an unnatural setting, such as a laboratory where the animals are caged, will not be typical of the animals' normal behavior. If the researcher remains unobtrusive while performing the observation, the data obtained could be invaluable because the observed interaction of the animals takes place in a real-life, natural setting.

There are many disadvantages to the observational method, however. The researcher must spend a considerable amount of time in the natural setting in order to observe a full spectrum of behavior and not affect the behavior of the animals in the surroundings. Also, the cause of any behavior cannot be determined. Although many different patterns of behavior can be observed, the researcher can only make inferences as to the cause of such behaviors.

PLANNING AND CONDUCTING SURVEYS

SIMPLE RANDOM SAMPLING

With a simple random sampling procedure, every member of the population has an equal probability of being selected for the sample. If a population consists of 100 members, each member has one chance out of one hundred of being selected. This procedure does not introduce any biases about who gets chosen because every person has an equal chance of being selected as a subject. The advantage of this technique is that it provides a sample of subjects whose responses represent those of the general population. A good method for choosing a random sample is to use a table of random numbers, or to create a computer program in which a sample can be randomly generated from a given population.

CHARACTERISTICS OF A WELL-DESIGNED AND WELL-CONDUCTED SURVEY

When constructing a survey, it is important for the researcher to carefully determine what is being studied before beginning the study. The survey questions must relate to the research questions, and the researcher must be specific in the wording of such questions.

The following are characteristics of a well-designed survey:

(1) The researcher should always use closed-ended rather than open-ended questions. With closed-ended questions, only a limited number of response alternatives are given; open-ended questions, however, allow subjects to answer in any way they like, with an unlimited number of response types. The open-ended question "What do you do when you are depressed?" can yield many different answers. The following closed-ended question requires that the subject give one specific answer:

"What, of the following, do you do when you are depressed?"

A. sleep

B. cry

C. shop

D. yell

E. eat

The alternative choices can be coded before hand, allowing the researcher to quickly and efficiently interpret the data. It would be very difficult to score results from open-ended questions in a consistent and unbiased fashion; utilizing closed-ended questions involves a much more structured approach to analyzing data.

(2) Once the questions are constructed, they should be tested on individuals who are not included as subjects in the study. Any "bad" questions, including ambiguous or "double-barreled" questions, should not be used in the survey. An example of an ambiguous question is "How do you feel about politics?"; a better question would be "Which political party do you support?" (giving multiple choice answers for the subjects' selection) because a specific answer will be obtained. Double-barreled questions, such as "Do you agree that teachers should be concerned with students' performance in school and their social life?" ask more than one thing, and the researcher will be unable to determine if the subject agrees with the first, second or both portions of the sentence.

(3) The study should be free of interviewer bias. It has been shown that sex, age and race of the experimenter can influence the way a subject responds. A problem may also exist if more than one experimenter conducts the survey; different personalities and appearances might have an effect on the way the subject will respond.

(4) The order of question presentation should be randomized between subjects. It is best to avoid questions with negative connotations, if possible, as they increase the likelihood that a response set will be generated by the person responding to the survey. A response set is a pattern of individual responses to questions that is not related to the content of the questions. In general, it is best to ask positive questions first, as not to offend or intimidate the subject. The subject may feel ill at ease if the survey begins with a question such as "Do you cheat on your tax return?" and may not answer the questions truthfully. The questions should be randomized within the survey, and presented in a different order for each subject.

SAMPLING ERROR: THE VARIATION INHERENT IN A SURVEY

Every researcher wishes to perform the perfect study; since it will rarely ever be the case that such an occurrence will happen, some source of sampling error will be evident in every survey. Error arises from the fact that the sample of subjects selected does not provide a perfectly accurate representation of the population or when individuals not from the population are included in the sample. If, for example, you wish to study the effects of weight on the self-esteem of Americans, you would not survey only obese individuals.

In an ideal study, every member of the population would be questioned, and the sampling error would be zero; because this is not possible, some degree of sampling error, however small, will be present in all studies. This error is typically quite small, and approaches zero as the sample size increases. An invalid or biased sample yields data that are altered in some consistent fashion away from the parameter values.

To prevent a great amount of sampling error, the researcher should always carefully examine the population and decide which variables to measure, making sure to be aware of bias in a survey.

Sources of Bias in Surveys

Many different factors can contribute to bias in a given survey. Some examples of bias are:

(1) *Interviewer bias*. The researcher must be wary of inadvertently showing approval or disapproval when the subject responds. This subconscious approval by the researcher could influence how the subject responds to future questions. If the subject is reinforced for giving a positive response, the subject might continue to answer the following questions in a positive manner, even if the subject's feelings are to the contrary.

(2) *Non-randomized question bias*. Presenting questions non-randomly could result in possible bias of the results. The order of the questions could have an effect on the responses of the subject. A randomized presentation of questions solves the problem of social desirability—wanting to look good and socially acceptable to the experimenter.

(3) *Restricting subject population*. Restricting any sample to a particular group could have severe consequences on the reliability of experimental results. For example, imagine if a researcher chooses subjects from a college campus: if the researcher selects students who exit a particular classroom (Statistics 101) at 8:00 a.m. every day, the sample is restricted to a population with a mathematical interest and an inclination for rising early. The researcher should choose a sample from students from all classes, at all campus locations, at different times during the day. The results from a limited sample of the population cannot be generalized to the entire population because the sample is not representative of the whole population.

STRATIFYING TO REDUCE VARIATION

To reduce variation in a survey, sometimes a procedure called stratification is used. This procedure helps ensure that several of the characteristics of the population are represented in the survey sample. First, the experimenter determines characteristics relevant to the study; then, subjects who possess these characteristics are selected. The population is divided into subgroups (or "strata"). Random sampling techniques are then employed to select sample members from each stratum. A number of dimensions could be used to divide the population. The dimensions used should be relevant to the problem under study. For example, a survey of intellectual attitudes may be stratified into the following dimensions: age, amount of education, and gender. Stratifying on the basis of height or eye color would be ridiculous. The advantage of stratified random sampling is that we can be assured that the sample will accurately reflect the numerical composition of the various subgroups. This type of accuracy is especially important when some subgroups comprise very small percentages of the population. For instance, if Italian-Americans comprise 6% of the population in a given region of 100,000 individuals, a simple random sample of 100 individuals might not include any Italian-Americans. A stratified random sample, on the other hand, would include six Italian-Americans chosen randomly from the population, thus ensuring that a representative amount of Italian-Americans can be studied.

☞ Drill: Planning and Conducting Surveys

DIRECTIONS: Select the best answer.

1. A well-designed survey should contain

    (A) interviewer bias.

    (B) double-barreled questions.

    (C) randomized presentation of questions.

    (D) open-ended questions.

2. Stratifying a survey sample will provide which of the following?

    (A) Reduced variation

    (B) Increased sample size

    (C) Biased results

    (D) Subject restriction

3. The sampling method in which every member of a population has an equal chance of being selected for the sample is

    (A) stratified random sampling.

    (B) simple random sampling.

(C)   quota sampling.

(D)   cluster sampling.

4.   Which of the following methods can be used to present a survey?

I.   Questionnaire

II.   Interview

III.   Field observation

(A)   I only   (C)   I and II

(B)   II only   (D)   I and III

5.   An advantage of using the survey method of data collection is

(A)   minimal expense.

(B)   discovery of cause-and-effect relationships.

(C)   freedom to manipulate variables.

(D)   observing the subject in a natural environment.

DIRECTIONS: Determine the correct responses from the information provided in questions 6 and 7.

---

6.   You wish to construct a survey to find out about teenagers' feelings towards the Advanced Placement examinations. List five sample questions you would use in your survey, and describe what type of questions should be used in the construction of the survey. Also note what type of questions should be avoided, and provide explanations for why these questions should be omitted from your survey.

7.   The following questions were constructed by an absent-minded professor for inclusion in a survey about political attitudes. Describe why these questions are not ideal, and provide five alternative questions to be used in the survey.

a.   What do you like about politics?

b.   Do you agree that Clinton supports health care and education?

c.   Why would you choose to vote?

d.   Do you think that the debates accurately reflect the opinions of Republicans and Democrats?

e.   What is the worst thing about politics?

Answers to Drill Questions

1.   **(C)**   The correct answer is (C). A good survey should be free of interviewer bias; blinding techniques (where the experimenter and/or the subject are blind to the treatment being given) serve to reduce any interviewer bias. Interviewers should be instructed to present the survey in a standardized manner in order to reduce such bias. Double-barreled questions should be avoided because these questions ask more than one thing; the results are quite difficult to decipher and analyze. Open-ended questions allow the subject to answer in a vague or uninterpretable fashion; such questions should always be avoided when constructing a survey. The randomized presentation of questions helps to eliminate bias in a given survey, and should always be employed when giving a survey.

2.   **(A)**   The correct answer is (A). The purpose of stratifying a sample is to include those individuals representative of the large population who may not be present in a small, selected sample of subjects. Stratification will not affect the size of the sample, nor will the results become biased. On the contrary, such stratification can remove bias from the sample. The restriction of subjects can occur when the experimenter chooses members of a restricted population, such as subjects from one particular classroom.

3.   **(B)**   The correct answer is (B). Stratified random sampling requires that the researcher examine the population before beginning the study, separating the population into different strata; each member of the population does not have an equal chance of being selected for the sample. Quota sampling involves a sample that reflects the numerical composition of various subgroups in the population. Cluster sampling is used when the researcher wishes to sample members from an unusual or very large population (for instance, all volunteers from mental health hospitals from across the country); rather than sampling randomly from the entire population, "clusters" of desired individuals are identified, and samples are selected from such clusters. In simple random sampling, every member of the population has an equal chance of being selected.

4.   **(C)**   The correct answer is (C). Both questionnaires and interviews are useful in presenting a survey to a designated sample. An observation requires that the subject remain passive and the researcher make detailed notes and observations regarding behavioral patterns.

5.   **(A)**   The correct answer is (A). The survey method can be performed with minimal time and expense. The discovery of cause-and-effect

relationships and the freedom to manipulate variables are both benefits of the experimental procedure, not the survey. The observational method allows for the observance of behavior in a natural environment.

6.   Here is a possible answer. In constructing a survey studying the feelings of teenagers towards the Advanced Placement examinations, the following types of questions should be used:

    a.   Are you currently taking an Advanced Placement examination?

    b.   Of the following choices, which best describes how you feel about the AP examination:

        i.   great opportunity

        ii.   waste of time

        iii.   I volunteered to take the exam

        iv.   I am forced to take the exam

    c.   How many Advanced Placement examinations have you taken, if any?

    d.   What, in your opinion, is the best aspect of the AP examination?

        i.   college credit

        ii.   intellectual challenge

        iii.   interesting material

        iv.   good practice for college

    e.   List your favorite AP subject:_____.

These questions are specific, and closed-ended, requiring the subject to report a concise answer which can easily be analyzed by the researcher. All answers can be quantified (even question "e," because only a certain number of AP examinations exist).

Questions to be avoided in forming a survey are double-barreled questions, which ask more than one question of the subject (such as, "What do you think about the AP examination and review course?"), and ambiguous questions which cannot easily be interpreted by the experimenter (for instance, "What do you think about Statistics?"). Open-ended questions, which allow the subject to answer in a vague, unspecified fashion, should also be avoided when constructing a survey.

7.   Here is a possible answer. The above questions should not be used in a survey for the following reasons: questions (a), (c), and (e) are vague open-ended questions which do not require a specific answer. The answers to such questions are often difficult to code by the experimenter, and sometimes conflict with what the researcher is actually trying to find out. Questions (b) and (d) ask more than one question of the subject; if this information is desired, the researcher should break down this question into two separate inquiries. Better corresponding questions are:

a.   Do you prefer the Republican Party or the Democratic Party?

b.   Do you agree that Clinton supports health care?

c.   Out of the following choices, what is the strongest reason why you vote:

   i.   I feel obligated to vote

   ii.   I vote because my friends vote

   iii.   I want to show my support of a particular political party

   iv.   I want to be active in choosing an American President

d.   Do you think that the debates accurately reflect the opinions of Republicans?

e.   What do you dislike most about politics:

   i.   I do not dislike anything about politics

   ii.   I dislike political representatives

   iii.   I dislike the election process

   iv.   I dislike the Democratic government

These questions are much more specific, and allow the researcher to easily code and analyze the results. They are closed-ended and force the subject to answer in a distinct manner. The use of closed-ended questions makes the job of analyzing the results much easier for the researcher, and also produces a much more reliable study.

PLANNING AND CONDUCTING EXPERIMENTS

EXPERIMENTS VERSUS OBSERVATIONAL STUDIES VERSUS SURVEYS

An experiment is the most direct and conclusive approach to testing a hypothesis about a cause-effect relationship between two variables (a variable is anything that can vary). In a psychological experiment, a variable is used as a test behavior, such as the performance of a subject on a given task or the number of responses made by the subject. The experimenter can choose the variables to be measured, and set the desired manipulations of the variables. The benefits of conducting an experiment include having control over potentially confounding variables (by manipulating one variable and holding all extraneous variables constant) and maintaining freedom to choose any appropriate manipulation. However, such a method is often costly because of recruitment of subjects and preparation of the laboratory for the experiment. An experiment can also be quite time consuming, and it could potentially produce biased results due to unnatural laboratory settings which cannot be generalized to the study's population. Results which are obtained in an artificial and sterile environment will not necessarily apply to a natural, real-life situation because of the difference of conditions and the constraints placed on the subjects.

A **survey** involves the use of self-report measurement techniques, such as questionnaires or interviews, to measure human attitudes, behavior and demographics. The survey allows a researcher to study the change in behavior or attitudes over time.

The benefit of this type of research is that it allows the researcher to generalize results to a large population with minimal time and expense.

Surveys can be mailed to subjects, or administered in groups. However, caution is advised when generalizing any results to a given population. A small subject sample can be representative of a large population, as evidenced by surveys such as the Gallup Poll, which measures political views over a geographical region using a small sample of subjects from that region. The subjects should, however, be representative of the population in order to generalize the results to a large population. Self-report measures are limited by the subjects' honesty and by their ability to observe and remember their own behaviors or moods.

The aim of observational studies is to describe the behavior of an individual or set of individuals without systematically investigating relationships between specific variables. Naturalistic observation is necessary in studying issues that are not responsive to experimentation, such as giving birth or committing suicide. Observations are limited by the great amount of time they take, by realistic constraints on a researcher's ability to observe ongoing behavior without disrupting it, and by the difficulty of coding results in a form that can be used for later statistical analyses. Variables must be operationally defined in order to be studied empirically. The operational definition is a definition of a variable in terms of the techniques or operations the researcher uses to measure or manipulate it. In this way, the researcher is forced to discuss abstract concepts in concrete terms. For instance, a researcher may be interested in studying hostility. "Hostility" could be defined in a number of ways: the loudness of a subject, the number of shocks presented by a subject, blood pressure, etc. The researcher must decide on an operation definition before implementing the study.

The naturalistic observation provides a rich source of observations of behavior as it normally occurs, but typically it does not allow us to interpret that behavior. It is difficult to determine cause-and-effect relationships; we are only provided with a list of events, connected by time. If the researcher records the following events: "Father enters the kitchen. The child hides beneath the table," we cannot conclude that the entrance of the father caused the child to hide under the table. Rather, we can only connect these events by their time frame. Although the ultimate cause of events cannot be determined, observational studies provide us with information with which many different hypotheses about the cause of different behaviors can be formed.

None of these methods can be considered the "best" method for collecting data; each method has both positive and negative aspects. It is up to the researcher to consider all factors and determine the most appropriate method of data collection taking into consideration what is being studied, the time frame of the study, the availability of subjects, and sources of funding. One psychological researcher may prefer to always conduct experiments, whereas an animal behaviorist will achieve more relevant results from an observational study.

CONFOUNDING, CONTROL GROUPS, PLACEBO EFFECTS, BLINDING

Confounding occurs when some extraneous variable has not been controlled for by the experimenter. If the experimenter wishes to find out the effects of stress on test-taking, for example, the independent variable would be the amount of stress produced by the experimenter (that is, imposing a large penalty for poor performance "High-Stress Condition" or imposing no penalty for poor performance "Low-Stress Condition"). The dependent variable would be the performance of the subject on the test. Confounding could occur if a third variable is not accounted for by the experimenter. Several types of confounding include maturation (any naturally occurring change within an individual which may be responsible for the results), history (any outside event that is not part of the manipulation which may be responsible for the results) and the effects the testing procedure itself has on the subject. For example, one group could be tested in the morning, and another group could be examined in the evening. This extraneous variable could have an effect on the performance of the subject, which would be unrelated to the stress level imposed. In this manner, the time of day can be a confounding factor, because although stress could have an effect on test performance, other factors could also contribute to the observed results. Many confounding factors may be present in a single study; to prevent influence of such factors, a control group should be employed.

A **control group** is used for comparison with the experimental group. The control group does not receive the manipulation of the experiment, while the experimental group does receive the intervention. The use of a control group makes it possible to eliminate other explanations for the result of the manipulations. The two groups should be equal across all dimensions except for the intervention. When comparing a treatment group to a control group, if the results show improvement among the treatment condition, the researcher can conclude that any differences between the two groups is due to the treatment, as long as other variables are controlled for.

Research involving drugs sometimes produces a special kind of subject expectation. Consider the following example: A drug is given to patients suffering from mental depression (Group 1), while another group receives no drug (Group 2). The results indicate that Group 1 has improved greatly over Group 2. Although it seems that the drug is the cause of the difference in results, it may not be the only factor leading to improvement. The placebo effect refers to a subject's expectations about a given treatment, in this case, the influence of the drug. To counteract any effects of expectations, a placebo treatment should be given. In this case, one group would receive the drug, and another group would receive a sugar pill (the "placebo" or "fake pill"); both sets of subjects are unaware of which treatment they are receiving. If the placebo group improves in addition to improvement of the drug treatment group, the result could be attributed to the placebo effect. Other sorts of treatments besides drugs can also influence subjects' expectations. For example, subjects receiving psychotherapy may improve simply because they believe psychotherapy will help them.

Sometimes the expectations of a subject or an experimenter can influence the results. In order to prevent expectancy effects, the experimenter should use **blinding** techniques.

In a single-blind experiment, the subject is unaware of whether a placebo or the actual drug is being administered. In a double-blind experiment, neither the subject nor the experimenter knows whether the placebo or actual drug is being given. Blinding prevents expectancy effects, both by the subject and by the experimenter. An overzealous researcher who knows when the real drug is being given may cue the patient to act in a certain way or be more lenient in interpreting the results. A blind procedure ensures that expectancy effects are "controlled for"; such effects are prevented from exerting any influence on the experiment. Not knowing who is in what group, the blind observer has no basis for having different expectations for different subjects. Ideally, to prevent bias due to placebo effects, subjects should be kept blind regarding the treatment they are receiving or its possible effects. The experimenter should also be kept blind as to which treatment is being administered in an ideal experiment.

TREATMENTS, EXPERIMENTAL UNITS, AND RANDOMIZATION

When designing an experiment, the researcher will devise **treatment** conditions based on what is to be examined. In the stress/exercise example, the two groups received two different treatments (that is, exercise and no exercise) in order to study the effects of exercise on stress. Subjects in the different treatment conditions are compared to see if a significant difference exists between the two groups.

It is important for the researcher to determine the **experimental units** (the coding scheme used to analyze experimental results) before undertaking the actual experiment. A measurement scale consists of a mathematical system associated with a specific, empirical measurement procedure. The numbers represent attributes of real persons, objects, or events. A post-hoc comparison (that is, choosing a coding scheme after the actual experiment takes place) lends itself to biased results because the experimenter could be overly optimistic in interpreting the results, conforming results to a given hypothesis. For instance, the experimenter may wish to determine the effect of studying on the performance of students on the AP Statistics examination. The experimenter needs to categorize exercise and performance on the test into different quantified levels; studying can be quantified in the following manner (0 = no studying, 1 = one hour studying per day, 2 = two hours of studying per day, etc.). The score on the examination (0 – 5) is the quantified performance level. The experimental units are pre-determined...

It may be difficult to keep a variable constant. The most obvious such variable is any characteristic of the subjects; a third variable, unknown to the experimenter, may exert influence on the results of the experiment. Perhaps income is somehow related to stress and exercise; the influence of this "extra" variable needs to be removed. The process of **randomization** allows for this elimination of extraneous variables. When two groups are randomized, the subjects are assigned to groups in a random fashion. In this way, extraneous variables are just as likely to affect one group as the other, therefore not affecting the results. This ability to randomly assign subjects to groups is an important difference between the experimental and correlational methods (surveys and observational studies).

COMPLETELY RANDOMIZED DESIGN FOR TWO TREATMENTS

One type of experimental design is completely randomized design for two treatments; in this type of set-up, an independent variable is varied in (at least) two ways. This type of experimental design ensures that there will be a minimal amount of bias due to extraneous factors. In such a study, the experimenter would randomly assign subjects to each of the treatments; this type of assignment helps to control for unwanted variables. The two groups will receive different treatments (ideally, one group will serve as a control group for comparison), and the results from each manipulation will be compared. When using two treatments, randomization is essential to ensure that one treatment is just as likely to affect an individual in one group as in the other group. The following diagram represents the two treatment design:

	Treatment	Response	
Control Group	X	Y_1	Compare these responses
Expt. Group 1	X_2	Y_2	

The experimental (expt.) group receives a treatment (X_2) and the control group does not receive a treatment (X). The responses from the trials (Y_1 from control group, Y_2 from experimental group) are then compared to examine any differences in response. Through a series of statistical analyses (in this case, a *t*-test would be appropriate), the researcher can determine if the result is significant and if the hypothesis is correct.

An example of this design is an examination of the effect of jogging on self-esteem. Subjects will be randomly assigned to one of the two treatment groups: one group will serve as the control group (refraining from jogging), and one group will receive the treatment (jogging 2 miles each day). The two groups will be assessed on a measure of self-esteem (for instance, a questionnaire) and the results of the questionnaire from the two groups will be compared. The random assignment of subjects to the groups will reduce bias in the study.

Theoretically, all possible extraneous variables are controlled if enough subjects are included in the study. As most researchers do not have access to unlimited subjects and unlimited funding, some bias may be present in the experimental design.

RANDOMIZED PAIRED COMPARISON DESIGN

Sometimes a researcher wishes to conduct within-subject comparisons, in addition to across-subject comparisons. For instance, the experimenter may wish to determine the effect of exercise versus no exercise on stress using husband/wife pairs. A **randomized paired comparison** would best fit this type of study. The husband/wife teams would be randomly assigned to a condition; the results must be compared across subjects (that is, Group 1 compared to Group 2), and within subjects (husband compared to wife). In this type of experimental design, we can find out if significant differences exist not only between groups, but between genders. However, because we cannot randomly assign husbands to wives (or vice-versa), the results should be interpreted with caution.

REPLICATION, BLOCKING, AND GENERALIZABILITY OF RESULTS

In many areas of research, the basic experimental procedure is repeated many times. Each repetition of the basic experiment is called a **block** of trials. To control for order effects when there are many such blocks of trials, the order of presentation should be randomly determined

for each experiment. Randomized blocking should be used in the initial experiment and when replicating a study to control for possible effects of ordering.

Can the results of a completed research project be generalized to other subject populations, to other age groups and to other ways of manipulating or measuring the variables? Internal validity is the adequacy of the procedures and design of the research. External validity is the extent to which the findings may be generalized. Research conducted in a laboratory setting presents the advantage of allowing the experimenter control over most extraneous variables. However, we are presented with the question of whether the artificiality of the laboratory setting limits the ability to generalize what is observed in the laboratory to real-life settings.

Replication is a way of overcoming any problems of generalization that occur in a single study. If an unexpected finding is obtained, a researcher will frequently attempt a replication to see if the same results occur. An exact replication is an attempt to replicate exactly the procedures of a study to see if the same results are obtained. A failure to replicate could mean that the original results are invalid, but it could also mean that the replication attempt was flawed. A single failure to replicate is not adequate cause for discarding the original research finding. Repeated failures, however, do lead to reconsideration of the original findings. The procedures for use with a single subject can be replicated with other subjects, greatly enhancing the **generalizability** of the results.

One way to view the sampling process is to imagine that the population is a bowl full of gumballs; a handful of gumballs is considered the sample. If the sample is unbiased, we can generalize the results from the handful of gumballs to the entire bowl.

☞ Drill: Planning and Conducting Experiments

> **DIRECTIONS:** Select the best answer.

1. To eliminate influence of confounding variables, the experimenter should

   (A) use a control group.

   (B) have a placebo effect.

    (C)   increase sample size.

    (D)   eliminate a control group.

2.   To ensure that the results of an experiment can be generalized from a small sample to a larger population, the researcher should

    (A)   use blocks of trials.

    (B)   replicate the study.

    (C)   use stratified sampling.

    (D)   use a randomized paired comparison design.

3.   A subject's expectations about the influence of treatment is called

    (A)   placebo effect.   (C)   sampling effect.

    (B)   blocking.   (D)   blinding effect.

4.   To study a cause-and-effect relationship between variables, which of the following methods of data collection should be used

    (A)   observational study.

    (B)   survey (presentation of questionnaire).

    (C)   survey (use of one-on-one interview).

    (D)   experiment.

5.   What is a characteristic of a well-constructed experiment?

    (A)   Non-randomized sampling techniques

    (B)   Closed-ended questions

    (C)   Use of a control group

    (D)   Interviewer bias

DIRECTIONS: Determine the correct responses from the information provided in questions 6 and 7.

6.   Construct your own experiment: state a hypothesis, describe the independent and dependent variables, and the treatment conditions. Describe the manipulation of the independent variables, and state the possible effect this manipulation will have on the dependent variable.

7. A friend asks for advice on an experiment she would like to perform. She wishes to test the effect of alcohol on the motor skills of women. State the advantages and disadvantages of the experimental method for this particular study, and provide suggestions for how such a study might be implemented.

Answers to Drill Questions

1. **(A)** The correct answer is (A). To remove the possible influence of confounding factors, a control group should be used; this group does not receive the manipulation and is compared to the group(s) receiving the manipulation. A placebo effect refers to the expectations of the subjects; Increasing the sample size is a good idea when attempting to control for sampling error, but it will not have an effect on confounding variables. Eliminating a control group will add more influence from possible confounding factors.

2. **(B)** The correct answer is (B). Results can be safely generalized from a sample to a population when a study has been replicated. If the same results are obtained more than once, the study is considered reliable, and the results can be generalized to a population outside of the experimental setting. Using blocks of trials will serve to prevent effects of order potentially biasing the experiment. Stratified random sampling requires that the researcher examine the population before beginning the study, separating the population into different strata; each member of the population does not have an equal chance of being selected for the sample. A randomized paired comparison design is sometimes an optimal method of experiment design; however, this depends on the conditions of the experiment and the variables being measured. The results of any type of experiment, constructed with any experimental design, can only be safely generalized if the experiment is replicated and the same results are observed.

3. **(A)** The correct answer is (A). The placebo effect refers to a subject's expectations about the effect of treatment (such as a drug for the treatment of depression). Blocking serves to reduce the possible effects of order from presentation of questions. No "sampling effect" exists; the implications for different types of sampling can potentially affect the experiment, but not the expectations of a subject. Blinding serves to reduce the placebo effect (a subject's expectations).

4. **(D)** The correct answer is (D). The experiment is the only method which can explain a cause-and-effect relationship between two or more

variables. An observation is simply observing the behavior of an organism, without interference by the researcher. The survey is used to collect data regarding individuals' attitudes or demographics of a particular topic.

5. **(C)** The correct answer is (C). A good experiment will always use a control group (a group which does not receive a manipulation of the independent variable) to serve as a comparison to other treatment groups. Non-randomized sampling techniques and the presence of interviewer bias could contribute to biased results. Closed-ended questions are useful in constructing a valid survey, but have little or no relevance to an experiment.

6. Here is a possible answer:

Hypothesis: Exercise reduces the rate of depression in college students.

For this experiment, the subjects will be chosen from a local college and randomly assigned to one of three groups. The experimental design will be a randomized three-group design. The independent variable (the variable to be manipulated) is the amount of exercise per day. One third of the subjects (Group 1), chosen randomly, will refrain from exercise. One third of the subjects (Group 2) will exercise one half hour every other day, and the last third of the subjects (Group 3) will be required to exercise one hour every other day.

At the end of every week, the subjects will be given a brief battery of neuropsychological tests to determine rate of depression on a 100 point scale (0–20 = not depressed, 21–40 = mildly depressed, 41–60 = moderately depressed, 61– 80 = severely depressed, 81–100 = extremely depressed/suicidal). These tests will be standardized before the beginning of the experiment, and tested on individuals not included in the study.

The expected results of this manipulation are the following: the individuals who exercised the most (one hour every other day) will be less depressed than those who exercised one hour every other day or not at all. The two groups who did in fact exercise (Group 2 and Group 3) will be compared to each other, as well as to the control group (the group who abstained from exercise—Group 1). A great benefit of the experiment is the ability to explore many different relations between variables.

7. Here is a possible answer:

The advantages of the experimental method for the given study are:

(1) Ability to choose and manipulate the independent variables; and

(2) Ability to determine cause-and-effect relationships

The disadvantages of the experimental method are:

(1) *Generalization*. These results should be interpreted with caution if they are to be generalized to the population of women as a whole, and cannot be generalized to humans (including men) as a whole group. The conditions of the experiment restrict the behavior of the subjects, and therefore one must use caution in generalizing results to a population outside of the sample.

(2) *Ethical considerations*. Use of a substance such as alcohol poses a risk to subjects; the subjects must give full consent, as with any study.

To perform an experiment on the effect of alcohol on the motor skills of women, subjects should be randomly assigned to different treatment groups. One group should serve as a control group, and other groups should receive different levels of alcohol (the independent variable). The dependent variable is the performance of the subjects on certain motor tasks, which are administered to the subjects at different points during the study. The experimenter and the subjects should be blind to the treatment groups to prevent placebo effects. Such an experiment should be conducted with much caution due to the nature of the variables.

CHAPTER 4
ANTICIPATING PATTERNS

Chapter 4

ANTICIPATING PATTERNS

REVIEW OF LAWS OF LARGE NUMBERS

There are two Laws of Large Numbers: the Weak Law of Large Numbers and the Strong Law of Large Numbers. In combination, these are known as the Laws of Large Numbers and will be our focus in this section.

We will see that both the Strong Law of Large Numbers and the Weak Law of Large Numbers can be stated in terms of types of convergence. One may also recognize a similarity between the Weak Law of Large Numbers and Chebyshev's inequality. In fact, Chebyshev's inequality is often used to prove the Weak Law of Large Numbers, and Chebyshev was the first to prove the Weak Law of Large Numbers.

Let M be the population mean of X, or

$$E[X] = M.$$

Suppose that a simple random sample of size n is taken, each with the distribution of X. Let $X^*(n)$ be the sample mean, or

$$X^*(n) = \Sigma_{i=1 \text{ to } n} X_i/n.$$

The Weak Law of Large Numbers states that as n increases, $X^*(n)$ will tend to become closer and closer to M. In particular,

$$\lim_{n \text{ to infinity}} P\{| X^*(n) - M | > k\} = 0 \text{ for all positive } k,$$

or, alternatively,

$$\lim_{n \text{ to infinity}} P\{| X^*(n) - M | < k\} = 1 \text{ for all positive } k.$$

This says that with high probability, in fact probability tending to one, the sample mean and the population mean will be within k of each other, for any value of k. This is equivalently stated as with low probability, in fact probability tending to zero, the sample mean differs from the population mean by more than k.

The Weak Law of Large Numbers does not apply only to simple random samples (that is, independent sampling from the same population). We will confine our attention to independent random variables, but we will allow them to have different distributions. In fact, our only interest in the distributions of these random variables will be in their first two moments (i.e., their means and variances).

Let $X^*(n)$ be the sample mean of the n independent random variables, even if they have different distributions. That is,

$$X^*(n) = \Sigma_{i = 1 \text{ to } n} X_i / n.$$

Let $\quad M(n) = E[X^*(n)]$

$$= E[\Sigma_{i = 1 \text{ to } n} X_i / n]$$

$$= \Sigma_{i = 1 \text{ to } n} E[X_i] / n.$$

Let $V(X_i)$ be the variance of the random variable X_i. If $V[X^*(n)]$ tends to zero as n tends to infinity, then the Weak Law of Large Numbers holds, or

$$\lim_{n \text{ to infinity}} P\{| X^*(n) - M(n) | > k\} = 0 \text{ for all positive } k,$$

or, alternatively,

$$\lim_{n \text{ to infinity}} P\{| X^*(n) - M(n) | < k\} = 1 \text{ for all positive } k,$$

even if the component random variables have different distributions.

Notice that

$$V[X^*(n)] = V[\Sigma_{i = 1 \text{ to } n} X_i / n]$$

$$= (1/n^2) V[\Sigma_{i = 1 \text{ to } n} X_i]$$

$$= (1/n^2) \Sigma_{i = 1 \text{ to } n} V(X_i),$$

so this is the quantity which must tend to zero in the limit as n tends to infinity.

The Strong Law of Large Numbers states that, under certain conditions, almost all sequences of $X^*(n)$, considered as a sequence, will converge to M, assuming that a simple random sample was employed. Of course, if the different component random variables are allowed to have different distributions, then M may depend upon the sample size n. The formal statement is

$$P\{X^*(n) \text{ tends to } M\} = 1.$$

The Strong Law of Large Numbers implies the Weak Law of Large Numbers, but the reverse implication does not hold.

CONDITIONAL PROBABILITIES AND INDEPENDENCE

In this section, we will consider a variety of rules and properties that will make our probability calculations easier. We will discuss "the probability of rolling an eight" or "the probability of drawing an ace of spaces from a deck of cards," but in most application cases we are interested in the probability of a number of related events. For simplicity, we will mostly consider situations where there are only two events; on occasion,  we will look at larger problems. First, in order to fully understand related events we need to review set theory.

When combining sets there are two basis operations—union and intersection. In the union of sets A_1 and A_2 ($A_1 \cup A_2$), we are looking at the elements that belong to A_1 alone, to A_2 alone, or to both A_1 and A_2. The operation $\cup$ translates into the word "OR" where $A_1 \cup A_2$ is the set of elements in A_1 *or* A_2 or to both A_1 and A_2. We now want to examine the intersection of the sets A_1 and A_2 ($A_1 \cap A_2$). Here, we are looking at only the elements that are in both sets. The operation $\cap$ translates into the word "AND" where $A_1 \cap A_2$ is the set of elements which belong both to A_1 *and* to A_2. These ideas can also be represented using Venn diagrams.

We now want to consider the probability of related sets. In general, the probability of the union of two events is given by the formula

$$P(A_1 \cup A_2) = P(A_1) + P(A_2) - P(A_1 \cap A_2)$$

Notice that besides the addition of probability of each event, we must subtract the probability of the intersection of the two events. This is done because the intersection has been counted twice (once in A_1 and once in A_2), and the final answer should reflect it only once. Our formula can be simplified if the events are disjoint or mutually exclusive ($A_1 \cap A_2 = \varnothing$) as follows:

$$P(A_1 \cup A_2) = P(A_1) + P(A_2)$$

In this special case, we know that the probability of the intersection of the events is equal to zero. In order for these formulas to be useful, we must next compute the probabilities on the right hand side of the equations.

EXAMPLE

A single fair die is rolled. What is the probability of rolling an even number OR a number less than or equal to 4?

SOLUTION

Let A_1 = the event of rolling an even number = {2, 4, 6}

Let A_2 = the event of rolling a number ≤ 4 = {1, 2, 3, 4}

Since a die has six sides and each side is equally likely, we also know that

$$P(A_1) = \frac{3}{6} = \frac{1}{2} \text{ and } P(A_2) = \frac{4}{6} = \frac{2}{3}.$$

Elements of the intersection of these two events must satisfy both the conditions of A_1 and of A_2. Therefore,

$$A_1 \cap A_2 = \{2, 4\} \text{ and } P(A_1 \cap A_2) = \frac{2}{6} = \frac{1}{3}.$$

Finally, we can calculate $P(A_1 \cup A_2)$ with the help of our general formula.

$$P(A_1 \cup A_2) = P(A_1) + P(A_2) - P(A_1 \cap A_2)$$

$$= \frac{1}{2} + \frac{2}{3} - \frac{1}{3} = \frac{5}{6}$$

EXAMPLE

A single fair die is rolled. What is the probability of rolling a one OR a five?

SOLUTION

Let A_1 = the event of rolling a one = {1}

Let A_2 = the event of rolling a five = {5}

Since a die has six sides and each side is likely to be equal, we also know that

$$P(A_1) = \frac{1}{6} \text{ and } P(A_2) = \frac{1}{6}.$$

Elements of the intersection of these two events must satisfy both the conditions of A_1 and of A_2. In this example the two events cannot happen at the same time, because they are mutually exclusive. Therefore,

$$A_1 \cap A_2 = \emptyset \text{ and } P(A_1 \cap A_2) = 0$$

Finally, we can calculate $P(A_1 \cup A_2)$ with the help of our formula in the case of disjoint events.

$$P(A_1 \cup A_2) = P(A_1) + P(A_2)$$

$$= \frac{1}{6} + \frac{1}{6} = \frac{2}{6} = \frac{1}{3}$$

EXAMPLE

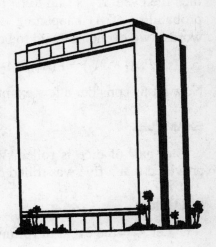

There is a 1 percent chance that the primary security system at a nuclear plant will fail. When this happens, the backup system is used. There is also a 1 percent chance that the backup system will fail. What is the probability that both systems will fail?

SOLUTION

Let A_1 = the event the primary system fails.

Let A_2 = the event the backup system fails.

We are given that the $P(A_1) = 0.01$ and $P(A_2) = 0.01$. Notice neither of the two systems can be simultaneously running; therefore, the events A_1 and A_2 are independent of each other. In this case,

$$P(A_1 \cap A_2) = P(A_1) \times P(A_2)$$

$$= (0.01)(0.01) = 0.0001$$

Sometimes it is interesting to know if an event will occur provided that another event has already happened. This idea is referred to as **conditional probability** and is denoted by

$$P(A_2 \mid A_1) = \text{the conditional probability of } A_2 \text{ occuring given}$$

that A_1 has occured.

In general this type of probability can be found using the following formula.

$$P(A_2 \mid A_1) = \frac{P(A_1 \cap A_2)}{P(A_1)}$$

Notice that here it is assumed that $P(A_1)$ is greater than zero. A more useful form of this definition is the multiplication rule for conditional probabilities.

$$P(A_1 \cap A_2) = P(A_1)P(A_2 \mid A_1)$$

As before, we can also discuss a special case here. If A_1 and A_2 are two events such that $P(A_2 \mid A_1) = P(A_2)$ and $P(A_1)P(A_2) > 0$ and $P(A_1) > 0$, then the event A_2 is said to be independent of event A_1. In other words, the probability of A_2 happening does not depend on A_1 occurring. In other words, two events are said to be independent if

$$P(A_1 \cap A_2) = P(A_1)P(A_2)$$

Now let us consider a few examples of conditional probability.

EXAMPLE

A pair of dice is rolled. What is the probability of rolling an eight, provided that a five was rolled on the first die?

SOLUTION

Let A_1 = the event of rolling an 8 on a pair of dice.

Let A_2 = the event of rolling a 5 on the first die.

Since there is only one way of rolling a 5 on a fair die, we know that $P(A_2) = {}^1/_6$. We also know that

$A_1 \cap A_2$ = the event of getting a 5 on the first die and

8 as a total sum.

The only one way that $A_1 \cap A_2$ can occur is if we must get a 3 on the second die. When rolling two dice there are 36 equal likely possible outcomes. Therefore, the $P(A_1 \cap A_2) = {}^1/_{36}$.

Using our formula for conditional probabilities we get

$$P(A_1 \mid A_2) = \frac{P(A_1 \cap A_2)}{P(A_2)}$$

$$= \frac{\frac{1}{36}}{\frac{1}{6}} = \frac{1}{6}$$

EXAMPLE

A pair of dice is rolled. What is the probability of rolling an 8, provided that a 1 was rolled on the first die?

SOLUTION

Let A_1 = the event of rolling an 8 on a pair of dice.

Let A_2 = the event of rolling a 1 on the first die.

Since there is only one way of rolling a one on a fair die, we know that $P(A_2) = \frac{1}{6}$. We also know that

$A_1 \cap A_2$ = the event of getting a 1 on the first die and

8 as a total sum.

The only one way that $A_1 \cap A_2$ can occur is if we must get a 7 on the second die (which is impossible). Therefore, $P(A_1 \cap A_2) = 0$, because the events A_1 and A_2 are disjoint and cannot occur at the same time.

Using our formula for conditional probabilities we get

$$P(A_1 \mid A_2) = \frac{P(A_1 \cap A_2)}{P(A_2)}$$

$$= \frac{0}{\frac{1}{6}} = 0$$

EXAMPLE

A die is rolled. What is the probability of rolling a one provided that an odd number is rolled?

SOLUTION

Let A_1 = the event of rolling a 1 = $\{1\}$.

Let A_2 = the event of rolling an odd number = $\{1, 3, 5\}$.

Since there are three odd numbers on a fair die, we know that $P(A_2) = \frac{3}{6} = \frac{1}{2}$. We also know that

$A_1 \cap A_2$ = the event of getting a 1 and odd.

Since 1 is odd, we know that the $P(A_1 \cap A_2) = P(A_1) = \frac{1}{6}$.

Using our formula for conditional probabilities we get

$$P(A_1 \mid A_2) = \frac{P(A_1 \cap A_2)}{P(A_2)} = \frac{P(A_1)}{P(A_2)}$$

$$= \frac{\frac{1}{6}}{\frac{1}{2}} = \frac{1}{3}$$

EXAMPLE

Two dice are rolled. What is the probability of rolling a 5 on the second die provided that a 3 is rolled on the first die?

SOLUTION

Let A_1 = the event of rolling a 3 on the first die.

Let A_2 = the event of rolling a 5 on the second die.

Since there is only one way of rolling a five and only one way of rolling a three on a fair die, we know that $P(A_1) = P(A_2) = \frac{1}{6}$. We also know that these events are independent of each other. Therefore,

$$P(A_1 \mid A_2) = P(A_1) = \frac{1}{6}$$

DISCRETE RANDOM VARIABLES

Random variables are typically either discrete or continuous, although there are other types. For example, some random variables are mixed, with both continuous and discrete components, and others, such as random variables whose support is the Cantor set, are neither. Discrete variables are the simplest random variables to understand, so these are presented first. Instead of a probability density function, we will speak of a probability mass function, $f_X(k)$, to be interpreted as the probability that X, a discrete random variable, takes on the value k, or

$$f_X(k) = P\{X = k\}.$$

Specifying that a random variable is discrete still allows for much flexibility, and many subclasses of discrete random variables have been defined. These will be explored in the remainder of Chapter Four. As discussed earlier, a discrete random variable is supported by a finite or countably infinite set of points.

The mean of a discrete random variable is defined as

$$M_X = \Sigma_k [k][f_X(k)]$$

$$= \Sigma_k[k][P\{X=k\}],$$

where the sum extends over the values of k in the support of X. The mean, or expected value, provides a commonly used measure of central tendency of the random variable X. Notice that the expected value need not be a value assumed by X with positive probability. For example, if $P\{X=1\} = 0.5$ and $P\{X=2\} = 0.5$, then

$$M_X = (1)(0.5) + (2)(0.5)$$
$$= 0.5 + 1.0$$
$$= 1.5$$

But 1.5 is not in the support of X and, consequently, $P\{X=1.5\} = 0$. What is true in general, however, is that the expected value of X is in the convex hull of the support of X (that is, it can be written as a convex combination of the elements in the support of X).

REVIEW OF UNIFORM RANDOM VARIABLES

A discrete random variable is uniform if its probability mass function is constant (i.e., does not change) over the range of its support. As an example, let X be a discrete random variable such that

$$P\{X=1\} = 0.5$$

and $P\{X=2\} = 0.5.$

Since $0.5 + 0.5 = 1$, all the mass has been exhausted, and we know that $\{1, 2\}$ is the entire support of X. We also know that the probability mass function assumes only the value 0.5 on the range of this support. Therefore, X is uniformly distributed. For enhanced clarity, one should specify that X is a uniformly distributed discrete random variable, because continuous random variables can also be uniformly distributed.

If we let Y be a discrete random variable such that

$$P\{Y=1\} = 0.4$$

and $P\{Y=5\} = 0.6,$

then Y is not uniformly distributed, because the probability mass function takes on different values (0.4 and 0.6) on the range of the support of Y.

In general, the value of the probability mass function will be the inverse of the number of points in the range of the support of a uniformly distributed random variable. For example, if X is uniformly distributed on the range $\{0, 1, 8, 9, 12\}$, then the value of the probability mass function is

$^1/_5$, or 0.2, on all five points. The value 0.2 is required to ensure that X is, in fact, a random variable (otherwise, the probability mass function would not sum to 1). The interpretation is that X takes on the values $\{0, 1, 8, 9, 12\}$ with probability 0.2 each, so each value is equally likely, or uniformly likely.

The expected value of a uniformly distributed discrete random variable is the unweighted arithmetic average of the points in its support. This is seen by applying the general formula for the expected value of a discrete random variable to the case of a uniformly distributed discrete random variable. In particular, if we let n denote the number of points in the support of X, then

$$M_X = \Sigma_k [k][P\{X = k\}]$$

$$= \Sigma_k [k] \left[\frac{1}{n}\right],$$

which is seen to be the unweighted arithmetic mean of the points in the support of X. The expected value of X is also often denoted by $E[X]$. For example, if X is a discrete random variable which is uniformly distributed on the points $\{1, 2, 3, 4, 5\}$, then its probability mass function is $^1/_5$, or 0.2, on each of these points, and its expected value is

$$M_X = (1)(0.2) + (2)(0.2) + (3)(0.2) + (4)(0.2) + (5)(0.2)$$

$$= 0.2 + 0.4 + 0.6 + 0.8 + 1.0$$

$$= 3.0$$

The cumulative distribution function of a discrete uniformly distributed random variable is a step function, ranging from zero to one, which increases by $^1/_n$ at each point in the support of X, where n is the number of points in the support of X. For example, if X is a discrete random variable which is uniformly distributed on the points $\{1, 2, 3, 4, 5\}$, then its cumulative distribution function is

$$F_X(k) = 0 \text{ for } k < 1;$$

$$= 0.2 \text{ for } 1 \leq k < 2;$$

$$= 0.4 \text{ for } 2 \leq k < 3;$$

$$= 0.6 \text{ for } 3 \leq k < 4;$$

$$= 0.8 \text{ for } 4 \leq k < 5;$$

and $\qquad = 1.0 \text{ for } k \geq 5.$

REVIEW OF BERNOULLI RANDOM VARIABLES

A discrete random variable has a Bernoulli distribution if it can take on only the values of zero and one. We let p be the probability that the Bernoulli random variable assumes the value 1, and $q = 1 - p$ is the probability that it assumes the value zero. Therefore, the probability mass function of a Bernoulli random variable is

$P\{X = k\} = 1 - p$ for $k = 0$;

$P\{X = k\} = p$ for $k = 1$;

and $P\{X = k\} = 0$ for other k.

This probability mass function can be conveniently written as

$P\{X = k\} = p^k(1 - p)^{1-k}$ for $k = 0, 1$;

and $P\{X = k\} = 0$ for other k.

The expected value of X, a Bernoulli random variable, is

$E[X] = (0)(1 - p) + (1)(p)$

$= 0 + p$

$= p$

The cumulative distribution function of X, a Bernoulli random variable, is

$F_X(k) = 0$ for $k < 0$;

$F_X(k) = 1 - p$ for $0 \leq k < 1$;

and $F_X(k) = 1$ for $1 \leq k$.

Bernoulli random variables are used to model single dichotomous (having two possible outcomes) events. Regardless of the two possibilities, the Bernoulli model is applicable, as the outcomes can be coded as zero and one. For example, the single toss of a coin may be regarded as a Bernoulli random variable if we use the convention that tails corresponds to $X = 0$ and heads corresponds to $X = 1$. The only two possible outcomes are heads and tails. Likewise, randomly selecting a patient from a hospital and recording the gender of this patient would also qualify as a Bernoulli random variable if we code male to be zero and female to be one. Here, the only possible outcomes are male and female. The particular choice of codes is irrelevant. That is, the model would fit as well if we had coded male as one and female as zero.

REVIEW OF BINOMIAL RANDOM VARIABLES

The Bernoulli distribution is quite useful, but it is limited by the fact that it allows only for a single dichotomous trial. The binomial distribution is more general than the Bernoulli distribution in that an arbitrary number of dichotomous trials are allowed, as long as each trial is independent of the others and has common success probability. The three conditions that define a binomial random variable are:

1. A series of dichotomous trials occur;

2. Each trial is independent of other trials; and

3. Each trial has the same success probability.

That is, each dichotomous trial is a Bernoulli random variable, and each has the same value of p.

For example, consider tossing a coin five times, and let X record the number of heads observed. Now X may take the values $\{0, 1, 2, 3, 4, 5\}$. We may define $X1$ as

$X1 = 0$ if the first toss results in tails

and $\quad X1 = 1$ if the first toss results in heads.

We may similarly define $X2$, $X3$, $X4$, and $X5$. Now

$$X = X1 + X2 + X3 + X4 + X5.$$

Each of the five random variables recording the outcome of a given toss is Bernoulli distributed. It is reasonable to assume independence across the different trials. Since the same coin is being used, the probability of heads is constant (the same) for each trial. Therefore, X has a binomial distribution.

The Bernoulli distribution is characterized by only one parameter, p, which is the success probability. However, the binomial distribution is characterized by two parameters: p, the common success probability for each trial, and n, the number of trials. In our example in which we tossed a coin five times, $n = 5$. These two parameters determine the probability mass function, the expected value, and the cumulative distribution function of the binomial random variable.

The probability mass function of a binomial random variable is derived by calculating the probability of each outcome (an outcome is a sequence of n successes and failures, where n is the number of trials) and grouping the outcomes by the number of successes. As a simple example, consider the case of $n = 2$. If we denote successes by S and failures by F, then the outcomes are $\{SS, SF, FS, FF\}$. We would group these as

two successes	$\{SS\}$,
one success	$\{SF, FS\}$,
and no successes	$\{FF\}$.

To find the probability of a given outcome, it is necessary to multiply the probabilities of the results of each of the n trials. For example, consider the sequence $\{SF\}$. We must multiply the probability of a success on the first trial by the probability of a failure on the second trial, or

$$P\{SF\} = P\{S1\}P\{F2\},$$

where $\{S1\}$ denotes a success on the first trial and $\{F2\}$ denotes a failure on the second trial. We will learn the rationale for this multiplication in the chapter on independence. Returning to the example,

$$P\{S1\} = p \text{ and } P\{F2\} = 1 - p.$$

Therefore,
$$P\{SF\} = P\{S1\}P\{F2\}$$
$$= p(1 - p)$$

If we list each outcome and its associated probability, we obtain

$\{SS\}$	p^2	two successes,
$\{SF\}$	$p(1-p)$	one success,
$\{FS\}$	$(1-p)p$	one success,
and $\{FF\}$	$(1-p)^2$	no successes.

Grouping again by the number of successes gives the probability mass function of the number of successes, which has a binomial distribution. We obtain

$$P\{X = 0\} = P\{FF\} = (1-p)^2;$$
$$P\{X = 1\} = P\{SF \cup FS\} = P\{SF\} + P\{FS\}$$
$$= p(1-p) + (1-p)p = 2p(1-p);$$
$$P\{X = 2\} = P\{SS\} = p^2;$$

and $\quad P\{X = k\} = 0$ for other k.

Notice that this defines a true probability mass function, because this function is non-negative and sums to one, which is seen as follows:

$$(1 - p)^2 + 2p(1 - p) + p^2 = (1 - 2p + p^2) + (2p - 2p^2) + p^2$$
$$= 1 - 2p + 2p + p^2 - 2p^2 + p^2$$
$$= 1$$

The question now becomes how to find the probability mass function when $n > 2$. We may use the same approach that yielded the probability mass function for the case of $n = 2$. Specifically, we enumerate the outcomes, find the probability of each, and group them by the number of successes.

The first point to notice is that, in the case of $n = 2$, the probability of any outcome depended only on the number of successes. That is, any sequence with k successes and $n - k$ (in this case, $2 - k$) failures had probability $p^k(1 - p)^{2-k}$. This will still be true for $n > 2$, with the obvious modification that the probability of any outcome with k successes and $n - k$ failures is $p^k(1 - k)^{n - k}$. The order in which the successes and failures occur does not influence the probability. There are k successes, and the probability of success on any one trial is p. Therefore, we must multiply p k times, resulting in p^k. Likewise, there are $n - k$ failures, and each trial will result in failure with probability $1 - k$. Therefore, we must multiply $1 - pn - k$ times, resulting in $(1 - p)^{n-k}$. Finally, we multiply these two quantities to arrive at $p^k(1 - k)^{n-k}$, the probability of any outcome with k successes and $n - k$ failures.

The remaining task, then, is to count the number of outcomes with k successes and $n - k$ failures. This must be done for each k. This is a problem of combinations, because the problem can be formulated as finding the number of ways to find k locations among n locations in which to place the successes. This is equivalent to finding the $n - k$ locations in which to place the failures. From our earlier development, we recognize this to be

$$C(n, k) = C(n, n - k) = \frac{n!}{[(k!)\,(n - k)!]}.$$

Therefore, the probability of k successes in n trials is

$$C(n, k)p^k(1 - p)^{n - k}.$$

This is the binomial probability mass function.

The range (or support) of a binomial random variable with parameters n and p is the set of non-negative integers not exceeding n. Since n must be a non-negative integer (since n is the number of trials), n is included in the range, which is therefore $\{1, 2, 3, ..., n\}$. This obvious fact is often forgotten when the binomial is compared to the Poisson.

It is possible to derive the expected value of a binomial random variable directly from the definition of the probability mass function. However, it is both simpler and more intuitive to utilize the fact that a binomial random variable with parameters n and p may be expressed as the sum of n Bernoulli random variables, each with parameter p. By the linearity property of the expected value, then, the expected value of the binomial random variable is the sum of the expected values of the n Bernoulli random variables. We recall from the previous section that the expected value of a Bernoulli random variable with parameter p is p. If we let X have a binomial distribution with parameters n and p, denoted by (n, p), and we let $X_1, X_2, ..., X_n$ be n independent Bernoulli random variables, each with parameter p, then

$$E[X] = E[\Sigma_{i = 1 \text{ to } n} X_i]$$
$$= \Sigma_{i = 1 \text{ to } n} E[X_i]$$
$$= \Sigma_{i = 1 \text{ to } n} p$$
$$= np$$

This is the expected value of a binomial random variable with parameters n and p.

The cumulative distribution function of a binomial random variable is found by summing the probability mass function over the appropriate range. For example, if we wish to find

$$F_X(k) = P\{X \leq k\},$$

then we recognize that for a binomial random variable to be less than or equal to k, it would need to be zero, one, two, or any other non-negative integer less than or equal to k. We would simply add the probability mass function over this range. Unfortunately, there is no general formula which applies to all cases. For small n, it is a simple matter to perform the addition with a calculator or a computer. For larger n, tables exist which provide the values of the cumulative distribution function for binomial random variables.

REVIEW OF MULTINOMIAL RANDOM VARIABLES

The multinomial distribution is more general than the binomial in that it allows for more than two outcomes. This fact is evident from the prefix: "bi" indicates two, while "multi" indicates more than two. This prefix refers to the number of possible outcomes in a given trial.

An example of a trinomial distribution is the number of points awarded in a soccer game. In the first round of the 1994 World Cup, three points were awarded for a win, one point was awarded for a tie, and no points were awarded for a loss. Here, there are three possible outcomes, so the binomial model would not be appropriate.

Of course, the multinomial distribution can accommodate random variables which may take on more than three outcomes as well. To be a random variable, each possible outcome must be numerically valued. Thus, if we define a variable to take the values "win," "lose," or "tie" as the outcome of a soccer game, then this variable is not a random variable. We would first need to code these outcomes into numerical values. The number of points awarded is one such method of coding.

Other examples of multinomial random variables are the responses people make when asked their favorite color (if the outcomes are coded into numerical values), the winning candidate in an election with more than two candidates (if the outcomes are coded into numerical values), and the number facing up when a pair of dice is tossed. What makes the multinomial distribution interesting is that, like the binomial distribution, it can accommodate more than one trial. Thus, we may treat repeated tosses of pairs of dice as a multinomial random variable.

You may recall that the Bernoulli random variable was characterized by a single parameter. This was the success probability of the one trial. The binomial random variable was characterized by a pair of parameters. These were n, the number of trials, and p, the success probability on each trial. The multinomial random variable is characterized by k parameters, where k is the number of possible outcomes of any trial. These parameters are $p(i)$, the probability of the ith outcome, $i = 1, 2, ..., k - 1$, and n, the number of trials. We need not specify $p(k)$ because we know that

$$p(1) + p(2) + ... + p(k) = 1,$$

so $$p(k) = 1 - p(1) - p(2) - ... - p(k-1)$$

is determined by the specification of the other probabilities.

A typical problem in the study of multinomial random variables involves calculating the probability of a given configuration. For example,

suppose that a single die is tossed three times. What is the probability of obtaining one four and two threes? To solve this, we recognize that there are three tosses, and hence three trials, so $n = 3$. Each of the six outcomes in the toss of a single die is equally likely, so $p(i) = 1/6$ for $i = 1, 2, 3, 4, 5, 6$. We have now characterized the multinomial distribution relevant to this problem. Now we proceed by enumerating all possibilities. These are too numerous to list (there are $6^3 = 216$ such possibilities), but we may speak of them by allowing the first toss to take any of the six possible values, likewise for the second, and likewise for the third. We must list all possibilities which are favorable to the event we wish to study, namely one four and two threes. These possibilities are {433, 343, 334}. There are three such possibilities, so the remaining task is to find the

probability of each. Since these are mutually exclusive events, we may add these probabilities to find the probability of one four and two threes.

Notice that the 216 outcomes, in general, are not equally likely. If they were, then we would have been able to stop here and declare the probability equal to $3/216$. This will turn out to be the solution in this problem, and the 216 outcomes are equally likely in this problem, but that is only because each outcome on a given trial is equally likely.

Consider the outcome {433}. The probability of obtaining a four on the first toss is $1/6$. The probability of obtaining a three on the second toss is also $1/6$. The probability of obtaining a three on the third toss is also $1/6$. The three tosses are assumed to be independent, so we may multiply these probabilities. We obtain $1/216$ as the probability of {433}. We may likewise calculate the probability of {343} and {334} as $1/216$ each. Adding these probabilities gives the probability of one four and two threes as $3/216$.

Even though we did not enumerate all possible outcomes, we did enumerate those outcomes which were favorable to the event we were studying. In this example, there were only three favorable outcomes. In other problems, there may be significantly more favorable outcomes, and in these cases enumeration is quite inefficient. It will turn out that these favorable outcomes are all permutations of each other. In the previous example, the favorable outcomes were {433, 343, 334}, which are all seen to be permutations of each other. It will turn out that order does not matter, so the probability is the same for all of these permutations. What we need is a method for counting the number of such permutations and a method for finding the probability of any of them.

It should be clear that the number of outcomes which are favorable to a given event is the number of permutations of the items specified in the definition of a favorable event. In the case of the earlier example, the number of outcomes which were favorable to the event of one four and two threes was the number of permutations of one four and two threes. Since there are three locations for the four (i.e., in the first toss, the second toss, or the third toss), there are three such permutations, or three out-comes favorable to the event in question. In general, the number of permu-tations of n items when $n(1)$ are of a given type, $n(2)$ of another type, and so on up to $n(k)$ of the kth type is

$$\frac{n!}{[n(1)!\, n(2)!\ldots n(k)!]},$$

where $n(1) + n(2) + \ldots + n(k) = n$. To check the validity of this formula in the case we just studied, notice that $k = 2$ (we are only interested in two types of items, fours and threes), $n(1) = 1$ (one four), and $n(2) = 2$ (two threes). Also, $n = 3$ (three tosses). The formula yields

$$\frac{n!}{[n(1)!\, n(2)!]} = \frac{3!}{[(1!)\,(2!)]}$$
$$= \frac{6}{[(1)\,(2)]}$$
$$= \frac{6}{2}$$
$$= 3,$$

which agrees with our answer. Also, notice that when $k = 2$, this formula reduces to

$$\frac{n!}{[n(1)!\, n(2)!]}$$

but $n(1) + n(2) = n,$

so $n(2) = n - n(1).$

If we rewrite the formula, we obtain

$$\frac{n!}{\{n(1)!\,[n-n(1)!]\}} = C(n, n(1)),$$

which is in agreement with the binomial formula.

As a more complicated example, consider ten tosses of a pair of dice. What is the expected number of sevens? What is the probability of three fours, three sixes, three sevens, and one eight?

The probability of rolling a seven on any one toss was previously seen to be $1/6$. We may define a binomial random variable by declaring a seven to be a success and everything else to be a failure. If we call this binomial random variable X, then

$$E[X] = np$$

$$= (10)\left(\frac{1}{6}\right)$$

$$= \frac{10}{6}$$

$$= 1.667$$

The probability of three fours, three sixes, three sevens, and one eight is found by using the multinomial formula. There are

$$\frac{10!}{[3!\,3!\,3!\,1!]}$$

permutations with three fours, three sixes, three sevens, and one eight. The probability of each such outcome is

$$\left(\frac{1}{6}\right)^3 \left(\frac{1}{6}\right)^3 \left(\frac{1}{6}\right)^3 \left(\frac{1}{6}\right)^1 = \left(\frac{1}{6}\right)^{10}$$

Therefore, the probability of this event is given by

$$P\{\text{three fours, three sixes, three sevens, and one eight}\}$$

$$= \frac{10!}{[3!\,3!\,3!\,1!]}\left(\frac{1}{6}\right)^{10}.$$

The expected value, probability mass function, and cumulative distribution function of a multinomial random variable are not very useful concepts, because there is no one numerical outcome. The outcome consists of various counts. A binomial random variable takes on a single value (the number of successes). A multinomial random variable is technically not a random variable by the definition provided earlier, but it is a random variable if we allow for vector-valued outcomes. That is, the outcome consists of a vector of counts. In the previous example, the vector would have been

$$(0, 0, 3, 0, 3, 3, 1, 0, 0, 0, 0),$$

corresponding to no twos, no threes, three fours, etc.

REVIEW OF GEOMETRIC RANDOM VARIABLES

Geometric random variables are similar to binomial random variables, with one important difference. A binomial random variable is the number of successes in a given number of trials. A geometric random

variable is the number of trials required to observe the first success. For example, if we toss a coin until we observe a heads and then record the number of tosses required, then, under fairly reasonable assumptions, the random variable defined as the number of required tosses follows a geometric distribution. The required assumptions are that each trial must result in either a success or a failure, the probability of success is constant across trials, and the results of all trials are independent. These are the same assumptions underlying the binomial distribution.

As an example, consider a batter who hits 0.250. How many at-bats would we expect this batter to require before getting a hit? A more appropriate question might be "what is the probability that k at-bats are required prior to this player getting his first hit?" To answer this question, notice that if k at-bats are required, then the first $(k - 1)$ at-bats must have resulted in outs, and then the kth at-bat must be a hit. Since the probability of a success on any given at-bat is 0.250, the probability of an out is $1 - 0.250 = 0.750$. Since the at-bats are independent, the probability of $(k - 1)$ outs followed by a hit is $(0.750)^{(k-1)} (0.250)$. This is the probability of the batter requiring k at-bats to record his first hit.

The geometric distribution is characterized by a single parameter, p, which is the success probability on any given trial. With this information, we may compute $P\{X = k\}$, where X is a geometric random variable (p), as

$$P\{X = k\} = P\{(k-1) \text{ failures followed by a success}\}$$
$$= P\{\text{failure}\}^{(k-1)} P\{\text{success}\}$$
$$= (1-p)^{(k-1)} p$$

This is the probability mass function for positive integer k. The probability mass function is zero for any other value of k, because the observed value must be a positive integer in order to be interpreted as the required number of trials to achieve a success.

Using the theory of infinite sequences, it can be shown that the expected value of a geometric random variable is $1/p$. Some textbooks state that the expected value of a geometric random variable is

$$\frac{(1-p)}{p}.$$

The apparent discrepancy is due to alternative parameterizations of the geometric distribution. If we let the random variable Y be the number of failures prior to the first success and let the random variable X be the number of trials required to achieve the first success, then $X = Y + 1$. Therefore,

$$E[X] = E[Y] + 1.$$

Some textbooks would call X a geometric random variable, while others call Y a geometric random variable. We consider X to be a geometric random variable. Now,

$$E[Y] = \frac{(1-p)}{p},$$

so $\qquad E[X] = E[Y + 1]$
$$= E[Y] + 1,$$

and $\qquad E = \left[\frac{(1-p)}{p}\right] + 1$

$$= \left(\frac{1}{p}\right) - \left(\frac{p}{p}\right) + \left(\frac{p}{p}\right)$$

$$= \frac{1}{p}$$

The cumulative distribution function of a geometric random variable may be easily found by noting that if X is a geometric random variable with parameter p, then

$$F_X(k) = P\{X \leq k\}$$

$$= 1 - P\{X > k\}$$

But the event $\{X > k\}$ may be simplified, because X is greater than k if more than k trials are required to produce the first success. This is equivalent to specifying that the first $(k-1)$ trials result in failures. The probability of this is $(1-p)^{k-1}$. Then,

$$F_X(k) = P\{X \leq k\}$$

$$= 1 - P\{X > k\}$$

$$= 1 - (1-p)^{k-1}$$

REVIEW OF NEGATIVE BINOMIAL RANDOM VARIABLES

The negative binomial distribution generalizes the geometric distribution, in that it allows for additional successes prior to the success at which we stop the trials. Recall that the interpretation of the geometric random variable was the number of trials required to observe the first success. However, a geometric random variable would not be appropriate if our interest was in the number of trials required to observe the second success, or the third success, or, indeed, any success other than the first one. The negative binomial distribution helps to bridge this gap.

For example, consider tossing a fair coin until the second heads is observed. In particular, let X denote the number of trials required to observe two successes. Then X has a negative binomial distribution, and X is a negative binomial random variable.

A negative binomial random variable is characterized by a pair of parameters. The first parameter is the success probability on any given trial, denoted p. The second parameter is the number of successes required, denoted n. We will derive the probability mass function in a manner similar to that used to derive the probability mass function for the geometric distribution.

We derive the probability mass function of the negative binomial distribution by finding the probability that a negative binomial random variable takes on the value k for all values k. We notice that the negative binomial random variable X takes on the value k if k trials are required to observe n successes. Clearly, then, k cannot be less than n. Also, since k is the required number of trials, k must be valued as an integer. Thus, we may restrict attention to values of k which are positive integers at least as large as n. For such k, we notice that $X = k$ if k trials are required to observe n successes; therefore, there are n successes and $k - n$ failures in the k trials. Since we did not stop prior to the kth trial, we also know that the nth success did not occur prior to the kth trial. Thus, the nth success must have occurred on the kth trial. To summarize, we have $(n - 1)$ successes and $(k - n)$ failures in the first $(k - 1)$ trials, followed by a success on the kth trial. The probability of this event is the probability that X takes on the value k, or $P\{X = k\}$.

We find the probability of this event the same way we found the probability mass function for the binomial distribution. There are many outcomes which would lead to the event $\{X = k\}$. Each of these outcomes is a permutation of the $(n - 1)$ successes and $(k - n)$ failures in the first $(k - 1)$ trials. Each of these outcomes results in n successes and $(k - n)$ failures, so the probability of any of these outcomes is $p^n(1 - p)^{k-n}$. The remaining task is to find the number of outcomes which lead to the event $\{X = k\}$. This question is tantamount to asking how many permutations there are of $(n - 1)$ successes and $(k - n)$ failures in the first $(k - 1)$ trials. The answer is

$$C(k - 1, n - 1), \text{ or } \frac{(k-1)!}{[(n-1)!\,(k-n)!]}.$$

Now,

$$P\{X = k\} = \frac{(k-1)!}{[(n-1)!\,(k-n)!]p^n(1-p)^{k-n}} \text{ for integer } k, k \geq n.$$

Just as a binomial random variable with parameters n and p can be viewed as a sum of n Bernoulli random variables, each with parameter p, likewise a negative binomial random variable with parameters n and p can be viewed as a sum of n geometric random variables, each with parameter p. Then we may find the expected value of a negative binomial random variable X, with parameters n and p, by letting $X1, X2, ..., Xn$ be geometric random variables, each with parameter p. Then

$$E[X] = E[\Sigma_{i=1 \text{ to } n}Xi]$$

$$= \Sigma_{i-1 \text{ to } n}E[Xi]$$

$$= \Sigma_{i=1 \text{ to } n} \frac{1}{p}$$

$$= \frac{n}{p}$$

Notice that as n becomes larger, the expected value becomes larger. This is reasonable, because we would expect more trials to be required if we require more successes. In addition, as p becomes larger, the expected value becomes smaller. If a success becomes more likely on any given trial, then fewer trials should be expected to be required to observe a given number of successes.

REVIEW OF POISSON RANDOM VARIABLES

Poisson random variables are derived from count data under a fairly broad set of assumptions. The details of the assumptions are beyond the scope of this book, but in summary, we will treat any random variable which counts the number of some occurrence for which no upper limit may be assigned a priori as Poisson. As examples, we may consider many of the random variables discussed in the earlier section on random variables which were said to be countably infinite. This would include the number  of phone calls received in a day, the number of thunderstorms in a year, the number of cars passing a given intersection in an hour, or the number of goals scored in a soccer game. At this point, it might be a good idea to review the section on random variables to better understand the concept that no upper limit exists on these random variables.

The possible values that a Poisson random variable can assume are the set of non-negative integers, or $\{0, 1, 2, ...\}$. A Poisson random variable is characterized by a single parameter, L. If X is a Poisson random variable with parameter L, then

$E[X] = L$,

so L is the mean of X. The probability mass function of a Poisson random variable is given by

$$P\{X = k\} = \frac{e^{-L}L^k}{k!} \text{ for } k = 0, 1, \dots.$$

Here, let us suppose that $e = 2.71828\dots$

As previously mentioned, the expected value of a Poisson random variable with parameter L is L, or $E[X] = L$, if X is a Poisson random variable with parameter L. When we learn about higher moments in a later chapter, we will see that the variance of a Poisson random variable with parameter L is also L.

REVIEW OF HYPERGEOMETRIC RANDOM VARIABLES

The hypergeometric distribution is used primarily for contingency tables, or cross-classified data. For example, patients in a hospital may be classified both by age (over 40 or under 40) and by gender (male or female). Thus, each patient would be cross-classified. In this example, suppose that the total numbers of males, females, patients over 40, and patients under 40 were known. All that remains to be determined is the number of males over 40. If we knew this, then by subtraction we would also know the number of males under 40, the number of females over 40, and the number of females under 40. The distribution of any one of these quantities is said to be hypergeometric.

The hypergeometric distribution is most frequently applied to the tag-recapture model for estimating the size of a biological population and to testing for defective items. As an example of the first application, let us say we want to know the number of fish in a lake. A number of fish from this lake are captured, tagged, and released back into the lake for redistribution among the population-at-large. After a given period of time, more fish are captured. The random quantity is the number of fish among the second batch to be captured who were also captured in the first batch. This number may be determined by counting the number of fish in the second batch who have tags.

The population size is fixed (but unknown to the experimenter), and the numbers of fish captured in the first batch, not captured in the first batch, captured in the second batch, and not captured in the second batch are also fixed. Thus, all margins are fixed. The number of fish who were captured in both batches follows the hypergeometric distribution. The cross-classification in this example refers to the classification as either captured or not captured in the first batch and either captured or not captured in the second batch.

In the second application of the hypergeometric distribution, testing for defective items, the typical problem involves a number of items received, of which some are defective and some are not. A sample of these items is taken, and each item in the sample is tested. The random quantity is the number of items in the sample which are defective. The cross-classification in this example refers to classifying each item as defective or not and as belonging to the sample or not. Each margin is fixed, as it is known ahead of time how many items will be sampled, and the numbers of defective items and non-defective items in the population are fixed (but not known to the experimenter).

When testing for defective items, it should be mentioned that if the sampling is with replacement, then the binomial model is the appropriate one. In the more realistic case of sampling without replacement, however, the hypergeometric model becomes the appropriate one. Therefore, we will assume throughout this section that sampling is performed without replacement, and thus that the hypergeometric model is appropriate.

The probability mass function of the hypergeometric distribution is derived by considering the probability that a hypergeometric random variable takes on any given value. To demonstrate the method of finding this probability, consider again testing for defective items. We may represent the situation with the following table:

	Sampled	Not Sampled	Total
Defective	X	$D - X$	D
Not Defective	$S - X$	$N - D - S + X$	$N - D$
Total	S	$N - S$	N

We let D be the (unknown) number of defective items, N the (known) total number of items, and S the (known) number of items sampled. Finally, X is the number of defective items in the sample. For X to take on the value k, we would require that there be k defective items in the sample and $S - X$ non-defective items in the sample. The number of ways to pick k defective items out of the D total defective items is $C(D, k)$. Likewise, the number of ways to pick $S - X$ non-defective items out of the $N - D$ total non-defective items is $C(N - D, S - k)$. Multiplying these quantities together provides the total number of ways that X could be k. All outcomes from this sampling scheme are equally likely, so to obtain the probability that X takes on the value k we must divide this number by the total number of possible outcomes (samples). We are selecting S items out of N, so there are $C(N, S)$ total outcomes possible. Thus,

$$P\{X = k\} = \frac{C(D, k)\, D(N - D, S - k)}{C(N, S)}.$$

This is the hypergeometric probability mass function. We must note that the possible values of k are such that each cell in the table is non-negative. In addition, no cell in the table can exceed the margin. Thus, we obtain

$0 \leq k \leq D,$

$0 \leq D - k \leq D,$

$0 \leq S - k \leq N - D,$

$0 \leq N - D - S + k \leq N - D,$

$0 \leq k \leq S,$

$0 \leq D - k \leq N - S,$

$0 \leq S - k \leq S,$

and $\quad 0 \leq N - D - S + k \leq N - S.$

Each of these inequalities makes good intuitive sense if one considers what would happen if it did not hold. For example, if the first inequality did not hold, then either there would be a negative number of defective items in the sample or there would be more defective items in the sample than there are in the entire batch. Clearly, this is impossible.

Many of these inequalities are redundant, and we can summarize them in the following set of inequalities:

$0 \leq k,$

$D + S - N \leq k,$

$k \leq D,$

and $\quad k \leq S.$

This can also be written as

$\mathrm{MAX}(0, D + S - N) \leq k \leq \mathrm{MIN}(D, S).$

MATHEMATICAL EXPECTATION OF DISCRETE RANDOM VARIABLES

Let X be a discrete random variable defined on a sample space $S = \{x_1, x_2, ..., x_n\}$, having a finite range $S_X = \{x_1, x_2, ..., x_n\}$ with point probabilities $Q(x_i) = 1/n$. The possible outcomes of the random experiment in S_X have average

$$\mu = \sum_{i=1}^{n} \frac{x_i}{n} = \sum_{i=1}^{n} x_i \frac{1}{n} = \sum_{i=1}^{n} x_i Q(x_i)$$

If some discrete model other than the equally likelihood model applies, then some values of X are more likely to occur than others. Then the equation defining, μ may be viewed as defining a weighted average of the outcomes, where each x_i is weighted by its point probability. This weighted average is called the mean of X or the expected value of X

EXPECTED VALUE OF A DISCRETE RANDOM VARIABLE

Let X be a discrete random variable with range $S_X = \{x_1, x_2, ..., x_n\}$ and a probability point function Q. The expected value (or mean) of X, denoted by $E(X)$, is defined as

$$E(X) = \sum_{i=1}^{n} x_i Q(x_i)$$

For example, let X be the first digit that results from a call to the random number generator in a computer system. Then $S_X = \{0, 1, 2, ..., 9\}$, and $Q(x_i) = 0.1$. Thus,

$$E(X) = \sum_{i=1}^{n} x_i Q(x_i) = (0)\,(.1) + (1)\,(.1) + ... + (9)\,(.1)$$

$$= 0.1\,(0 + 1 + 2 + ... + 9)$$

$$= 0.1\,(45)$$

$$= 4.5$$

Note that the expected value of X is not an outcome to be expected since an outcome for this experiment can never be 4.5.

PROPERTIES OF EXPECTED VALUES

1. Let X be a random variable defined on a sample space S, and let c be any constant. Then

i) $E(cX) = cE(X)$

ii) $E(X + c) = E(X) + c$

2.   Let $X_1, X_2, \ldots, X_n$ be random variables defined on the same sample space S. Then

$$E(X_1 + X_2 + \ldots + X_n) = E(X_1) + E(X_2) + \ldots + E(X_n)$$

CALCULATION OF EXPECTED VALUE

The expected value can be calculated explicitly for random variables with standard probability functions such as the following.

1.   **Random Variables With Uniform Probability Functions**

If X is a random variable with $S_x = \{x_1, x_2, \ldots x_n\}$ and a uniform probability point function $Q(x_i) = 1/n$, then

$$E(X) = \frac{\sum\limits_{i=1}^{n} x_i}{n}$$

2.   **Bernoulli Random Variables**

Let X be a Bernoulli random variable defined on a sample space S, $S_X = \{0, 1\}$, and $Q(1) = p$, where p is the probability of success in a trial. Then

$$E(X) = P$$

3.   **Binomial Random Variables**

Let X be a Binomial random variable and $S_x = x_1, x_2, \ldots, x_n$ be the number of successes in n trials with probability p for success on each trial. Then

$$E(X) = np$$

4.   **Independent Random Variables**

If X and Y are independent random variables , then

$$E(XY) = E(X) \times E(Y)$$

EXPECTATION OF A FUNCTION OF A RANDOM VARIABLE

If X is a random variable, then X defines a function from a sample space S to the set of real numbers. If g is a real-values function defined over the set of real numbers, then the composition of X and g, denoted by $g(X)$, is also a function from the sample space S to the set of real numbers.

Thus, $g(X)$ is itself a random variable. Let $Y = g(X)$. Then Y is called a function of the random variable X.

If X is a random variable with range $S_X = \{x_1, x_2, ..., x_n\}$,

$$E(X) = \sum_{i=1}^{n} x_i \, QX(x_i), \text{ and } Y = g(X) \text{ is a random variable of } X, \text{ then}$$

$$E(Y) = E(g(X)) = \sum_{i=1}^{n} g(x_i) Q_X(x_i)$$

A special case of the function g occurs when g is the sum of two other functions g_1 and g_2. For example $Y = X^2 + X$ can be written as

$$Y = (X)^2 + X; \text{ so if } g_1(X) = X^2 \text{ and } g_2(X) = X,$$

then $g(X) = g_1(X) + g_2(X)$.

Let X be a random variable defined on a sample space S, let g_1 and g_2 be two functions whose domains include S_X. If $Y = g_1(X) + g_2(X)$, then

$$E(Y) = E(g_1(X)) + E(g_2(X))$$

Some other properties for the expected value of a function of a random variable are the following.

1. If X is a finite random variable and a and b are arbitrary real numbers, then

    $$E(aX + b) = aE(X) + b$$

2. If X is a finite random variable and a and b are arbitrary real numbers, then

    i) $E(aX) = aE(X)$

    ii) $E(X + b) = E(X) + b$

    iii) $E(b) = b$

    iv) $E(X - E(X)) = 0$

VARIANCE OF DISCRETE RANDOM VARIABLES

The mean or expected value of a random variable is useful in describing the center or balancing point of its distribution. Suppose, however, that the random variables X, Y, and Z have the same expected value. That is, $E(X) = E(Y) = E(Z)$, then the probability functions of these variables are not necessarily identical. A quantity which measures the spread or variability is based on the expected value of the "square deviations from the mean." This measure is called the variance.

Variance

Let X be a random variable defined on a sample space S with range $S_X = \{x_1, x_2, \ldots x_n\}$ a probability point function Q, and an expected value $E(X)$. Then the variance of the random variable X, denoted by $V(X)$, is defined as

$$V(X) = E((X - E(X))^2)$$

$$= \sum_{i=1}^{n} (x_i - E(X)^2)\, Q(x_i)$$

Since $V(X)$ is a function of squared deviations from the mean, it measures the variability in squared units of X. Frequently, it is desirable and useful to have a measure in the original units of X. To accomplish this, we take the positive square root of $V(X)$. That is, X and σ_X have the same units. Because of its importance and practicality, we define the square root of $V(X)$ formally.

Standard Deviation

The square root of the variance of a random variable X is called the standard deviation of X and denoted by

$$\sigma_X = \sqrt{V(X)}$$

For example, if X denotes the uppermost face when a fair die is tossed, then $E(X)$, $V(X)$, and σ_X can be calculated as follows.

$$E(X) = \sum_{i=1}^{6} x_i Q(x_i) = 1\left(\frac{1}{6}\right) + 2\left(\frac{1}{6}\right) + 3\left(\frac{1}{6}\right) + 4\left(\frac{1}{6}\right) + 5\left(\frac{1}{6}\right) + 6\left(\frac{1}{6}\right)$$

$$= 3.5$$

$$V(X) = \sum_{i=1}^{6} (x_i - E(X))^2\, Q(x_1)$$

$$= \sum_{i=1}^{6} (x_i - 3.5)^2 Q(x_i)$$

$$= \frac{35}{12}$$

and

$$\sigma_X = \sqrt{V(X)} = \sqrt{\frac{35}{12}}$$

COMPUTING FORMULA FOR V(X)

If the mean $E(X)$ of a random variable is not an integer, then using the formula

$$V(X) = \sum_{i=1}^{n} (x_i - E(X))^2 \, Q(x_i)$$

to compute the variance of the random variable X is cumbersome. The following formula gives us an easier way to compute it.

If X is a random variable with a variance $V(X)$, then

$$V(X) = E(X^2) - (E(X))^2$$

PROPERTIES OF VARIANCE FOR A SINGLE RANDOM VARIABLE

1. If X is a finite random variable, and a and b are arbitrary real numbers, then

   $$V(aX + b) = a^2 \, V(X)$$

2. If X is a finite random variable, and a and b are arbitrary real numbers, then

   i) $V(X + b) = V(X)$

   ii) $V(aX) = a^2 V(X)$

3. If X is a random variable with a uniform probability point function for n values, then

   $$V(X) = \frac{1}{n} \sum_{i=1}^{n} (x_i - E(X))^2$$

   $$= \frac{1}{n} \sum_{i=1}^{n} x^2_i - E(X))^2$$

4. If X is a Bernoulli random variable with $S_X = \{0, 1\}$, then

   $$V(X) = pq$$

   where $p = Q(1)$ and $q = 1 - p$

5. If X is a binomial random variable for n trials, where p is the probability of a success on each trial, then

$$V(X) = np(1 - p) = npq$$

where $p + q = 1$

INDEPENDENT RANDOM VARIABLES

Similar to our discussion earlier in the chapter, random variables are independent if for every pair of X and Y values:

$$P(X,Y) = P_x(X) \times P_y(Y) \text{ (discrete case)}$$

$$f(x,y) = f_x(X) \times f_y(Y) \text{ (continuous)}$$

Then the random variables X and Y are independent.

If X and Y are independent, then the probability of X happening is in no way related to Y occurring. If two coins are flipped, the first coin has no control over the outcome of the other coin. Random variables that are not independent are dependent.

EXAMPLE

Suppose that the successive daily changes of the price of a given stock are assumed to be independent and identically distributed random variables with probability mass function given by

$$P(\text{daily change is } I) = \begin{cases} 2 & \text{with probability } 0.20 \\ 1 & \text{with probability } 0.30 \\ 0 & \text{with probability } 0.25 \\ -1 & \text{with probability } 0.10 \\ -2 & \text{with probability } 0.15 \end{cases}$$

What is the probability that the stock's price will fluctuate by 2, 1, 0, and 2 points in the next four days?

SOLUTION

Let X denote the change in the stock price on a given day. Thus, $X = X_1 + X_2 + X_3 + X_4$. Since we are assuming that the random variables are independent and identically distributed we know that

$$P(X_1 = 2, X_2 = 1, X_3 = 0, X_4 = 2)$$
$$= P(X_1 = 2) \times P(X_2 = 1) \times P(X_3 = 0) \times P(X_4 = 2)$$

$$= (0.20)\,(0.30)\,(0.25)\,(0.20) = 0.003$$

Now that we understand independent random variables, we want to consider their mean and standard deviation. When working with random variables the mean is often referred to as the **expectation**. We can calculate the expectation of a random variable X using

$$E[X] = P(X = a_1) \times a_1 + P(X = a_2) \times a_2 + \dots + P(X = a_n) \times a_n$$

In the above formula, a_i takes on all of the possible values of the random variable X.

EXAMPLE

Let X be the number of heads in 5 tosses of a fair coin. Find the expectation of X.

SOLUTION

Since X is the number of heads in five tosses of a fair coin, we know that

$$E[X] = E[X_1 + X_2 + X_3 + X_4 + X_5]$$

$$= \frac{1}{2} + \frac{1}{2} + \frac{1}{2} + \frac{1}{2} + \frac{1}{2}$$

$$= 5 \times \frac{1}{2} = 2\frac{1}{2}$$

EXAMPLE

An electronics company has recently sent in bids for four jobs that will earn them 7, 13, 15, and 25 million dollars profit respectively. If the probabilities of getting the bids are 0.6, 0.2, 0.7, and 0.5 respectively, what is their expected total profit?

SOLUTION

Let X equal the company's profit from the bid jobs. Therefore, the expected value of X can be calculated by

$$E[X] = E[X_1 + X_2 + X_3 + X_4]$$

$$= E[X_1] + E[X_2] + E[X_3] + E[X_4]$$

$$= [7(0.6) + 0(0.4)] + [13(0.2) + 0(0.8)]$$

$$+ 15(0.7) + 0(0.3)\,] + [25(0.5) + 0(0.5)]$$

$$+ 4.2 + 2.6 + 10.5 + 12.5$$

$$= 29.8$$

Thus, the company's expected profit is 29.8 million dollars.

EXAMPLE

Suppose a set of trading cards has 12 different subsets and suppose that each time one obtains a card it is equally likely to be any one of the different subsets. Compute the expected number of different subsets that are contained in a package of 8 cards.

SOLUTION

Let X denote the number of different subsets in a package of 8 cards. If

$$X = X_1 + X_2 + \ldots + X_{12}$$

where $X_i = 1$ if at least one subset i card is contained in the package of 8 and $X_i = 0$ otherwise, we can now compute $E[X_i]$.

$$E[X_i] = P(X_i \geq 1)$$

$$= 1 - P(\textit{No type i card})$$

$$= 1 - \left(\frac{11}{12}\right)^8$$

We can now combine the X_i's together and calculate $E[X]$.

$$E[X] = E[X_1] + [X_2] + \ldots + E[X_{12}]$$

$$= 12 \times \left[1 - \left(\frac{11}{12}\right)^8\right] \approx 6.018$$

Even though the expectation (or mean) is very useful, in some cases more information is needed. A useful value is the variance of a random variable (denoted by Var). Recall that the standard deviation is the positive square root of the variance. This standard deviation helps us determine how much the values are spread out. We can use expectations to define the variance of a random variable. This formula is

$$Var(X) - E[X^2] - (E[X])^2$$

The next two examples consider the topic of rolling dice. Let us begin by calculating the expectation of rolling a single die. Let R equal the value obtained from rolling a die. Since $P(R = 1) = P(R = 2) = P(R = 3) =$

$P(R = 4) = P(R = 5) = P(R = 6) = {}^1/_6$, we can quickly evaluate $E[R]$.

$$E[R] = 1 \times \frac{1}{6} + 2 \times \frac{1}{6} + 3 \times \frac{1}{6} + 4 \times \frac{1}{6} + 5 \times \frac{1}{6} + 6 \times \frac{1}{6}$$

$$E[R] = \frac{7}{2}$$

Therefore, the expected value of rolling a single die is 3.5.

EXAMPLE

Calculate the expected sum obtained when 6 independent rolls of a die are made.

SOLUTION

Let X denote the sum of the 6 independent rolls.

$$X = X_1 + X_2 + X_3 + X_4 + X_5 + X_6$$

We can now find $E[X]$.

$$E[X] = E[X_1] + E[X_2] + \ldots + E[X_6]$$

$$= \frac{7}{2} + \frac{7}{2} + \ldots + \frac{7}{2} = 6 \times \frac{7}{2} = 21$$

Therefore, if we roll a die six times the sum that we expect to get is 21.

EXAMPLE

Compute the variance of X when X represents the outcome when we roll a fair die.

SOLUTION

Since $P(X = I) = {}^1/_6$ for $I = 1, 2, \ldots, 6$, we can obtain $E[X^2]$.

$$E[X^2] = (1)^2 \times \frac{1}{6} + (2)^2 \times \frac{1}{6} + (3)^2 \times \frac{1}{6} + (4)^2 \times \frac{1}{6} + (5)^2 \times \frac{1}{6} + (6)^2 \times \frac{1}{6}$$

$$= \frac{1}{6} + \frac{2}{3} + \frac{3}{2} + \frac{8}{3} + \frac{25}{6} + 6$$

$$E[X^2] = \frac{91}{6} = 15.167$$

With this information we are finally able to compute the variance of X.

$$Var(X) = E[X^2] - (E[X])^2$$

$$= \frac{91}{6} - \left(\frac{7}{2}\right)^2 = \frac{35}{12}$$

$$Var(X) = 2.917$$

NORMAL DISTRIBUTION

REVIEW OF NORMAL RANDOM VARIABLES

The normal distribution is the most commonly used of all probabilistic distributions in all areas of statistical application. There are many reasons for this prevalence, not the least of which are closure under the process of averaging and the central limit theorem. Closure under the process of averaging ensures that the mean of a set of normal random variables is also a random variable with a normal distribution. The central limit theorem appears in many forms, so actually it is a collection of theorems, but for our purposes we will simplify this collection and consider the central limit theorem to state that whenever the sample size is large enough, say, for example, there are at least 30 observations, then the mean of these observations follows, approximately, the normal distribution. Of course if the original random variables are normally distributed, then we do not require the central limit theorem to tell us that the mean is approximately normally distributed, because we know from closure under the process of averaging that the mean is exactly normally distributed. But the central limit theorem applies even when the original random variables are not normally distributed.

The probability density function of a normal random variable is of no use to us, but it is worth noting that when plotted it gives the familiar bell-shaped curve so commonly referred to in the statistical literature. The cumulative distribution function of a normal random variable cannot be written in closed (algebraic) form. Tables are required, but fortunately these tables are fairly wide-spread. Almost every introductory statistical text has a normal table in the back of the book.

The normal distribution is characterized by two parameters. These are the mean and the variance. Each set of these parameters gives rise to a different normal distribution. The mean can be any real number, positive or negative. The variance must be non-negative, but otherwise is arbitrary. If a book were to include tables of the cumulative distribution function of each of these normal distributions, then there would not be enough paper in the world to fit all of these tables. Fortunately, this is not necessary.

Any linear function of a normally distributed random variable is also a normally distributed random variable. To illustrate, let X be a normally distributed random variable with mean M and standard deviation S. Let $Y = aX + b$ be an arbitrary linear function of X. Then Y is a normally distributed random variable with mean $aM + b$ and standard deviation aS. The importance of this fact will be seen when we discuss the standard normal distribution and its tabulated distribution.

There are two key properties of the normal distribution which allow for tabulation of the cumulative distribution function of only a single normal distribution. First, the normal probability density function is symmetric about the mean. Second, when we standardize a normal random variable by subtracting from it its mean and then dividing it by its standard deviation (to be discussed in a future chapter), the result is a normal random variable with mean zero and standard deviation one. This is known as a standard normal random variable, and this is the one which is most commonly tabulated in textbooks.

If X is distributed normally with mean two and standard deviation three, and we are asked to find the probability that $X > 4$ (for example), then we define Z to be $(X - 2) / 3$. Now Z is also a random variable, and it turns out that Z is normally distributed with mean zero and standard deviation one. Then

$$P\{X > 4\} = P\left\{\frac{(X-2)}{3} > \frac{(4-2)}{3}\right\}$$

$$= P\left\{Z > \frac{2}{3}\right\}$$

This probability can be looked up in any normal table.

To save space, most normal tables only tabulate non-negative values. Thus, they cannot be used directly to answer questions about negative numbers. If a question involves negative numbers, such as, find $P\{X > -3\}$, then we use the fact that the normal distribution is symmetric about its mean. Mathematically, this symmetry is described by stating that if X is a normal random variable with mean M and standard deviation S, then for any value k it is true that

$$P\{X > M + k\} = P\{X < M - k\}$$

and $\quad P\{X < M + k\} = P\{X > M - k\}.$

Returning to our example, X is a normal random variable with mean two and standard deviation three. We first must write -3 as a deviation from the mean ($-3 = 2 - 5$). Then we use the symmetry to obtain

$$P\{X > -3\} = P\{X > 2 - 5\}$$

$$= P\{X < 2 + 5\}$$

$$= P\{X < 7\}$$

$$= P\left\{\frac{(X-2)}{3} < \frac{(7-2)}{3}\right\}$$

$$= P\left\{Z < \frac{5}{3}\right\}$$

$$= P\{Z < 1.67\}$$

and this probability can again be looked up in any normal table. Typically, Z is used to denote the standard normal distribution.

The strategy for solving problems which ask for probabilities involving the normal distribution is first to write what is being asked for. Typically, this will be of the form

$$P\{X > k\}$$

or $\qquad P\{X < k\}$

for some given k, and the mean and standard deviation of X will be given as M and S. Our next step is to equate this probability to one involving X after being standardized. Of course whatever we do to one side of the inequality must also be done to the other side of the inequality. Thus, k must be "standardized" as well. Then we obtain

$$P\{X > k\} = P\left\{\frac{(X-M)}{S} > \frac{(k-M)}{S}\right\}$$

or $\qquad P\{X < k\} = P\left\{\frac{(X-M)}{S} < \frac{(k-M)}{S}\right\}.$

Now we replace the quantity $(X - M) / S$ with Z, since any normal random variable which is standardized has a standard normal (Z) distribution. We obtain

$$P\{X > k\} = P\{Z > (k - M) / S\}$$

or $\qquad P\{X < k\} = P\{Z < (k - M) / S\}.$

The numbers k, M, and S are all known so we can evaluate the right-hand side of the inequality in the expression. If the result is non-negative, then we look it up in the table for the standard normal distribution. If, however, it is negative, then we use the symmetry of the normal distribution about its mean and look up the absolute value of this quantity in the table of the normal distribution, being careful to change the direction of the inequality.

Different books have different types of tables for the normal cumulative distribution, but all contain equivalent information. That is, from any one such table any other such table can be derived. These tables are typically indexed by cutoffs. The tables may contain

1. the probability of a standard normal random variable exceeding this cutoff (which is one minus the cumulative distribution function),

2. the probability of a standard normal random variable being less than this cutoff (this would directly give the cumulative distribution function of the standard normal distribution),

3. the probability of a standard normal random variable falling between zero and the cutoff (which is the cumulative distribution function minus 0.5), or

4. the probability of a standard normal random variable falling within plus or minus the absolute value of the cutoff (which is twice what is tabulated in tables of the third type).

This book provides a table of the second type, so it provides the cumulative distribution function directly. Thus, there is no need for transformations if one wishes to evaluate the cumulative distribution function of the standard normal distribution. For example,

$$P\{Z < 0.14\} = 0.5557,$$

as seen from the table. A more realistic example may ask for $P\{X > -0.5\}$ when X is a random variable with a normal distribution with mean 0.2 and standard deviation 1.4. Then we would need to calculate

$$P\{X > -0.5\} = P\left\{\frac{(X - 0.2)}{1.4} > \frac{(-0.5 - 0.2)}{1.4}\right\}$$

$$= P\left\{Z > \frac{(-0.7)}{1.4}\right\}$$

$$= P\{Z > -0.5\}$$

$$= 1 - P\{Z < -0.5\}$$
$$= 1 - P\{Z > 0.5\}$$
$$= P\{Z < 0.5\}$$
$$= 0.6915$$

It was merely a coincidence that the problem $P\{X < -0.5\}$ converted to $P\{Z < -0.5\}$ after the standardization. Typically, the cutoff for X will not be the same as the cutoff for Z.

SAMPLING DISTRIBUTIONS

SAMPLING DISTRIBUTION OF THE MEAN

If all possible samples of size n are selected from a population of size N, and the mean of some characteristic (e.g., age) is calculated, these values, along with their respective probability of occurrence, make up the sampling distribution. The number of possible samples of size n that can be drawn from a population of size N is determined using the following formula for a number of combinations:

$$N_n^C = \frac{N!}{n!(N-n)!}$$

EXAMPLE

The number of possible samples of size 10 that can be selected from a population of 100 objects is:

$$_{100}C_{10} = \frac{100!}{10!\,90!} = 17,310,309,000,000.$$

Note that two samples are different if at least **one** object or value is different.

If it were possible to select every one of these 17,310,309,000,000 samples and calculate the mean age and the probability of occurrence for each, the resulting distribution would be approximately (asshown on the following page); where:

$$\mu = \frac{\Sigma \bar{x}}{N^c n}$$

= The mean of the Sampling Distribution (will be the same as the population mean).

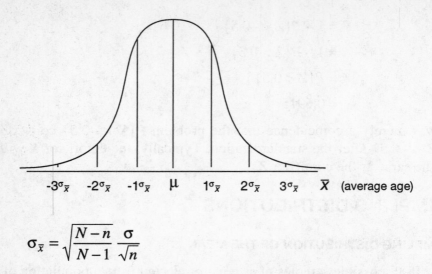

$$\sigma_{\bar{x}} = \sqrt{\frac{N-n}{N-1}} \frac{\sigma}{\sqrt{n}}$$

= The Standard Error of the Mean (the standard deviation of the sampling distribution).

Note that the figure shown on the pervious page looks very much like the normal distribution presented earlier. It does approach the normal distribution; however, the two are not identical at this point unless the population from which the sample is drawn is normally distributed; i.e., the percentage of areas under the curve between $\pm 1\sigma$, $\pm 2\sigma$, and $\pm 3\sigma$ are not identical to those areas specified by the normal distribution, except in the case of a normally distributed population. More discussion of this will be included later.

SAMPLING DISTRIBUTION OF THE PROPORTION

The explanation of the sampling distribution of the proportion parallels that of the sampling distribution of the mean. The only dif-ference is that the distribution consists of sample proportions of some characteristic (e.g., percentage of smokers) and their respective probability of occurrence. The number of possible samples of size n from a population of size N would be calculated in the same manner as discussed earlier. The resulting distribution would look as follows:

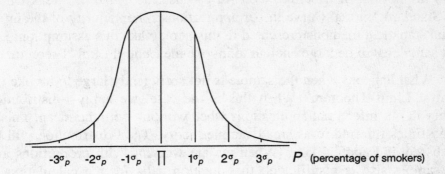

$-3\sigma_p$ $-2\sigma_p$ $-1\sigma_p$ Π $1\sigma_p$ $2\sigma_p$ $3\sigma_p$ P (percentage of smokers)

where:

$$\Pi = \frac{\Sigma\, p}{N^c n}$$

= The mean of the Sampling Distribution (will be the same as the population proportion).

$$\sigma_p = \sqrt{\frac{N-n}{N-1}}\,\sqrt{\Pi(1-\Pi)/n}$$

= The Standard Error of The Proportion (the standard deviation of the Sampling Distribution).

A similar discussion applies concerning the relationship between this distribution and the normal distribution as that presented for the sampling distribution of the mean.

THE CENTRAL LIMIT THEOREM

The Central Limit Theorem states:

Regardless of the shape formed by the data values in the population, the shape of the values making up the sampling distribution of the mean ($\overline{X}$'s) will approach a normal distribution having a mean of μ and a standard deviation of σ_x if the sample size is 30 or greater. Likewise, for the sampling distribution of the proportion (p's), if the sample is 50 or greater, this distribution approaches the normal distribution with a mean of Π and a standard deviation of σ_p, when both $n\,\Pi \geq 5$ and $n(1-\Pi) \geq 5$.

What this theorem is telling us is that if we take sufficiently large samples (n $\geq$ 30 for the mean and n $\geq$ 50 for the proportion), then we may use normal curve theory in applying statistical inference. That is, if we can assume that our distribution of sample means or sample proportions follows the normal distribution, then we can use the Table of Areas Under the Standard Normal Curve in our applications. The majority of the inferential statistical methods presented in this book make this assumption; i.e., that samples will be large enough to invoke the Central Limit Theorem.

What happens when the sample is not sufficiently large to invoke the Central Limit Theorem? When this is the case, we apply t-distribution theory in our inferential applications when working with the mean. This is many times referred to as small sample theory. The t-distribution will be discussed and applied later. When we are working with proportions and the sample size is insufficient, the situation calls for the calculation of probabilities and statistical procedures involving the binomial distribution which is beyond the scope of this book. Examples follow illustrating the application of the Central Limit Theorem to practical situations.

EXAMPLE

Assume that 1500 students have graduated from the M.B.A. program at XYZ University and their average starting salary is $29,500 with a standard deviation of $2,000. If a sample of 50 students is randomly selected, what is the probability that the average starting salary will be at least $30,000?

SOLUTION

1. Ascertain that the existing conditions allow for the use of the normal approximation.

    Yes, $n \geq 30$.

2. Sketch the distribution of $\bar{X}$'s and locate the area specified.

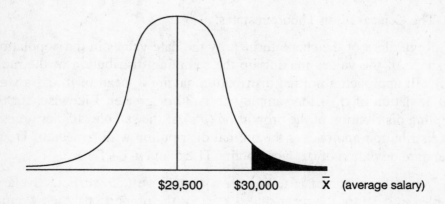

$29,500 \qquad $30,000 \qquad \bar{X}$ (average salary)

3. Calculate the Z value.

$$Z = \frac{\bar{x} - \mu}{\sigma_{\bar{x}}}$$

$$= \frac{\bar{x} - \mu}{\frac{\sigma}{\sqrt{n}}}$$

$$= \frac{30,000 - 29,500}{\frac{2,000}{\sqrt{50}}}$$

$$= 1.77.$$

4. Determine the area from the mean to $\bar{X} = 30,000$ ($Z = 1.77$) using the Table of Areas Under the Normal Curve.

   If $Z = 1.77$, area = .46164.

5. Determine the specified probability.

   $P(\bar{X} \geq 30,000) = .5 - .46164 = .03836.$

EXAMPLE

Assume that the Borg Corporation employs 1,600 people, 160 of whom are identified as problem employees due to absenteeism. If a random sample of 100 employees is selected, what is the probability that between 12% and 15% are problem employees with regard to absenteeism?

SOLUTION

1. Ascertain that the existing conditions allow the use of the normal distribution.

   Yes, $n \geq 50$

   $n \, \Pi = 100 \, (.10) = 10$

   $n \, (1 - \Pi) = 100 \, (.90) = 90.$

2. Sketch the distribution of p's and locate the area specified.

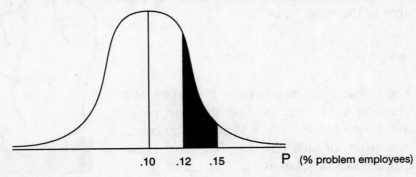

.10   .12   .15   P (% problem employees)

3.   Calculate Z values.

$$z = \frac{P_1 - \Pi}{s_p} \qquad\qquad z = \frac{P_2 - \Pi}{s_p}$$

$$= \frac{P_1 - \Pi}{\sqrt{\Pi(1 - \Pi)/n}} \qquad\qquad = \frac{P_2 - \Pi}{\sqrt{\Pi(1 - \Pi)/n}}$$

$$= \frac{.12 - .10}{\sqrt{(.10)(.90)/100}} \qquad\qquad = \frac{.15 - .10}{\sqrt{(.10)(.90)/100}}$$

$$= .67 \qquad\qquad\qquad\qquad = 1.67$$

4.   Determine the areas from the mean to $P = .12$ and $P = .15$ using the Table of Areas Under the Normal Curve.

If $Z = .67$, area $= .2486$.

If $Z = 1.67$, area $= .4525$.

5.   Determine the specified probability.

$$P(.12 \le p \le .15) = .4525 - .2486$$

$$= .2039.$$

SAMPLING DISTRIBUTION OF PROPORTIONS

Suppose that for an infinite population the probability of occurrence of an event (i.e., its success) is p. Then the probability of its failure is $q = 1 - p$.

EXAMPLE

The population is all possible tosses of a coin (we always assume a coin, a die, etc., to be fair). The probability of the event "tails" is

$$p = \frac{1}{2}.$$

All possible samples of size n are drawn from this population and for each sample the proportion P of success is determined. For n tosses of the coin, P is the proportion of tails obtained. We have a sampling distribution of proportions. Its mean μ_P and standard deviation σ_P are given by

$$\mu_p = p$$

$$\sigma_P = \sqrt{\frac{p(1-p)}{n}} = \sqrt{\frac{pq}{n}}$$

The above equations are valid for a finite population and sampling with replacement. For large values of n the sampling distribution is close to the normal distribution. For finite populations and sampling without replacement the mean μ_P is

$$\mu_P = p$$

and the standard deviation σ_P is

$$\sigma_P = \sqrt{p(1-p)}$$

SAMPLING DISTRIBUTION OF SUMS AND DIFFERENCES

Two populations are given. From the first population we draw samples of size n_1 and compute a statistic s_1. Thus, we obtain a sampling distribution for the statistic s_1 with the mean μ_{s_1} and standard deviation σ_{s_1}.

Similarly, from the second population we draw samples of size n_2, compute a statistic s_2 and find μ_{s_2} and σ_{s_2}. From all possible combinations of these samples from the two populations we can determine a distribution of the sums, $s_1 + s_2$, which is called the sampling distribution of sums of the statistics. We can also find a distribution of the differences, $s_1 - s_2$, which is called the sampling distribution of differences of the statistics. The mean and standard deviation of the sampling distribution is

for the sum

$$\mu_{s_1 + s_2} = \mu_{s_1} + \mu_{s_2}$$

$$\sigma_{s_1 + s_2} = \sqrt{\sigma_{s_1}^2 + \sigma_{s_2}^2}$$

for the difference

$$\mu_{s_1 - s_2} = \mu_{s_1} - \mu_{s_2}$$

$$\sigma_{s_1 - s_2} = \sqrt{\sigma_{s_1}^2 + \sigma_{s_2}^2}$$

The samples have to be independent, that is, do not depend on each other.

EXAMPLE

Suppose f_1 can be any of the elements of the population 3, 5, 7 and f_2 any of the elements of the population 2, 4. Then

$$\mu_{f_1} = \text{mean of population } f_1 = \frac{3+5+7}{3} = 5$$

$$\mu_{f_2} = \text{mean of population } f_2 = \frac{2+4}{2} = 3$$

Now, let us consider the population consisting of the sums of any number of f_1 and any number of f_2.

3 + 2	5 + 2	7 + 2
3 + 4	5 + 4	7 + 4

or

5	7	9
7	9	11

The mean $\mu_{f_1+f_2}$ is

$$\mu_{f_1+f_2} = \frac{48}{6} = 8$$

This result is in agreement with the general rule

$$8 = \mu_{f_1+f_2} = \mu_{f_1} + \mu_{f_2} = 5 + 3$$

The standard deviations are

$$\sigma^2_{f_1} = \frac{(3-5)^2 + (5-5)^2 + (7-5)^2}{3} = 2.667$$

$$\sigma_{f_1} = 1.633$$

$$\sigma^2_{f_2} = \frac{(2-3)^2 + (4-3)^2}{2} = 1$$

and $\quad \sigma_{f_2} = 1$

Similarly, we compute $\sigma_{f_1+f_2}$

$$\sigma^2_{f_1+f_2} = \frac{(5-8)^2 + (7-8)^2 + (9-8)^2 + (7-8)^2 + (9-8)^2 + (1-8)^2}{6}$$

$$= 3.667$$

$$\sigma_{f_1+f_2} = 1.915$$

That agrees with the general formula

$$\sigma_{f_1+f_2} = \sqrt{\sigma_{f_1}^2 + \sigma_{f_2}^2}$$

for independent samples.

Suppose s_1 and s_2 are the sample means from the two populations, which we denote by $\bar{x}_1$ and $\bar{x}_2$. Then, for infinite populations (or finite populations and sampling with replacement) with means μ_1 and μ_2 and standard deviations σ_1 and σ_2 respectively, the sampling distribution of the sums (or the differences) of means is

for sums

$$\mu_{\bar{x}_1+\bar{x}_2} = \mu_{\bar{x}_1} + \mu_{\bar{x}_2} = \mu_1 + \mu_2$$

$$\sigma_{\bar{x}_1+\bar{x}_2} = \sqrt{\sigma_{\bar{x}_1}^2 + \sigma_{\bar{x}_2}^2} = \sqrt{\frac{\sigma_1^2}{n_1} + \frac{\sigma_2^2}{n_2}}$$

for differences

$$\mu_{\bar{x}_1-\bar{x}_2} = \mu_{\bar{x}_1} - \mu_{\bar{x}_2}$$

$$\sigma_{\bar{x}_1-\bar{x}_2} = \sqrt{\sigma_{\bar{x}_1}^2 + \sigma_{\bar{x}_2}^2} = \sqrt{\frac{\sigma_1^2}{n_1} + \frac{\sigma_2^2}{n_2}}$$

where n_1 and n_2 are sizes of samples.

EXAMPLE

Two producers manufacture tires. The mean lifetime of tires made by A is 120,000 miles with a standard deviation of 20,000 miles, while the mean lifetime of tires made by B is 80,000 miles with a standard deviation of 10,000 miles.

Random samples of 200 tires of each brand are tested. What is the probability that tires made by A will have a mean lifetime which is at least 45,000 miles more than the tires made by B? $\bar{x}_A$ and $\bar{x}_B$ denote the mean lifetimes of samples A and B respectively. Then

$$\mu_{\bar{x}_A - \bar{x}_B} = \mu_{\bar{x}_A} - \mu_{\bar{x}_B} = 120,000 - 80,000 = 40,000 \text{ miles}$$

$$\sigma_{\bar{x}_A - \bar{x}_B} = \sqrt{\frac{\sigma_A^2}{n_A} + \frac{\sigma_B^2}{n_B}} = \sqrt{\frac{(20,000)^2}{200} + \frac{(10,000)^2}{200}}$$

$$= 1,581$$

The standardized variable for the difference in means is

$$z = \frac{(\bar{x}_A - \bar{x}_B) - (\mu_{\bar{x}_A - \bar{x}_B})}{\sigma_{\bar{x}_A - \bar{x}_B}} = \frac{(\bar{x}_A - \bar{x}_B) - 40,000}{1,581}$$

For large samples the distribution is normal. For the difference 45,000 miles

$$z = \frac{45,000 - 40,000}{1,581} = 3.16$$

Hence

required probability = area under normal curve to right of z

$$= 3.16 = 0.5 - 0.4992 = 0.0008$$

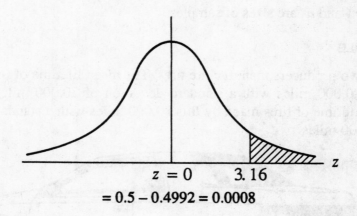

$$z = 0 \qquad 3.16$$

$$= 0.5 - 0.4992 = 0.0008$$

☞ Drill: Anticipating Patterns

> **DIRECTIONS:** Determine the correct response from the information provided

1. Two balls are to be randomly selected without replacement from a jar containing 10 balls numbered 1 through 10. If we bet that at least one of the balls drawn has a number of 8 or greater, what is the probability that we will win the bet?

2. A box contains 5 red, 6 white, and 7 blue balls. A ball is chosen at random from the box, and it is noted that the chosen ball is not white. What is the probability that the chosen ball is red?

3. A hospital blood test is 97% effective in detecting the presence of a disease. However, the test also yields a "false positive" result for 1.1% of the heathy people tested. If 0.9% of the population actually have the disease, what is the probability a person has the disease given that the test result is positive?

4. A bus company has discovered that 13 percent of the people who make reservations do not show up for their trip. Consequently, the company decides to take a risk and take more reservations than available seats, hoping that enough people fail to show up so that an overflow does not occur. If the bus seats 55 passengers and the company takes 58 reservations, what is the probability of an overflow?

5. If X is a geometric random variable with the parameter $p = 1/4$, what is $P(X \leq 3)$?

6. If X is a discrete random variable and we know that

    $P(X \leq 13) = 0.7310$

and $P(X \geq 13) = 0.5960$

   then what is $P(X = 13)$?

7. Let X be a discrete random variable with density function $f(x)$. If

    $f(2) = 0.4$,

    $f(5) = 0.1$,

$$f(7) = t,$$

$$f(11) = 0.2,$$

and $f(x) = 0$

then what is the value of t?

8. Calculate the expected sum obtained when eight independent rolls of a fair die are made.

9. If 12 balls are randomly selected from a jar containing 26 red balls and 51 blue balls, find the expected number of red balls selected.

10. Mike and Kelley play a game. Mike flips a fair coin. If it comes up heads, Kelley pays him $2. If it comes up tails, Kelley rolls a die. If the result is an even number, Kelley pays Mike $1; if the result is an odd number, then Mike pays Kelley $6. What is Mike's expected payoff (average amount he will win or lose)?

11. Let X be a normal random variable with parameters $\mu = 10$ and $\sigma^2 = 144$. What is $P(16 < X < 22)$?

12. If you flip a fair coin 576 times, what is the probability you will get between 276 and 300 heads?

13. Let C be a normal random variable with parameters $\mu = -7$ and $\sigma^2 = 16$. If C has a cumulative distribution function of $F(a) = 0.9$, what is a?

14. The score that a student receives on an entrance exam is a normally distributive random variable with a mean of 543 and a variance of 961. If a score of 582 is needed to be accepted at the college of the student's choice, what is the probability that the student will be accepted?

15. A final examination is regarded as being good if the test scores of those taking the examination can be approximated by a normal density function. The professor uses the test scores to estimate the normal parameters μ and σ^2 and then assigns the letter grades. Those who score above $\mu + 1.25\sigma$ are assigned an A. Students receiving scores between μ and $\mu + 1.25\sigma$ are assigned a B. Scores between μ -0.75σ and μ receive a C. A grade of D is given to students scoring between μ -1.5σ and μ -0.75σ, and F is given for scores below μ

-1.5σ. Given this situation, what is the probability of a student receiving an A, B, C, D, and F?

16. Estimate the mean and variance for

    20, 9, 18, 14, 24, 10, 11, 10, 19, 15, 21, 16.

17. Suppose an intuitive calculus class consisting of 10 people have the following scores on a one hundred point examination.

    48, 63, 77, 78, 81, 83, 88, 92, 97, 99

    Calculate the mean and standard deviation.

18. During an election, candidates normally conduct polls to determine their position in the race. You know that in a group of 30 eligible voters, 11 support your candidate. If you ask a sample of 5 voters whom they support, what is the probability that 3, 4, and 5 will side your way?

19. It is known that light bulbs produced by company will be defective, independently of each other, with a probability of 0.02. The company sells the light bulbs in boxes of four and offers a money-back guarantee that at the most one of the four light bulbs are defective. What is the probability of the company replacing the packages sold?

20. A warehouse buyer buys items in lots of 20. The company's policy is to inspect five components randomly from a lot and to accept the lot only if all five are nondefective. If 27 percent of the lots have six defective components and 73 percent have only two, what proportion of the lots does the buyer reject?

Answers to Drill Questions

1.   Let X denote the largest number selected. Then X is the random variable taking on the values of 2, 3, 4, ..., 10. If we suppose that each of the

$$\binom{10}{2}$$

possible selections are equally likely to occur, then

$$P(X = i) = \frac{\binom{i-1}{1}}{\binom{10}{2}}$$

$i = 2, 3, 4, \ldots, 10$

Hence as the event $\{X \geq 8\}$ is the union of the disjoint events $\{X = I\}$ for $I = 8, 9,$ and 10, it follows that the probability of our winning the bet is given by

$$P(X \geq 8) = P(X = 8) + P(X = 9) + P(X = 10)$$

$$= \frac{\binom{7}{1}}{\binom{10}{2}} + \frac{\binom{8}{1}}{\binom{10}{2}} + \frac{\binom{9}{1}}{\binom{10}{2}}$$

$$= \frac{7}{45} + \frac{8}{45} + \frac{9}{45} = \frac{24}{45}$$

$$P(X \geq 8) = 0.5333$$

2.   Let A = the event of getting a red ball.

   Let B = the event of getting a ball that is not white.

Therefore,

$$P(A) = \frac{5}{18} \text{ and } P(B) = \frac{12}{18}$$

$A \cap B$ = the event of a ball that is both red and not white

   = the event of getting a red ball

   = A

(This is only true because A and B are disjoint events.)

Thus,

$$P(A \cap B) = P(A) = \frac{5}{18}$$

Hence,

$$P(A \mid B) = \frac{P(A \cap B)}{P(B)} = \frac{P(A)}{P(B)}$$

$$= \frac{\frac{5}{18}}{\frac{12}{18}} = \frac{5}{12}$$

$$P(A \mid B) \approx 0.4167$$

3.   Let A = the event that the person has the disease.

Let B = the event that the result is positive.

Therefore,

$$P(A) = 0.09, P(B \mid A) = 0.97,$$

and $P(A^c) = 0.991$.

Since the "false positive" results 1.1% of the time, the probability is 0.011 that the test results imply the patient has the disease when they really do not.

Hence,

$$P(A \mid B) = \frac{P(A \cap B)}{P(B)}$$

$$= \frac{P(B \mid A)\,P(A)}{P(B \mid A)\,P(A) + P(B \mid A^C)\,P(A^C)}$$

$$= \frac{(0.97)\,(0.009)}{(0.97)\,(0.09) + (0.011)\,(0.991)}$$

$$P(A \mid B) \approx 0.4447$$

4.   If a "success" is when a person shows up for the trip, then we have a binomial distribution (X) with $n = 58$ and $p = 0.87$ (100% - 13% no shows).

$$P(X = 56) = \binom{58}{56}(0.87)^{56}(0.13)^2$$

$$P(X = 56) \approx 0.0114614$$

$$P(X = 57) = \binom{58}{57}(0.87)^{57}(0.13)^1$$

$$P(X = 57) \approx 0.0026913$$

$$P(X = 58) = \binom{58}{58}(0.87)^{58}(0.13)^0$$

$$P(X = 58) \approx 0.0003105$$

Thus,

$$P(X \geq 56) = P(X = 56) + P(X = 57) + P(X = 58)$$

$$\approx 0.0114614 + 0.0026913 + 0.0003105$$

$$P(X \geq 56) \approx 0.0144632$$

Therefore, there is approximately a 1.4 percent chance that more than 55 people will show up.

5. $P(X \leq 3) = p + p(1 - p) + p(1 - p)^2$

$$= \frac{1}{4} + \frac{1}{4} \times \frac{3}{4} + \frac{1}{4} \times \frac{3}{4} \times \frac{3}{4}$$

$P(X \leq 3) \approx 0.5781$

6. $P(X \leq 13) + P(X \geq 13)$

$= [P(X < 13) + P(X = 13)] + [P(X = 13) + P(X > 13)]$

$= [P(X < 13) + P(X = 13) + P(X > 13)] + P(X > 13)$

$0.731 + 0.596 = [1] + P(X = 13)$

$1.327 = 1 + P(X = 13)$

$0.327 = P(X = 13)$

7. We know that the total probability must equal 1.

Therefore,

$f(2) + f(5) + f(7) + f(11) + f(x) = 1$

$0.4 + 0.1 + t + 0.2 + 0 = 1$

$0.7 + t + 1$

$t = 0.3$

8.   We can begin by calculating the expected value for a single roll (R).

$$P(R = 1) = P(R = 2) = P(R = 3) = P(R = 4)$$

$$= P(R = 5) = P(R = 6) = \frac{1}{6}$$

$$E[R] = 1 \times \frac{1}{6} + 2 \times \frac{1}{6} + 3 \times \frac{1}{6} + 4 \times \frac{1}{6} + 5 \times \frac{1}{6} + 6 \times \frac{1}{6} = \frac{7}{2}$$

Now let X denote the sum of the 8 independent rolls.

$$X = X_1 + X_2 + X_3 + X_4 + X_5 + X_6 + X_7 + X_8$$

$$E[X] = E[X_1 + X_2 \ldots + X_8]$$

$$= E[X_1] + E[X_2] + \ldots + E[X_8]$$

$$= \frac{7}{2} + \frac{7}{2} + \frac{7}{2} + \frac{7}{2} + \frac{7}{2} + \frac{7}{2} + \frac{7}{2} + \frac{7}{2}$$

$$= 8 \times \frac{7}{2} = 28$$

$$E[X] = 28$$

9.   Let X denote the number of red balls selected.

$$X = X_1 + X_2 + X_3 + \ldots + X_{12}$$

where

$X_i = 1$ if the ith ball selected is red

$X_i = 0$ otherwise

Since the ith ball selected is equally likely to be any of the 77 $(51 + 26)$, we have

$$E[X_i] = \frac{26}{77} \approx 0.3376623$$

Thus,

$$E[X] = E[X_1 + X_2 + X_3 + \ldots + X_{12}]$$

$$= E[X_1] + E[X_2] + E[X_3] + \ldots + E[X_{12}]$$

$$\approx 0.3376623 + 0.3376623 + \ldots + 0.3376623$$

$$\approx 12(0.3376623) = 4.0519481$$

Therefore, we would expected 4 red balls to be drawn.

10. We know that if the coin is a fair one heads and tails have a 50% chance. Likewise, even and odd on the roll of the die also have a 50% chance of coming up (assuming the die is also fair). In summary we have

Head ($^1/_2$)	$\rightarrow$	$\rightarrow$	Mike gets $2
Tails ($^1/_2$)	$\rightarrow$	Even ($^1/_4$) $\rightarrow$	Mike gets $1
	$\rightarrow$	Odd ($^1/_4$) $\rightarrow$	Mike pays $6

The fractions above are the probability that each outcome will be obtained while following the arrows.

Thus,

$$E[\text{Mike}] = E[\text{Head}] + E[\text{Tail/Even}] + E[\text{Tail/Odd}]$$

$$= \frac{1}{2}(2) + \frac{1}{4}(1) + \frac{1}{4}(-6)$$

$$= \frac{1}{4}$$

Therefore, Mike will lose an average of 25 cents per game.

11. $P(16 < X < 22)$

$$= P\left(\frac{16-10}{12} < \frac{X-10}{12} < \frac{22-10}{12}\right)$$

$$= P\left(\frac{1}{2} < Z < 1\right) = \phi(1) - \phi\left(\frac{1}{2}\right)$$

$$= 0.8413 - 0.6915$$

$$P(16 < X < 22) = 0.1498$$

12. With a fair coin ($n = 576$) we know that the probability of getting a head is 0.5. We must now calculate the μ and σ^2.

$$\mu = np = 576(0.5) = 288$$

$$\sigma^2 = np(1-p) = 576(0.5)(0.5) = 144$$

Therefore,

$$P(276 < X < 300)$$

$$= P\left(\frac{276-288}{12} < \frac{X-288}{12} < \frac{300-288}{12}\right)$$

$$= P(-1 < Z < 1) = \Phi(1) - \Phi(-1) \ \Phi(1) - [1 - \Phi(1)] = 2\Phi(1) - 1$$

$$= 2(0.8413) - 1 = 0.6826$$

$$P(276 < X < 300) = 0.6826$$

13. $F(a) = 0.9$

$$P(C \leq a) = 0.9$$

$$P\left(\frac{C+7}{4} \leq \frac{a+7}{4}\right) = 0.9$$

$$\Phi\left(\frac{a+7}{4}\right) = 0.9$$

From the table we see that $\Phi(1.28) = 0.8997 \approx 0.9$. Thus,

$$\frac{a+7}{4} \approx 1.28$$

$$a \approx -1.88$$

14. Let X = the score a student gets on the exam.

$$P(X \geq 582)$$

$$= P\left(\frac{X - 543)}{31} \geq \frac{582 - 543}{31}\right)$$

$$\approx P(Z \geq 1.26) \approx 1 - \Phi(1.26)$$

$$\approx 1 - 0.8962 \approx 0.1038$$

Therefore, approximately 10% of the students will be accepted.

15. For an A:

$$P(X > \mu + 1.25\sigma) = P(Z > 1.25)$$

$$= 1 - \Phi(1.25) = 1 - 0.8944 = 0.1056$$

For a B:

$$P(\mu < X < \mu + 1.25\sigma) = P(0 < Z < 1.25)$$

$$= \Phi(1.25) - \Phi(0) = 0.8944 - 0.5 = 0.3944$$

For a C:

$$P(\mu - 0.75\sigma < X < \mu = P(-0.75 < Z < 0)$$

$$= \Phi(0) - \Phi(-0.75) = \Phi(0) + \Phi(0.75) - 1$$

$$= 0.5 + 0.7734 - 1 = 0.2734$$

For a D:

$$P(\mu - 1.5\sigma < X < \mu - 0.75\sigma) = P(-1.5 < Z < -0.75)$$

$$= \Phi(-0.75) - \Phi(-1.5) = \Phi(1.5) - \Phi(0.75)$$

$$= 0.9332 - 0.7734 = 0.1598$$

For a F:

$$P(X < \mu - 1.5\sigma) = P(Z < -1.5)$$

$$= \Phi(-1.5) = 1 - \Phi(1.5)$$

$$= 1 - 0.9332 = 0.0668$$

Therefore, approximately 11% of the class will receive an A grade on the final examination, 39% a B grade, 27% a C grade, 16% a D, and 7% will fail.

16.

$$\text{Mean} = \frac{20 + 9 + 18 + 14 + 24 + 10 + 11 + 10 + 19 + 15 + 21 + 16}{12}$$

$$= \frac{187}{12} \approx 15.583$$

$$\text{Variance} \approx \frac{(20 - 15.583)^2 + (9 - 15.583)^2 + \ldots + (16 - 15.583)^2}{12}$$

$$\approx \frac{19.206944 + 43.340278 + \ldots + 0.173611}{12}$$

$$\approx \frac{250.41667}{12} \approx 20.868056$$

17.

$$\text{Mean} = \frac{48 + 63 + 77 + 78 + 81 + 83 + 88 + 92 + 97 + 99}{10}$$

$$= \frac{806}{10} = 80.6$$

$$\text{Standard Deviation} = \sqrt{\frac{(48-80.6)^2 + (63-80.6)^2 + \ldots + (99-80.6)^2}{10}}$$

$$= \sqrt{\frac{1062.76 + 309.76 + \ldots + 338.56}{10}}$$

$$= \sqrt{\frac{2190.4}{10}} = \sqrt{219.04} = 14.8$$

18. For the three eligible voters supporting your candidate, the probability is

$$P(X=3) = \frac{\binom{11}{3}\binom{19}{2}}{\binom{30}{5}}$$

$$= \frac{(165)(171)}{142,506} \approx 0.198$$

For the four eligible voters supporting your candidate, the probability is

$$P(X=4) = \frac{\binom{11}{4}\binom{19}{1}}{\binom{30}{5}}$$

$$= \frac{(330)(19)}{142,506} \approx 0.044$$

For the five eligible voters supporting your candidate, the probability is

$$P(X=5) = \frac{\binom{11}{5}\binom{19}{0}}{\binom{30}{5}}$$

$$= \frac{(462)(1)}{142,506} \approx 0.003$$

19. If X is the number of defective light bulbs in a package, then X is a binomial random variable with parameters (4,0.02). Hence, the probability that a package will have to be replaced is

$$1 - P(X = 0) - P(X = 1)$$

$$= 1 - \binom{4}{0}(0.02)^0(0.98)^4 - \binom{4}{1}(0.02)^1(0.098)^3$$

$$\approx 1 - 0.9223682 - 0.0752954$$

$$\approx 0.0023364$$

Therefore, only 0.2% of the packages will have to be replaced.

20. Let A denote the event that the buyer accepts a lot.

$$P(A) = P(A \mid 6 \text{ defective}) (0.27) + P(A \mid 2 \text{ defective}) (0.73)$$

$$= \frac{\binom{6}{0}\binom{14}{5}}{\binom{20}{5}} \times (0.27) + \frac{\binom{2}{0}\binom{18}{5}}{\binom{20}{5}} \times (0.73)$$

$$\approx 0.0348646 + 0.4034211 \approx 0.4382856$$

Thus,

$$P(A^c) = 1 - P(A)$$

$$\approx 1 - 0.4382856 \approx 0.5617144$$

Therefore, the buyer will reject approximately 56% of the lots.

CHAPTER 5
STATISTICAL INFERENCES

Chapter 5

STATISTICAL INFERENCES

CONFIDENCE INTERVALS

In estimating a population parameter, we need to distinguish between a point estimate and an interval estimate. A point estimate is a single guess about the value of a population parameter. In contrast, an interval estimate specifies a range of values which are most likely to include the population parameter. The confidence interval is the range of the estimate we are making.

The probability that we associate with a confidence interval actually including the true population parameter is called the **confidence level**. Thus, the confidence level expressed as a percentage tells us how much confidence we have that the interval we are estimating contains the true population parameter.

EXAMPLE

"We are 95 percent confident that the mean lies in the interval from 25 to 35." This indicates that if we would draw a large number of samples from the population and find a confidence interval for each sample, then about 95 percent of the intervals would contain the population mean μ.

The confidence level is usually expressed by $(1 - \alpha)100\%$. When expressed as a probability, it is called the **confidence coefficient** and is denoted as $1 - \alpha$.

CONFIDENCE INTERVAL ESTIMATION FOR THE POPULATION MEAN FOR LARGE SAMPLES

For large samples ($n \geq 30$), we use the sample mean $\bar{x}$ to estimate the population mean μ. Based on the central limit theorem, we know the following properties of $\bar{x}$ for large samples:

(a) The sampling distribution of $\bar{x}$ is approximately normally distributed.

(b) The mean of $\bar{x}$ or $\mu_{\bar{x}} = \mu$

(c) The standard deviation of $\bar{x}$, or $\sigma_{\bar{x}} = \sigma / \sqrt{n}$

Thus, when the sample size is large ($n \geq 30$), we use the normal distribution to construct a confidence interval for the population mean μ.

Note: A confidence interval formula for any population parameter will always be of the general form:

confidence interval

= estimate $\pm$ (critical value) $\times$ (standard deviation of estimate),

where the critical value is a value from either the normal distribution table or t distribution table.

CONFIDENCE INTERVAL FORMULA FOR A POPULATION MEAN μ FOR LARGE SAMPLES

The formula for a $(1 - \alpha)$ 100% confidence interval for μ is:

(1) when σ is known:

$$\bar{x} + z_{\alpha/2} \times \sigma_{\bar{x}} = \bar{x} + z_{\alpha/2} \times \frac{\sigma}{\sqrt{n}}$$

(2) when σ is unknown, we substitute s for σ:

$$\bar{x} + z_{\alpha/2} \times s_{\bar{x}} = \bar{x} \pm z_{\alpha/2} \times \frac{s}{\sqrt{n}}$$

where $\bar{x}$ = sample mean

σ = population standard deviation

n = sample size

z = z value obtained from the standard normal distribution table for a given confidence level

s = sample standard deviation

Also, it should be noted that z-value should be replaced with a t-value (with $n - 1$ degrees of freedom from the t-distribution) if the sample size is not sufficiently large (i.e., if is is not > 30).

EXAMPLE

The standard deviation of a population is 5. A sample of 40 observations selected from the population gives us a sample mean of 75. Determine a 95% confidence interval for the population mean.

SOLUTION

(1) The confidence level is 95% or .95. Since the sample size is greater than 30, we use the normal distribution to determine the confidence level. We need to find the z value for a 95% confidence level. We divide .95 by 2, obtaining .475. From the normal distribution table, we obtain 1.96 for the value of z. (See figure below.)

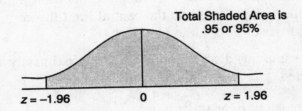

Total Shaded Area is .95 or 95%

$z = -1.96$ 0 $z = 1.96$

(2) Substituting the values back into the formula when σ is known, we obtain:

$$\bar{x} \pm z_{\alpha/2} \frac{\sigma}{\sqrt{n}} = 75 \pm 196\left(\frac{5}{\sqrt{40}}\right) = 73.45 \text{ to } 76.55$$

Thus we have a 95% confidence level that the mean μ is between 73.45 and 76.55.

EXAMPLE

A sample of 64 observations from a population produced a sample mean equal to 172 and a sample standard deviation equal to 17. Find a 99 percent confidence interval for the mean.

SOLUTION

1. The confidence level is 99% or .99. Since the sample size is larger than 30, we use the normal distribution to find the confidence interval. We divide .99 by 2, obtaining .495. From the standard normal distribution table, we obtain 2.58.

2. Substituting the values back into the formula when σ is unknown, we obtain:

$$\bar{x} \pm z_{\alpha/2} \frac{s}{\sqrt{n}} = 172 \pm (2.58)\left(\frac{17}{\sqrt{64}}\right)$$

$$= 172 \pm 5.48 = 166.52 \text{ to } 177.48$$

Thus, we have a 99% confidence level that the mean μ is between 166.52 and 177.48.

CONFIDENCE INTERVAL ESTIMATION FOR A POPULATION PROPORTION FOR LARGE SAMPLES

For large samples, we use the sample proportion $\hat{p}$ to estimate the population proportion p. Based on the central limit theorem, we know the following properties of $\hat{p}$ for large samples:

(a) The sampling distribution of $\hat{p}$ is approximately normally distributed.

(b) The mean of $\hat{p}$, or $\mu_{\hat{p}} = p$

(c) The standard deviation of $\hat{p}$, or $\sigma_{\hat{p}} = \sqrt{\dfrac{p(1-p)}{n}}$

Thus, we use the normal distribution to construct a confidence interval for the population proportion p under the following conditions:

(1) The sample is large. This means that $n\hat{p}$ and $n(1 - \hat{p})$ are both greater than 5.

(2) The sample standard deviation $s_{\hat{p}}$ is used as an estimate for $\sigma_{\hat{p}}$, since p is unknown.

Confidence Interval for a Population Proportion p

The formula for a $(1 - \alpha)$ 100% confidence interval for p is:

$$\hat{p} \pm z_{\alpha/2} \times \sigma_{\hat{p}} \cong \hat{p} \pm z_{\alpha/2} \times s_{\hat{p}}$$

$$\cong \hat{p} \pm z_{\alpha/2} \times \sqrt{\frac{\hat{p}(1-\hat{p})}{n}}$$

where $\hat{p}$ = sample proportion

= number of successes divided by number of trials

n = sample size

z = z value obtained from the standard normal distribution table

EXAMPLE

A random sample of 1000 car owners from across the United States were asked whether or not they used their seat belts on a regular basis. 85% of the car owners  said that they always used their seatbelts. Determine a 95% confidence interval for the proportion of all U. S. car owners who use their seat belts on a regular basis.

SOLUTION

From the given information we have, $n = 1000$, $\hat{p} = .85$, $1 - \hat{p} = .15$ and confidence level = 95% or .95.

(1) We verify that np and $n(1 - p)$ are both greater than 5.

$$n\hat{p} = 1000(.85) = 850$$

$$n(1 - \hat{p}) = 1000(.15) = 150$$

Thus, the sample is large and we use the normal distribution to construct a confidence interval for p.

(2) We need to find the z-value from the standard normal distribution table corresponding to a 95% confidence level.

Thus, the z value for $.95/2 = .475$ is 1.96.

(3) We substitute the values back into the formula for p.

$$\hat{p} \pm z_{\alpha/2}\sqrt{\hat{p}(1-\hat{p})/n} = .85 \pm 1.96\sqrt{(.85)(.15)/1000}$$

$$= .85 \pm .0221 = .828 \text{ to } .872$$

Thus, we are 95% confident that the population proportion is between .828 and .872 based on our sample.

CONFIDENCE INTERVAL FOR A DIFFERENCE BETWEEN TWO POPULATION MEANS FOR LARGE SAMPLES

Suppose $\bar{x}_1$ is the mean of a large sample from a normal population with population mean μ_1, and $\bar{x}_2$ is the mean of a large sample from a normal population with population mean μ_2. Then $(\bar{x}_1 - \bar{x}_2)$ is used to estimate the difference between population means $(\mu_1 - \mu_2)$ and has the following properties based on the central limit theorem:

1. The mean of $\bar{x}_1 - \bar{x}_2$, or $\mu_{\bar{x}_1 - \bar{x}_2} = \mu_1 - \mu_2$

2. The standard deviation of $\bar{x}_1 - \bar{x}_2 = \sigma_{\bar{x}_1 - \bar{x}_2} = \sqrt{\dfrac{\sigma_1^2}{n_1} + \dfrac{\sigma_2^2}{n_2}}$

3. The sampling distribution of $\bar{x}_1 - \bar{x}_2$ is approximately normal.

4. $z = \bar{x}_1 - \bar{x}_2$ is a standard normal random variable where

$$\Pr(-z_{\alpha/2} < \frac{\bar{x} - \bar{y} - (\mu_1 - \mu_2)}{\sqrt{\dfrac{\sigma_1^2}{n_1} + \dfrac{\sigma_2^2}{n_2}}} < z_{\alpha/2} = 1 - \alpha$$

Thus, we use the normal distribution to construct a confidence interval about the difference between two population means $\mu_1 - \mu_2$ under the following conditions:

1. The sample sizes n_1 and n_2 are sufficently large. That is, $n_1 \geq 30$ and $n_2 \geq 30$.

2. The two samples are selected independently. That is, the data selected from one sample cannot be related to the data selected from the other sample.

CONFIDENCE INTERVAL FORMULA FOR $\mu_1 - \mu_2$

The formula for a $(1 - \alpha)$ 100% confidence interval for $\mu_1 - \mu_2$ is:

(1) when σ is known:

$$(\bar{x}_1 - \bar{x}_2) \pm z_{\alpha/2} \times \sigma_{\bar{x}_1 - \bar{x}_2} = (\bar{x}_1 - \bar{x}_2) \pm z_{\alpha/2} \times \sqrt{\dfrac{\sigma_1^2}{n_1} + \dfrac{\sigma_2^2}{n_2}}$$

(2)   when σ is unknown:

$$(\bar{x}_1 - \bar{x}_2) \pm z_{\alpha/2} \times S_{\bar{x}_1 - \bar{x}_2} = (\bar{x}_1 - \bar{x}_2) \pm z_{\alpha/2} \times \sqrt{\frac{S_1^2}{n_1} + \frac{S_2^2}{n_2}}$$

where n_1 and n_2 = sample size drawn from population 1 and population 2

$(n_1 \geq 30$ and $n_2 \geq 30)$

σ_1 and σ_2 = standard deviation of population 1 and population 2

s_1 and s_2 = sample standard deviation of population 1 and population 2

$\bar{x}_1$ and $\bar{x}_2$ = mean of the sample from population 1 and population 2

z = z-value obtained from the standard normal distribution table for a given confidence level

EXAMPLE

Find a 95% confidence interval for the difference in mean math test scores of advanced American and German 10th grade students based on the following test study results.

	Sample Size	Sample Mean	Sample Standard Deviation
Americans	300	95	4.5
Germans	250	90.5	4.1

Steps to follow:

Step 1: Check to see if sample sizes are large and independent. Yes— sample sizes are 300 and 250 and drawn from two independent samples.

Step 2: Find the appropriate z-value (confidence coefficient). Since the confidence level is .95, we divide .95 by 2, obtaining .475. From the standard normal distribution table, we obtain a z-value of 1.96.

Step 3: Substitute the appropriate values back into the formula when σ is unknown.

$$95 - 90.5 \pm (1.96) \sqrt{\frac{(4.5)^2}{300} + \frac{(4.1)^2}{250}}$$

$$4.5 \pm .719$$

Therefore, we are 95% confident that the difference in mean math test scores is between 3.78 and 5.22.

CONFIDENCE INTERVAL FOR THE DIFFERENCE BETWEEN TWO POPULATION PROPORTIONS FOR LARGE SAMPLES

For large and independent samples, we use the difference between two sample proportions $\hat{p}_1 - \hat{p}_2$ to estimate the difference between two population proportions $p_1 - p_2$.

Based on the central limit theorem, we arrive at the following properties of $\hat{p}_1 - \hat{p}_2$ for large and independent samples:

(a) The sampling distribution of $\hat{p}_1 - \hat{p}_2$ is approximately normally distributed.

(b) The mean of $\hat{p}_1 - \hat{p}_2$, or $\mu_{\hat{p}_1 - \hat{p}_2} = p_1 - p_2$

(c) The standard deviation of $\hat{p}_1 - \hat{p}_2$, or

$$\sigma_{\hat{p}_1 - \hat{p}_2} = \sqrt{\frac{p_1(1-p_1)}{n} + \frac{p_2(1-p_2)}{n}}$$

Thus, we use the normal distribution to construct a confidence interval about the difference between two population proportions $p_1 - p_2$ under the following conditions:

(1) The two samples are large and independent. This means $n_1 p_1$, $n_1(1 - p_1)$, $n_2 p_2$ and $n_2(1 - p_2)$ should be all greater than 5.

(2) The sample standard deviation $s_{\hat{p}_1 - \hat{p}_2}$ is used as an estimate for $\sigma_{\hat{p}_1 - \hat{p}_2}$, since p_1 and p_2 are unknown.

CONFIDENCE INTERVAL FORMULA FOR $p_1 - p_2$

The formula for a $(1 - \alpha)\,100\%$ confidence interval for $p_1 - p_2$ is:

$$(\hat{p}_1 - \hat{p}_2) \pm z_{\alpha/2} \sigma_{\hat{p}_1 - \hat{p}_2} \cong (\hat{p}_1 - \hat{p}_2) \pm z_{\alpha/2} s_{\hat{p}_1 - \hat{p}_2}$$

$$\cong (\hat{p}_1 - \hat{p}_2) \pm z_{\alpha/2} \times \sqrt{\frac{\hat{p}_1(1-\hat{p}_1)}{n_1} + \frac{\hat{p}_2(1-\hat{p}_2)}{n_2}}$$

where $\hat{p}_1 = x_1 / n_1$

and $\hat{p}_2 = x_2 / n_2$

with x_1 and x_2 = no. of elements of the characteristic we seek for each sample

and n_1 and n_2 = sample sizes respectively.

EXAMPLE

An individual owns two pizza stores in different sections of New York City. He conducts a survey to estimate the percentage of customers who feel that the pizza is superior at each of these stores. Based on a sample of 225 customers in the first store, he discovers that 140 customers find the pizza superior. In the second store, a sample of 275 customers shows that 162 customers find the pizza superior.

Construct a 95% confidence interval for the difference between the proportions of customers at the two pizza stores who find the pizza superior.

SOLUTION

Pizza Store 1:

$n_1 = 225, x_1 = 140$

Pizza Store 2:

$n_2 = 275, x_2 = 162$

(1) We calculate $\hat{p}_1, \hat{p}_2, 1 - \hat{p}_1$, and $1 - \hat{p}_2$ as follows:

$\hat{p}_1 = x_1 / n_1 = 140/225 = .622$

$1 - \hat{p}_1 = 1 - .622 = .378$

$\hat{p}_2 = x_2 / n_2 = 162/275 = .589$

$1 - \hat{p}_2 = 1 - .589 = .411$

(2) We verify that the two samples are large.

Thus, we check if

$n_1 \hat{p}_1, n_1 (1 - \hat{p}_1), n_2\hat{p}_2, n_2 (1 - \hat{p}_2)$

are all greater than 5.

$n_1 \hat{p}_1 = (225)(.622) = 140,$

$n_1(1 - \hat{p}_1) = (225)(.378) = 85$

$$n_2 \hat{p}_2 = (275)(.589) = 162,$$

$$n_2(1 - \hat{p}_2) = (275)(.411) = 113$$

Thus, the two samples are large and we use the normal distribution to construct the confidence interval for $p_1 - p_2$.

(3) We need to find the z-value from the standard normal distribution table corresponding to a 95% confidence level.

Thus, the z-value for $.95/2 = .475$ is 1.96.

(4) We substitute these values into the confidence interval formula for $p_1 - p_2$.

$$(\hat{p}_1 - \hat{p}_2) \pm z_{\alpha/2} \times \sqrt{\frac{\hat{p}_1(1 - \hat{p}_1)}{n_1} + \frac{\hat{p}_2(1 - \hat{p}_2)}{n_2}}$$

$$(.622 - .589) \pm 1.96 \times \sqrt{\frac{(.622)(.378)}{225} + \frac{(.589)(.411)}{275}}$$

$$= .033 \pm 1.96 \, (.0439)$$

$$= .033 \pm .086 = -053 \text{ to } .119$$

Thus, we are 95% confident that the difference between the two population proportions is between $-.053$ and $.119$.

CONFIDENCE INTERVAL ABOUT THE DIFFERENCE BETWEEN TWO POPULATION MEANS FOR PAIRED SAMPLES—LARGE SAMPLE CASE

Definition of Paired (Dependent or Matched) Samples

Two samples are paired (matched or dependent) samples if each data value obtained from the first sample is paired with a data value obtained from the second sample, and both sets of data values are derived from the same source.

EXAMPLE

A hundred participants were randomly selected to participate in a medical study to investigate the effects of a low-fat diet on lowering cholesterol levels. Cholesterol levels for each individual were recorded before the diet and then six months later. Let μ_d be the mean reduction in cholesterol level due to the low-fat diet for the population of all adults. Construct a 90% confidence level for μ_d.

SOLUTION

In this example, both sets of data values are collected from the same 100 persons. We have a before and after cholesterol level for each individual.

We call the difference between cholesterol levels the paired difference and refer to it as d. Thus, $d = x_1 - x_2$, where x_1 is the before cholesterol level in sample 1 and x_2 is the after cholesterol level in sample 2 on the first individual; $d_2 \ldots d_{100}$ are obtained accordingly.

We treat the paired differences (di) as one sample, and use the sample mean of the paired differences (d = $\Sigma di/n$) to construct a confidence interval about the population mean for paired differences (μ_d).

CONFIDENCE INTERVAL FOR μ_d—LARGE SAMPLES

When the number of paired differences is sufficiently large ($n \geq 30$), we use the normal distribution to find a confidence interval about the population mean for the paired differences (μ_d). This is based on the central limit theorem, which indicates that the sampling distribution of the sample mean of the paired differences ($\bar{d}$) is approximately normally distributed for large n.

Thus, the following formula is used to construct a $(1 - \alpha)$ 100% confidence interval for μ_d:

(1) when σ is known:

$$\bar{d} \pm z_{\alpha/2}\sigma_{\bar{d}} = \bar{d} \pm z_{\alpha/2}\frac{\sigma_d}{\sqrt{n}}$$

(2) when σ is unknown, we substitute s for σ:

$$\bar{d} \pm z_{\alpha/2}s_{\bar{d}} = \bar{d} \pm z_{\alpha/2}\frac{s_d}{\sqrt{n}}$$

where σ_d = population standard deviation of the paired differences

z = value obtained from the nornal distribution table based on the given confidence level

s_d = sample standard deviation of the paired differences

$$= \sqrt{\frac{\Sigma d_2 - \frac{(\Sigma d)^2}{n}}{n-1}} = \sqrt{\frac{\Sigma(di - \hat{d})^2}{n-1}}$$

Note: When $n < 30$, you would use $t_{\alpha/2}$, $n-1$ instead of $Z_{\alpha/2}$ here.

EXAMPLE

Find a confidence interval for μ_d based on the following information:

$n = 35$, $\overline{d} = 32.5$, $s_d = 12.1$, confidence level = 95%

SOLUTION

Since the confidence level is .95, we divide .95 by 2, obtaining .475. From the normal distribution table, we obtain a z-value of 1.96.

We substitute the appropriate values back into the formula:

$$\overline{d} \pm z_{\alpha/2} \frac{s_d}{\sqrt{n}} = 32.5 \pm 1.96 \left(\frac{12.1}{\sqrt{35}} \right)$$

$32.5 \pm 4.01 = 28.49$ to 36.51

Thus we can say with 95% confidence that μ_d is between 28.49 and 36.51 based on our sample.

HYPOTHESIS TESTING

REASONS FOR TESTING HYPOTHESES

The Random House Dictionary defines the term hypothesis as an unproved or unverified assumption that can be either used or accepted as probable in the light of established facts. This definition applies as well to a statistical interpretation of the term hypothesis. In statistical inference methodology, a hypothesis is a statement of a condition which is assumed to exist in a population and is tested using the results from a randomly selected sample. For example, a candidate for public office assumes that he will receive at least fifty percent of the votes in a particular election; the president of a bank may assume that his average balance per customer is $500; or the production manager of an assembly process may have reason to believe that the process is operating with only a 2% rate of defectives.

These statements or claims should not be used as statements of fact or belief unless there is some evidence of the validity of such statements. Therefore, prior to announcing these types of information either through advertisements or other means, tests should be conducted to determine whether or not the statements should be accepted and with what likelihood of accuracy. Therefore, randomly select voters, or customer accounts, or assembled items, etc. and use the results from these randomly selected sampling units to test against what is believed to be true in the population. Based on the outcome of the test, action might then be taken, for example, relative to changes in campaign strategy, new marketing strategy allowing incentives for the purpose of increasing customer bank balances, readjusting a machine, or swapping out workers.

Basically, hypothesis testing is performed to investigate preconceived assumptions about some condition in the population. Usually this condition can be expressed as an average of some characteristic or as a percentage of some characteristic of interest. Sample data are selected and either the sample average (mean) or percentage (proportion) is calculated in order to determine if this value could reasonably be assumed to exist within the hypothesized population.

STEPS IN HYPOTHESIS TESTING

Any hypothesis test, regardless of whether it involves means or proportions, can be solved following a step-by-step approach. The number of steps may vary from textbook to textbook, but the end results will be the same regardless of whether we use five steps, seven steps, or ten steps. Five steps are outlined below for solving hypothesis testing problems.

Step 1

a) State the null hypothesis (H_0), which is the statement that we test. As the term "null" implies, this is an assumption of "no relationship," or "no difference" concerning the parameter(s) of interest. For example:

H_0: $\mu = C$, $\mu \geq C$, $\mu \geq C$; i.e., the population mean is equal to some prespecified value of C, at least some prespecified value of C, or at most some prespecified value of C.

H_0: $\Pi = C$, $\Pi \geq C$, $\Pi \leq C$; i.e., the population proportion is equal to some prespecified value of C, at least some prespecified value of C, or at most some prespecified value of C.

H_0: $\mu_1 = \mu_2$, $\mu_1 \geq \mu_2$, $\mu_1 \leq \mu_2$; i.e., two population means are identical, or the mean of population 1 is greater than or equal to that of population 2, or the mean of population 1 is less than or equal to that of population 2.

H_0: $\Pi 1 = \Pi_2$, $\Pi_1 \geq \Pi_2$, $\Pi_1, \leq \Pi_2$; i.e., two population proportions are identical, or the proportion in population 1 is greater than or equal to that of population 2, or the proportion in population 1 is less than that of population 2.

b) State the alternative hypothesis (H_1) which is based on the belief of the investigator relative to the relationship between the parameter(s). Three options are available in basic hypothesis tests:

1. There is a "difference" in values being investigated. For example:

    H_1: $\mu \neq C$; i.e., the population mean is not the same as the prespecified value of C.

    H_1: $\Pi \neq C$; i.e., the population proportion is not the same as the prespecified value of C.

    H_1: $\mu_1 \neq \mu_2$; i.e., the two population means are not the same value.

    H_1: $\Pi_1 \neq \Pi_2$; i.e., the two population proportions are not the same value.

2. One value is "greater than" another value. For example:

    H_1: $\mu > C$; i.e., the population mean is greater than the prespecified value of C.

    H_1: $\Pi > C$; i.e., the population proportion is greater than the prespecified value of C.

    H_1: $\mu_1 > \mu_2$; i.e., the mean in population 1 is greater than the mean in population 2.

    H_1: $\Pi_1 > \Pi_2$; i.e., the proportion of some characteristic in population 1 is greater than the proportion of the same characteristic in population 2.

3. One value is "less than" another value. For example:

H_1: $\mu < C$; i.e., the population mean is less than the prespecified value of C.

H_1: $\Pi < C$; i.e., the population proportion is less than the prespecified value of C.

H_1: $\mu_1 < \mu_2$; i.e., the mean in population 1 is less than the mean in population 2.

H_1: $\Pi_1 < \Pi_2$; i.e., the proportion of some characteristic in population 1 is less than the proportion of the same characteristic in population 2.

Step 2

Specify the values given in the problem.

Step 3

Determine the appropriate distribution and a critical value from either:

A. The Table of Areas Under the Standard Normal Curve (Z); or

B. The Table of the Student's t-distribution (t), depending on which is appropriate for the particular problem being solved.

Step 4

Solve for the sample value of Z or t (whichever is appropriate) using the appropriate equation for the value.

Step 5

Draw a conclusion as to whether H_0 should be rejected or whether we should fail to reject H_0.

Rule A. If the absolute value of the computed value from Step 4 is greater than or equal to the absolute value of the table value from Step 3, reject the null hypothesis (H_0) and accept the alternative hypothesis (H_1).

Rule B. If the computed value from Step 4 is less than the absolute value of the table value from Step 3, fail to reject the null hypothesis

(H_0) which requires no action to be taken regarding H_1. This is simply an indication that the sample results are sufficient to allow us to reject the null hypothesis (H_0) This could be viewed as a lack of a definitive conclusion.

HYPOTHESIS TESTS ON MEANS

One of the most common types of hypothesis tests is that dealing with the testing of means. This type of test may deal with testing to determine if a population mean can be concluded to be equal to a prespecified value. The test may deal with small samples or large samples, and with the population standard deviation (σ) being known or unknown. Also, tests involving means may involve two populations and may be either independent tests or dependent (matched pairs) tests.

HYPOTHESIS TESTS ON PROPORTIONS

Another very common use of hypothesis testing deals with tests of proportions. In this situation, our interest is in testing to determine if the proportion of the population having a certain characteristic is as we assumed it to be; i.e., equal to some prespecified value. The procedures outlined previously for tests involving means apply for proportions, except forthe small sample case. When testing proportions, the exact test for a sample size less than 50 is based on the binomial distri-  bution. This procedure, however, is beyond the scope of the material presented in this text. Tests on proportions involve testing the relationship between two population proportions.

TYPE I AND TYPE II ERRORS

As the previous sections have illustrated, hypothesis testing does not lead us to absolutely definite outcomes. Just because the result of the test is to reject H_0, or fail to reject H_0, we are not 100% sure that we have reached the correct conclusion. The same is true in confidence interval estimation, or in any other statistical inference technique. The explanation for this is that in inferential procedures, we are always working with sample data. And sample data can never yield definitive results due to the presence of sampling error.

Errors in conclusions drawn in hypothesis testing are referred to as either Type I or Type II. These are defined as:

Type I error—the decision to reject the null hypothesis (H_0) when it is true and should not have been rejected.

Type II error—the decision to fail to reject the null hypothesis (H_0) when it is false and should have been rejected.

The probability of making a Type I error is denoted by α (alpha) the level of significance. As we have seen in previous examples, α *is* a predetermined value which is specified in a textbook problem or in a real life type situation and is specified by the user(s) of the information. This is the chance that the user(s) of the information are willing to take that the null hypothesis might be rejected in error; i.e. that we might conclude that a difference or relationship exists when it really does not. The choice of this probability should consider the possible consequences of an incorrect decision. For example, in medical research where life sustaining situations are being tested, one would likely be much more conservative in specifying a value for α than in some of the examples presented herein.

The probability of making a Type II error is denoted by β (beta). This is not a predetermined value set by the user(s) of the information, but a value that must be calculated once the result of the test is known. This procedure is not included in this text and for the most part, not of real concern to decision makers. The decision to fail to reject H_0 simply says that this particular sample does not provide enough evidence to support concluding otherwise. It is not a decision that is going to create life-threatening or devastating business decision situations. Many times it might, however, result in additional sample data being studied.

There are four possible outcomes in the decisions made from hypothesis testings. Two are in error and two are correct; they are easily illustrated in a table format as shown below.

H_0 **is**

	TRUE	FALSE
Reject H_0	TYPE I Error α	Correct Decision $1-\beta$
Fail to Reject H_0	Correct Decision $(1-\alpha)$	TYPE II Error β

This table may be interpreted as follows. The null hypothesis (H_0) is either true or false. If it is true and our test leads us to say that it is not, we have committed a Type I error. The chance of this happening is α; therefore, the chance that we reach the correct conclusion would be $(1 - \alpha)$. That is, we will either reach a correct or an incorrect conclusion and as we learned in elementary probability theory, the probability that an event occurs plus the probability that it does not occur sums to 1. By the same token, if H_0 is false and we fail to reject it, we have committed a Type II error and the probability that this will occur is β. Likewise, the probability that we reject H_0 when it is indeed false is $(1-\beta)$, using the same rationale.

HYPOTHESIS TESTING—SINGLE SAMPLE

HYPOTHESES TESTS ABOUT A POPULATION MEAN—LARGE SAMPLES

When the sample size is sufficiently large ($n \geq 30$), we use the normal distribution to test a hypothesis about the population mean. This is based on the central limit theorem which as we discussed previously indicates that the sampling distribution of the sample mean $\bar{x}$ is approximately normally distributed for large n. Furthermore, we find that this approximation improves as the sample size increases.

Since the test is based on the standard normal distribution, it is called the Z-test. We refer to the value obtained from the formula below as the test statistic for the sample mean $\bar{x}$, as our decision to reject or accept the null hypothesis is based on this value.

The test statistic for $\bar{x}$ is calculated as follows:

(1) When σ is known:

$$Z = \frac{\bar{x} - \mu_{\bar{x}}}{\sigma_{\bar{x}}}$$

$$= \frac{\bar{x} - \mu}{\frac{\sigma}{\sqrt{n}}}$$

(2) When σ is unknown, we substitute s for σ:

$$Z = \frac{\bar{x} - \mu_{\bar{x}}}{s_{\bar{x}}}$$

$$= \frac{\bar{x} - \mu}{\frac{s}{\sqrt{n}}}$$

Note: The test statistic for any sample statistic in a hypothesis test about a population parameter will always be of the general form:

$$\frac{\text{Estimate } - \text{ Population Parameter}}{\text{Standard Deviation of the Estimate}}$$

TWO-TAILED TEST OF A MEAN FOR LARGE SAMPLES

EXAMPLE

Perform a hypothesis test based on the following information:

$H_0: \mu = 30, H_a \mu \neq 30, n = 100, \bar{x} = 32, s = 3, \alpha = .05$

SOLUTION

Step 1

State the null and alternative hypothesis

$H_0: \mu = 30$

$H_a : \mu \neq 30$

(The $\neq$ sign in the alternative hypothesis indicates a two-tailed test.)

Step 2

Specify the values given in the problem

$\mu = 30$

$n = 100$

$\bar{x} = 32$

$s = 3$

$\alpha = .05$

Step 3

Determine the appropriate distribution and the critical values.

Since the sample size is large ($n \geq 30$), we use the normal distribution to do the test. We need to find the Z-values corresponding to the two critical points on our graph, which separate the rejection and non-rejection regions (see below).

Since we have a two-tailed test, we determine the area in each tail =

$\alpha/2 = .05/2 = .025$. To find the critical points, we first find the area between the mean and one of the critical points. This area is .4750 (.5 – .025). From the standard normal distribution table, we look for .4750 in the table, where Z has a value of 1.96. Since we have two critical points which are symmetrical, these values are –1.96 and 1.96.

Step 4

Calculate the value of the test statistic using the appropriate formula.

Since σ is not known, we use

$$z = \frac{\bar{x} - \mu}{\frac{s}{\sqrt{n}}}$$

$$= \frac{32 - 30}{\frac{3}{\sqrt{100}}}$$

$$= 6.67$$

Step 5

Draw a conclusion for the null hypothesis.

Since the calculated Z-value for $\bar{x} = 6.67 > 1.96$, we reject the null hypothesis, as this value falls within the rejection region. We conclude that the mean does not appear to equal 30.

When we reject the null hypothesis, we imply that the difference between the sample mean = 32 and the population mean = 30 is too large and may not be due to sampling error alone. The possibility still exists that the mean is equal to 30. If this is true, then the null hypothesis has been rejected incorrectly. This is a Type I error and the probability of this occurring is .05 (the level of significance).

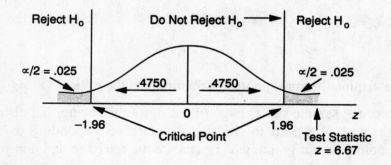

RIGHT-TAILED TEST OF A MEAN FOR LARGE SAMPLES

EXAMPLE

A random sample of 45 observations from a population provided a sample mean of 38.2 and a standard deviation of 8.2. Test H_0: $\mu \leq 40$ against H_a: $\mu > 40$ at the .05 level of significance.

SOLUTION

Step 1

State the null and alternative hypothesis.

H_0: $\mu \leq 40$

H_a: $\mu > 40$

(The > sign in the alternative hypothesis indicates a right-tail test.)

Step 2

Specify the values given in the problem.

$\mu = 40$

$n = 45$

$\bar{x} = 38.2$

$s = 8.2$

$\alpha = .05$

Step 3

Determine the appropriate distribution and the critical values.

Since the sample size is large ($n \geq 30$), we use the normal distribution to do the test. We need to find the Z-value corresponding to the critical point on our graph, which is on the right side of the graph.

Since this is a right-tailed test with only one rejection region, the area in the right tail is $\alpha = .05$. From the standard normal distribution table, we look for .45 in the the table (.5 − .05), which has a Z-value of 1.65.

Step 4

Calculate the value of the test statistic using the appropriate formula.

Since σ is not known, we use

$$Z = \frac{\bar{x} - \mu}{\frac{s}{\sqrt{n}}}$$

$$= \frac{38.2 - 40}{\frac{8.2}{\sqrt{45}}}$$

$$= -1.48$$

Step 5

Draw a conclusion for the null hypothesis.

Since the calculated Z-value = $-1.48 < 1.65$, we do not reject the null hypothesis, as this value falls within the nonrejection region. We interpret this to mean that it appears that $\mu \leq 40$, and the information we have from our sample is not enough to reject the null hypothesis.

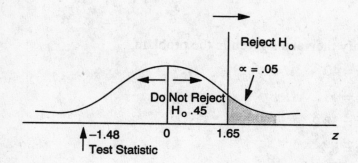

LEFT-TAILED TEST OF A MEAN FOR LARGE SAMPLES

EXAMPLE

A study claims that female working adults are spending an average of 12 hours weekly on housework. American Consumers conducted a survey to test this claim. A random sample of 150 working female adults showed that these women spent an average of 10 hours or less weekly on housework with a standard deviation of 2.4 hours. Test at the 1% significance level if working female adults are now spending less than 12 hours doing housework.

SOLUTION

Step 1

State the null and alternative hypothesis

$H_0: \mu = 12$

$H_a: \mu < 12$

(The $<$ sign in the alternative hypothesis indicates a left-tailed test.)

Step 2

Specify the values given in the problem.

$\mu = 12$

$n = 150$

$\bar{x} = 10$

$s = 2.4$

$\alpha = .01$

Step 3

Determine the appropriate distribution and the critical values.

Since the sample size is large ($n \geq 30$), we use the normal distribution to do the test. We need to find the Z-value corresponding to the critical point on our graph, which is on the left side of the graph.

Since this is a left-tailed test with only one rejection region, the area in the left tail is $\alpha = .01$. From the standard normal distribution table, we look for .49 in the table ($.5 - .01$), which has a Z-value of -2.33.

Step 4

Calculate the value of the test statistic using the appropriate formula.

Since σ is not known, we use

$$Z = \frac{\bar{x} - \mu}{\frac{s}{\sqrt{n}}}$$

$$= \frac{10 - 12}{\frac{2.4}{\sqrt{150}}}$$

$$= \frac{-2}{.196}$$
$$= -10.20$$

Step 5

Draw a conclusion for the null hypothesis.

Since the calculated Z-value for $\bar{x} = -10.20 < -2.33$, we reject the null hypothesis, as this value falls within the rejection region. It appears that the average weekly time that female working adults spend on house-work is less than 12 hours based on the American Consumers Study.

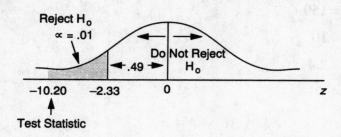

HYPOTHESES TESTS ABOUT A POPULATION MEAN—SMALL SAMPLES

When the sample size is small, we use the t-distribution to test a hypothesis about the mean μ. The central limit theorem does not apply to small samples and therefore we cannot assume that the sampling distribution of $\bar{x}$ is normally distributed.

Thus, we use the t distribution for hypothesis testing under the following conditions:

(1) The sample size is small.

(2) The sample is drawn from a population which is approximately normally distributed.

(3) The population standard deviation (σ) is unknown.

The test statistic for $\bar{x}$ is calculated as follows:

$$t = \frac{\bar{x} - \mu_{\bar{x}}}{s_{\bar{x}}}$$

$$= \frac{\bar{x} - \mu_{\bar{x}}}{\frac{s}{\sqrt{n}}}$$

where $df = n - 1$

We continue to use the same 5-step approach in hypothesis testing.

TWO-TAILED TEST OF A MEAN FOR SMALL SAMPLES

EXAMPLE

Perform a hypothesis test based on the following information: Assume that the population is normally distributed.

$H_0: \mu = 40$, $H_a : \mu \neq 40$, $n = 10$, $x = 30$, $s = 4.2$, $\alpha = .01$

SOLUTION

Step 1

State the null and alternative hypothesis.

$H_0: \mu = 40$

$H_a: \mu \neq 40$

(The $\neq$ sign in the alternative hypothesis indicates a two-tailed test)

Step 2

Specify the values given in the problem.

$n = 10$

$\mu = 40$

$\bar{x} = 30$

$s = 4.2$

$\alpha = .01$

Step 3

Determine the appropriate distribution and the critical values.

Since the sample size is small ($n < 30$), the population is normally distributed and σ is unknown, we use the t distribution to do the test. We need to find the t values corresponding to the two critical points on our graph, which separate the rejection and non-rejection regions.

A t-distribution requires a calculation of the degrees of freedom, which we do as follows:

$$df = n - 1 = 10 - 1 = 9$$

Since we have a two-tailed test, we determine the area in each tail $\alpha/2 = .01/2 = .005$. From the t-distribution table, the t value corresponding to 9 degrees of freedom and .005 area in each tail is 3.250. Since we have two critical points, which are symmetrical the critical values are -3.250 and 3.250.

Step 4

Calculate the value of the test statistic using the appropriate formula.

$$t = \frac{\bar{x} - \mu}{\frac{s}{\sqrt{n}}}$$

$$= \frac{30 - 40}{\frac{4.2}{\sqrt{10}}}$$

$$= \frac{-10}{1.328}$$

$$= -7.53$$

Step 5

Draw a conclusion for the null hypothesis.

Since the calculated t value for $\bar{x} = -7.53 < -3.250$, we reject the null hypothesis, as this value falls within the rejection region. We conclude that the mean does not appear to equal 40.

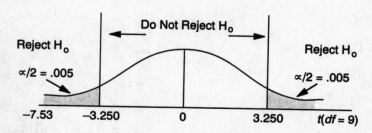

RIGHT-TAILED TEST OF A MEAN FOR SMALL SAMPLES

EXAMPLE

An entertainment center manufacturing company that specializes in do-it-yourself assembly kits claims that the mean completion time for its most popular kit is at most 72 hours. A random sample of 20 individuals purchasing this kit from this company showed that the mean completion time for this kit is 82 hours with a standard deviation of 4.5 hours. Assume that the completion time for the kit has a normal distribution, test at the 1% significance level if the completion time is greater than 72 hours.

SOLUTION

Step 1

State the null and alternative hypothesis.

H_0: $\mu \leq 72$

H_a: $\mu > 72$

(The > sign in the alternative hypothesis indicates a right-tail test.)

Step 2

Specify the values given in the problem.

$\mu = 72$

$n = 20$

$\overline{x} = 82$

$s = 4.5$

$\alpha = .01$

Step 3

Determine the appropriate distribution and the critical values.

Since the sample size is small ($n < 30$), the population is normally distributed and σ is unknown, we use the t distribution to do the test. We need to find the t value corresponding to the critical point on our graph, which is on the right side of the graph.

Since this is a right-tailed test with only one rejection region, the area in the right tail is $\alpha = .01$. From the t-distribution table, the t-value corresponding to 19 degrees of freedom ($n - 1 = 20 - 1$) and .01 area in the right tail is 2.539.

Step 4

Calculate the value of the test statistic using the appropriate formula.

$$t = \frac{\bar{x} - \mu}{\frac{s}{\sqrt{n}}}$$

$$= \frac{82 - 72}{\frac{4.5}{\sqrt{20}}}$$

$$= \frac{10}{1.006}$$

$$= 9.94$$

Step 5

Draw a conclusion for the null hypothesis.

Since the calculated t value for $\bar{x} = 9.94 > 2.539$, we reject the null hypothesis, as this value falls within the rejection region. We conclude that it appears that the average completion time is more than 72 hours.

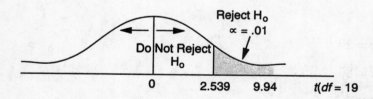

HYPOTHESIS TESTING FOR TWO POPULATIONS

HYPOTHESES TESTS FOR THE DIFFERENCE BETWEEN THE MEANS OF TWO POPULATIONS

The procedures to test a hypothesis about the difference between two population means $\mu_1 - \mu_2$ are similar to those we outlined previously to test a hypothesis about a single population mean μ.

We use the same five steps in hypothesis testing described earlier.

The null and alternative hypotheses for comparing the means of two independent samples may be stated in terms of either the population means μ_1 and μ_2 or the mean of the sampling distribution of $(\bar{x}_1 - \bar{x}_2)$. Both ways are correct and are listed below for reference.

(1) This describes a two-tailed test.

$$H_0: \mu_1 = \mu_2$$

or $$H_0: \mu_{(\bar{x}_1 \times \bar{x}_2)} = k,$$

where k is the value specified in the null hypothesis

$$H_a: \mu_1 \neq \mu_2$$

or $$H_0: \mu_{(\bar{x}_1 \times \bar{x}_2)} \neq k$$

(2) This describes a left-tailed test.

$$H_0: \mu_1 \geq \mu_2$$

or $$H_0: \mu_{(\bar{x}_1 - \bar{x}_2)} \geq k$$

$$H_a: \mu_1 < \mu_2$$

or $$H_a: \mu_{(\bar{x}_1 - \bar{x}_2)} < k$$

(3) This describes a right-tailed test.

$$H_0: \mu_1 \leq \mu_2$$

or $$H_0: \mu_{(\bar{x}_1 - \bar{x}_2)} \leq k$$

$$H_a: \mu_1 > \mu_2$$

or $$H_a: \mu_{(\bar{x}_1 - \bar{x}_2)} > k$$

Note: $\mu_{(\bar{x}_1 - \bar{x}_2)}$ simplifies to $\mu_1 - \mu_2$

EXAMPLE

We may want to test the hypothesis that the mean disability claims filed for teachers in California (population 1) is lower than the mean disability claim forms filed for teachers in New York State (population 2).

Our hypothesis will look like (2).

EXAMPLE

We may want to test the hypothesis of the form that the mean reading scores of female first graders in Los Angeles (population 1) is higher than the mean reading scores of male first graders in Los Angeles (population 2). Our hypothesis will look like (3).

HYPOTHESES TESTS ABOUT THE DIFFERENCE BETWEEN TWO MEANS FOR LARGE SAMPLES

We use the normal distribution in hypothesis testing for comparing two population means $\mu_1 - \mu_2$ under the following conditions:

1. The two samples are selected randomly and independently.

2. The sample sizes are sufficiently large ($n_1 \geq 30$ and $n_2 \geq 30$).

The test statistic for $\bar{x}_1 - \bar{x}_2$ is calculated as follows:

(1) When σ is known

$$Z = \frac{(\bar{x}_1 - \bar{x}_2) - (\mu_{\bar{x}_1 - \bar{x}_2})}{\sigma_{\bar{x}_1 - \bar{x}_2}}$$

$$= \frac{(\bar{x}_1 - \bar{x}_2) - (\mu_1 - \mu_2)}{\sqrt{\frac{\sigma_1^2}{n_1} + \frac{\sigma_2^2}{n_2}}}$$

where $\mu_{\bar{x}_1 - \bar{x}_2} = \mu_1 - \mu_2$

$$\sigma_{\bar{x}_1 - \bar{x}_2} = \sqrt{\frac{\sigma_1^2}{n_1} + \frac{\sigma_2^2}{n_2}}$$

(2) When σ is unknown, substitute s for σ in the formula above:

$$Z = \frac{(\bar{x}_1 - \bar{x}_2) - (\mu_{\bar{x}_1 - \bar{x}_2})}{S_{\bar{x}_1 - \bar{x}_2}}$$

$$= \frac{(\bar{x}_1 - \bar{x}_2) - (\mu_1 - \mu_2)}{\sqrt{\frac{s_1^2}{n_1} + \frac{s_2^2}{n_2}}}$$

where $S_{\bar{x}_1 - \bar{x}_2} = \sqrt{\frac{s_1^2}{n_1} + \frac{s_2^2}{n_2}}$

Note: We find the value of $(\mu_1 - \mu_2)$ above by substituting the value in the null hypothesis. The test statistic for $\bar{x}_1 - \bar{x}_2$ is approximately standard normal.

DECISION RULE REVIEW

Previously, in step 5 for hypothesis testing we formulated decision rules for either rejecting or accepting the null hypothesis. We review those rules for comparing two means below:

1. For a right-tailed test, if Z (calculated value) for $\bar{x}_1 - \bar{x}_2 \geq Z_\alpha$ (table value), we reject the null hypothesis and accept the alternative hypothesis.

2. For a left-tailed test, if Z (calculated value) for $\bar{x}_1 - \bar{x}_2 \leq Z_\alpha$ (table value), we reject the null hypothesis and accept the alternative hypothesis.

3. For a two-tailed test, if $|Z|$ (calculated value) for $\bar{x}_1 - \bar{x}_2 \geq Z_{\alpha 2}$ (table value or for $\bar{x}_1 - \bar{x}_2 < -Z_{\alpha/2}$), we reject the null hypothesis and acccept the alternative hypothesis.

TWO-TAILED TEST FOR COMPARING MEANS OF LARGE SAMPLES

EXAMPLE

Based on the following information, test the null hypothesis H_0: $\mu_1 = \mu_2$ versus the alternative hypothesis H_a: $\mu_1 \neq \mu_2$ at the .01 level of significance. Assume independent random samples. $\bar{x}_1 = 155$, $\bar{x}_2 = 145$, $n_1 = 60$, $n_2 = 70$, $s_1 = 12$, $s_2 = 10$.

SOLUTION

Step 1

State the null and alternative hypothesis.

$$H_0: \mu_1 = \mu_2$$

(which indicates $\mu_1 - \mu_2 = 0$)

$$H_a: \mu_1 \neq \mu_2$$

(The $\neq$ sign in the alternative hypothesis indicates a two-tailed test.)

Step 2

Specify the values given in the problem.

$$\bar{x}_1 = 155, n_1 = 60, s_1 = 12$$

$$\bar{x}_2 = 145, n_2 = 70, s_2 = 10$$

Step 3

Determine the appropriate distribution and the critical values.

Since both sample sizes are large ($n_1 \geq 30$ and $n_2 \geq 30$) and these are random and independent samples, we use the normal distribution to do the test. We need to find the Z-values corresponding to the two critical points on our graph.

Since we have a two-tailed test, we determine the area in each tail $\alpha/2 = .01/2 = .005$. Thus, the critical values of Z with .005 area in each tail are 2.58 and -2.58.

Step 4

Calculate the value of the test statistic using the appropriate formula.

Since σ is not known, we calculate the value of the test statistic for $\bar{x}_1 - \bar{x}_2$ as follows:

$$Z = \frac{(\bar{x}_1 - \bar{x}_2) - (\mu_1 - \mu_2)}{\sqrt{\frac{s_1^2}{n_1} + \frac{s_2^2}{n_1}}}$$

$$= \frac{(155 - 145) - 0}{\sqrt{\frac{(12)^2}{60} + \frac{(10)^2}{70}}}$$

$$= 5.11$$

Step 5

Draw a conclusion for the null hypothesis.

Since the calculated Z-value for $\bar{x}_1 - \bar{x}_2 = 5.11 > 2.58$, we reject the null hypothesis, as this value falls within the rejection region. Therefore, we can only say that it appears that the two population means are different based on our test.

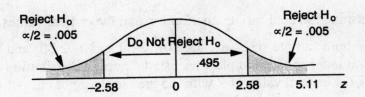

RIGHT-TAILED TEST FOR COMPARING MEANS OF LARGE SAMPLES

EXAMPLE

A recent study of reading achievement levels of American and French children was conducted. According to the results of the study, the mean score on a reading test given to 250 American 8-year-old children was 49.3 with a standard deviation of 6.2. A comparable reading test given to 244 French 8-year-old children showed a mean reading score of 47.2 with a standard deviation of 5.8. Test at the 5% significance level if the mean reading scores are higher for American children than French children. Assume random and independent samples.

SOLUTION

Step 1

State the null and alternative hypothesis.

$H_0: \mu_1 - \mu_2 \leq 0$

$H_a: \mu_1 - \mu_2 \geq 0$

(The $\geq$ sign in the alternative hypothesis indicates a right-tailed test.)

Step 2

Specify the values given in the problem.

$\bar{x}_1 = 49.3$, $n_1 = 250$, $s_1 = 6.2$

$\bar{x}_2 = 47.2$, $n_2 = 244$, $s_2 = 5.8$

Step 3

Determine the appropriate distribution and the critical values.

Since both sample sizes are large ($n_1 \geq 30$ and $n_2 \geq 30$) and these are random and independent samples, we use the normal distribution to do the test. Thus, the critical value of Z with .05 area in the right tail is 1.65.

Step 4

Calculate the value of the test statistic using the appropriate formula.

Since σ is not known, we calculate the value of the test statistic for $\bar{x}_1 - \bar{x}_2$ as follows:

$$Z = \frac{(\bar{x}_1 - \bar{x}_2) - (\mu_1 - \mu_2)}{\sqrt{\dfrac{s_1^2}{n_1} + \dfrac{s_2^2}{n_2}}}$$

$$= \frac{(49.3 - 47.2) - 0}{\sqrt{\dfrac{(6.2)^2}{250} + \dfrac{(5.8)^2}{244}}}$$

$$= -3.89$$

Step 5

Draw a conclusion for the null hypothesis.

Since the calculated Z-value for $\bar{x}_1 - \bar{x}_2 = 3.89 > 1.65$, we reject the null hypothesis, as this value falls within the rejection region. Therefore, we can say that the mean reading score for American children appears to be higher than the mean reading score for French children based on our study. However, we cannot conclude that this is definitely true.

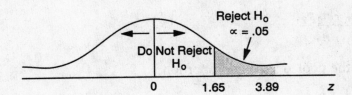

HYPOTHESES TESTS ABOUT THE DIFFERENCE BETWEEN TWO PROPORTIONS FOR LARGE SAMPLES

We use the normal distribution in hypothesis testing for comparing two population proportions $p_1 - p_2$ under the following conditions:

(1) The two samples are large (n_1 and $n_2 \geq 30$). Also, $n_1 p_1$, $n_1(1 - p_1)$, $n_2 p_2$ and $n_2(1 - p_2)$ should all be greater than 5.

(2) The two samples are selected randomly and independently.

Case 1

When testing a null hypothesis of the form $H_0: p_1 - p_2 = 0$, the test statistic for $\hat{p}_1 - \hat{p}_2$ is calculated as follows:

$$z = \frac{(\hat{p}_1 - \hat{p}_2) - (p_1 - p_2)}{\sigma \hat{p}_1 - \hat{p}_2}$$

$$= \frac{\hat{p}_1 - \hat{p}_2}{\sqrt{\dfrac{p_1 q_1}{n_1} + \dfrac{p_2 q_2}{n_2}}}$$

To find the best estimate for p_1 and p_2 we substitute $\hat{p}$ for both p_1 and p_2, since we know $p_1 = p_2$ from the null hypothesis. (Likewise, we substitute $\hat{q}$ for both q_1 and q_2.)

Thus, $$z \cong \frac{\hat{p}_1 - \hat{p}_2}{\sqrt{\hat{p}\hat{q}\left(\dfrac{1}{n_1} + \dfrac{1}{n_2}\right)}}$$

where $\hat{p} = \dfrac{x_1 + x_2}{n_1 + n_2}$

or $\dfrac{n_1\hat{p}_1 + n_2\hat{p}_2}{n_1 + n_2}$

($\hat{p}$ is called the pooled sample proportion.)

$$\hat{q} = 1 - \hat{p}$$

$$\hat{p}_1 = \dfrac{\hat{x}_1}{n_1}$$

and $\quad \hat{p}_2 = \dfrac{\hat{x}_2}{n_2}$

Case 2

When testing a null hypothesis of the form H_0: $p_1 - p_2 = K$ (where $K \neq 0$), the test statistic for $\hat{p}_1 - \hat{p}_2$ is calculated as follows:

$$z = \dfrac{(\hat{p}_1 - \hat{p}_2) - (p_1 - p_2)}{\sigma_{\hat{p}_1 - \hat{p}_2}}$$

$$\cong \dfrac{(\hat{p}_1 - \hat{p}_2) - (p_1 - p_2)}{S_{\hat{p}_1 - \hat{p}_2}}$$

$$\cong \dfrac{(\hat{p}_1 - \hat{p}_2) - (p_1 - p_2)}{\sqrt{\dfrac{\hat{p}_1\hat{q}_1}{n_1} + \dfrac{\hat{p}_2\hat{q}_2}{n_2}}}$$

where $\quad \hat{p}_1 = \dfrac{x_1}{n_1}$

and $\quad \hat{p}_2 = \dfrac{x_2}{n_2}$

$$\hat{q}_1 = 1 - \hat{p}_1 \text{ and } \hat{q}_2 = 1 - \hat{p}_2$$

EXAMPLE

A hardware store owner received a large shipment of light bulbs. Based on a sample of 500, 40 of the light bulbs were found to be defective. The manufacturer revamped the production process in order to improve the quality of the light bulbs, and believed this would improve them. The store owner received another shipment of light bulbs made from the new production process and 30 of the 500 light bulbs were defective. At the 5% significance level, test whether the manufacturer's belief is warranted.

SOLUTION

Step 1

State the null and alternative hypothesis.

$H_0: p_1 - p_2 = 0$

$H_a: p_1 - p_2 > 0$

(The > sign in the alternative hypothesis indicates a right-tailed test.)

Step 2

Specify the values given in the problem.

$x_1 = 40$ $n_1 = 500$

$x_2 = 30$ $n_2 = 500$

We calculate the sample proportions as follows:

$\hat{p}_1 = x_1 / n_1 = 40 / 500 = .08, 1 - \hat{p}_1 = .92$

$\hat{p}_2 = x_2 / n_2 = 30 / 500 = .06, 1 - \hat{p}_2 = .94$

Step 3

Determine the appropriate distribution and the critical values.

We verify that $n_1\hat{p}_1$, $n_1(1 - \hat{p}_1)$, $n_2 \hat{p}_2$, and $n_2(1 - \hat{p}_2)$ are all greater than 5.

$$n_1 \hat{p}_1 = (500)(.08) = 40, \; n_1(1 - \hat{p}_1) = (500)(.92) = 460$$

$$n_2 \hat{p}_2 = (500)(.06) = 30, \; n_2(1 - \hat{p}_2) = (500)(.94) = 470$$

Since both samples are large and independent, we use the normal distribution to do the test. The critical value of z with a .05 area in the right tail is 1.65.

Step 4

Calculate the value of the test statistic.

Since $p_1 - p_2 = 0$, we calculate the test statistic for $\hat{p}_1 - \hat{p}_2$ using the formula from Case 1 as follows:

$$Z = \frac{(\hat{p}_1 - \hat{p}_2)}{\sqrt{\hat{p}\hat{q}\left(\dfrac{1}{n_1} + \dfrac{1}{n_2}\right)}}$$

with $\hat{p} = x_1 + x_2 / n_1 + n_2 = 40 + 30 / 500 + 500 = 70 / 1000 = .07$

$\hat{q} = 1 - \hat{p} = 1 - .07 = .93$

Thus,

$$Z = \frac{(.08 - .06)}{\sqrt{(.07)(.93)\left(\dfrac{1}{500} + \dfrac{1}{500}\right)}}$$

$$= 1.25$$

Step 5

Draw a conclusion for the null hypothesis.

Since the calculated z value for $\hat{p}_1 - \hat{p}_2 = 1.25 < 1.65$ we do not reject the null hypothesis as this value falls within the nonrejection region. We interpret this to mean that the proportion of defective light bulbs from sample 1 does not appear to be greater than the proportion of defective light bulbs from sample 2. Thus, the manufacturer's belief is not warranted.

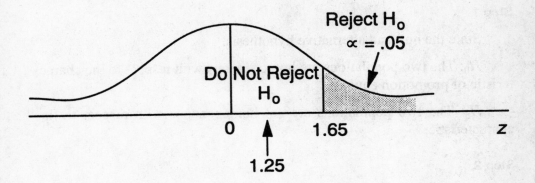

CHI-SQUARE APPLICATIONS

Homogeneity of Proportions—Test of Homogeneity

This test involves determining whether two (or more) different populations are similar (homogeneous) with respect to a certain characteristic.

We test the null hypothesis (H_0) that the different populations are homogeneous (similar) with respect to some characteristic against the alternative hypothesis (H_a) that they are not the same. The procedure is similar to the procedure for a test of independence that we discussed earlier.

EXAMPLE

A survey of male and female employees at a corporation was done with male and female employees asked whether they felt that promotion opportunities between male and female employees were equitable.

The results of those samples are given below.

Test the hypothesis that the appropriate populations are homogeneous at a 1% level of significance.

	Yes	No	Row Totals
Males	65	80	145
Females	55	50	105
Column Totals	120	130	250 Grand Total

SOLUTION

Step 1

State the null and alternative hypothesis.

H_0: The two populations are homogeneous with respect to the characteristic of promotion equity.

H_a: The two populations are not homogeneous with respect to this characteristic.

Step 2

Determine the appropriate distribution and the critical values.

We use the chi-square distribution to do the homogeneity test.

Since the significance level is 1% the area of the rejection region is .01, and it is in the right tail of the curve. (See graph below.)

The degrees of freedom are:

$$df = (R - 1)(C - 1) = (2 - 1)(2 - 1) = 1$$

Thus, the critical value for χ^2 with $df = 1$ and $\alpha = .01$ is 6.635.

Step 3

Calculate the value of the test statistic.

We calculate the expected frequencies for each cell as follows:

E = (row total) × (column total) / grand total

E for males and Yes cell = (145) (120) / 250 = 69.60

E for males and No cell = (145) (130) / 250 = 75.40

E for females and Yes cell = (105) (120) / 250 = 50.40

E for females and No cell = (105) (130) / 250 = 54.60

We apply the formula to determine the test statistic:

$$\chi^2 = \Sigma(O - E)^2 / E$$

$$= (65 - 69.6)^2 / 69.6 + (80 - 75.4)^2 / 75.4 + (55 - 50.4)^2 / 50.4$$

$$+ (50 - 54.6)^2 / 54.6$$

$$= .304 + .281 + .420 + .388 = 1.393$$

Step 4

Draw a conclusion for the null hypothesis.

Since the calculated χ^2 value $= 1.393 < 6.635$ we do not reject the null hypothesis, as this value falls in the nonrejection region. It appears that the two populations seem to be homogeneous with respect to the characteristic of promotion equity.

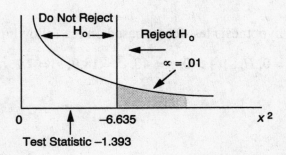

HYPOTHESES TESTS ABOUT THE DIFFERENCE BETWEEN TWO POPULATION MEANS FOR PAIRED SAMPLES—LARGE SAMPLE CASE

When the number of paired differences is sufficiently large ($n \geq 30$) we use the normal distribution to test a hypothesis about the population mean for paired differences (μ_d).

The test statistic for $\bar{d}$ is calculated as follows:

(1) when σ is known:

$$z = \frac{\bar{d} - \mu_{\bar{d}}}{\sigma_{\bar{d}}}$$

$$= \frac{\bar{d} - \mu_{\bar{d}}}{\frac{\sigma_d}{\sqrt{n}}}$$

where $\bar{d} = \Sigma \dfrac{di}{n}$

(2) when σ is unknown we substitute s for σ:

$$z = \frac{\bar{d} - \mu_{\bar{d}}}{s_{\bar{d}}}$$

$$= \frac{\bar{d} - \mu_{\bar{d}}}{\frac{s_d}{\sqrt{n}}}$$

where $s_d = \sqrt{\frac{\Sigma d^2 - \frac{(\Sigma d)^2}{n}}{n-1}} = \sqrt{\frac{\Sigma (di - \bar{d})^2}{n-1}}$

EXAMPLE

Perform a hypothesis test for μ_d based on the following information:

H_0: $\mu_{\bar{d}} = 0$, H_a: $\mu_{\bar{d}} > 0$, n = 40, $\bar{d}$ = 18.9, s_d = 7.2, α = .05

SOLUTION

Step 1

State the null and alternative hypothesis.

H_0: $\mu_d = 0$

H_a: $\mu_d > 0$

Step 2

Specify the values given in the problem.

$\mu_{\bar{d}} > 0$, n = 40, $\bar{d}$ = 18.9, s_d - 7.2, α = .05

Step 3

Determine the appropriate distribution and the critical values.

Since the sample size is large ($n \geq 30$), we use the normal distribution to do the test. The > sign in the alternative hypothesis indicates a right-tail test.

The area in the right tail is α = .05. From the standard normal distribution table we look for .45 in the table (.5 – .05) which has a z value of 1.65.

Step 4

Calculate the value of the test statistic, using the appropriate formula.

Since σ is not known, we use

$$z = \frac{\bar{d} - \mu_{\bar{d}}}{\frac{s_d}{\sqrt{n}}}$$

$$= \frac{18.9 - 0}{\frac{7.2}{\sqrt{40}}}$$

$$= \frac{18.9}{1.138} = 16.608$$

Step 5

Draw a conclusion for the null hypothesis.

Since the calculated z value $= 16.608 > 1.65$, we reject the null hypothesis as this value falls within the rejection region. We conclude that the mean of the population paired differences is not different from zero.

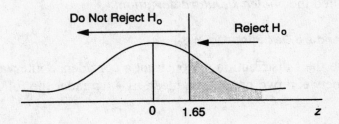

CONFIDENCE INTERVAL ABOUT THE DIFFERENCE BETWEEN TWO POPULATION MEANS—SMALL SAMPLE CASE

Equal Standard Deviations ($\sigma_1 = \sigma_2$)

We use the t-distribution to construct a confidence interval about the difference between two population means $\mu_1 - \mu_2$ under the following conditions:

1. The sample sizes n_1 and n_2 are small and independent. That is, $n_1 < 30$ and $n_2 < 30$.

2. The populations from which the two samples are drawn (x_1 and x_2 values) are approximately normally distributed.

3. The population standard deviations σ_1 and σ_2 are unknown but equal ($\sigma_1 = \sigma_2$).

We use the sample standard deviation $s_{\bar{x}_1 - \bar{x}_2}$ as an estimate for $\sigma_{\bar{x}_1 - \bar{x}_2}$ since σ is unknown.

Confidence Interval Formula for $\mu_1 - \mu_2$

A formula for a $(1 - \alpha)$ 100% confidence interval for $\mu_1 - \mu_2$ is:

$$(\bar{x}_1 - \bar{x}_2) \pm t_{\alpha/2} s_{\bar{x}_1 - x_2}$$

where $\quad s_{\bar{x}_1 - \bar{x}_2} = s_p \sqrt{\frac{1}{n_1} + \frac{1}{n_2}}$

and $\quad s_p = \sqrt{\dfrac{(n_1 - 1) s_1^2 + (n_2 - 1) s_2^2}{n_1 + n_2 - 2}}$

which is called the *pooled standard deviation*.

Unequal Standard Deviations ($\sigma_1 \neq \sigma_2$)

We use the *t*-distribution to construct a confidence interval about the difference between two population mean $\mu_1 - \mu_2$ under the following conditions:

1. The samples are small and independent. That is, $n_1 < 30$ and $n2 < 30$.

2. The populations from which the two samples are drawn are approximately normally distributed.

3. The population standard deviations are unknown and unequal ($\sigma_1 \neq \sigma_2$).

We use the sample standard deviation $s_{\bar{x}_1 - \bar{x}_2}$ as an estimate for $\sigma_{\bar{x}_1 - \bar{x}_2}$ since σ is unknown.

Confidence Interval Formula for $\mu_1 - \mu_2$

A formula for a $(1 - \alpha)$ 100% confidence interval for $\mu_1 - \mu_2$ is:

$$(\bar{x}_1 - \bar{x}_2) \pm t_{\alpha/2} \, s_{\bar{x}_1 - \bar{x}_2}$$

where $s_{\bar{x}_1 - \bar{x}_2} = \sqrt{\dfrac{s_1^2}{n_1} + \dfrac{s_2^2}{n_2}}$

$t = t$ value obtained from the t distribution table for a given confidence level and degrees of freedom calculated as

$$df = \frac{\left(\dfrac{s_1^2}{n_1} + \dfrac{s_2^2}{n_2}\right)}{\dfrac{\left(\dfrac{s_1^2}{n_1}\right)^2}{n_1 - 1} + \dfrac{\left(\dfrac{s_2^2}{n_2}\right)^2}{n_2 - 1}}$$

(Always round down this number)

$\bar{x}_1$ and $\bar{x}_2$ = sample means

n_1 and n_2 = sample sizes

$t = t$ value obtained from the t-distribution table for a given confidence level with $n_1 + n_2 - 2$ degrees of freedom

$\bar{x}_1$ and $\bar{x}_2$ = sample means

n_1 and n_2 = sample sizes

HYPOTHESES TESTS ABOUT THE DIFFERENCE BETWEEN TWO MEANS FOR SMALL-SAMPLES

Equal Standard Deviations ($\sigma_1 = \sigma_2$)

We use the t-distribution in hypothesis testing for comparing two population means $\mu_1 - \mu_2$ under the following conditions:

1. The two samples are small and independent. ($n_1 < 30$ and $n_2 < 30$).

2. The populations from which the two samples are drawn are approximately normally distributed.

3. The population standard deviations σ_1 and σ_2 are unknown but equal ($\sigma_1 = \sigma_2$).

These are the same three conditions we applied for constructing a confidence interval in the preceding section. The degrees of freedom for the t-distribution are calculated by $n_1 + n_2 - 2$.

The test statistic for $x_1 - x_2$ is calculated as follows:

$$t = \frac{(\bar{x}_1 - \bar{x}_2) - (\mu_1 - \mu_2)}{s_{\bar{x}_1 - \bar{x}_2}}$$

where $s_{\bar{x}_1 - \bar{x}_2} = s_p \sqrt{\dfrac{1}{n_1} + \dfrac{1}{n_2}}$

and $s_p = \sqrt{\dfrac{(n_1 - 1)\, s_1^2 + (n_2 - 1)\, s_2^2}{n_1 + n_2 - 2}}$

$\mu_1 - \mu_2 = $ value substituted from the null hypothesis

EXAMPLE

A sample of 22 male students enrolled in a first-year college chemistry course showed that the mean test scores on the final exam was 77.8 with a standard deviation of 7.1. A sample of 20 female students from the same chemistry course showed that the mean test score on the final exam was 79.2 with a standard deviation of 6.8. Assume that the test scores are normally distributed for all male and female students, with equal but unknown standard deviations.

(a) Test at the 2.5% significance level whether you can conclude that the mean final exam test scores in chemistry for all male students is lower than for all female students.

(b) Construct a 95% confidence interval for the difference between the mean final exam test scores in chemistry for all male and female students.

SOLUTION

Part (a)—Step 1

State the null and alternative hypothesis .

H_0: $\mu_1 - \mu_2 = 0$

H_a: $\mu_1 - \mu_2 < 0$

(The < sign in the alternative hypothesis indicates a left-tail test.)

Step 2

Specify the values given in the problem.

For male students $n_1 = 22 \; \bar{x}_1 = 77.8 \; s_1 = 7.1$

For female students $n_2 = 20 \; \bar{x}_2 = 79.2 \; s_2 = 6.8$

Step 3

Determine the appropriate distribution and the critical values.

Since both samples are small ($n_1 < 30$ and $n_2 < 30$), the populations are normally distributed and the standard deviations (σ_1 and σ_2) are unknown but equal, we use the t distribution to do the test. We need to find the t value corresponding to the critical point on the graph which is on the left side of the graph.

Since this is a left-tailed test with only one rejection region, the area in the left tail is $\alpha = .025$.

Degrees of freedom $= df = n_1 + n_2 - 2 = 22 + 20 - 2 = 40$

From the t distribution table, the t value corresponding to 40 degrees of freedom and .025 area in the left tail is -2.021.

Step 4

Calculate the value of the test statistic using the appropriate formula.

$$t = \frac{(\bar{x}_1 - \bar{x}_2) - (\mu_1 - \mu_2)}{s_{\bar{x}_1 - \bar{x}_2}}$$

First, we calculate $s_{\bar{x}_1 - \bar{x}_2}$ as follows:

$$s_p = \sqrt{\frac{(n_1 - 1)s_1^2 + (n_1 - 1)s_1^2}{n_1 + n_2 - 2}}$$

$$= \sqrt{\frac{(22 - 1)\,(7.1)^2 + (20 - 1)\,(6.8)^2}{22 + 20 - 2}}$$

$$= 6.9591$$

$$s_{\bar{x}_1 - \bar{x}_2} = s_p \sqrt{\frac{1}{n_1} + \frac{1}{n_2}}$$

$$= (6.9591) \sqrt{\frac{1}{22} + \frac{1}{20}}$$

$$= 2.150$$

Thus, $t = \dfrac{(\bar{x}_1 - \bar{x}_2) - (\mu_1 - \mu_2)}{s_{\bar{x}_1 - \bar{x}_2}}$

$$= (77.8 - 79.2) - \frac{0}{2.150}$$

$$= \frac{-1.4}{2.150}$$

$$= -.651$$

Step 5

Draw a conclusion for the null hypothesis.

Since the calculated t value $= -.651 > -2.021$ we do not reject the null hypothesis as this value falls within the nonrejection region. Therefore, we can conclude that there is no difference in the mean final exam chemistry test scores for male and female students.

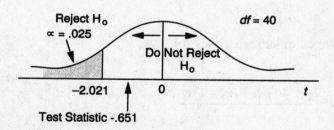

Part (b)

(1) The confidence level is 95% or .95. We use the t distribution to determine the confidence interval as explained in step 3 above.

To find the t value from the distribution table, we need to know the area in each tail of the curve ($\alpha/2$) and the degrees of freedom (df). Thus we have

Area in each tail $= ..5 - \alpha/2 = .5 - .95 / 2 = .025$

$df = n_1 + n_2 - 2 = 22 + 20 - 2 = 40$

Thus, from the t distribution table we obtain a t value of 2.021 and $s_{\bar{x}_1 - \bar{x}_2} = 2.150$ (see above calculation).

(2) Substituting the values back into the formula, we obtain:

$$(\bar{x}_1 - \bar{x}_2) \pm t_{\alpha/2} \; s_{\bar{x}_1 - \bar{x}_2} = (77.8 - 79.2) \pm (2.021)(2.150)$$

$$= -1.4 \pm 4.35 = -5.75 \text{ to } 2.95$$

Thus, we are 95% confident that the difference in mean chemistry final exam test scores is between -5.75 and 2.95.

The example below is the same example we discussed in the preceding section except here we assume unequal population standard deviations $(\sigma_1 \neq \sigma_2)$ where before we assumed equal standard deviations $(\sigma_1 = \sigma_2)$.

Unequal Standard Deviations ($\sigma_1 \neq \sigma_2$)

We use the t-distribution in hypothesis testing for comparing two population means $\mu_1 - \mu_2$ under the following conditions:

1. The two samples are small and independent ($n_1 < 30$ and $n_2 < 30$).

2. The populations from which the two samples are drawn are approximately normally distributed.

3. The population standard deviations are unknown and unequal $(\sigma_1 \neq \sigma_2)$.

The degrees of freedom for the t-distribution are calculated by the formula below:

$$df = \frac{\left(\dfrac{s_1^2}{n_1} + \dfrac{s_2^2}{n_2}\right)^2}{\dfrac{\left(\dfrac{s_1^2}{n_1}\right)^2}{n_1 - 1} + \dfrac{\left(\dfrac{s_2^2}{n_2}\right)^2}{n_2 - 1}}$$

(Always round down this number.)

The test statistic for $\bar{x}_1 - \bar{x}_2$ is calculated as follows:

$$t = \frac{(\bar{x}_1 - \bar{x}_2) - (\mu_1 - \mu_2)}{s_{\bar{x}_1 - \bar{x}_2}}$$

where $s_{\bar{x}_1 - \bar{x}_2} = \sqrt{\dfrac{s_1^2}{n_1} + \dfrac{s_2^2}{n_2}}$

$\mu_1 - \mu_2$ = value substituted from the null hypothesis

EXAMPLE

A sample of 22 male students enrolled in a first-year college chemistry course showed that the mean test scores on the final exam was 77.8 with a standard deviation of 7.1. A sample of 20 female students from the same chemistry course showed that the mean test score on the final exam was 79.2 with a standard deviation of 6.8. Assume  that the test scores are normally distributed for all male and female students with unequal population standard deviations.

(a)   Test at the 2.5% significance level whether you can conclude that the mean final exam test scores in chemistry is lower for all male students than for all female students.

(b)   Construct a 95% confidence interval for the difference between the mean final exam test scores in chemistry for all male and female students.

SOLUTION

Part (a)—Step 1

State the null and alternative hypothesis.

H_0: $\mu_1 - \mu_2 = 0$

H_a: $\mu_1 - \mu_2 < 0$

(The < sign in the alternative hypothesis indicates a left-tail test.)

Step 2

Specify the values given in the problem.

For male students $n_1 = 22, \bar{x}_1 = 77.8, s_1 = 7.1$

For female students $n_2 = 20, \bar{x}_2 = 79.2, s_2 = 6.8$

Step 3

Determine the appropriate distribution and the critical values.

Since both samples are small ($n_1 < 30$ and $n_2 < 30$) the populations are normally distributed and the standard deviations (σ_1 and σ_2) are unknown and unequal we use the t distribution to do the test. We need to find the t value corresponding to the critical point on the graph which is on the left side of the graph.

Since this is a left-tailed test with only one rejection region the area in the left tail is $\alpha = .025$. Now we calculate the degrees of freedom for the special case when $\sigma_1 \neq \sigma_2$.

$$df = \frac{\left(\frac{s_1^2}{n_1} + \frac{s_1^2}{n_1}\right)^2}{\frac{\left(\frac{s_1^2}{n_1}\right)^2}{n_1 - 1} + \frac{\left(\frac{s_2^2}{n_2}\right)^2}{n_2 - 1}}$$

$$= \frac{\left(\frac{(7.1)^2}{22} + \frac{(6.80)^2}{20}\right)^2}{\frac{\left(\frac{(7.1)^2}{22}\right)^2}{22 - 1} + \frac{\left(\frac{(6.80)^2}{20}\right)^2}{20 - 1}}$$

$$= 39.39$$

$$\cong 39$$

(Round down this number.)

From the t-distribution table the t-value corresponding to 39 degrees of freedom and .025 area in the left tail is -2.019.

Step 4

Calculate the value of the test statistic using the appropriate formula.

$$t = \frac{(\bar{x}_1 - \bar{x}_2) - (\mu_1 - \mu_2)}{s_{\bar{x}_1 - \bar{x}_2}}$$

First we calculate $s_{\bar{x}_1 - \bar{x}_2}$ as follows:

$$s_{\bar{x}_1 - \bar{x}_2} = \sqrt{\frac{s_1^2}{n_1} + \frac{s_2^2}{n_2}}$$

$$= \sqrt{\frac{(7.1)^2}{22} + \frac{(6.8)^2}{20}}$$

$$= 2.1455$$

Thus, $t = \dfrac{(\bar{x}_1 - \bar{x}_2) - (\mu_1 - \mu_2)}{s_{\bar{x}_1 - \bar{x}_2}}$

$$= \frac{(77.8 - 79.2) - 0}{2.1455}$$

$$= -.653$$

Step 5

Draw a conclusion for the null hypothesis.

Since the calculated t-value $= -.653 > -2.019$, we do not reject the null hypothesis as this value falls within the nonrejection region. Therefore we conclude that there is no difference in the mean final exam chemistry test scores for male and female students.

Note: When we compare the t value ($-.653$ and the degrees of freedom (39) with the previous section values of $-.651$ and 40 we see how close these values are. Thus, even if we assume $\sigma_1 = \sigma_2$ when this may not be true and use the previous section's results our error will be quite small provided the difference between the standard deviations is small.

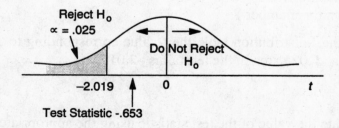

Part (b)

(1) The confidence level is 95% or .95. We use the t distribution to determine the confidence interval as explained in step 3 above.

To find the t value from the distribution table we need to know the area in each tail of the curve ($\alpha/2$) and the degrees of freedom (df). Thus we have

Area in each tail $= .5 - \alpha/2 = .5 - .95 / 2 = .025$

$df \cong 39$ (see above calculation.)

and $s_{\bar{x}_1 - \bar{x}_2} = \sqrt{\dfrac{s_1^2}{n_1} + \dfrac{s_2^2}{n_2}}$

$= 2.1455$

(see above calculation)

Thus, from the t-distribution table, we obtain a t-value of 2.019.

(2) Substituting the values back into the formula, we obtain:

$$\bar{x}_1 - \bar{x}_2) \pm t_{\alpha/2}\, s_{\bar{x}_1 - \bar{x}_2} = (77.8 - 79.2) \pm (2.019)(2.140)$$

$$= -1.4 \pm 4.33 = -5.73 \text{ to } 2.93$$

Thus, we are 95% confident that the difference in mean chemistry final exam test scores is between -5.73 and 2.93. Again, we see how close the confidence interval is to the previous section's confidence interval. Thus, even if we assume $\sigma_1 = \sigma_2$ when $\sigma_1 \neq \sigma_2$ and apply the previous section's formula our error will be quite small when the difference between the two standard deviations is small.

☞ Drill: Statistical Inferences

DIRECTIONS: Determine the correct responses from the information provided in questions 1 through 9.

1. In the production of size D cells for use as flashlight batteries, the standard deviation of operating life for all batteries is 3.0 hours, based on the known variability of battery ingredients. Distribution of the operating life for all batteries is approximately normal. A random sample has a mean operating life of 20.0 hours. Find a 90% confidence interval for the true mean life of the battery.

2. You select a random sample of 100 teardrops. The sample has an average salt concentration of .1 with a standard deviation of .01. Establish a 95% confidence interval for the mean saline concentration of the tears.

3. In the Idaho State Home for Runaway Girls, 25 residents were polled as to what age they ran away from home. The sample mean was 16 years old with a standard deviation of 1.8 years. Establish a 95% confidence interval for μ, the mean age at which runaway girls leave home in Idaho.

4. A random sample of 10 Miss America contestants had a mean age of 22.6 years with a standard deviation of 2 years. A random sample of 12 Miss U.S.A. candidates had a mean age of 19.6 with a standard deviation of 1.6. Assume the population variances are equal. Find a 90% confidence interval estimate for the difference between the population means.

5. Tom and Joe like to throw darts. Tom throws 100 times and hits the target 54 times; Joe throws 100 times and hits the target 49 times. Find a 95 percent confidence interval for $p_1 - p_2$ where p_1 represents the true proportion of hit in Tom's tosses, and p_2 represents the true proportion of hits in Joe's tosses.

6. Suppose you are a buyer of large supplies of light bulbs. You want to test, at the 5% significance level, the manufacturer's claim that his bulbs last more than 800 hours. You test 36 bulbs and find that the sample mean, $\bar{X}$, is 816 hours and the sample standard deviation $s = 70$ hours. Should you accept the claim?

7. A recent report claims that college non-graduates get married at an earlier age than college graduates. To support the claim, random samples of size 100 were selected from each group, and the mean age at the time of marriage was recorded. The mean and standard deviation of the college non-graduates were 22.5 years and 1.4 years respectively, while the mean and standard deviation of the college graduates were 23 years and standard deviation of the college graduates were 23 years and 1.8 years. Test the claims of the report at the .05 level of significance.

8. A group of babies all of whom weighed approximately the same at birth are randomly divided into two groups. The babies in sample 1

were fed formula A; those in sample 2 were fed formula B. The weight gains attained from birth to age six months were recorded for each baby. The results were as follows: sample 1: 5, 7, 8, 9, 6, 7, 10, 8, 6; sample 2: 9, 10, 8, 6, 8, 7, 9. We desire to know whether either formula A or formula B is more effective than the other in producing weight gains. Test for this at the .05 level of significance.

9. An electrical company claimed that at least 95% of the parts which they supplied on a government contract conformed to specifications. A sample of 400 parts was tested, and 45 did not meet specifications. Can we accept the company's claim at a .05 level of significance?

Answers to Drill Questions

1. Let μ = the true mean life of the battery.

   Let σ = the standard deviation of operating life.

   We know from the standard normal table:

   $Pr(-1.645 < \text{standard normal quantity} < 1.645) = .90.$

   Our main stumbling block now is the lack of an appropirate standard normal quantity involving μ. But we know that if a population is normally distributed with mean μ and standard deviation σ, an extracted sample mean will be normally distributed with expectation m and standard deviation.

   $$\frac{\sigma}{\sqrt{n}}$$

   (n is the sample size.) Let's standardize the sample mean.

   $$\frac{\overline{X} - E(\overline{X})}{\sqrt{\text{Var } \overline{X}}}$$

   is standard normal. In our case

   $$\frac{\overline{X} - E(\overline{X})}{\sqrt{\text{Var } \overline{X}}} = \frac{20.0 - \mu}{3.0/\sqrt{n}}.$$

   We have obtained a standard normal quantity involving μ. Therefore

   $$-1.645 < \frac{20.0 - \mu}{3.0/\sqrt{n}} < 1.645$$

is a 90 percent C. I.

Multiplying by $\dfrac{3.0}{\sqrt{n}}$:

$$-\frac{4.94}{\sqrt{n}} < 20.0 - \mu < \frac{4.94}{\sqrt{n}}.$$

Subtracting 20:

$$-\frac{4.94}{\sqrt{n}} - 20 < -\mu < \frac{4.94}{\sqrt{n}} - 20.$$

Multiply by -1:

$$20 - \frac{4.94}{\sqrt{n}} < \mu < 20 + \frac{4.94}{\sqrt{n}}.$$

Our required confidence interval is

$$20 - \frac{4.94}{\sqrt{n}} < \mu < 20 + \frac{4.94}{\sqrt{n}}.$$

2. We have a large sample, 100. The Law of Large Numbers will allow us to use the sample standard deviation, S, as an estimate for the population deviation σ. The Central Limit Theorem tells us

$$\frac{(\overline{X} - \sigma)\sqrt{n}}{\sigma}$$

is approximately standard normal. We will assume then that is standard normal. Therefore, from the table,

$$\Pr\left(-1.96 < \frac{(\overline{X} - \mu)\sqrt{n}}{S} < 1.96\right) = .95.$$

Substituting .1 for $\overline{X}$, 100 for n, and .01 for S, the inequality within the parenthesis becomes

$$-1.96 < \frac{(.1 - \mu)\sqrt{100}}{.01} < 1.96.$$

Multiply through by $\dfrac{.01}{\sqrt{100}}$:

$-.002 < .1 - \mu < .002.$

Subtract .1:

$-1.002 < -\mu < -.098$

Multiple by -1 to obtain the final answer:

$.098 < \mu < 1.002.$

This is a 95% confidence interval for m, the true but unknown salt concentration of audience tears.

3.   We do not know precisely the population standard deviation and our sample is not large, 25. We might be all right in using the sample deviation to approximate the real one, but it is better to be safe and use a *t*-statistic. We know

$$\frac{\overline{X} - \mu}{\sigma / \sqrt{n}}$$

is a standard normal random variable. Also note that

$$\sqrt{\frac{\Sigma(X_i - \overline{X})^2}{\sigma^2 (n-1)}}$$

is the square root of a Chi-square random variable with $n - 1$ degrees of freedom divided by $n - 1$. The quotient of these two quantities

$$\frac{(\overline{X} - \mu) / (\sigma / \sqrt{n})}{\sqrt{\Sigma(X_i - \overline{X})^2 / \sigma^2 (n-1)}}$$

is a *t* random variable with $n - 1$ degrees of freedom. Factoring

$$\frac{(\overline{X} - \mu) / (\sigma / \sqrt{n})}{\sqrt{\Sigma(X_i - \overline{X})^2 / \sigma^2 (n-1)}} = \frac{\frac{1}{\sigma} \frac{(\overline{X} - \mu)}{1 / \sqrt{n}}}{\frac{1}{\sigma} \sqrt{\Sigma(X_i - \overline{X})^2 / (n-1)}}$$

The denominator is now the sample standard deviation, S. A convenient form for our *t*-statistic ($n - 1$ d.o.f.). is

$$\frac{\overline{X} - \mu}{S / \sqrt{n}}$$

In our case $n - 1 = 25 - 1 = 24$. From t-tables we see that

$$\Pr(- 2.064 < t_{(24)} < 2.064) = .95.$$

Inserting our t-statistic:

$$\Pr\left(-2.064 < \frac{\overline{X} - \mu}{S/\sqrt{n}} < 2.064\right) = .95.$$

It is the interval,

$$-2.064 < \frac{\overline{X} - \mu}{S/\sqrt{n}} < 2.064,$$

with which we are concerned. Substituting our values

$$\overline{X} = 16, \ S = 1.8, \ \sqrt{n} = \sqrt{25} = 5,$$

we see the result is

$$-2.064 < \frac{16 - \mu}{1.8/5} < 2.064.$$

Multiplying through by $\dfrac{1.8}{5}$:

$$- .743 < 16 - \mu < .743.$$

Subtracting 16:

$$- 16.743 < - \mu < - 15.267.$$

Multiplying by -1:

$$15.267 < \mu < 16.743.$$

Thus a 95% confidence interval for the true mean age at which Idaho girls run away from home is (15.267, 16.743).

4.   We have small samples with a common unknown variance. We have already derived the general conficence interval for this type of problem. The interval we obtained was

$$\left((\overline{X} - \overline{Y}) - b\sqrt{\frac{(n-1)S_1^2 + (m-1)S_2^2}{n + m - 2}\left(\frac{1}{n} + \frac{1}{m}\right)},\right.$$

$$(\bar{X} - \bar{Y}) + b \sqrt{\frac{(n-1)S_1^2 + (m-1)S_2^2}{n+m-2} \left(\frac{1}{n} + \frac{1}{m}\right)}.$$

The problem tells us $\bar{X} = 22.6$, $S_1^2 = 2^2 = 4$, $n = 10$ $\bar{Y} = 19.6$, $S_2^2 = 1.6^2 = 2.56$, and $m = 12$. Since $m + n - 2 = 12 + 10 - 2 = 20$, b will be the value such that

$$\Pr(-b < t(20) < b) = .95.$$

A glance at the t tables reveals $b = 1.725$. Inserting the known values, our interval becomes

$$\left((22.6 - 19.6) - 1.725 \sqrt{\frac{(10-1)4 + (12-1)2.56}{12+10-2} \left(\frac{1}{10} + \frac{1}{12}\right)}, \right.$$

$$\left. (22.6 - 19.6) + 1.725 \sqrt{\frac{(10-1)4 + (12-1)2.56}{12+10-2} \left(\frac{1}{10} + \frac{1}{12}\right)} \right).$$

Combining yields:

$$\left(3 - 1.725 \sqrt{\frac{36 + (11)2.56}{20} \left(\frac{22}{120}\right)}, \right.$$

$$\left. 3 - 1.725 \sqrt{\frac{36 + (11)2.56}{20} \left(\frac{22}{120}\right)} \right).$$

Further simplification changes our result to

$$(3 - 1.725 \,(.767), 3 + 1.725 \,(.767).$$

Equivalently we have $(3 - 1.32, 3 + 1.32)$ or $(1.68, 4.32)$ as the 90% confidence interval for the difference in ages between Miss America contestants and Miss U.S.A, contestants.

5. Previously, we applied the Central Limit Theorem to the statistic

$$\frac{Y_1}{n_1} - \frac{Y_2}{n_2}$$

we arrived at an approximate standard normal random variable,

$$\frac{(\frac{Y_1}{n_1} - \frac{Y_2}{n_2}) - (p_1 - p_2)}{\sqrt{\frac{p_1(1-p_1)}{n_1} + \frac{p_2(1-p_2)}{n_2}}}. \tag{1}$$

After estimating the denominator by substituting

$$\frac{Y_1}{n_1} \text{ for } p_1 \text{ and } \frac{Y_2}{n_2} \text{ for } p_2,$$

we "pivoted" (1) into the following confidence interval for $p_1 - p_2$.

$$\left(\left(\frac{Y_1}{n_1} - \frac{Y_2}{n_2} \right) - Z_{\alpha/2} \sqrt{\frac{\frac{Y_1}{n_1} \left(1 + \frac{Y_1}{n_1} \right)}{n_1} + \frac{\frac{Y_2}{n_2} \left(1 + \frac{Y_2}{n_2} \right)}{n_2}}, \right.$$

$$\left. \left(\frac{Y_1}{n_1} - \frac{Y_2}{n_2} \right) + Z_{\alpha/2} \sqrt{\frac{\frac{Y_1}{n_1} \left(1 + \frac{Y_1}{n_1} \right)}{n_1} + \frac{\frac{Y_2}{n_2} \left(1 + \frac{Y_2}{n_2} \right)}{n_2}} \right). \tag{2}$$

In the present problem $1 - \alpha = .95$. Hence $\alpha = .05$, $\alpha/2 = .025$ and $z_{\alpha/2} = 1.96$. Also $Y_1 = 54$, $Y_2 = 49$, and $n_1 = n_2 = 100$. Therefore

$$Z_{\alpha/2} \sqrt{\frac{\frac{Y_1}{n_1} \left(1 + \frac{Y_1}{n_1} \right)}{n_1} + \frac{\frac{Y_2}{n_2} \left(1 + \frac{Y_2}{n_2} \right)}{n_2}}$$

$$= 1.96 \sqrt{\frac{\frac{54}{100} \left(1 - \frac{54}{100} \right)}{100} + \frac{\frac{49}{100} \left(1 - \frac{49}{100} \right)}{100}}$$

$$= 1.96 \sqrt{\frac{\frac{54}{100} \left(\frac{46}{100} \right) + \frac{49}{100} \left(\frac{51}{100} \right)}{100}}$$

$$= 1.96 \sqrt{\frac{(.54)(.46) + (.49)(.51)}{100}}$$

$$= 1.96 \sqrt{\frac{.4983}{100}}$$

$$= 1.96 \sqrt{.004983}$$

$$= 1.96 (.0706)$$

$$= .138.$$

In addition

$$\frac{Y_1}{n_1} - \frac{Y_2}{n_2} = \frac{54}{100} - \frac{49}{100} = \frac{5}{100} = .05.$$

Therefore (2) reduces to

$$(.05 - .138, .05 + .138) \text{ or } (-.88, .188).$$

6. Establish the hypotheses

$$H_0: \mu = 800 \text{ hours, and } H_1: \mu > 800 \text{ hours.}$$

We know by the Central Limit Theorem that the sampling distribution of the sample means is approximately normal, because $n = 36 > 30$. the rejection area for H_0 is shown in the diagram:

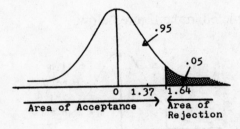

The shaded area represents 5% of the area under the standard normal curve. The table of z-scores gives $z = 1.64$ for a 5% rejection area. Now compute the z-value corresponding to the sample mean $\overline{X} = 816$.

$$z = \frac{\overline{X} - \mu_0}{\sigma_{\overline{X}}},$$

where μ_0 is the mean of the null hypothesis and $\sigma_{\overline{X}}$ is the standard deviation of the sampling distribution of means, which is equal to the quotient of the population standard deviation s and the square root of the sample size:

$$\sigma_{\overline{X}} = \frac{\sigma}{\sqrt{n}}.$$

We do not know the population standard deviation, so we approximate it by the sample standard deviation $s = 70$. Making substitutions in the formula for z, we have

$$z = \frac{\overline{X} - \mu}{\sigma_{\overline{X}}} = \frac{\overline{X} - \mu_0}{\sigma / \sqrt{n}} = \frac{\overline{X} - \mu_0}{s / \sqrt{n}} = \frac{816 - 800}{70 / \sqrt{36}} = \frac{16}{11.67} = 1.37.$$

This z-value falls in the acceptance region $(-\infty, 1.64)$ for H_0, $\mu = 800$ hours. Therefore, you should reject, at the 5% level, the manufacturer's claim that $\mu > 800$.

7.   The wording of the problem calls for a one-tailed test. If we let $\mu_1 =$ average age at which non-graduates marry and $\mu_2 =$ average age at which graduates marry, we have for our hypotheses:

H_0: $\mu_1 - \mu_2 \geq 0$

H_1: $\mu_1 - \mu_2 < 0$.

This problem is depicted in the figure below.

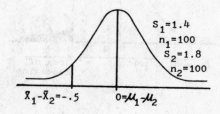

The statistic

$$\frac{(\overline{X}_1 - \overline{X}_2) - (\mu_1 - \mu_2)}{\sigma_{\overline{X}_1 - \overline{X}_2}}$$

is approximately normally distributed with a mean of 0 and a standard deviation of 1 when the size of the samples is large ($n_1 + n_2 > 30$).

Our decision rule for a level of significance of $\alpha = .05$ is: reject H_0 if $Z < -1.64$; accept H_0 if $Z \geq -1.64$. We must calculate

$$Z = \frac{(\overline{X}_1 - \overline{X}_2) - 0}{S_{\overline{X}_1 - \overline{X}_2}}$$

where $S_{\overline{X}_1 - \overline{X}_2} = \sqrt{\dfrac{S_1^2}{n_1} + \dfrac{S_2^2}{n_2}}$.

For the data of this problem we have

$$S_{\overline{X}_1 - \overline{X}_2} = \sqrt{\frac{(1.4)^2}{100} + \frac{(1.8)^2}{100}}$$

$$= \sqrt{\frac{1.96}{100} + \frac{3.24}{100}}$$

$$= \sqrt{.0520}$$

$$= .229$$

and $\quad z = \dfrac{(22.5 - 23) - 0}{.229}$

$$= \frac{-.5}{.229}$$

$$= -2.18.$$

Since $-2.18 < -1.64$, we reject H_0 and conclude at a 5% level of significance that college non-graduates do marry at an earlier age than college graduates.

8. Since we have no preconceived notions about which formula may be more effective in producing weight gains, we will use a two-tailed test. We have

$$H_0: \mu_A - \mu_B = 0$$

$$H_1: \mu_A - \mu_B \neq 0.$$

The statistic

$$\frac{(\overline{X}_1 - \overline{X}_2) - (\mu_1 - \mu_2)}{S_{\overline{X}_1 - \overline{X}_2}}$$

has a t-distribution when $n_1 + n_2 \leq 30$.

At a .05 level of significance our decision rule is: reject H_0 if $t > 2.145$ or $t < 2.145$ (critical t value for $n_1 + n_2 - 2 = 9 + 7 - 2 = 14$ df's is 2.145); accept H_0 if $-2.145 \leq t \leq 2.145$. We must calculate

$$t = \frac{(\overline{X}_1 - \overline{X}_2) - 0}{S_{\overline{X}_1 - \overline{X}_2}}$$

where $S_{\overline{X}_1 - \overline{X}_2} = \sqrt{\dfrac{(n_1 - 1)S_1^2 + (n_2 - 1)S_2^2}{n_1 + n_2 - 2}} \sqrt{\dfrac{1}{n_1} + \dfrac{1}{n_2}}$.

But first we must calculate $\overline{X}_1$, $\overline{X}_2$, S_1, and S_2.

$$\overline{X}_1 = \frac{\Sigma X_1}{n_1} = \frac{5 + 7 + \ldots + 6}{9} = \frac{66}{9} = 7.33.$$

$$\overline{X}_2 = \frac{\Sigma X_2}{n_2} = \frac{9 + 10 + \ldots + 9}{7} = \frac{57}{7} = 8.14.$$

To calculate S_1 and S_2, it is helpful to set up the following chart.

X_1	X_2	X_1^2	X_2^3
5	9	25	81
7	10	49	100
8	8	64	64
9	6	81	36
6	8	36	64
7	7	49	49
10	9	100	81
8	57	64	475
6		36	
66		504	

$$S_1 = \sqrt{\frac{n_1 \Sigma X_1^2 - (\Sigma X_1)^2}{n_1 (n_1 - 1)}}$$

$$= \sqrt{\frac{9(504) - (66)^2}{9(8)}}$$

$$= \sqrt{\frac{4536 - 4356}{9(8)}}$$

$$= \sqrt{\frac{180}{72}}$$

$$= 1.58;$$

$$S_2 = \sqrt{\frac{n_2 \Sigma X_2^2 - (\Sigma X_2)^2}{n_2 (n_2 - 1)}}$$

$$= \sqrt{\frac{7(475) - (57)^2}{7(6)}}$$

$$= \sqrt{\frac{3325 - 3249}{7(6)}}$$

$$= \sqrt{\frac{76}{42}}$$

$$= 1.35.$$

Now we can calculate

$$S_{\bar{X}_1 - \bar{X}_2} = \sqrt{\frac{8(1.58)^2 + 6(1.35)^2}{14}} \sqrt{\frac{1}{9} + \frac{1}{7}}$$

$$= \sqrt{\frac{8(2.50) + 6(1.82)}{14}} \sqrt{.2540}$$

$$= \sqrt{\frac{20 + 10.92}{14}} (.50)$$

$$= (1.49)(.50)$$

$$= .745$$

and $\quad t = \dfrac{(7.33 - 8.14) - 0}{.745}$

$$= -\frac{.81}{.745}$$

$$= -1.09.$$

Since $-2.145 \le -1.09 \le 2.145$, we accept H_0 and conclude that there is no difference in the abilities of formula A and formula B to produce weight gains in babies during the period from birth to age 6 months at a .05 level of significance.

9.   In this problem we wish to determine whether the sample proportion of parts which did meet specifications,

$$\bar{p} = \frac{355}{400} = .8875,$$

is significantly small so as to reject the company's claim that at least 95% of the parts conformed to specifications. Therefore we have for our alternate hypothesis,

$$H_1: p < .95.$$

Our null hypothesis is thus

$$H_0: p = .95.$$

This problem may be depicted by the following diagram. The statistic

$$\frac{(\bar{p} - p)}{\sigma_p}$$

has approximately a normal distribution with a mean of 0 and a standard deviation of 1.

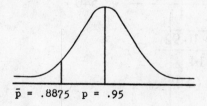

$$\bar{p} = .8875 \quad p = .95$$

We must calculate

$$Z = \frac{\bar{p} - p}{\sigma_{\bar{p}}}$$

For the data of this problem we have

where $\sigma_{\bar{p}} = \sqrt{\dfrac{.95(.05)}{400}} = .011$

and $Z = \dfrac{.8875 - .95}{.011} = \dfrac{-.0625}{.011} = -5.7.$

For a level of significance, a, of .05, and a one-tailed test, our decision rule is: reject H_0 if $Z < -2.33$; accept $H_0 \geq -2.33$.

Since $-5.7 < 2.33$ we reject H_0 and conclude that the company's claim that at least 95% of the parts conformed to specifications is not justified.

▼
PRACTICE
TEST 1

AP EXAMINATION IN STATISTICS

Test 1

Section I

TIME: 90 Minutes
35 Multiple-Choice Questions

(Answer sheets appear in the back of this book.)

DIRECTIONS: For each question or incomplete statement in this section, select the best answer from among the five choices and fill in the corresponding oval on the answer sheet.

1. Cars are grouped into the following classes:

    I. Subcompact
    II. Compact
    III. Midsize
    IV. Large

    This data is

    (A) ordinal.

    (B) nominal.

    (C) ratio.

    (D) interval.

    (E) cannot be determined.

2. A machine stamps out metal pieces. The machine operator checks every tenth piece to make sure the size is correct. This is an example of

    (A) random sampling.

    (B) systematic sampling.

    (C) stratified sampling.

    (D) cluster sampling.

    (E) quota sampling.

3. A numerical sample is grouped into the following classes:

    I.   0 – 8   IV. 27 – 35
    II. 9 – 17   V.   36 – 44
    III. 18 – 26   VI. 45 – 53

The width, or real size, of these classes is

(A) 8.0.

(B) 8.5.

(C) 9.0.

(D) 9.5.

(E) 10.0.

4. Given the following lengths of time in minutes it takes 20 students to get to school who do not take the school bus:

    15 13 17 16 35 28   5 16 18 21
    40 37 12 25   7 23 41 32 36 17

If you want to classify this data into five classes starting at lower limit zero, what is the smallest first class you can have? Zero to

(A) 6

(B) 7

(C) 8

(D) 9

(E) 10

5. Given the ogive of a frequency distribution, which classes have equal frequencies?

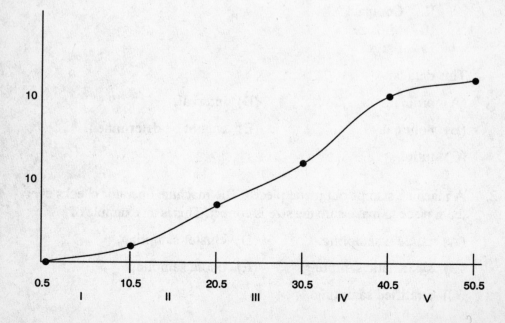

238

(A) I & V   (D) III & V

(B) II & III   (E) None of the above.

(C) III & IV

6. We know that the mean weight of ten body-builders is 257.5 pounds. We have the following list of weights for the first eight athletes but have lost the weights of Big Ned and Muscular Marv. What does Marv weigh if we know that he weighs 10 pounds more than Ned?

Body Builder	Weight (in Pounds)
1	250
2	282
3	260
4	245
5	237
6	291
7	249
8	291

(A) 235 pounds.   (D) 262 pounds.

(B) 240 pounds.   (E) 270 pounds.

(C) 245 pounds.

7. The diagram shows the graph of a frequency distribution.

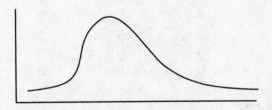

From left to right, what is the order of measures of central location?

(A) Median - mode - mean

(B) Mode - median - mean

(C) Mean - median - mode

(D) Mean - mode - median

(E) Can't tell from the diagram

8.   Given the frequency table:

Class	Class Boundaries	Frequency
I	0.5 – 10.5	6
II	10.5 – 20.5	8
III	20.5 - 30.5	12
IV	30.5 - 40.5	7
V	40.5 - 50.5	5
VI	50.5 - 60.5	2

What is the median for this grouped data?

(A) 20.5   (D) 30

(B) 25.5   (E) 30.5

(C) 27.5

9.   Which of the following four sets of data have the smallest and largest standard deviations?

I	II	III	IV
1	1	1	1
2	5	1	3
3	5	1	3
4	5	1	3
5	5	5	5
6	5	9	7
7	5	9	7
8	5	9	7
9	9	9	9

Smallest/largest:

(A) II/I   (D) II/IV

(B) III/I   (E) II/III

(C) IV/I

10. Three grinding machines—I, II, and III—produce the same metal pieces. The machines are tested periodically by checking a sample of the pieces from each of the machines. In one testing, the following results were obtained:

	Mean Diameter	Standard Deviation
Machine I	0.0032	0.00021
Machine II	0.0036	0.00024
Machine III	0.0033	0.00029

Which is the correct rank of machines in order of *decreasing* consistency?

(A) I, II, III   (D) II, III, I

(B) I, III, II   (E) III, II, I

(C) II, I, III

11. Polly takes three standardized tests. She scores 600 on all three. Using standard scores, or z-scores, rank her performance on the three tests from best to worst if the means and standard deviations for the tests are as follows:

	Mean	Standard Deviation
Test I	500	80
Test II	470	120
Test III	560	30

Her rankings are:

(A) I, II, III   (D) I, III, II

(B) III, II, I   (E) III, I, II

(C) II, I, III

12. Given the following three sets of data:

I	10	15	20	22	25	30				
II	10	12	18	19	23	24	26	30		
III	10	14	15	16	18	24	25	26	28	30

Which sets of data would be represented by the same boxplot?

(A) I and II
(D) All of the above

(B) I and III
(E) None of the above

(C) II and III

13. Thirty percent of the people attending a basketball game are under 21 years of age. Sixty percent are male. If 20 percent of all the people are males under 21, and one person is chosen at random for a prize, what is the probability that the answer will be someone under 21 and/or a male?

(A) 30%
(D) 80%

(B) 60%
(E) 90%

(C) 70%

14. A package of ten calculators shipped to a store contains two defective calculators. What is the probability of buying two of the calculators and ending up with exactly one of the defective ones?

(A) 20%
(D) 36%

(B) 25%
(E) 50%

(C) 33%

15. A neighborhood association runs a lottery. They sell 5,000 tickets at $1.00 per ticket and award prizes of $1,000, $500, and $200 to the lucky winners. What is the expected gain or loss of a person who buys one ticket?

(A) Loss of $1.00
(D) Gain of $.20

(B) Loss of $.66
(E) Gain of $1,700

(C) Loss of $.34

16. A coin is flipped 10 times in Trial I, 20 times in Trial II, and 40 times in Trial III. The probability of getting heads between 40% and 60% (inclusive) heads is

(A) equal in all three trials.

(B) greatest in Trial I and least in Trial III.

(C) greatest in III and least in I.

(D) greatest in III and least in II.

(E) not able to be determined.

17. If one-third of students applying to Yarvard College are accepted, what is the probability that one of the next three students applying to Yarvard will be accepted?

(A) 25%

(B) 30%

(C) 33%

(D) 38%

(E) 44%

18. Given a normal curve distribution, what is the area of the curve between $z = -1.37$ and $z = -2.05$?

(A) 0.0651

(B) 0.4349

(C) 0.8945

(D) 0.1055

(E) 0.3945

19. A food-processing plant fills bags of potatoes called 50-pound bags. Investigators discover that only 4% of the bags actually weigh more than 50 pounds. If the weights of the bags form a normal distribution, what is the actual mean weight of the bags of potatoes if the standard deviation of this population is 2.0?

(A) 45.0 pounds

(B) 46.5 pounds

(C) 48.0 pounds

(D) 49.5 pounds

(E) 50.0 pounds

20. A researcher is suddenly granted extra money for her study and realizes that she can double the size of her already large sample. If she decides to do this, what will happen to the size of her confidence interval?

(A) It will double in size.

(B) It will be multiplied by a factor of approximately 1.4.

(C) It will remain unchanged.

(D) It will be multiplied by a factor of approximately 0.7.

(E) It will be halved.

21. A random sample of 150 high school boys is taken to determine what proportion watch at least an hour of cartoons on television each week. If 40% of the sample watch television, what is the confidence interval at the 95% confidence level for the true percentage of high school boys who watch at least an hour of cartoons?

(A) $0.39 < p < 0.41$ (D) $0.34 < p < 0.46$

(B) $0.30 < p < 0.40$ (E) $0.32 < p < 0.48$

(C) $0.35 < p < 0.45$

22. A radio station is scheduling time slots for the coming baseball season and believes that a typical game lasts three hours. A researcher hired by the station decides to choose at random 60 games played during the first month of the season and accepts the value of three hours if the average game lasts between 170 and 190 minutes. What is the probability of a Type I error to the nearest percent if the standard deviation is a half hour?

(A) 0%   (D) 5%

(B) 1%   (E) 10%

(C) 2%

23. On the average, Robin the Hood hits the bull's eye on the target 25% of the time. He steps up to the line to shoot four arrows at the target. How many times will he hit the bull's eye?

(A) 0 or 1   (D) 2

(B) 1   (E) 0, 1, 2, 3, or 4

(C) 0, 1, or 2

24. The value of t in the t-test for the correlation coefficient is given by the formula

$$t = r\sqrt{\frac{n-2}{1-r^2}}$$

with the number of degrees of freedom given by $n - 2$. Six pairs of independent and dependent variables are measured in a two-tailed situation, and a value for the correlation coefficient of 0.8 is determined. For this data, what is the minimum value of a, the level of significance, at which you could reject the null hypothesis? (The null hypothesis states that there is no significant relationship between the independent and dependent variables.)

(A) 0.20

(D) 0.02

(B) 0.10

(E) 0.01

(C) 0.05

25. Given the regression line shown. What is the approximate value of the correlation coefficient represented by this line?

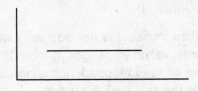

(A) −1

(D) +0.7

(B) −0.7

(E) +1

(C) 0

26. Using the goodness of fit test, an investigator wants to show that people have clear preferences among ten different brands of laundry detergents. If he surveys 100 people, which of the following would prove his point at the 0.01 level of significance?

(A) $\chi^2 > 135.8$

(D) $\chi^2 > 21.67$

(B) $\chi^2 > 23.21$

(E) $\chi^2 > 140.2$

(C) $\chi^2 < 135.8$

27. When attempting to show the relationship between two variables, a regression line can be drawn and the correlation coefficient, r, can be calculated. The y-intercept and slope of the regression are denoted b_0 and b_1 respectively. Consider the following statements:

I. $r = b_0$
II. $r = b_1$
III. r and b have the same sign

Which of the statements above are always true?

(A) I only

(B) II only

(C) III only

(D) I & III only

(E) None of the statements are always true.

28. When studying the relationship between an independent and a dependent variable, under what condition might it be invalid to use a regression line to predict future values of the dependent variable? Consider the following possibilities:

I. The independent variable is not normally distributed.
II. The dependent variable is not normally distributed for specific values of the independent variable.
III. We go outside the range of the independent variable.

It might be invalid in situation(s)

(A) I only.

(B) II only.

(C) III only.

(D) I & II only.

(E) II & III only.

29. Two variables are studied and the correlation coefficient, r, is determined to have the value -0.05. Consider the following statement about the relationship between the variables:

I. There is a strong relationship.
II. There is a weak relationship.
III. As one increases, the other increases.
IV. As one increases, the other decreases.
V. A causal connection between variables has been proven.

Which of the following are true?

(A) I & III

(B) II & III

(C) I & IV

(D) II & IV

(E) I, III, & V

30. When doing an experiment using an experimental group and a control group, it is most important that

(A) the two groups are similar.

(B) the groups have clearly different backgrounds.

(C) the experimental group be more interested in the research than the control group.

(D) the control group's interest be maintained.

(E) the two groups be allowed to communicate with each other as much as possible.

31. The issue in research design that relates to the researcher's awareness of the experimental or control status of the subjects is referred to as

(A) quota sampling.   (D) statistical regression.

(B) blinding.   (E) selection bias.

(C) placebo effect.

32. A test is developed to measure reading ability. It actually measures two separate factors—the ability to read aloud and reading comprehension—as if they were one. A better statistical approach would be to measure these factors separately. This raises the experimental issue of

(A) confounding.   (D) randomization.

(B) placebo effect.   (E) replication.

(C) blinding.

33. In experimental design, replication is an important practice to help deal with the issue of

(A) generalization.   (D) attrition.

(B) internal validity.   (E) ex-post facto design.

(C) randomization.

34. Two independent samples of size 100 are studied and their means compared. At the 0.04 level of significance, what is the critical statistic, or key value of z, that determines whether or not the difference between the means is significant?

(A) ±1.75   (D) ±2.33

(B) ±1.96   (E) ±0.04

(C) ±2.05

35. The values of a probability distribution are 1, 2, 3, and 4, with probabilities of 0.1, 0.2, 0.3, and 0.4 respectively. What is the variance for this distribution?

(A) 0   (D) 0.3

(B) 1   (E) 3

(C) 0.25

Section II

TIME: 90 Minutes
6 Free-Response Questions

DIRECTIONS: Show all your work. Grading will be based on both the methods used and the accuracy of the final answers. Please make sure that all procedures are clearly shown.

Part 1: Open-Ended

1.   A study was developed to compare how long two different brands of pens lasts. It was determined that fifty Brand X pens last an average of 25.3 hours of writing with a standard deviation of 5.1 hours; sixty Brand Y pens last an average of 22.8 hours with a standard deviation of 5.8 hours. We want to determine at the 0.05 level of significance if the difference between these two sample means are significant.

   a.   What is the null hypothesis?

   b.   What is the alternative hypothesis?

   c.   Under what conditions will we reject the null hypothesis?

   d.   Determine your result.

   e.   State which company—the Brand X company or the Brand Y company—would be happier with the results of this study and briefly explain why.

2.   The following table shows the assessed values and the selling prices of five houses constituting a random sample of all the houses sold recently in a rural area.

Assessed Value (Thousands of $)	Selling Price (Thousands of $)
77	108
59	97
73	98
94	145
47	52

Fitting a least-square line relating the selling price to the assessed value taken as the independent variable, find each of the following:

a.   The slope of the least-square line, b_1

b.   The y-intercept of the least-square line, b_0

c.   The selling price of a house assessed at $100,000 if it followed the least-square line

d.   The possible assessed value of a house that sells for $80,000

3.   A small college has 200 students, each of whom is required to take at least one major subject, English, math, or history. One semester, 80 students take history, 45 take math, and 75 take English. For all three subjects, there are 20 students who take just that subject and no other major. There are also ten students who take all three major subjects simultaneously. There are also students who are taking two of the majors. Three students are to be chosen at random to attend a national student conference. What is the probability that at least one student will be chosen who is taking both math and English but not history?

4.   An opaque jar contains seven marbles that are identical except for color: four are red, and three are green. A game is played in which one marble at a time is taken out of the jar (and not replaced). The game ends when either three red marbles or two green marbles have been removed from the jar.

a.   Draw a tree diagram that indicates all of the different sequences of picks that can occur.

b.   On the average, if the game is played many times, what percent of the games will end on the third pick?

5.   A school district in a large suburban area is trying to determine if student absences are distributed equally throughout the school week. Choosing a five-day week at random, a researcher surveys all of the schools in the district and comes up with the following data:

Day of Week	Number of Absent Students
Monday	73
Tuesday	57
Wednesday	48
Thursday	59
Friday	68

Use the χ^2 test to determine if student absences are distributed equally at the $\alpha = 0.10$ level of significance.

Part 2: Investigative Task

1.   It rains on Paradise Island about 40% of the time. A travel agent is signing people up to go on a five-day tour of the island, and she wants to know what the chances are of getting two days of rain in a row at any time during the five days while the other three days are nice. She asks you to make this determination. You decide to do a simulation experiment setting up 40 five-day trials.

   a.   Explain how you set up the trials using a random number table.

   b.   Show on the random number table how you carry out the trial.

   c.   Set up a frequency table with your results.

   d.   Write a brief report. In this report, discuss your results and compare your results with the theoretical prediction for this situation.

AP STATISTICS

Test 1

ANSWER KEY

Section I

1.	(A)	10.	(A)	19.	(B)	28.	(E)
2.	(B)	11.	(E)	20.	(D)	29.	(D)
3.	(C)	12.	(A)	21.	(E)	30.	(A)
4.	(C)	13.	(C)	22.	(B)	31.	(B)
5.	(A)	14.	(D)	23.	(E)	32.	(A)
6.	(B)	15.	(B)	24.	(B)	33.	(A)
7.	(B)	16.	(C)	25.	(C)	34.	(C)
8.	(B)	17.	(E)	26.	(D)	35.	(B)
9.	(E)	18.	(A)	27.	(C)		

DETAILED EXPLANATIONS
OF ANSWERS

Test 1

Section I

1.   **(A)**   The data cannot be ratio or interval, because there are no numerical values. There is order in the classes, because the size of the cars increases with class. If there was no order, the data would be nominal. For example, if a class of mopeds was added at the end, the data would become nominal.

2.   **(B)**   Choosing data in a regular sequence is systematic sampling. The machine operator is choosing data (the metal pieces) in a regular sequence (every tenth piece).

3.   **(C)**   The width of a class is the difference between the boundaries of the class. For class 2, the boundaries are 8.5 and 17.5. The difference is 9. Note that the difference between the lower or upper limits of successive classes will also give the width.

4.   **(C)**   The largest element is 41. Therefore, the five classes must include both 0 and 41. If the width were 8, it would not be large enough to include both values in five classes, so the width must be 9. The difference between the limits of a class is 1 less than the width, so the difference between limits of a class is 8 $(9 - 1)$. Therefore, the upper limit of the first class is 8 $(0 + 8)$. Question #3 shows a good representation of the classes for this question.

5.   **(A)**   The ogive shows the cumulative frequency. The amount of increase from lower to upper boundary of each class shows the number added by that class, or the frequency of that class. Both class I and class V add 2 to the cumulative frequency so they have equal frequencies.

6.   **(B)**   If the average weight of the athletes is 257.5, and there are 10 athletes, the total weight must be 10×257.5 or 2,575 pounds. The sum of

the weights of the eight athletes whose weights we know is 2,105 pounds. That means there are 2,575 − 2,105 = 470 pounds to be added by Ned and Marv. If Marv's weight is m and Ned's weight is 10 pounds less, or m − 10, then m + (m − 10) = 470. Solving this equation yields m = 240, so Marv weighs 240 pounds.

7.　**(B)**　The high point of the graph represents the mode; therefore the mode is furthest left. The median is to the right of the mode, because the curve spreads to the right, therefore the middle term is to the right of the highest point. The higher values off to the right shown by the curve slowly descending toward the x-axis increases the value of the mean. A good example of this is given by the scores on a difficult test where most of the students do poorly, but a few do very well. The high scores of the best students will pull the mean up above the median.

8.　**(B)**　First find the halfway point: 40/2 = 20. Locate the class that contains the 20th term: Class III. Subtract from the halfway point the cumulative frequency of Classes I and II: 20 −14 = 6. Divide this quantity by the frequency of the median class to see how far along the median is in this class: 6/12 = 0.5. Multiply this by the width of the class to locate the median within the class: 0.5x10 = 5. Add this to the lower boundary of the median class and you have the median: 20.5 + 5 = 25.5. This can be expressed by the following equation:

$$\text{Median} = \left[\frac{\frac{n}{2} - cf}{f} \right] (\text{Size}) + LB$$

where: n: total frequency

cf: cumulative frequency of class below median class

f: frequency of median class

Size: size of median class (width)

LB: lower boundary of median class

9.　**(E)**　Standard deviation represents the spread of the data around the mean, not variety of terms. In II, only two terms are separate from the mean, and this by a total distance of 8. In III, the total distance from the mean of eight terms is 32.

10. **(A)**   Decreasing consistency is the same as increasing variation, which is measured by the coefficient of variation:

$$V = \frac{s}{\bar{x}}.$$

(or $V = \frac{s}{\bar{x}} \cdot 100\%$ expressing V as a percent)

Making this calculation for the three machines yields:

$$V_I = 0.0656 \,,\ V_{II} = 0.0666 \,,\ V_{III} = 0.0878.$$

In order of increasing variation, the order is $V_I < V_{II} < V_{III}$, so the correct order is I, II, and III.

11. **(E)**   Standard score is given by the equation:

$$z = \frac{x - \mu}{\sigma}$$

Substituting her score of 600 for x, and the means and standard deviations as given in the table, the results are:

$$z_I = 1.25 \,,\ z_{II} = 1.08 \,,\ z_{III} = 1.33.$$

In order of decreasing z-scores, the order is $z_{III} > z_{II} > z_I$. Therefore, the correct order is III, I, II.

12. **(A)**   A boxplot shows five key points. From left to right, they are the lowest value, first quartile, median, third quartile, and the highest value. Data sets I and II have the following in common:

> lowest value = 10;
> first quartile = 15;
> median = 21;
> third quartile = 25;
> highest value = 30.

Data set III has the third quartile equal to 26, so it would have a different boxplot.

13. **(C)**   There are two ways to determine the probability the winner would be someone under 21 and/or male. One way is using the probability formula for union and the second way is using a Venn diagram. Make C

represent children or people under 21 years of age, and M to represent males. The formula for the union is

$$P(C \cup M) = P(C) + P(M) - P(C \cap M).$$

Substitution yields

$$P(C \cup M) = 30\% + 60\% - 20\% = 70\%.$$

The other method is shown in the Venn diagram.

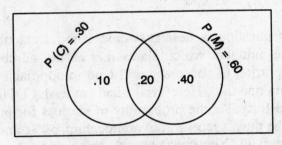

$$.10 + .20 + .40 = .70 \text{ or } 70\%$$

14. **(D)**   This is a hypergeometric distribution and is done using the following method:

The formula is:

$$f(x) = \frac{\binom{a}{x}\binom{b}{n-x}}{\binom{a+b}{n}} \text{ or } f(x) = \frac{{}_aC_x \, b \cdot C_{(n-x)}}{{}_{(a+b)}C_n}$$

where a and b are complementary parts of a whole, x is the number chosen of type a and n is the total number chosen.

Here

$$a = 2, b = 8, x = 1, n = 2$$

so

$$f(1) = \frac{\binom{2}{1}\binom{8}{1}}{\binom{10}{2}} = \frac{(2)(8)}{(45)} = .36 \text{ or } 36\%.$$

15. **(B)** This uses the formula for expected value,

$$E(X) = \sum x_i p_i.$$

The probability of losing \$1 is 1. The probability of winning each prize is 1/5000, or 0.0002. So the formula yields:

$$E(X) = (-\$1)(1) + (\$1000)(0.0002) + (\$500)(0.0002) +$$
$$(\$200)(0.0002) + \text{(for completeness)} (\$0)(0.9994)$$

$$\text{so } E(X) = -\$0.66$$

16. **(C)** This question is best answered without calculation by using the law of large numbers which states that as the number of trials increases, the proportion of successes will tend to approach the probability of success for any one trial. Here Trial I had ten trials, Trial II had twenty, and Trial III had forty. As the probability of success for one trial is 50%, Trial III should be most successful in approaching 50%, and Trial I should be the least successful. You could also do this using a binomial distribution table or calculating z using the continuity correction and using the normal distribution table.

17. **(E)** This is answered by using the binomial distribution formula:

$$f(x) = \binom{n}{x} p^x (1 - p)^{n-x}$$

$$f(1) = \binom{3}{1} \left(\frac{1}{3}\right)^1 \left(\frac{2}{3}\right)^2$$

$$f(1) = (3)\left(\frac{1}{3}\right)\left(\frac{4}{9}\right)$$

$$f(1) \approx .44 \text{ or } 44\%$$

p is the probability of a success on any trial
n is the total number of trials
x is the number of successes

18. **(A)** Use the table for the normal distribution, Table A. Subtract from the area to the left of $z = -1.37$ the area to the left of $z = -2.05$. $0.0853 - 0.0202 = 0.0651$. Note that many students are probably more familiar with the standard normal distribution tables that give the area under the normal curve between the given value of z and $z = 0$. Teachers

may want to have their students become acquainted with the left-tailed version of the table used on this test.

19. **(B)**   The fact that four percent of the bags weigh more than 50 pounds implies the value of z. Once we have the value of z, we can determine the value of μ in the formula for z.

$$z = \frac{x - \mu}{\sigma}.$$

The normal wave for this situation is:

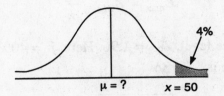

Note that the mean weight is supposed to be 50 pounds, but it clearly is less than 50. So in the equation, we look for μ not x. From the normal curve area table, $z \approx 1.75$ when the tail area = 4% or .04. So the equation then becomes

$$1.75 = \frac{50 - \mu}{2.0}$$

so $3.5 = 50\ \mu$ and $\mu = 46.5$ pounds.

20. **(D)**   A confidence interval is given by: $\bar{x} - E_{max} < \mu < \bar{x} + E_{max}$ where

$$E_{max} = \frac{Z_{\frac{2}{2}} \cdot \sigma}{\sqrt{n}}$$

So the size of the interval is $2\,E_{max}$. In this situation, because $Z_{2/2}$ and σ remain constant,

$$E_1 \cdot \sqrt{n_1} = E_2 \cdot \sqrt{n_1}$$

$$\text{So } E_2 = \frac{\sqrt{n_1}}{\sqrt{n_2}}\,E_1$$

If $n_2 = 2n_1$,

$$E_z = \frac{E_1}{\sqrt{2}}$$

$$\text{or } E_2 \approx 0.7E_1$$

21. **(E)** The confidence interval for a proportion is given by

$$\hat{p} - E_{max} < p < \hat{p} + E_{max}$$

where

$$E_{max} = Z_{2/2}\sqrt{\frac{\hat{p}\hat{q}}{n}}$$

For a 95% confidence level, $Z_{2/2} = 1.96$. Here $\hat{p} = 40\%$ or 0.40 and $\hat{q} = 1 - \hat{p} = 60\%$ or 0.60. n is 150. So

$$E_{max} = 1.96 \cdot \sqrt{\frac{(0.40)((0.60)}{150}} = 0.0784 \approx 0.08.$$

The confidence interval is

$$0.40 - 0.08 < p < 0.40 + 0.03$$

or

$$0.32 < p < 0.48$$

22. **(B)** A Type I error for a two-tailed situation is given by the area shaded under the normal curve.

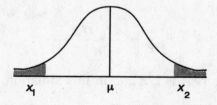

It is important to do this problem in consistent units. To avoid fractions, use minutes.

$$\mu = 3 \text{ hours} = 180 \text{ minutes}, x_1 = 170 \text{ minutes}, x_2 = 190 \text{ minutes},$$
$$\sigma = \tfrac{1}{2} \text{ hour} = 30 \text{ minutes}$$

$$z_1 = \frac{x_1 - \mu}{\frac{\sigma}{\sqrt{n}}}$$

$$= \frac{170 - 180}{\frac{30}{\sqrt{60}}}$$

$$= -2.58$$

By symmetry, $Z_2 = 2.58$.

From the normal curve table, the area to the left of $Z = -2.58$ is 0.0049. So the whole area under the curve is 2×0.0049 or $0.0098 \approx 1\%$.

23. **(E)**   Although Robin the Hood hits the bull's eye an *average* of one time out of four, he does not hit it exactly once each time he shoots four arrows. He would hit it not at all or four times or anywhere in between.

24. **(B)**   Given that $r = 0.8$ and $n = 6$, we use the formula for t to calculate

$$t = .8\sqrt{\frac{4}{1-.64}} = 2.67$$

Using the critical t-value table, with $\propto \not\!/2$, because it is a two-tailed situation, we get the following $t_\propto$ values for $d.f = n - 2 = 4$.

$\propto$	t_2
0.20	1.533
0.10	2.132
0.05	2.776
0.02	3.747
0.01	4.604

Since $t = 2.67$ is greater than 2.132 ($t_{0.10}$) but not greater than 2.776 ($t_{0.05}$), the minimum value of μ at which you could reject the null hypothesis is $\propto = 0.10$

25. **(C)**   A horizontal regression line indicates that the dependent variable does not change as the independent variable does. Therefore, there is no distinguishable relationship between the variables, and $r = 0$.

26. **(D)**   In order to use the χ^2 table, we must know the degrees of freedom, which is one less than the number of categories, not the number of participants. In this case, there are ten categories so the degrees of freedom = 9, and the associated value of χ^2 is 21.67. Note that the numbers in the question are taken from the table that will be included with the test, which may be different than the χ^2 table that the students have in their textbook.

27. **(C)**   The relationship between b and r is given by $b = r(s/s)$. Since s and s are always positive, r and b always have the same sign. However, as is clear from the formula, they will generally not have the same value. Since b is the y-intercept of the regression line, there is no relationship between b and r.

28. **(E)**   Consider the possibilities. I: The independent variable is chosen according to plan or availability by the researcher and whether or not it is normally distributed is irrelevant. II: If the dependent variable is not normally distributed for particular values of the independent variable, the validity of predictions are called into question. III: If we go outside the range of the independent variable, the conditions may be different from those under which the experiment was carried out and the relationship between variables may change. Therefore II and III can make predictions invalid.

29. **(D)**   The closer the absolute value of r is to 1, the stronger the relationship between the variables. The closer it is to 0, the weaker the relationship. Therefore 0.05 implies a weak relationship, and the negative sign implies that as the independent variable increases, the dependent one decreases. The question of causality does not even come into this weak a relationship. Therefore II and IV are the true statements.

30. **(A)**   When comparing how an experimental group changes after experiencing a research intervention and how a control group changes after *not* experiencing the same research intervention, it is critical that the two groups be as similar as possible. Otherwise, changes may be observed in the two groups that reflect differences between the groups rather than the effects of the experiment. The four other answers are either counterproductive or irrelevant for the success of the experiment.

31. **(B)**   Blinding refers to the practice of keeping the researcher purposely uninformed about the experimental or control status of the subjects

the researcher is working with. It was discovered that if the researcher was aware of this status, he or she could subconsciously bias the results of the research because of his or her desire to prove the experimental hypothesis.

32. **(A)**   Confounding refers to the practice of measuring as one entity a collection of factors that are not necessarily related and should be measured separately. If the researcher does not separate the factors properly, he/she can get incorrect or misleading results.

33. **(A)**   Replication is the practice of repeating previous studies in the attempt to determine whether the results of the earlier research can be accepted under similar situations or generalized to different ones. The more the earlier results can be confirmed under different conditions, the more generally valid the results may be considered.

34. **(C)**   The point here is to see if the student can determine the critical statistic at a less typical level of significance, not 0.01 or 0.05. This is a two-tailed situation, so the total area of 0.04 must be divided between left- and right-tailed areas of 0.02. The value of z associated with this tail-area as taken from the normal distribution table is 2.05.

35. **(B)**   First we determine the mean, given by $u = x p$. Therefore

$$u = 1(.1) + 2(.2) + 3(.3) + 4(.4) = 3.$$

Then we determine the variance, using the expression $o = (x \, u \,) \, p$. Therefore

$$o = (1 - 3) \, (.1) + (2 - 3) \, (.2) + (3 - 3) \, (.3)$$
$$+ (4 - 3) \, (.4) = 1.$$

Section II

Part 1

1. a.   The null hypothesis is that the brands of pens last the same amount of time: $\mu_x = \mu_y$

   b.   The alternative hypothesis is that they do *not* last the same amount of time: $\mu_x \neq \mu_y$

   c.   We reject the null hypothesis at $Z < -1.96$ or $Z > 1.96$

   d.
$$Z = \frac{\bar{X}_x - \bar{X}_y}{\sqrt{\dfrac{s_x^2}{n_x} + \dfrac{s_y^2}{n_y}}}$$

$$Z = \frac{25.3 - 22.8}{\sqrt{\dfrac{(5.1)^2}{50} + \dfrac{(5.8)^2}{60}}}$$

$$Z = 2.40$$

Since $Z > 1.96$, we reject the null hypothesis. We can conclude at the 0.05 level of significance that the amount of time the different brands last are not equal.

   e.   The Brand X company would be happier with the results of this study, because their pens last longer than Brand Y pens, and the statistical analysis of the results indicates that the time difference is meaningful. In other words, the difference is not just due to chance.

2. a.   The slope is given by

$$\frac{\sum (x_i - \bar{x})(y_i - \bar{y})}{\sum (x_i - \bar{x})^2}$$

x	$x - \bar{x}$	$(x - \bar{x})^2$	y	$y - \bar{y}$	$(x - \bar{x})(y - \bar{y})$
77	7	49	108	8	56
59	−11	121	97	−3	33
73	3	9	98	−2	−6
94	24	576	145	45	1080
47	−23	529	52	−48	1104

$$\sum (x - \bar{x})^2 = 1,284 \qquad\qquad \sum = 2267$$

$$\Sigma_x = 350 \qquad\qquad \Sigma_y = 350$$
$$\bar{x} = 70 \qquad\qquad \bar{y} = 100$$

So $b_1 = \dfrac{2267}{1284} = 1.77$

b. $b_0 = \bar{y} - b, \bar{x}$

$b_0 = 100 - (1.77)(70)$

$b_0 = -23.9$ or $-\$23,900$

c. $\hat{y} = b_0 + b, x$

$\hat{y} = -23.9 + 1.77(100)$

$\hat{y} = 153.1$ or $\$153,100$

d. $x = \dfrac{\hat{y} - b_0}{b_1}$

$x = \dfrac{80 - (-23.9)}{1.77}$

$x = 58.7$ or $\$58,700$

3. This problem is best done using a Venn Diagram.

E: English
M: Math
H: History

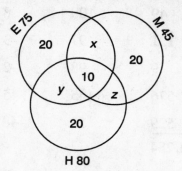

We first must determine x, y and z. By inspecting the diagram we get

I. $x + y \quad = 75 - (20 + 10) = 45$

II. $x + z = 45 - (20 + 10) = 15$

III. $y + z = 80 - (20 + 10) = 50$

Subtracting II. from I.,

$y - z = 30$

and III

$y + z = 50$

combining

$2y = 80$
$y = 40$

so $x = 5$

and $z = 10$

There are, therefore, $10 + x$, or 15 students, taking math and English but not history.

The probability of choosing at least one from the group of 15 students is the same as

(1 – probability of choosing *none* of the 15 students).

To get the probability of choosing none, we use the hypergeometric equation:

$$f(x) = \frac{\binom{a}{x}\binom{b}{n-x}}{\binom{a+b}{n}}$$

Here, $a + b = 200$, $a = 15$, $b = 185$, $x = 0$, $n = 3$

$$f(o) = \frac{\binom{15}{0}\binom{185}{3}}{\binom{200}{3}}$$

So

$$f(o) = \frac{(1)(1,038,220)}{1,313,400}$$
$$= .79$$

Therefore, the probability of choosing at least one of the fifteen students is $(1 - .79)$ or 0.21, or 21%.

4. a.   R : RED
          G : GREEN
          ○ : GAME OVER
          ● : THIRD PICK

Probability of each
pick is written on
the branch

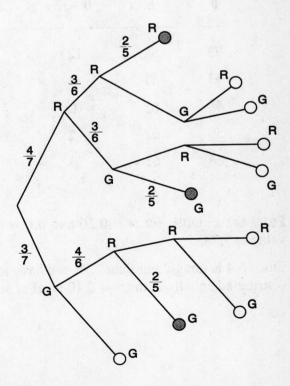

b.   Probability of game ending on the third pick is given by sum of the products of the probabilities.

$$P(3) = \frac{4}{7}\cdot\frac{3}{6}\cdot\frac{2}{5} + \frac{4}{7}\cdot\frac{3}{6}\cdot\frac{2}{5} + \frac{3}{7}\cdot\frac{4}{6}\cdot\frac{2}{5}$$

$$= 3\left(\frac{24}{210}\right)$$

$$= .343 \approx 34\%$$

5.   The formula for the x^2 goodness–of–fit test is:

$$x^2 = \sum \frac{(0-E)^2}{E},$$

where 0 represents the observed values and E the expected values, and

$$E = \frac{\sum 0}{n}$$

0	E	0 – E	$(0-E)^2$	$\dfrac{(0-E)^2}{E}$
73	61	12	144	2.4
57	61	–4	16	0.3
48	61	–13	169	2.8
59	61	–2	4	0.1
68	61	7	49	0.8
				$\sum = 6.4$

From the x^2 table, for $\alpha = 0.10$ and d.f. $= \cap - 1 = 5 - 1 = 4$, the critical value is 7.78.

Since 6.4 is not greater than 7.78, we have to say that student absences *are* distributed equally at the $\alpha = 0.10$ level of significance.

Section II

Part 2

1. One way of setting up the trials is as follows:

    a. Start in the top left-hand corner of the table and go across horizontally in groups of 5. Take digits 1, 2, 3, 4 for rain and digits 5, 6, 7, 8, 9, 0 for sun.

    b. Two tables shown on table.

    c. Weeks with two days in a row rain and the rest nice = 6

        All other weeks = S4

    d. The theoretical prediction for this situation is as follows: Use the binomial formula,

$$f(x) = \binom{n}{x} p^x (1 - p)^{n-x}$$

here $x = 2$, $n = 5$, $p = 0.4$.

So

$$f(2) = \binom{5}{2}(.4)^2(.6)^3$$
$$f(2) = (10)(.16)(.216)$$
$$f(2) = 0.3456$$

This is the probability that two out of the next five days will have rain. However, we want to know how many times we will get two days in a *row* of rain. The total number of sequences is given by the formula

$$\frac{n!}{x_1! x_2!},$$

where n is the total and the x's are repeat elements in the sequence. If x_1 are rainy days, and x_2 sunny, $n = 5$, $x_1 = 2$, and $x_2 = 3$.

Random Numbers*

SRRRR	SSSSR					
04433	80674	24520	18222	10610	05794	37515
60298	47829	72648	37414	75755	04717	29899
67884	59651	67533	68123	17730	95862	08034
89512	32155	51906	61662	64130	16688	37275
32653	01895	12506	88535	36553	23757	34209
95913	15405	13772	76638	48423	25018	99041
55864	21694	13122	44115	01601	50541	00147
35334	49810	91601	40617	72876	33967	73830
57729	32196	76487	11622	96297	24160	09903
86648	13697	63677	70119	94739	25875	38829
30574	47609	07967	32422	76791	39725	53711
81307	43694	83580	79974	45929	85113	72268
02410	54905	79007	54939	21410	86980	91772
18969	75274	52233	62319	08598	09066	95288
87863	82384	66860	62297	80198	19347	73234
68397	71708	15438	62311	72844	60203	46412
28529	54447	58729	10854	99058	18260	38765
44285	06372	15867	70418	57012	72122	36634
86299	83430	33571	23309	57040	29285	67870
84842	68668	90894	61658	15001	94055	36308
56970	83609	52098	04184	54967	72938	56834
83125	71257	60490	44369	66130	72936	69848
55503	52423	02464	26241	68779	66388	75242
47019	76273	33203	29608	54553	25971	69573
84828	32592	79526	29554	84580	37859	28504
68921	08141	79227	05748	51276	57143	31926
36458	96045	30424	98420	72925	40729	22337
95752	59445	36847	87729	81679	59126	59437
26768	47323	58454	56958	20575	76746	49878
42613	37056	43636	58085	06766	60227	96414
95457	30566	65482	25596	02678	54592	63607
95276	17894	63564	95958	39750	64379	46059
66954	52324	64776	92345	95110	59448	77249
17457	18481	14113	62462	02798	54977	48349
03704	36872	83214	59337	01695	60666	97410
21538	86497	33210	60337	27976	70611	08250
57178	67619	98310	70348	11317	71623	55510
31048	97558	94953	55866	96283	46620	52087
69799	55380	16498	80733	96422	58078	99643
90595	61867	59231	17772	67831	33317	00520
?????	?????	98939	78784	09977	29398	93896
15340	93460	57477	13898	48431	72936	78160
64079	42483	36512	56186	99098	48850	72527
63491	05546	67118	62063	74958	20946	28147
92003	63868	41034	28260	79708	00770	88643
52360	46658	66511	04172	73085	11795	52594
74622	12142	68355	65635	21828	39539	18988
04157	50079	61343	64315	70836	82857	35335
86003	60070	66241	32836	27573	11479	94114
41268	80187	20351	09636	84668	42486	71303

*Based on parts of *Tables of 105,000 Random Decimal Digits.* Interstate Commerce Commission. Bureau of Transport Economics and Statistics, Washington, D.C.

$$\frac{5!}{2! \cdot 3!} = 10.$$

So the total number of sequences is 10. The total number with two rainy days in a row is shown as follows: (R = Rain, S = Sun)

Day:	1	2	3	4	5
	R	R	S	S	S
	S	R	R	S	S
	S	S	R	R	S
	S	S	S	R	R

So, 4 out of 10 sequences have two rainy days in a row, or 40%. Therefore, 40% of .3456 represents the probability of getting two rainy days in a row. This is 0.138.

If we run 40 trials (0.138)(40) = 5.5 or approximately 6 of them should give us two rainy days in a row with the rest nice. This was our result.

Report: I simulated 40 five-day periods. Out of these, six, or approximately 15%, contained two rainy days in a row with the other three nice. This is what the people going on your tours can expect. The simulated result was very close to the result predicted by probability theory, which is 13.8%.

PRACTICE TEST 2

AP EXAMINATION IN STATISTICS

Test 2

Section I

TIME: 90 Minutes
35 Multiple-Choice Questions

(Answer sheets appear in the back of this book.)

DIRECTIONS: For each question or incomplete statement in this section, select the best answer from among the five choices and fill in the corresponding oval on the answer sheet.

1. A study measures the number of cars passing through a certain tollbooth each day during a two-week period. This data is

   (A) ordinal.

   (B) nominal.

   (C) ratio.

   (D) interval.

   (E) can't tell

2. In doing an investigation of health care coverage in a metropolitan area, a researcher surveys every resident in a particular three-block area. This is an example of

   (A) random sampling.

   (B) systematic sampling.

   (C) stratified sampling.

   (D) cluster sampling.

   (E) a combination of random and systematic sampling.

3. The class limits of a numerical sample are given as follows:

Class	Limits
I	10 – 19
II	20 – 29
III	30 – 39
IV	40 – 49
V	50 – 59
VI	60 – 69

What are the class boundaries of Class IV?

(A) 40, 49

(D) 39, 50

(B) 39.9, 49.1

(E) 39.5, 49.5

(C) 39.95, 49.05

4. A frequency table representing a group of 100 people and the amount of time they watch television on a certain day is shown.

Time (in Minutes)	Number of People
0 – 59	12
60 – 119	15
120 – 179	18
180 – 239	25
240 – 299	20
300 – 359	7
360 – 419	3

What is wrong with this table?

(A) Unequal class size

(D) Mistake in frequencies

(B) Overlapping classes

(E) Nothing is wrong with the table.

(C) Missing class values

5. Given the stemplot shown

1	3 7 6 4
2	2 8 9 3 7 4
3	6 8 8 2 1
4	6 2

What is the relationship between mean, median, and mode for this data?

(A) mean = mode > median   (D) mean = median = mode

(B) mode = median < mean   (E) mean = median < mode

(C) mean = median > mode

6. In a study of people's work habits, 16 federal employees are chosen at random, and the number of days they worked during one month is determined. The average number of days worked per person is 20. If 12 of the people worked 19 days during the month, how many days did the other four people work?

(A) 20   (D) 23

(B) 21   (E) 24

(C) 22

7. A frequency distribution is skewed left. This means the order of measures of central tendency from left to right are

(A) median-mode-mean   (D) mean-mode-median

(B) mode-median-mean   (E) mode mean median

(C) mean-median-mode

8. Given the following table of grouped data—what is the mode of this data given as a single value?

Class	Class Limits	Frequency
I	50 – 54	12
II	55 – 59	17
III	60 – 64	9
IV	65 – 69	4
V	70 – 74	2
VI	75 – 79	1

The mode is

(A) 22.   (D) 57.

(B) 23.   (E) 59.5.

(C) 64.5.

9. Standardized test scores of all the high school seniors in one school in a large city are used for two studies. In the first study, the seniors are studied just for their own school, i.e. as a population. In the second study, the seniors are assumed to represent all the seniors in the city, i.e. as a sample. What is the relationship between the means and standard deviations in the two studies?

    (A) The mean is higher in first study, and the standard deviations are equal.

    (B) The mean is higher in second study, and the standard deviations are equal.

    (C) The means are equal, and the standard deviation is higher in first study.

    (D) The means are equal, and the standard deviation is higher in second study.

    (E) The means and standard deviations are equal in both studies.

10. If a set of data follows a normal curve distribution, and 50% of the data lies in a region centered around the mean between values of 60 and 100, 95% of the data lies in a region centered around the mean between approximate values of

    (A) 70 and 90.   (D) 30 and 130.

    (B) 50 and 110.   (E) 20 and 140.

    (C) 40 and 120.

11. The top ten tennis players are given the following ranking scores:

Player	Score
A	100
B	97
C	93
D	88
E	87
F	84
G	83
H	83
I	80
J	78

What is the percentile rank among these ten players of Player E?

(A) 47%   (D) 60%

(B) 50%   (E) 87%

(C) 55%

12. In a sample of twelve people in an exercise class, their ages are given as follows:

    20 22 24 26 28 29 29 30 31 33 35 37

    What is the interquartile range for this data?

(A) 0   (D) 7

(B) 2.5   (E) 8.5

(C) 5

13. A deck of playing cards has 52 total cards of which 12 are picture cards. What is the probability of choosing 3 cards in a row without replacement and getting 3 picture cards (approximately)?

(A) 0.1%   (D) 2%

(B) 0.5%   (E) 6%

(C) 1%

14. One hundred state parks are surveyed around the country. Forty-five have boating areas, and 75 have hiking trails. Forty percent of the parks that have hiking trails have boating areas. If you choose a park at random from the list of parks that have boating areas, what is the probability that the park you choose will have hiking trails?

(A) $\dfrac{1}{5}$ (D) $\dfrac{3}{4}$

(B) $\dfrac{1}{2}$ (E) $\dfrac{5}{6}$

(C) $\dfrac{2}{3}$

15. If a couple getting married today can be expected to have 0, 1, 2, 3, 4, or 5 children with probabilities of 20%, 20%, 30%, 20%, 8%, and 2% respectively, what is the average number of children, to the nearest tenth, couples getting married today have?

    (A) 1.0   (D) 2.2

    (B) 1.8   (E) 2.8

    (C) 2.0

16. Stan brings a bag of five different-colored marbles to his multiple-choice statistics test which has possible answers A through E for each question. What is the probability Stan will get at least a 40 percent on a 20-question test if he takes a marble from the bag at random to guess the answer for each question?

    (A) 3%   (D) 20%

    (B) 8%   (E) 40%

    (C) 15%

17. A die is a cube with six faces. Each face displays dots representing one of the numbers from 1 to 6, and each die contains all six numbers. If a *pair* of dice are thrown 100 times, what is the approximate number of times that a sum of 7 or 11 will appear on the top faces of the two dice?

    (A) 8   (D) 37

    (B) 15   (E) 50

    (C) 22

18. Given a normal curve distribution, what is the value of z if the area under the curve to the right of z is .0075?

    (A) −2.43   (D) +1.44

    (B) −0.07   (E) +2.43

    (C) +0.07

19. A well-balanced coin is flipped 10,000 times. What is the probability of getting more than 5,100 heads?

    (A) 42.17%   (D) 2.01%

    (B) 2.28%   (E) 2.00%

    (C) 2.22%

20. In an experiment done with a sample of size $n = 100$, the limits of the confidence interval are 16.6 and 18.0. If the standard deviation is 3.0, at approximately what degree of confidence was the experiment done?

    (A) 90%

    (B) 95%

    (C) 98%

    (D) 99%

    (E) You cannot tell from the given information.

21. A consulting firm is studying the effectiveness of an on-the-job computer training course given throughout a large government agency. How large a sample of employees should the firm study if they want to be accurate within 8% of the true proportion at the 99% confidence level? (From an earlier study, they can assume that the course is effective for about 65% of the employees.)

    (A) 76   (D) 22

    (B) 52   (E) 236

    (C) 62

22. A drug company has published results of medical tests that claim that a certain medication is effective in 60% of the cases of a rare disease. A medical researcher questions this result, although she does not know whether she thinks it is high or low. She only has 12 people to test with the medication. What test statistic, or key value of t, should she check her results against if she wants to limit the possibility of a Type I error to at the most 1.0%?

    (A) 2.681   (D) 3.055

    (B) 2.764   (E) 4.025

    (C) 3.106

23. We compare the two regression lines representing the relationship between two variables, Graph M and Graph N. Consider the following statements relating the correlation coefficient for the two representations:

I. r_M and r_N are both negative
II. $|r_M| < |r_N|$
III. $r_M < r_N$

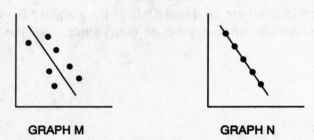

GRAPH M   GRAPH N

Which statements are correct?

(A) I only

(B) II only

(C) III only

(D) I and II only

(E) all of them

24. A researcher is studying the food preferences of a group of children. She finds that 70% of them like chocolate ice cream, 40% like strawberry ice cream, and 30% like both chocolate and strawberry ice cream. If we choose a child at random from this group, what is the probability that he/she will either like chocolate or like strawberry ice cream, but not like both?

(A) 10%

(B) 20%

(C) 30%

(D) 50%

(E) 80%

25. A sociologist is studying the relationship between church attendance and donations to charity. He sets up a table as follows:

Attendance	Large Donations	Average Donations	Small Donations
Often (more than once a week)			
Average (once a week)			
Occasional (between average & never)			
Never			

What would prove at the 0.05 level of significance that the amount of a donation is related to church attendance?

(A) $\chi^2 > 12.59$

(B) $\chi^2 > 14.06$

(C) $\chi^2 > 21.02$

(D) $\chi^2 > 11.07$

(E) $\chi^2 > 16.01$

26. A regression line having variables x and y is determined to have the equation:

$$\hat{y} = 65 + 2x$$

Assuming conditions are met to use the regression line for prediction, for what numerical value of the independent variable will the ratio of the dependent variable to the independent variable be 2:1?

(A) 15

(B) 25

(C) −65

(D) there are many infinite values

(E) there is no such value

27. In finding the relationship between two variables, the equation of the regression line is determined to be:

$$\hat{y} = 250 - 3x$$

The five values of the independent variable used in the experiment were: 2, 5, 8, 9, and 11. What is $\bar{y}$?

(A) 250

(B) 247

(C) 229

(D) 206

(E) cannot be determined

28. A researcher performs an experiment, changing the value of the independent variable x and recording values of the dependent variable y. She calculates the value of the correlation coefficient to be $r = 0.7$, and draws the associated regression line. What percentage of the variation in y cannot be attributed to changes in x and the associated relationship indicated on the regression line?

    (A) 70%

    (B) 49%

    (C) 30%

    (D) 51%

    (E) There is not enough information provided.

29. When studying the relationship between two variables, the correlation coefficient is calculated to equal +0.95. Consider the following statements.

    I.   There is a strong relationship between the variables.
    II. There is a weak relationship between the variables.
    III. As one increases the other increases.
    IV. As one increases the other decreases.
    V.   A causal connection between the variables has been proven.

    Which of the statements are true?

    (A) I and III   (D) II and IV

    (B) II and III   (E) I, III, and V

    (C) I and IV

30. The Placebo Effect refers to changes

    (A) in the experimental group caused by the administration of the independent variable.

    (B) in the experimental group caused by separation from real-life conditions.

    (C) in the experimental group caused by evaluating the dependent variable.

    (D) in the control group caused by the attention of the experiment itself.

    (E) in both groups caused by lack of randomization of selection.

31. The expermental design practice of subject matching is important in dealing with the issue of

    (A) attrition.

    (B) confounding.

    (C) measurement bias.

    (D) placebo effect.

    (E) selection bias.

32. Two teams, *A* and *B*, play a series in which the first team to win two games wins the series. Team *A* has won the first game. What is the probability that Team *B* will win the series if the teams can be considered to be equal in strength?

    (A) $\dfrac{1}{8}$

    (B) $\dfrac{1}{6}$

    (C) $\dfrac{1}{4}$

    (D) $\dfrac{1}{3}$

    (E) $\dfrac{1}{2}$

33. Blocking is an attempt to deal with the effect on the data of

    (A) researcher bias.

    (B) extraneous factors.

    (C) overgeneralization.

    (D) poor measuring devices.

    (E) premature closure of research.

34. The test scores of eight students are compared before and after a new computerized teaching method is put into effect. What is the critical value of *t* that is used to determine if the new method had the effect of increasing scores at the 0.05 level of significance when you subtract the before scores from the after scores for each student?

    (A) –1.860

    (B) +1.895

    (C) –1.895

    (D) +2.365

    (E) –2.365

35. When two variables are investigated for a relationship, it is discovered that the greatest absolute value of r is attained when the data is fit to a regression curve following the equation

$$y = ax^b$$

What is this kind of regression called?

(A) Exponential regression   (D) Quartic regression

(B) Power regression   (E) Logarithmic regression

(C) Linear regression

Section II

TIME: 90 Minutes
        6 Free-Response Questions

> **DIRECTIONS**: Show all your work. Grading will be based on both the methods used and the accuracy of the final answers. Please make sure that all procedures are clearly shown.

Part 1: Open-Ended

1. The physical condition of seven people is tested after one year's membership in a health club and is compared with their condition before they joined the club. The trainer at the health club claims that membership has improved the health of the seven people. One measure of health is resting pulse rate, with a lower rate generally better (although a rate of zero is *not* good). Let's check at the 0.01 level of significance. The table shows the results.

Member	Pulse Rate Before Membership	Pulse Rate After Membership
1	78	72
2	89	74
3	92	86
4	80	93
5	103	84
6	77	84
7	83	81

Give each of the following:

a.   the null hypothesis.

b.   the alternative hypothesis.

c.   the number of degrees of freedom.

d.   the conditions under which the null is rejected.

e.   the results and conclusion assuming the standard deviation equals 11.3. Can we accept the trainer's claim?

f. questions about the investigation or suggestions that could improve it.

2. State A has a state lottery in which you pick six numbers out of a total 40. If you pick all six correctly, you will become an instant millionaire. In an effort to get some of the lottery income, State B begins a lottery with the offer of a big win if you pick only five numbers. However, to make it more interesting, they increase the total numbers to 48.

   a. Which state lottery does the participant have the better chance of winning? Explain your answer.

   b. If we want to use a coin to demonstrate how difficult it is to win a lottery, how many heads would we have to flip in a row to duplicate winning a lottery when the probability of doing so is one chance in a million?

3. A consumer advocacy group is trying to determine the average useful life of a muffler installed on a particular make of car. We can assume that the standard deviation is a half year.

   a. How big a random sample of these cars should the researchers use to be able to assert with 95% confidence that the sample mean will be off by at most one month?

   b. If the researchers decide that they would prefer to operate at the 99% confidence level, but they can't increase the size of the sample above what they were planning to use already, how big a maximum error must they be willing to allow?

4. A small liberal arts college decides to study the relationship between students' scores on the PSAT verbal test and their grades in a mandatory freshman English composition course. The results are shown in the table.

Student	PSAT Score	English Course Grade
A	47	73
B	49	85
C	50	70
D	60	89
E	62	92
F	71	98

a. Determine the value of the correlation coefficient for the relationship between these variables. The standard deviations for the PSAT scores and for the English grades are 9.4 and 11.0 respectively.

b. Discuss the meaning of the correlation coefficient in terms of the variables being studied.

c. Discuss whether we can say that a significant relationship exists between the PSAT scores and the course grades at the $\alpha = 0.05$ level of significance using the formula for the t test:

$$t = r\sqrt{\frac{n-2}{1-r^2}} \text{ where } d.f. = n - 2$$

5. A railroad freight car filled with coal weighs on the averge 72 tons with a standard deviation of 12 tons. A train of fifty coal cars is compiled. The engine assigned to pull the train can pull a maximum weight of 3,400 tons.

a. What is the probability that the engine will be able to pull the train?

b. If one coal car is removed from the train, what is the new probability that the engine could pull the train?

c. How many coal cars would have to be removed from the original train of fifty cars to give the engine a 50% chance of pulling the train?

Part 2: Investigative Task

1.   The World Series and professional basketball and hockey playoffs involve two teams playing a series in which the first team to win four games wins the series. Our question does not involve the issue of who wins but rather how long the series lasts.

Compare the two series. In the first series, the two teams are evenly matched. In the second series, one team will beat the other on the average 70% of the time.

Simulate 40 series, 20 in which the teams are evenly matched, and 20 in which one team wins an average of 70% of the time.

   a.   Explain how you will do the simulations using a random number table.

   b.   Start in the top left hand corner of the random number table and use columns for your experiment. Draw lines clearly on the table after each series.

   c.   Tally your data and then enter it in a frequency table.

   d.   Determine the average lengths of the two kinds of series and briefly summarize your results.

   e.   Explain what general method you would use on this data to decide whether or not any difference you attained is statistically significant.

AP STATISTICS

Test 2

ANSWER KEY

Section I

1.	(C)	10.	(E)	19.	(C)	28.	(D)
2.	(D)	11.	(C)	20.	(C)	29.	(A)
3.	(E)	12.	(D)	21.	(E)	30.	(D)
4.	(E)	13.	(A)	22.	(C)	31.	(E)
5.	(E)	14.	(C)	23.	(D)	32.	(C)
6.	(D)	15.	(B)	24.	(D)	33.	(B)
7.	(C)	16.	(A)	25.	(A)	34.	(B)
8.	(D)	17.	(B)	26.	(E)	35.	(B)
9.	(D)	18.	(E)	27.	(C)		

DETAILED EXPLANATIONS OF ANSWERS

Test 2

Section I

1. **(C)** The data is ratio, because the same intervals or differences between values mean the same thing no matter what the value of the data, and there is a meaningful zero.

2. **(D)** The study of the people in one small geographical area when the population covers a large area is called cluster sampling. The sample area may be chosen at random, but the investigation of the people in the chosen area is called cluster sampling, not random sampling.

3. **(E)** Class boundaries are halfway between upper and lower limits of successive classes. Therefore the lower class boundary of Class IV is halfway between the upper limit of Class III and the lower limit of Class IV, which is located at $(39 + 40)/2 = 39.5$. Similarly, the upper class boundary of Class IV is located halfway between the upper class limit of Class IV and the lower class limit of Class V, or at $(49 + 50)/2$, or 49.5.

4. **(E)** None of the mistakes listed in (A) through (D) are evident in the frequency table. Therefore, there are no mistakes.

5. **(E)** The mean is the sum of the data, 476, divided by the number of terms, 17, which yields 28. The median is the ninth term—determined by $(n + 1)/2$, or $18/2 = 9$—when the terms are listed in order. This is also 28. The mode is the term which occurs the most, which is 38. Therefore, mean = median < mode.

6. **(D)** This is an example of a weighted mean problem, where the weighted mean is given, and the mean of one of the partial weights has to be determined. The equation is

$$\bar{x}_w = \frac{\sum w_i x_i}{\sum w_i}$$

where w_i is the weight or number of a particular value x_i. Here

$$\bar{x}_w = 20$$
$$w_1 = 12$$
$$x_1 = 19 \text{ days}$$
$$w_2 = 4$$
$$x_2 = ?$$
$$\sum w = 12 + 4 = 16$$

So,

$$20 = \frac{(12)(19) + 4x}{16}$$

Solving for x, yields $4x = 320 - 228$ or $x = 23$ days.

7. **(C)** Negatively skewed data may be represented by a curve as shown.

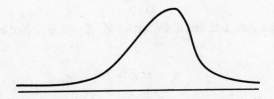

For this curve, the highest point represents the mode, which is on the right. Because the data spreads to the left, the median is to the left of the mode. Because there are are a few values of the data which are quite low, off to the left, the value of the mean is dropped below that of the median. So the order from left to right is: mean-median-mode

8. **(D)** The modal class is the class with the greatest frequency, in this case, Class II with frequency 17. The mode is considered to be located at the center of this class, halfway between 55 and 59, or 57.

9. **(D)** If you compare equations for the means and standard deviations for samples and populations, the only difference is in the

denominators of the standard deviations. For a population, the denominator under the square root is *N*, whereas the denominator under the square root for a sample is *n* − *1*. The −*1* makes the denominator of the sample expression smaller than the population expression, and therefore makes the *whole* expression larger for the sample than it is for the population. So the means are the same, and the standard deviation for the sample is larger than that for the population.

10. **(E)**   Using the standard normal probability table, we know that when the area under the normal curve to the left of Z is approximately equal to 0.25 i.e, when half the area under curve lies between +Z and −Z, Z = 0.675. We know that

$$Z = \frac{x - \mu}{\sigma}$$

We know *x* = 60 and μ, halfway between 60 and 100, is 80. Solving the formula for σ yields

$$\sigma = \frac{x - \mu}{Z}$$
$$= \frac{60 - 80}{-.675}$$
$$= 29.6$$

If 95% of the area lies between +Z and −Z, Z = 1.96. Solving the formula for *X* yields

$$x = \sigma Z + \mu$$

or

$$x = (29.6)(1.96) + 80$$
$$\approx 138$$

The closest answer is 140.

11. **(C)**   Percentile is calculated by counting the number of terms below the one you are interested in, adding 0.5 to this value, and determining what percent this number is of the total number of terms. In this case there are five people below Player E, and a total of ten players. The percentile is given by

$$\frac{(5 + 0.5)}{10} \text{ or } 55\%.$$

12. **(D)** The interquartile range is given by $Q_3 - Q_1 \cdot Q_3$ is given by counting 75% or three-quarters of the way up the list of terms and then a half term more. In this case 75% of 12 terms is 9 terms, and a half term more is halfway between the ninth and tenth terms, which is halfway between 31 and 33, or at 32. Similarly, Q_1 is given by counting 25% or one-quarter of the way up the list of terms, which takes us to 25% of 12, or the third term. A half term more brings us halfway between the third and fourth terms, or halway between 24 and 26, or at 25. The interquartile range, then, is $32 - 25$, or 7.

13. **(A)** This can be done in two different ways. First, multiply probabilities, and we get (12/52)(11/51)(10/50), which equals 0.00995 or approximately 0.1%. Second, we can use the hypergeometric formula, which yields the same answer as the first method. The hypergeometric formula is:

$$f(x) = \frac{{}_aC_x \cdot {}_bC_{(n-x)}}{{}_{(a+b)}C_n}$$

where a and b are C complementary parts of a whole, x is the number chosen out of a, and n is the total number chosen.

Here

$$f(3) = \frac{\binom{12}{3}\binom{40}{0}}{\binom{52}{3}}$$

$$f(3) = \frac{(220)(1)}{(22,100)}$$

$$f(3) = .00995$$

$$f(3) \approx 0.1\%$$

14. **(C)** There are two convenient ways to do this problem. Either set up a conditional probability table, or draw the appropriate Venn diagram. Here is the conditional probability table:

	H	H'	
B	30	15	45
B'	45	10	55
	75	25	100

B: Parks with boating

H: Parks with hiking

The Venn diagram is drawn as follows:

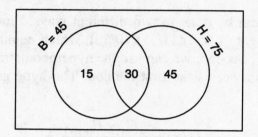

Students should be careful with the expression "Forty percent of the parks that have hiking have boating," since this means that 40% of 75, or 30 of the parks with hiking have boating. To conclude, look at the total number of parks with boating (45) and see how many of them have hiking (30), so the final answer is 30/45, or 2/3. Formally,

$$P\left(\frac{H}{B}\right) = \frac{P(H \cap B)}{P(B)}$$
$$= \frac{30}{45}$$
$$= \frac{2}{3}$$

15. **(B)** Use the equation for expectation: $E(X) = \sum x_i p_i$, where in this case, x_i is the number of children, and p_i is the probability of having that number.

$$E(X) = 0(.20) + 1(.20) + 2(.30) + 4(.08) + 5(.02)$$
$$E(X) = 1.82, \text{ or } 1.8 \text{ to the nearest tenth}$$

16. **(A)** This problem is easy to do with a binomial distribution table. If one is available, $n = 20$, $x = 8, 9, 10$, etc., for $p = 0.2$. We get a value of 8 for x since 40% of 20 is 8. Just add the values in the table, which in this

case are, for 8, 9, and 10, 0.022, 0.007, and 0.002 respectively, which totals to 0.031, or approximately 3%. If this table is not available, use the binomial equation once, for $x = 8$.

$$f(x) = {_nC_x}\, p^x \, (1-p)^{n-x}$$
$$f(8) = {_{20}C_8}\, (0.2)^8 \, (0.8)^{12} = .022.$$

At this point, the student should look at the possible answers, realize that $f(9)$ and $f(10)$ will drop off quickly in value, and conclude that the sum will have to be around 3%. (They will drop off quickly in value because the mean is $(0.2)\,(20) = 4$, and 9 and 10 are further from the mean. The student might approach this using the normal curve approximation to the binomial distribution. Using the standard normal distribution table will yield, for z calculated at 1.96, a tail area of 0.025. Using the t-distribution table and interpolating for 19 degrees of freedom will yield a tail area of approximately 0.035. In both cases, the closest answer is 3%.

17. **(B)**   There are six times six or thirty-six ways to throw sums of 2 to 12 with two dice. There are six ways to throw a 7. With the first number representing the first die, and the second number representing the second, the six ways are $1 + 6$; $2 + 5$; $3 + 4$; $4 + 3$; $5 + 2$; and $6 + 1$. There are two ways to throw an 11: $5 + 6$ and $6 + 5$. So there are six plus two or eight ways to throw a 7 or an 11. Out of thirty-six total ways, eight represents $8/36$ or $2/9$ of the total. If the dice are thrown 100 times, a sum of 7 or 11 will appear $2/9$ of the time, or

$$\left(\frac{2}{9}\right) \cdot 100 \approx 22 \text{ times.}$$

18. **(E)**   Using the standard normal probability table, the z associated with a tail area of 0.0075 is +2.43. Since this is an area to the *right* of z, the value of z must be positive.

19. **(C)**   Use the normal curve approximation to the binomial distribution.

$$\mu = nP$$
$$= (10,000)(.5)$$
$$\mu = 5,000$$
$$\sigma = \sqrt{\mu p(1-p)}$$
$$= \sqrt{5000(.5)}$$

$$= \sqrt{2500}$$

$$\underline{\sigma = 50}$$

$$z = \frac{x - \mu}{\sigma}$$

$$= \frac{5100.5 - 5000}{50} \text{ by the continuity correction.}$$

$$= \frac{100.5}{50}$$

$$\underline{\underline{z = 2.01}}$$

The tail area for z is <u>0.0222</u>, as shown in the normal curve table.

20. **(C)** The size of the confidence interval is given by $\left(\bar{x} + E_{max}\right) - \left(\bar{x} - E_{max}\right)$ which equals $2E_{max}$. So

$$E_{max} = \frac{1}{2} \text{ (size of confidence interval)}$$

Here the size of the interval is $18.0 - 16.6$ or 1.4 so

$$E_{max} = \frac{1}{2} (1.4) = 0.7.$$

We know

$$z_{\alpha/2} = \frac{E}{\dfrac{\sigma}{\sqrt{n}}}$$

Here

$$z_{\alpha/2} = \frac{0.7}{\dfrac{8.0}{\sqrt{100}}}$$

or

$$\underline{z_{\alpha/2} = 2.33}$$

From the normal curve table,

$$\frac{\alpha}{2} \approx 0.01$$

so

$$\alpha \approx 0.02$$

So the degree of confidence is given by

$$1 - \alpha$$

or

$$1 - .02$$

which equals .98 or 98%.

21. **(E)** For a proportion,

$$z_{\alpha/2} = \frac{E\max}{\sigma \hat{p}}, \text{ where } \sigma\hat{p} = \sqrt{\frac{p(1-p)}{n}}$$

so

$$z_{\alpha/2} = \frac{E}{\sqrt{\dfrac{p(1-p)}{n}}}$$

we want to find n so solving for n yields

$$z_{\alpha/2} = \frac{E\sqrt{n}}{\sqrt{p(1-p)}}$$

or

$$\sqrt{n} = \sqrt{p(1-p)} \cdot \frac{z_{\alpha/2}}{E}$$

squaring

$$n = p(1-p)\left(\frac{z_{\alpha/2}}{E_{\max}}\right)^2$$

Here

$$p = .65, 1-p = .85, z_{\alpha/2} = 575, \text{ and } E_{\max} = 0.08$$

so

$$n = (.65)(.35)\left(\frac{2.575}{0.08}\right)^2$$

$$n = 235.7$$

so $n = 236$.

22. **(C)** With 12 people, $n = 12$ and $df = n - 1 = 11$. Since she does not know whether she thinks the earlier conclusion is high or low, she is doing a two-tailed test. If $\alpha = 1.0\%$ or 0.01, $\alpha/2 = 0.005$. From the t-distribution table, for $df = 11$ and tail probability .005, $t = 3.106$.

23. **(D)** In relating the independent and dependent variables, Graph N shows a strong relationship, because the points are right on or close to the line. Graph M, with points scattered off the line, shows a weaker, less clear relationship, with a stronger relationship $| r_N | > | r_M |$. However, since both lines slant down as they move to the right, the slopes and correlation coefficients are negative. So r_N is close in value to -1, while r_M is closer to zero than r_N. Therefore $r_N < r_M$. So looking at our choices, I and II are both true; III is not.

24. **(D)** This question is best answered using a Venn Diagram. $P(C) = 70\%$; $P(S) = 40\%$; $P(C \cap S) = 30\%$.

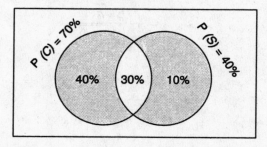

From the diagram, $40\% + 10\% = 50\%$. Alternatively the formula for the shaded area is

$$P(C) + P(S) - 2 \cdot P(C \cap S) \text{ or } 70\% + 40\% - 2(30\%) = 50\%$$

25. **(A)** In this x^2 test for independence, the number of degrees of freedom is given by $(R - 1)(C - 1)$, where R is the number of rows and C is the number of columns. Here $R = 4$ and $C = 3$, so $DF = (4 - 1)(3 - 1) = 6$. Using the x^2 table, the critical x^2 value is 12.59 at the 0.05 level of significance.

26. **(E)** If the dependent variable is going to have double the value of the independent variable, the equation is $\hat{y} = 2x$. So the regression line value of $\hat{y}$ will have to equal $2x$. So $65 + 2x = 2x$. Subtracting $2x$ from both sides yields $65 = 0$, which is impossible. So there is no value of x that will allow the dependent variable to have double the value of the independent variable.

27. **(C)** For the regression line $\hat{y} = b_0 + b_1x$, the averages of the variables follow the same relationship: $\bar{y} = b_0 + b_1\bar{x}$

Here

$$\bar{x} = \frac{\sum x_i}{n} = \frac{2+5+8+9+11}{5} = 7$$

so

$$\bar{y} = 250 - 3\bar{x} = 250 - 3(7)$$
$$\bar{y} = 229$$

28. **(D)** The coefficient of determination, r^2, gives the percentage of the variation in y that can be attributed to changes in x through the relationship revealed in the associated regression line. Here, $r^2 = 0.7^2 = 0.49$. So 0.49 of the variation in y can be attributed to changes in x, and $1 - 0.49 = 0.51$ therefore cannot be attributed.

29. **(A)** If $|r|$ is close to 1, there is a strong relationship. When r is positive, the slope of the regression line is positive and y increases when x does. Unfortunately, an $|r|$ close to 1 does not prove causality, since the variables might be varying in a similar way by coincidence. Depending on the actual research situation, $|r|$ close to 1 might suggest the strong possibility of causality, but it does not always prove it. Therefore I and III are true.

30. **(D)** The classic Placebo Effect is the improvement in the patient when given a pill that has no medicinal value. This effect has been generalized to the change in the control subject who is *not* subjected to the independent variable, or the experimental intervention, but still changes as a result of the attention involved in being part of the experiment itself.

31. **(E)** Subject matching is the practice of taking pairs of similar people and randomly assigning one to the experimental group and the

other to the control group. This is done to make the two groups as similar as possible and to make it more likely that changes observed in the groups are due to the experiment and not due to differences in the backgrounds or characteristics of the group members.

32. **(C)** The probability that *B* will win the next game is 0.5. In order for *B* to win the series, they must win the next game also. The probability of doing that is also 0.5. Multiplying probabilities,

$$(0.5)(0.5) = 0.25 \text{ or } \frac{1}{4}.$$

33. **(B)** Blocking involves dividing the data into different blocks representing different levels of an extraneous factor. Without dealing for the extraneous factor in this manner, either experimental error could increase, or the data would be limited to less heterogeneous groups and could not be generalized as widely. An example would be studying the physical fitness of college students and not accounting for the different environments of the students in a big-city school and of those in a small school in a rural environment. Students with comparable fitness levels within their own schools could be blocked together to make the research more generalizable.

34. **(B)** For the *t*-test, the value of the degree of freedom is one less than the size of the sample. In this case *n* = 8, so *df* = 7. This is a one-tailed test because the researcher is trying to determine whether one method is better than another one. According to the *t* distribution table, the critical *t* value for *df* = 7 is 1.895. This should be a positive value since we are subtracting before scores from after scores, and the after scores should be higher if the new teaching method is having an effect.

35. **(B)** This relationship is a power regression. The closest one in appearance is the exponential regression, given by $y = ab^x$. As the value of *x* increases, the exponential regression curve will eventually rise more sharply than the power regression curve.

Section II

Part 1

1. a.   The null hypothesis is that the rates are equal: $\mu_B = \mu_A$ B: Before; A: After.

    b.   The trainer from the health club claims that members pulse rate is lower: $\mu_A < \mu_B$ of $\mu_A - \mu_B < 0$

    c.   d.f. $= n - 1 = 6$

    d.   Null is rejected if $t < -3.143$

x_B	x_A	$x_B - x_A$
78	72	−6
89	74	−15
92	86	−6
80	93	13
103	84	−19
77	84	7
83	81	−2

$$\sum(x_A - x_B) = -28$$

$$\overline{x_A - x_B} = \frac{-28}{7} = -4$$

$$t = \frac{(\overline{x_A - x_B}) - (\mu_A - \mu_B)}{\dfrac{s}{\sqrt{n}}}$$

$$t = \frac{-4 - 0}{\dfrac{11.3}{\sqrt{7}}}$$

$$t = -0.94$$

    e.   We cannot reject the null hypothesis because t is not less than −3.143. Therefore, we cannot accept the trainer's claim.

f.   There are many other factors that affect health besides participation in a health club. Physical illness, diet and nutrition, stress level, and
the use of alcohol or drugs are all factors that can affect health. Did the
researcher conducting the control for any of these factors? If so, which
factors and how did they control these factors? Also, people who are
members of health clubs can go to the club on a regular schedule or
irregularly. They can also go frequently (a few times a week) or infre-
quently (once a month). What was the participation rate of the people
chosen for the study?

2.   a.   The probability of picking 6 numbers correctly out of 40 is

$$\frac{1}{\binom{40}{6}}$$

or 1 out of 8,888,880. The probability of picking 5 numbers correctly out
of 48 is

$$\frac{1}{\binom{48}{5}}$$

or 1 out of 1,712,304. Obviously the participant has a better chance playing in State B.

b.   The probability of flipping n heads in a row with a balanced
coin is

$$P = \frac{1}{2^n}.$$

If $P = \dfrac{1}{1,000,000}$, then

$$\frac{1}{2^n} = \frac{1}{1,000,000}$$

or $2^n = 1,000,000$. Taking the log of both sides yields

$$\log 2^n = \log 1,000,000$$

or

$$n \log 2 = 6.$$
$$\log 2 = .35103$$

so

$$n = 19.93$$

or

$$n \approx 20.$$

So we would have to flip 20 heads in a row.

3. a.   The size of the sample is given by

$$n = \left(\frac{z\sigma}{E}\right)^2$$

Here, for confidence level = 95%, $z = 1.96$. If we use months as our time units, $\sigma = 6$ and $E = 1$. So,

$$n = \left[\frac{(1.96)(6)}{(1)}\right]^2$$
$$n = 138.29$$

Sample sizes are always rounded up to the next whole number, so

$$n = 139.$$

   b.   Solving the equation above for E,

$$E = \frac{z \cdot \sigma}{\sqrt{n}}$$

for confidence level = 99%, $z = 2.575$. So

$$E = \frac{(2.575)(6)}{\sqrt{139}}$$

or

$$E = 1.31$$

Therefore they would have to allow a maximum error of 1.31 months instead of 1 month.

4. a.

x	$x - \bar{x}$	y	$y - \bar{y}$	$(x - \bar{x})(y - \bar{y})$
47	−9.5	78	−11.5	109.25
49	−7.5	85	0.5	−3.75
50	−6.5	70	−14.5	94.25
60	3.5	89	4.5	15.75
62	5.5	92	7.5	41.25
71	14.5	98	13.5	195.75

$$\Sigma_x = 339 \qquad \Sigma_y = 507$$

$$\bar{x} = \frac{339}{6} = 56.5 \qquad \bar{y} = \frac{507}{6} = 84.5$$

$$\Sigma(x - \bar{x})(y - \bar{y}) = 452.5$$

$$r = \frac{1}{n-1} \Sigma \left(\frac{x - \bar{x}}{s_x} \right) \left(\frac{y - \bar{y}}{s_y} \right)$$

$$= \frac{1}{5} \frac{(452.5)}{(9.40)(11.0)}$$

$$r = 0.875$$

b. This value of r indicates a fairly strong positive correlation between PSAT scores and college performance.

c. $$t = r\sqrt{\frac{n-2}{1-r^2}}$$

$$= (.875)\sqrt{\frac{6-2}{1-(.875)^2}}$$

$$t = 3.61$$

From the t-table, the critical t values are $\neq 2.776$ since $3.61 > 2.776$. A significant relationship does exist.

5. a. The maximum weight the engine can pull is 3,400 tons or

$$\frac{3,400}{50} = 68 \text{ tons/car (average car weight)}$$

Represented on the normal curve,

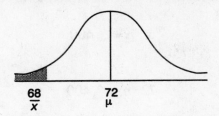

68
$\overline{x}$

72
μ

we see that the shaded area represents the probability of the engine pulling the train.

$$z = \frac{\overline{x} - \mu}{\frac{\sigma}{\sqrt{n}}}$$

so

$$z = \frac{68 - 72}{\frac{12}{\sqrt{50}}}$$

or

$$z = 2.36$$

The area to the left of z is approximately 0.01 or 1%. The probability is 1%.

b.   We use the same reasoning, but n is now 49. The engine could pull an average coal car weighing

$$\frac{3,400}{49} = 69.4 \text{ tons}$$

$$z = \frac{69.4 - 72}{\frac{12}{\sqrt{49}}}$$

$$z = -1.52.$$

The area to the left of z is 0.0643 or approximately 0.06 or 6%.

c.   For the engine to have a 50% chance of pulling the train, the average weight of the train should equal 3,400 tons. This means that the product of the average car weight and the number of cars should equal 3,400. So,

$$\bar{x} \cdot n = 3,400$$

or

$$72 \cdot n = 3,400$$

or

$$n = 47.2$$

to the nearest whole number, $n = 47$. Therefore three coal cars would have to be removed for the engine to have about a 50% chance of pulling the train. Checking this result yields

$$\bar{x} = \frac{3,400}{47} = 72.3 \text{ tons}$$

$$z = \frac{72.3 - 72}{\frac{12}{\sqrt{47}}}$$

$$z = 0.17$$

The area to the left of z is .5675 or 57%. This is somewhat greater than 50%, but we cannot get closer because n has to be a whole number.

Section II

Part 2

1. a. Call the teams *A* and *B*. For the even series, let any five digits represent a team *A* win and the other five digits a team *B* win. For example, digits 0, 1, 2, 3, and 4 could represent a team *A* win, while digits 5, 6, 7, 8, and 9 would represent a team *B* win. Another method could have even digits represent a team *A* win and odd digits a team *B* win. This is the method used in part 2 here.

For the uneven series, let any 7 digits represent a team *A* win and the other 3 digits a team *B* win. For example, digits 1, 2, 3, 4, 5, 6, and 7 could represent team *A* winning, while digits 8, 9, and 0 would represent team *B* winning. This is the method used in part 2 here. Another method could have non-perfect squares represent team *A* winning (2, 3, 5, 6, 7, 8, 0) and perfect squares represent team *B* winning (1, 4, 9).

b. and c.   Random Numbers*

Series 1 Start	Series 2 Start					
24418	23608	91507	76455	54941	72711	39406
57404	73678	08272	62941	02349	71389	45605
77644	98489	86268	73652	98210	44546	27174
68366	65614	01443	07067	11826	91326	29664
64472	72294	95432	53555	96810	17100	35066
88205	37913	98633	81009	81060	33449	68055
98455	78685	71250	10329	56135	80647	51404
48977	36794	56054	59243	57361	65304	93258
93077	72941	92779	23581	24548	56415	61927
84533	26564	91583	83411	66504	02036	02922
11338	12903	14514	27585	45068	05520	56321
23853	68500	92274	87026	99717	01542	72990
94096	74920	25822	98026	05394	61840	83089
83160	82362	09350	98536	38155	42661	02363
97425	47335	69709	01386	74319	04318	99387
83951	11954	24317	20345	18134	90062	10761
93085	35203	05740	03026	92012	42710	24650
33762	83193	58045	89880	78101	44392	53767
49665	85397	85137	30496	23469	42846	94810
37541	82627	80051	72521	35342	56119	97190
22145	85304	35348	82854	55846	18076	12415
27153	08662	61078	52433	22184	33998	87436
00301	49425	66682	25442	83668	66236	79655
43815	43272	73778	63469	50083	70696	13558
14689	86482	74157	46012	97765	27552	49617

Random Numbers (continued)

16680	55936	82453	19532	49988	13176	94219
86938	60429	01137	86168	78257	86249	46134
33944	29219	73161	46061	30946	22210	79302
16045	67736	18608	18198	19468	76358	69203
37044	52523	25627	64107	30806	80857	84383
61471	45322	35340	35132	42163	69332	98851
47422	21296	16785	66393	39249	51463	95963
24133	39719	14484	58613	88717	29289	77360
67253	67064	10748	16006	16767	57345	42285
62382	76941	01635	35829	77516	98468	51686
98011	16503	09201	03523	87192	66483	55649
37366	24386	20654	85117	74078	64120	04643
73587	83993	51476	05221	94119	20108	78101
33583	68291	50547	96085	62180	27453	18567
02878	33223	39199	49536	56199	05993	71201
91498	41673	17195	33175	04994	09879	70337
91127	19815	30219	55591	21725	53827	78862
12997	55013	18662	81724	24305	37661	18956
96098	13651	15393	69995	14762	69734	89150
97627	17837	10472	18983	28387	99781	52977
40064	47981	31484	76603	54088	91095	00010
16239	68743	71374	55863	22672	91609	51514
58354	24913	20435	30965	17453	65623	93058
52567	65085	60220	84641	18273	49604	47418
06236	29052	91392	07551	83532	68131	56970

d.   The average length of a series for even teams, series 1, was

$$\frac{[3(4) + 8(5) + 3(6) + 6(7)]}{20}$$

or

$$\frac{112}{20} = 5.6 \text{ games.}$$

With uneven teams, series 2, the average length was

$$\frac{[10(4) + 5(5) + 2(6) + 3(7)]}{20}$$

or

$$\frac{98}{20} = 4.9 \text{ games.}$$

This result suggests that when the teams are evenly matched, the series lasts longer.

e.   We can either decide on a level of significance, usually 0.05 or 0.01, or use *p*-values. Here, we will let $\propto = 0.05$. Assuming a normal curve distribution, the equation for comparing means of independent samples is

$$z = \frac{\bar{x}_1 - \bar{x}_2}{\sqrt{\dfrac{s_1^2}{n_1} + \dfrac{s_2^2}{n_2}}}.$$

We can calculate s_1 and s_2 using

$$s = \sqrt{\frac{\sum x^2 - \dfrac{(\sum x)^2}{n}}{n-1}}.$$

Using this equation yields $s_1 = 1.10$ and $s_2 = 1.12$.

Substituting all values into the z-equation gives

$$z = \frac{5.6 - 4.9}{\sqrt{\dfrac{(110)^2}{20} + \dfrac{(1.12)^2}{20}}}$$

$$z = 1.99$$

The critical z-value for $\propto = 0.05$ is ± 1.96. Since $1.99 > 1.96$, the difference between the means is significant at the 0.05 level of significance.

Note the following:

(1)   The difference between means would *not* be signficant at the $\propto = 0.01$ level of significance because then the critical z-value is ± 2.575.

(2)   Because $n < 30$ for each set of data, it would be technically correct to use t instead of z. If this is done, $t = 1.99$, but the critical t-value at $\propto = 0.05$ is 2.093, so the difference is *not* significant.

(3)   Theoretical determinations of the average number of games can be made. For the even series

$$\mu = \sum x \cdot f(x)$$

$$\mu = 4\left(\frac{1}{16}\right) + 5\left(\frac{1}{8}\right) + 6\left(\frac{5}{32}\right) + 7\left(\frac{5}{32}\right)$$

$$\mu = 5.81 \text{ games}$$

For the uneven series, the determinations of $f(x)$ for $x = 4, 5, 6, 7$ are a little more complicated, but when performed yield $\mu = 5.33$ games.

Both of our simulated results were relatively close to the theoretically predicted values, 5.6 to 5.81 for the even series and 4.9 to 5.33 for the uneven series.

PRACTICE
TEST 3

AP EXAMINATION IN STATISTICS

Test 3

Section I

TIME: 90 Minutes
35 Multiple-Choice Questions

(Answer sheets appear in the back of this book.)

DIRECTIONS: For each question or incomplete statement in this section, select the best answer from among the five choices and fill in the corresponding oval on the answer sheet.

---

1. The scattergraph below shows the relationship between scores on a music test and scores on a video game. Which of the following numbers best represents the correlation between these two measures?

   (A) 0.95   (D) −0.08

   (B) −0.85   (E) 0.76

   (C) 0.42

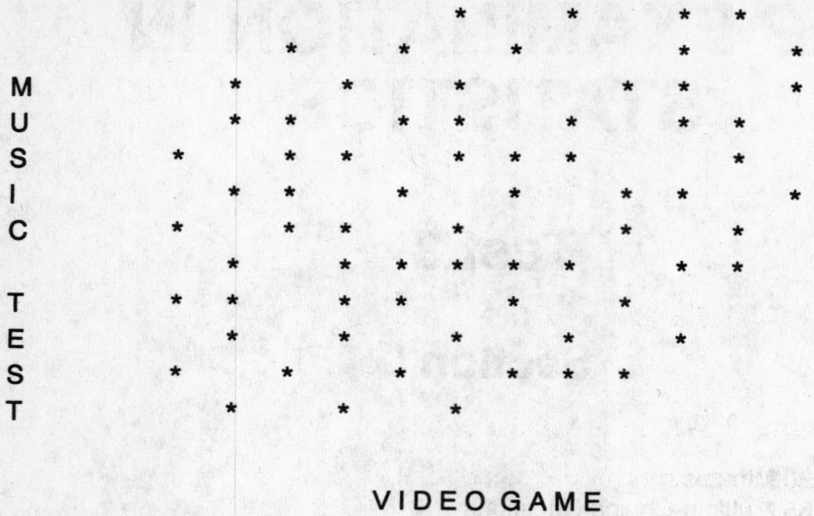

```
M
U
S
I
C

T
E
S
T
```

VIDEO GAME

2. The mean score on a certain standardized test is 500, and the variance is 625. Assuming that Anna's score on this test is a random variable with the same mean and variance as the population, what is the probability that Anna's score falls between 475 and 525?

    (A) 1
    (B) .8413
    (C) .6826

    (D) .1587
    (E) .1335

3. The sanitation department in one city recorded the odometer readings of their older trucks and found that the mean reading was 149, and the standard deviation of the readings was 15. It was later discovered that the readings actually reflected distances above 100. To correct this, a clerk was instructed to add 100 to each of the original readings. All measures are in thousands of miles. The standard deviation of the corrected readings should be

    (A) 1500.
    (B) 150.
    (C) 115.

    (D) 15.
    (E) none of the above.

4. The graph shows the distribution of scores on a standardized mental test. A school counselor deals exclusively with children with exceptional abilities and those who are mentally challenged. He knows that a child who walks into his office has already obtained a score that falls in one of the shaded regions in the graph. If Albert appears in the counselor's office, he must be among

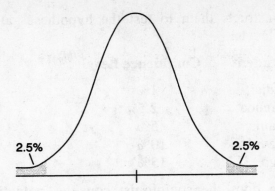

2.5%   2.5%

(A) the top 2.5% of the population.

(B) the bottom 2.5% of the population.

(C) the extreme 5% of the population.

(D) the middle 95% of the population.

(E) the top 97.5% of the population.

5. The table below shows the numbers of male and female students who prefer WordPerfect and Microsoft Word as their word processing software in their writing class. If there were no difference between male students' and female students' choice of a word processor, how many female students should be using WordPerfect?

Choices of Word Processors by Male and Female Students

	Male Students	Female Students	Total
Microsoft Word	7	26	33
WordPerfect	9	6	15
Total	16	32	48

(A) 6   (D) 16

(B) 8   (E) 22

(C) 10

6. In order to test the hypothesis that high school dropouts have a lower self-esteem than those who graduate, a sociologist instructs her students to design their own interview schedules and administer them to representative samples of high school dropouts and graduates. The students analyze their sets of data independently. Based on her knowledge of the students' demonstrated research experi-

ence, she instructs them to test the hypotheses at the following confidence levels:

Student	Confidence Level
Adjai	1%
Brenda	2.5%
Cain	5%
David	10%
Ego	15%

Whose data does the sociologist consider potentially the most reliable?

(A) Adjai

(B) Brenda

(C) Cain

(D) David

(E) Ego

7. A winery hires a group of wine tasters to rate three fruit wines: cherry, grape and strawberry. On the suspicion that the order of tasting would probably affect the tasters' ratings, the manager decides to divide the tasters into three groups and to have them taste the wines in different orders. Which of the following designs is a true Latin square?

(A)

	First	Second	Third
Cherry	Group 3	Group 2	Group 1
Grape	Group 1	Group 3	Group 2
Strawberry	Group 2	Group 1	Group 1

(B)

	First	Second	Third
Cherry	Group 1	Group 3	Group 2
Grape	Group 3	Group 1	Group 2
Strawberry	Group 2	Group 3	Group 1

(C)

	First	Second	Third
Cherry	Group 1	Group 2	Group 3
Grape	Group 3	Group 2	Group 1
Strawberry	Group 2	Group 1	Group 3

(D)

	First	Second	Third
Cherry	Group 3	Group 2	Group 1
Grape	Group 2	Group 3	Group 2
Strawberry	Group 1	Group 1	Group 3

(E)	**First**	**Second**	**Third**
Cherry	Group 3	Group 1	Group 2
Grape	Group 2	Group 3	Group 1
Strawberry	Group 1	Group 2	Group 3

8. Which of the following is *not* a measure of dispersion in a set of data?

   (A) Inter-quartile range   (D) Standard deviation

   (B) Mode   (E) Variance

   (C) Range

9. A few weeks before city council elections, a sociologist must conduct a poll to predict potential winners. With a limited budget, he must conduct the poll in a single location and on one day. In which of the following locations is he likely to obtain the fairest sample?

   (A) A supermarket   (D) A beauty salon

   (B) A movie theater   (E) A church

   (C) A golf club

10. The following frequency table shows how many pairs of shoes of different sizes a shoe store sold in a week. The modal shoe size sold was probably

Size	Pairs
5.5 to under 7.5	25
7.5 to under 9.5	59
9.5 to under 11.5	126
11.5 and larger	84

    (A) under 7.5.   (D) 11.5.

    (B) 7.5.   (E) above 11.5.

    (C) 10.

Use this information to answer questions 11 to 14.

The following frequency chart shows the approximate annual salaries of workers in a computer manufacturing company (in thousands of dollars).

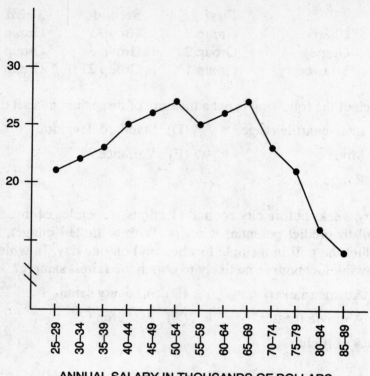

ANNUAL SALARY IN THOUSANDS OF DOLLARS

11. How many workers earn $70,000 or higher?

    (A) 23   (D) 74

    (B) 51   (E) not shown

    (C) 68

12. How many workers earn less than $45,000?

    (A) 118   (D) 26

    (B) 91   (E) not given

    (C) 65

13. To the nearest $100, what is the mean salary of workers who earn over $49,000 but less than $70,000?

    (A) $62,500   (D) $59,200

    (B) $61,700   (E) $57,000

    (C) $59,500

14. To the nearest $50, what is the mean salary of workers who earn $65,000 or more?

   (A) $75,450

   (B) $67,000

   (C) $78,400

   (D) $77,000

   (E) not given

15. A researcher has established that the more highly educated a person is, the greater his/her earning capacity. This suggests that, given a person's educational attainment, we can predict his/her earning capacity. Which of the following statements is true?

   (A) Predictions of earning capacity from educational attainment are uniformly reliable whether they are made from values of educational attainment within or outside the recorded range.

   (B) Predictions of earning capacity from educational attainment are more reliable when made from values of educational attainment below the recorded range of educational attainment than those made from values of educational attainment above the recorded range.

   (C) Predictions of earning capacity from educational attainment are more reliable when made from values of educational attainment above the recorded range of educational attainment than those made from values of educational attainment below the recorded range.

   (D) Predictions of earning capacity from educational attainment are more reliable when made from values of educational attainment within the range of recorded values than those made from values of educational attainment outside the recorded range.

   (E) Predictions of earning capacity from educational attainment are less reliable when made from values of educational attainment within the recorded range than those made from values of educational attainment outside the recorded range.

16. Assuming that a linear relationship has been established between time spent watching violent movies (shown along the horizontal axis) and time spent on war games (shown on the vertical axis), which of the following prediction interval graphs (shown in dotted lines) best represents the relationship?

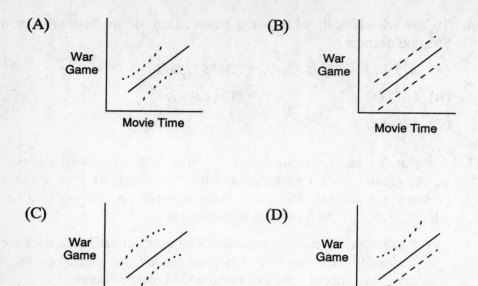

(E)   None of the above graphs

17. In a study of the relationship between study skills and test scores, five tutors took samples of the same size from a large number of students who had enrolled in a skills development class in a college. Each tutor predicted test scores from the corresponding study skills ratings and then computed the mean square error from the data. Which of the following mean square error values indicates the most accurate predictions of test scores from study skills ratings?

(A) 345.37   (D) 501.54

(B) 463.63   (E) 529.83

(C) 493.896

18. A dentist found that the coefficient of correlation between the time patients spend brushing their teeth and the whiteness of those teeth was 0.8. This suggests that

(A) 80% of people who brush their teeth have white teeth.

(B) 80% of the variations in the whiteness of people's teeth can be explained by variations in the time they spend brushing their teeth.

(C) 36% of the variations in the whiteness of people's teeth can be explained by variations in the time they spend brushing their teeth.

(D) 64% of the variations in the time people spend brushing their teeth can be explained by variations in the degree of whiteness of their teeth.

(E) 64% of the variations in the whiteness of people's teeth can be explained by variations in the time they spend brushing their teeth.

19. If the coefficient of correlation between two variables is 0.93, then the corresponding coefficient of determination would be

(A) 0.07.   (D) 0.93.

(B) 0.14.   (E) 0.96.

(C) 0.86.

20. Which of the following considerations compel(s) the researcher to employ random sampling whenever possible?

    I.   Random selection minimizes bias.
    II. Most test statistics assume a random distribution of the underlying phenomenon.
    III. Random selection saves time and labor.

(A) I and II   (D) I only

(B) II and III   (E) III only

(C) I and III

21. After scoring a statistics test, a teacher discovered that:

    I.   The scores ranged from 52 to 96 points.
    II. The median score was 81.
    III. 25 percent of the students scored 64 points or less.
    IV. 75 percent of the students scored 92 points or less.

Which of the following expressions would yield the closest value of the inter-quartile range?

(A) $\dfrac{81-52}{2}$ (D) $\dfrac{92-52}{2}$

(B) $\dfrac{96-64}{2}$ (E) none of these

(C) $\dfrac{92-64}{2}$

22. Which of the following are good reasons for blocking data in an experiment involving multiple measures?

   I.   To reduce within-subject variability
   II. To make statistical analysis more manageable
   III. To aid interpretation of the results of subsequent analyses
   IV. To increase the reliability of the data

   (A) I and II   (D) I and III

   (B) II and III   (E) II and IV

   (C) III and IV

23. Many football players and sports fans have such large feet that their sneakers have to be custom made. In a football stadium, which of the following would be an appropriate measure of the average shoe size of the players and spectators combined?

   (A) The mean   (D) The range

   (B) The median   (E) Any of the above

   (C) The mode

24. The table shows the numbers of women and men under 35 years old, by age group, serving as volunteer fire fighters in one city. The fire chief wishes to test the null hypothesis that there is no significant difference between the distributions of male and female volunteers in the various age categories. Which of the following figures most closely approximates the chi-square value associated with the difference between the observed and the expected frequencies in this table?

Distribution of Volunteer Fire Fighters by Gender

	18 - 24	25 - 29	30 - 34
Female	17	23	30
Male	22	40	36
Total	39	63	66

(A) 6.149

(B) 1.590

(C) 1.138

(D) 1.026

(E) 0.443

Use this information to answer questions 25 and 26.

In a class of 28, 11 students take engineering courses, 16 take biology, and 16 study chemistry. Five of the students study both engineering and biology; 9 study both biology and chemistry, and 3 study both chemistry and engineering. Two of the students study biology, chemistry, and engineering. The names of the 28 students are placed in a bag and a teacher draws a name blindly.

25. The first name drawn is that of a biology student. What is the probability that this student also studies chemistry?

(A) $\frac{9}{16}$

(B) $\frac{16}{49}$

(C) $\frac{9}{28}$

(D) $\frac{4}{7}$

(E) $\frac{16}{23}$

26. The first name drawn is that of an engineering student. What is the probability that this student also studies biology?

(A) $\frac{5}{28}$

(B) $\frac{8}{11}$

(C) $\frac{11}{49}$

(D) $\frac{5}{16}$

(E) $\frac{11}{28}$

Use this information to answer questions 27 to 29.

The following cumulative frequency histogram shows the distribution of social studies test scores obtained by seniors in one high school.

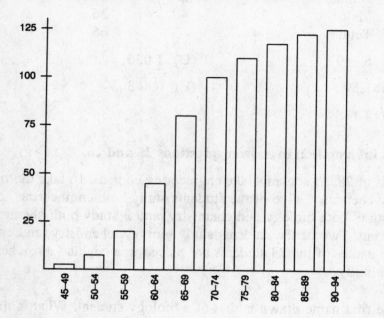

27. What is the median score on the test?

(A) 72

(D) 62.5

(B) 69.5

(E) 62

(C) 67

28. What score corresponds to the 80th percentile?

(A) 80

(D) 69.5

(B) 74.5

(E) 67

(C) 73

29. What percentile corresponds to a score of 64.5?

(A) 62.5

(D) 59.5

(B) 64.5

(E) 36

(C) 62

30. The table shows science test scores obtained by groups of fourth-graders in different rooms.

Group A: 82 74 69 92 84 75 81 90 77 83 88 81 76 79 84 73 83 85 90 96
Group B: 64 72 67 81 77 60 80 74 68 64 79 72 64 66 76 74 81 83 65 73
Group C: 89 76 83 90 88 79 75 85 77 81 80 92 73 69 88 74 73 78 69 82
Group D: 89 92 74 86 90 70 82 85 78 75 81 88 91 73 85 86 92 77 87 79

Working cooperatively, four high school students constructed the following boxplots to provide a pictorial summary of the data.

Which of the following plots accurately represents the set of data on which it is based?

(A) Group A

(B) Group B

(C) Group C

(D) Group D

(E) none of them

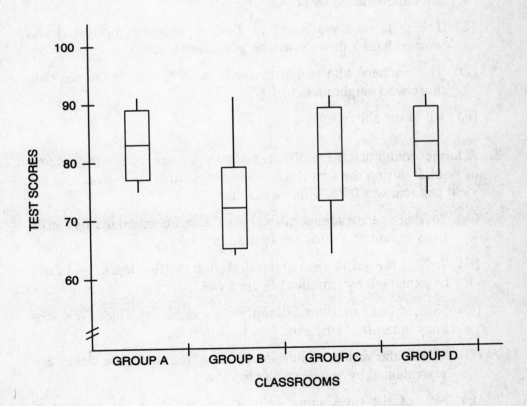

31. In 1994, the mean mathematics scores of graduating boys and girls were 87 and 82. The difference was statistically significant at the 99% level. In 1995, the school was segregated; boys and girls were located in different wings, under entirely different administrations and staff. At the end of the school year, the mean scores of the graduating boys and girls on a common mathematics test were 88 and 87, respectively. The one-point difference was not statistically significant.

Which of the following arguments, put forward by anti-segregation advocates, merit(s) serious attention as plausible explanations for the girls' "catching up with the boys"?

(A) The boys and girls who graduated in 1996 had equal mathematical ability, while the boys who graduated in 1995 were more mathematically inclined than the girls.

(B) Girls learn mathematical concepts and perform better when they are not distracted by boys.

(C) The girls who graduated in 1996 were more motivated and worked harder than those who graduated in 1995.

(D) The teachers who taught the girls in 1996 worked harder than those who taught them in 1995.

(E) All of the above.

32. A farmer found that the coefficient of correlation between the amount of rainfall during the first three weeks of planting their crop, and the yield per acre was 0.76. This means that

(A) 76% of the variations in crop yield can be explained by variations in rainfall during the first three weeks.

(B) 76% of the variations in rainfall during the first three weeks can be explained by variations in crop yield.

(C) 58% of the variations in crop yield can be explained by variations in rainfall during the first three weeks.

(D) 58% of the variations in rainfall during the first three weeks can be explained by variations in crop yield.

(E) 76% of the time, crop yield is dependent on the amount of rainfall during the first three weeks.

33. Let $r^2 = 0.75$ be the coefficient of determination for the regression of years as an actor on the actor's popularity (measured by the size of the fan club). This means that the coefficient of correlation between years as an actor **and** popularity is

(A) 0.75　　　　　　　(D) 0.25

(B) 0.87　　　　　　　(E) 0.17

(C) 0.56

Use this information to answer questions 34 and 35.

A sociology professor challenged four of her students with the task of designing and conducting independent studies to test the hypothesis that exposure to violent movies induces violent behaviors in teenagers. The movie identified as the most potent for this study is "Reasons and Methods to Kill." and tendency to commit violence is measured by an attitude questionnaire on which teenagers rate their willingness to commit violence. Here is a summary of the research designs employed by the students.

	Design 1	Design 2	Design 3	Design 4
Sample size	48	48	24	48
No. of groups	2	2	1	2
Composition	in each group, 12 boys and 12 girls who never saw the movie before	in one group, 12 boys and 12 girls who never saw the movie before; same numbers who saw the movie in next group	12 boys, 12 girls who have seen the movie before	in each group, 12 boys and 12 girls who never saw the movie before
How selected from population	random selection	random selection	random selection	random selection
How assigned to groups	randomly	—	—	matched in pairs, by gender, on pretest score
Pretest?	yes	no	yes	yes
Treatment	one group saw the real movie; the other group watched a comedy	none	everybody saw the real movie	one group saw the real movie; the other group did not
Posttest	yes	yes	yes	yes
Analysis	t-test for significance of diff. between change scores	t-test for diff. between independent means	t-test for significance of change scores	t-test for significance of diff. between change scores

34. Which of the research designs best illustrate(s) basic principles of a scientific experiment?

    (A) 1 and 2
    (B) 2 and 3
    (C) 2 and 4

    (D) 1 and 4
    (E) none of them

35. Which of these research designs would potentially yield the most generalizable result?

    (A) 1
    (B) 2
    (C) 3

    (D) 4
    (E) none of them

Section II

TIME: 90 Minutes
6 Free-Response Questions

DIRECTIONS: Show all your work. Grading will be based on both the methods used and the accuracy of the final answers. Please make sure that all procedures are clearly shown.

Part 1: Open-Ended

1. In an exploratory study designed to investigate the relationship between mathematical reasoning and age in the age range 10 to 19, a single spatial reasoning test was administered to groups of five boys and five girls randomly selected at each age level. Here are the scores. The scores in the table are the median scores of the 10 students in each group.

Relationship between Age and Spatial Reasoning Test Score

Position (i)	1	2	3	4	5	6	7	8	9	10
Age (a)	10	11	12	13	14	15	16	17	18	19
Score (s)	65	63	70	73	81	79	81	80	83	85

Assuming that a linear relationship exists, compute m, the slope of the regression of age on spatial reasoning test score. You may use the formula

$$m = \frac{\sum(a_i - \bar{a})(s_i - \bar{s})}{\sum(a_i - \bar{a})^2}$$

where a_i is the age of group i; $\bar{a}$ is the mean age of all groups; s_i is the spatial test score of group i; and $\bar{s}$ is the mean spatial test score of all groups [$i = 1, 2, 3, ..., 10$].

2. A final examination in geology consists of a set of open-ended questions and a set of 10 multiple-choice questions. Anjie took her time to answer the open-ended questions and is confident that she has already scored 85 points from that section. However, discovering that she has

not enough time to answer the questions in the multiple-choice section, she resorts to random guessing. There are five options per question and the minimum score for an A grade is 90.

a.   If Anjie guesses randomly without first eliminating any of the options, what is the probability that Anjie selects the correct answer for a particular item?

b.   What is the probability that Anjie would earn a grade of an A?

3.   A computer software company employs a total of 25 persons. The following figures show their annual gross earnings:

1.   One Manager: $95,000

2.   One Senior Analyst: $85,000

3.   Four Programmers: $30,000 each

4.   Five Salespersons: $21,000 each

5.   14 Others (dispatchers, secretaries, receptionists, etc.): $18,000 each

a.   In a dispute between the company and the workers, which of the three averages (mean, median or mode) would the union representatives quote to support their claim that the company is "robbing" the workers?

b.   Which average would the company's attorney use to suggest that the company pays highly competitive salaries? Use figures in this question to explain your answer.

4.   The passing score on a standardized reasoning test is 75. The mean score on the test is $\mu = 70$ and the variance is $\sigma^2 = 100$. Assuming that Judy's score on this test is a random variate with the same mean and variance as the general population, what is the probability that she passes?

5.   An assistant teacher graded 15 essays anonymously. Using a basic calculator, she found that the average rating was 81. The assistant teacher used a secret code to identify the students who submitted the essays in order to record their ratings. Ann, fearing that she had failed, sneaked in and stole her own paper before the secret code was used. [She planned to ask for a chance to re-submit or to claim a higher rating than she actually earned on her essay.] If the homeroom teacher finds that the average rating of the remaining essays was 83, what was Ann's essay rating?

Part 2: Investigative Task

1. A philosophy professor administered a pretest to his 250 students at the beginning of the semester. He graded all the papers and arranged them alphabetically. Eager to get a quick preview of the caliber of students in his new class, he asked his graduate assistant to compute the mean score of the first 25 papers on the pile. The obtained average was 85.65. The professor does not trust the method by which the graduate assistant selected the sample. He gives *you* 25 minutes to obtain a *better* estimate of the population mean from a sample of 25. The scores, rearranged in alphabetical order of the names of students by department and gender, are presented in Table 1.

Table 1: Philosophy Test Scores by Department and Gender

Age Range	Social Sciences		Science & Technology	
	Female Students	Male Students	Female Students	Male Students
17 to 25 years	92 91 89 94 91	82 81 88 83	76 76 83 77	87 86 83 89 86
	89 92 83 91 91	81 88 82 84	75 84 76 78	83 87 90 85 85
	88 85 91 84 87	81 80 87 80	75 75 83 80	81 77 85 77 80
	90 86 90 87 88	85 80 82 84	75 79 82 75	84 79 84 80 81
	93 92 89 94 91	81 84 82 82	81 84 82 82	89 85 85 84 80
	89 93 83 91 90	87 80 87 85	77 76 83 78	86 84 81 85 88
	88 84 91 84 87	81 87 86 80	76 84 77 79	83 83 79 90 83
	90 86 90 87 87	81 87 87 85		90 78 82 77 82
	93 91 90 89 93			78 79
	92			
26 years and over	81 89 87 82 89	92 91 88 93	87 86 84 88	89 88 85 90 88
	87 81 83 89 89	91 89 92 94	86 84 87 89	86 89 91 87 87
	86 84 89 84 86	90 90 87 96	86 85 82 91	96 93 87 93 89
	88 85 88 86 86	91 96 87 90	86	92 88 92 89 90
	82 83 82 89 84	86 90 86 87		87 86 95 88 85
	82 89 83 85 82	93		95 87
	82 88 86 82 86			
	88 81 87 81 88			
	88			

   a. Count the number of scores in each subgroup and enter the numbers in the rows headed "Number" in Table .

   b. Enter the corresponding range of scores in each subgroup in the rows headed "Range."

Table 2: Philosophy Test Scores by Department and Gender

		Social Sciences		Science & Technology	
Age Range		Female Students	Male Students	Female Students	Male Students
17 to 25 yrs	Number	_____	_____	_____	_____
	Range	___ to ___	___ to ___	___ to ___	___ to ___
26 yrs and over	Number	_____	_____	_____	_____
	Range	___ to ___	___ to ___	___ to ___	___ to ___

c. Select a representative sample of 25 scores from the data table and compute the necessary statistics to test the hypothesis that the graduate assistant's initial sample was sufficiently representative of the entire philosophy class. Test at the 95% level of confidence. Explain, briefly, how you selected your sample.

AP STATISTICS

Test 3

ANSWER KEY

Section I

1.	(C)	10.	(C)	19.	(C)	28.	(B)
2.	(C)	11.	(D)	20.	(A)	29.	(E)
3.	(D)	12.	(B)	21.	(C)	30.	(A)
4.	(C)	13.	(C)	22.	(A)	31.	(E)
5.	(C)	14.	(A)	23.	(B)	32.	(C)
6.	(A)	15.	(D)	24.	(C)	33.	(B)
7.	(E)	16.	(A)	25.	(A)	34.	(D)
8.	(B)	17.	(A)	26.	(D)	35.	(D)
9.	(A)	18.	(E)	27.	(C)		

DETAILED EXPLANATIONS
OF ANSWERS

Test 3

Section I

1.　**(C)**　One way to answer this question is to draw a ring around the plots, as shown in the figure below. If the ring is circular, we would expect a zero correlation, but if all the points fall in a straight line, this would represent a perfect correlation. A narrow ellipse would suggest a high correlation. The ring is more like an ellipse than like a circle. This suggests a low to moderate correlation between scores on the music test and the video game.

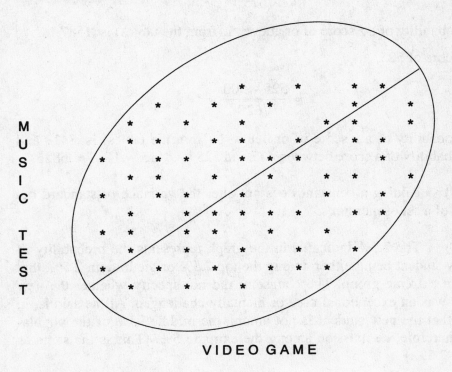

M
U
S
I
C

T
E
S
T

VIDEO GAME

In order to determine whether the correlation is positive or negative, we may want to draw the major axis of the ellipse, as shown in the picture. As can be seen, this major axis runs from the lower left to the upper right of the quadrant, suggesting a positive correlation. Based on the shape of the ring and the inclination of the axis, 0.42, choice (C) is probably the closest estimate of the correlation coefficient.

[In the absence of scale values, it is not possible to draw a precise regression line. However, the function of the visually drawn "axis" is to aid visualization of the direction of the regression line. Note that the same conclusion could also be reached without actually drawing the ring and the "axis."]

2. **(C)** The probability that Anna scores better than 475 may be computed as follows:

For a score of 475,

$$z = \frac{475 - 500}{\sqrt{625}} = -1$$

The probability of a z score of or above -1 (from the tables) is .1587

For a score of 525,

$$z = \frac{525 - 500}{\sqrt{625}} = 1$$

The probability of a z score of or below 1 (from the tables) is .8413 and the probability of a score between 475 and 525 is $.8413 - .1587 = .6826$.

3. **(D)** Adding a constant does not alter the variance or standard deviation of a set of measures.

4. **(C)** The 2.5% indicated in the graph represents the probability of the new student being either among the top 2.5% or the bottom 2.5%, that is, in an extreme group. The counselor did not specify whether the new student was an exceptional case or mentally challenged. All he said is, in effect, that the new student is not among the middle 95% of the population. Therefore, he must be among the extreme 5%. [This is the same as 2.5% + 2.5%.]

5.   **(C)**   Using the marginal totals, 15 and 32, and the grand total 48, the required number may be computed as follows:

$$\frac{(15 \times 32)}{48} = 10.$$

6.   **(A)**   When the expression "confidence level" is used, fractions greater than .5 (and equivalent percent figures higher than 50) represent progressively higher confidence and that the obtained result is reliable and can be replicated. Thus a 99% confidence level expresses greater confidence than 95% in the reliability of the result under consideration. However, it is very common that researchers use the complements of the larger fractions (or percent figures). Thus the following terms are used interchangeably:

  99% confidence level and *1% confidence level*

  95% confidence level and *5% confidence level*

  90% confidence level and *10% confidence level*

and so on. When the larger percent figures (usually 90% or higher) are used, the higher they are, the more confidence they express. When the smaller complements are used (usually 10% or less), the smaller they are, the greater confidence they express. Thus 1% expresses higher confidence than 2.5% or 5%. Hence, 1 percent expresses the highest confidence.

7.   **(E)**   Perhaps the surest way to test the correctness of the design is to add the numerals that identify the groups, by row and by column. For a 3 by 3 design, where 1, 2 and 3 are used as labels, the sum of the numerals is $(1 + 2 + 3) = 6$. Only design (E) satisfies this condition.

8.   **(B)**   The mode is a measure of central tendency, not dispersion.

9.   **(A)**   People of a wider range of interests are more likely to be found at the supermarket than in any of the other locations.

10.   **(C)**   The intervals under 11.5 are equal and the 9.5-to-under-11.5 interval carries the highest frequency. So the modal frequency should lie there. The midpoint of this interval is 10.

11.   **(D)**   The workers who earn $70,000 or higher are in the last four brackets, namely, 70–74 to 85–89. The frequencies are, respectively, 23, 21, 16 and 14, and their sum is 74.

12. **(B)** The workers who earn less than $45,000 are in the first four brackets, namely 25–29, 30–34, 35–39 and 40–44. Reading from the graph, we find that the frequencies are, respectively, 21, 22, 23 and 25. The sum of these frequencies is 91.

13. **(C)** The workers who earn over $49,000 but less than $70,000 are in the four brackets 50-54 to 65-69. The mid-points of these intervals are, respectively,

$$\frac{(50 + 54)}{2} = 52;$$

$$\frac{(55 + 59)}{2} = 57;$$

$$\frac{(60 + 64)}{2} = 62; \text{ and}$$

$$\frac{(65 + 69)}{2} = 67$$

Reading from the graph, we notice that the frequencies are, respectively, 27, 25, 26 and 27, and the sum of these frequencies is 105. The combined earnings of these people is

$$\frac{(52 \times 27 + 57 \times 25 + 62 \times 26 + 67 \times 27)}{105} = 59.5238$$

If we multiply this figure by $1000, we obtain $59,523, which, to the nearest $100 becomes $59,500.

14. **(A)** The workers who earn $65,000 or more are those who fall in the 65-69 to 85-89 intervals. The mid-points of these intervals are, respectively,

$$\frac{(65 + 69)}{2} = 67;$$

$$\frac{(70 + 74)}{2} = 72;$$

$$\frac{(75 + 79)}{2} = 77;$$

$$\frac{(80 + 84)}{2} = 82; \text{ and}$$

$$\frac{(85 + 89)}{2} = 87.$$

Reading from the graph, we find that the corresponding frequencies are, respectively, 27, 23, 21, 16, and 14. The sum of these frequencies is 27 + 23 + 21 + 16 + 14 = 101. The combined earnings of these people is

$$\frac{(67 \times 27 + 72 \times 23 + 77 \times 21 + 82 \times 16 + 87 \times 14)}{101} = 75.3663$$

On multiplying this figure by $1000, we obtain $75,450, to the nearest $50.

15. **(D)** Predictions of values of a dependent variable (*y*) made from values of the independent variable outside the range of observed values are generally less reliable than those made from values within the observed range.

16. **(A)** Prediction intervals are narrower near the mean than they are away from this mean. Note that the interval widens on both sides of the regression line, which is not the case in choice (E), hence this choice too must be rejected.

17. **(A)** If all other factors are held constant, smaller mean square error values are associated with progressively accurate predictions. The number 345.37 (option A) is the smallest in the given set.

18. **(E)** The correlation coefficient by itself says nothing about percentages. Hence choices (A) and (B) must be eliminated. However, the coefficient of determination, which can be derived from the correlation coefficient by squaring, may tell us about percentages in appropriate situations. So a correlation coefficient of .8 yields a coefficient of determination of .64. In question 18, this tells us that 64% of the variations in the whiteness of people's teeth can be explained by variations in the time they spend brushing their teeth. It would be ridiculous to think of the whiteness of people's teeth influencing the time they spend brushing their teeth, except, perhaps, that they could be encouraged to brush longer, or become complacent and brush for shorter times on seeing their teeth whiter. Choice (D) is not tenable.

19. **(C)** The coefficient of determination can be derived by squaring the correlation coefficient. Thus, if the correlation coefficient is .93, then the coefficient of determination must be .93 × .93 = .86.

20. **(A)** Although random selection often saves time and labor (iii), there are situations when other methods are more expedient. For example, taking the first set of people who arrive at a certain location, the nearest subjects available to the researcher, and so on. The need to minimize bias (i) and the assumption of a random distribution of the underlying principles (ii) are usually intricately related and are almost always of major concern.

21. **(C)** The inter-quartile range is computed as the mean of the first and third quartiles.

22. **(A)** The main reasons for blocking are (I) and (II). Choice (C) is clearly false. The claims in choices (B), (D), and (E) are partially true and partially false. The "and" within each of these statements implies that both parts of the statements are true. Since this is not so, each compound statement, taken as a whole, must be considered false. (Remember that, in elementary logic, a conjunction is true only if all the constituent simple statements are individually true.)

23. **(B)** The distribution of shoe sizes would be skewed and open-ended, since the custom made shoes would be "off the scale." So the median would be the average of choice here.

24. **(C)** The table is repeated here, with the marginal totals included.

Distribution of Volunteer Fire Fighters, by Gender

	18 – 24	25 – 29	30 – 34	Total
Female	17	23	30	70
Male	22	40	36	98
Total	39	63	66	168

The expected frequency for female volunteers between ages 18 and 24 is computed as follows:

$$\frac{39 \times 70}{168} = 16.25.$$

This has been entered in the corresponding space in the next table. The expected frequency for female volunteers in the age range 25 to 29 is computed as follows:

$$\frac{63 \times 70}{168} = 26.25.$$

and this has been entered in the corresponding space in the table.

Distribution of Volunteer Fire Fighters, by Gender

	18 – 24	25 – 29	30 – 34	Total
Female	16.25	26.25	27.5	70
Male	22.75	36.75	38.5	98
Total	39	63	66	168

The relevant frequency for the female volunteers in the 30 to 34 age range has been similarly calculated (27.5) and entered in the corresponding cell. The expected frequencies for the male volunteers could be similarly computed. However, since there are only two rows, and the column totals must be constant, the expected frequencies for the male volunteers can easily be derived by subtracting the number of females in each column from the column total. For example, to obtain the expected frequency for the male volunteers in the 18 to 24 age range, we subtract

$$39 - 16.25 = 22.75.$$

The rest of the expected frequencies in the 'male' row are similarly obtained.

The elements of the chi-square statistic are obtained by substituting in the expression

$$\frac{(O - E)^2}{E}$$

where O is the observed frequency and E is the expected frequency.

For the cell in the top left corner, the observed frequency is $O = 17$ and the expected frequency (as calculated) is $E = 16.25$. Plugging these values in the above expression, we obtain

$$\frac{(17 - 16.25)^2}{16.25} = .035.$$

Similarly, for the next cell in the top row, we have

$$\frac{(23 - 26.25)^2}{26.25} = .402.$$

For the last cell in the top cell, we have

$$\frac{(30 - 27.5)^2}{27.5} = .227.$$

The figures from the second row are .025, .287 and .162. The sum of these values is

$$.035 + .402 + .227 + .025 + .287 + .162 = 1.138.$$

25. (A)   One of the easiest ways to visualize the task is by drawing a Venn diagram. Since the students take three distinct subjects, we need three circles to represent them. Also, since some students take two or more courses, the three circles must overlap, as shown below. We begin by filling in the regions where three circles intersect, then the regions where only two circles intersect. Finally we fill the remaining regions, as shown.

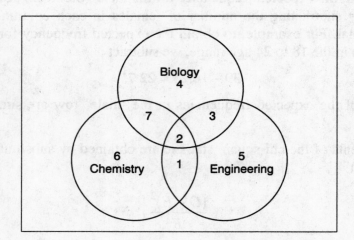

There are 28 students altogether, among whom 16 study biology. The probability of drawing the name of a biology student is $P(B) = 16/28$. There are nine students who study both biology and chemistry. The probability of drawing the name of a student who studies both these subjects is $P(B \cap C) = 9/28$. If the first name drawn is that of a biology student, the probability that this student is also a chemistry student is

$$P(C|B) = \frac{P(B \cap C)}{P(C)} = \frac{\dfrac{9}{28}}{\dfrac{16}{28}} = \frac{9}{16}.$$

26. **(D)**   We shall use the same Venn diagram employed in answering question 25. Among the 28 students, 16 study biology. The probability of drawing the name of a biology student is $P(B) = 16/28$. There are five students who study both biology and engineering. The probability of drawing the name of a student who studies both these subjects is $P(B \cap E) = 5/28$. If the first name drawn is that of an engineering student, the probability that this student is also a biology student is

$$P(E|B) = \frac{P(B \cap E)}{P(E)} = \frac{\frac{5}{28}}{\frac{16}{28}} = \frac{5}{16}.$$

27. **(C)**   The total number of students is 125 (from the graph) and half of this is 62.5. Careful examination of the graph indicates that the vertical axis is on a scale of 1 to 5. There are 45 scores below 65 as indicated in the 60–64 interval. There are 80 scores under 70 as shown in the 65–69 interval. This means that the median would fall in the 65–69 interval. So we must extract $62.5 - 45 = 16.5$ scores from the 65–69 interval and add to the 45 in the 65–69 interval to make up the 62.5. The big question is, "How do we go about this?" Here is one way to do it.

The difference between the numbers of scores in the 60–64 and the 65–69 intervals is $80 - 45 = 35$. We can assume that these 35 scores are spread evenly along the 65-69 interval. The width of this interval is 5 and these 35 scores must be spread evenly within it, so each score would cover 5/35 of this interval. Thus the 16.5 scores must cover

$$\frac{5}{35} \times 16.5 = 2.36.$$

If we add this to 64.5, the lower boundary of the 65–69 interval, we obtain 66.86, or 67, to the nearest integer.

28. **(B)**   The total number of scores is 125 (from the graph). 80% of 125 is 100. Therefore, the 80th percentile should fall in the 70–74 interval. The difference between the frequencies in the 65–69 and the 70–74 intervals is $100 - 80 = 20$. If we assume that these 20 scores are bunched together in the middle of the 70–75 interval, then the median should be $(70 + 74)/2 = 72$. (This answer is not one of the given choices.) However, if we assume that the 20 scores are spread evenly along the 70–74 interval, then the last of them should be hugging the upper boundary of the 70–74 interval, which is 74.5.

29. **(E)**   The boundary between the 60–64 and the 65–69 intervals 64.5. If we assume that the top score lies within the 60–64 interval, then we can trace the top of that bar to the vertical scale, which should read 45. (Remember that the vertical axis of this graph is drawn on a scale of 1 to 5.) Since there are 125 scores in the distribution, the percentile that corresponds to the score of 64.5 is

$$\frac{45}{125} \times 100 = 36.$$

30. **(A)**   If a boxplot is properly drawn, it should meet the following criteria: the top and bottom horizontal lines should mark the third and first quartiles, respectively; the middle horizontal line should mark the median and the top and bottom vertical "whiskers" should lead from the 90th and the 10th percentiles, respectively. Careful inspection shows that the plot for Room 1 choice (A) is the only one that satisfies these criteria.

31. **(E)**   At least, in principle, arguments (A) to (D) are all defensible. It may be argued that, if teachers worked harder, they would reach the girls and boys to the same degree and, so, the mathematically more able group would still excel. However, if the teachers worked infinitely harder, the more able group would reach their limits at some point and then only the less able group would continue to progress. Hence, even choice (D) is plausible.

32. **(C)**   The correlation coefficient cannot be converted to a percent figure directly. Therefore we must immediately reject choicess (A), (B), and (E). The coefficient of determination, however, can be derived from the correlation coefficient by squaring. Thus, the coefficient of determination derived from a correlation of .76 is .76 × .76 = .58. Now we can convert .58 to 58%. In this question, the amount of rainfall is clearly the independent variable and crop yield is the dependent variable. So amount of rainfall can, potentially, affect crop yield. Hence the correct interpretation of a correlation of .76 is that 58% of the variations in crop yield can be explained by variations in the amount of rainfall, choice (C), but not the other way round, as in choice (D).

33. **(B)**   The coefficient of determination is the square of the correlation coefficient. Therefore, the correlation coefficient must be the square root of the coefficient of determination. Thus the desired correlation

coefficient is $\sqrt{.75} = .87$. [Actually, in this particular question, the problem could simply be solved by solving the equation $r^2 = .75$.]

34. **(D)** In designs 1 and 4, there were real control groups and the independent variable (viewing the movie "Reasons and Methods to Kill") was manipulated. In design 2, "control" was simulated by selection, which does not necessarily eliminate potential confounding factors, such as discussion, that might either reinforce or discourage acting out the movie. In design 3, there was no independent control group.

35. **(D)** Although both designs 1 and 4 meet some basic requirements of a scientific experiment, design 4 is more generalizable: matching in pairs, by gender and pretest score, puts a tighter control than simple random selection, as in design 1.

Section II

Part 1

1. The calculations are shown in the table. Age figures are shown in column (1) and the spatial test scores are shown in column (4). Details are shown only in the first row.

Step 1. Calculate the mean age, the deviations from the mean and the sum of squares from the mean: The mean age, shown at the bottom of column (1), is $\bar{a}$ = 14.5. The deviation of each age figure from this mean is denoted $(a_i - \bar{a})$ and shown in column (2). The square of this deviation, denoted $(a_i - \bar{a})^2$, is shown in column (3).

Computation of data for slope of regression line

i	a_i	$(a_i - \bar{a})$	$(a_i - \bar{a})^2$	s_i	$(s_i - \bar{s})$	$(a_i - \bar{a})(s_i - \bar{s})$
	(1)	(2)	(3)	(4)	(5)	(6)
1	10	$(10 - 14.5) = -4.5$	$(-4.5)^2 = 20.25$	65	$(65 - 76) = -11$	$(-4.5)(-11) = 49.5$
2	11	-3.5	12.25	63	-13	45.5
3	12	-2.5	6.25	70	-6	15.0
4	13	-1.5	2.25	73	-3	4.5
5	14	-0.5	.25	81	5	-2.5
6	15	0.5	.25	79	3	1.5
7	16	1.5	2.25	81	5	7.5
8	17	2.5	6.25	80	4	10.0
9	18	3.5	12.25	83	7	24.5
10	19	4.5	20.25	85	9	40.5
Σ	145	0	82.50	760	0	196
Mean 14.5				76.0		

Step 2. Calculate the mean spatial test score and their deviations from the mean: The mean spatial test score, shown at the bottom of column (4), is $\bar{s}$ = 76. The deviation of each score from this mean is denoted $(s_i - \bar{s})$ and is shown in column (4).

Step 3. Calculate the cross-products of the deviations from the mean: The cross-products, denoted $(a_i - \bar{a})(s_i - \bar{s})$, are shown in column (5). From the last but one row (headed Σ), we observe that

(1) the sum of the cross-products of the deviations is $\Sigma(a_i - \bar{a})^2 = 82.5$

(2) the sum of the cross-products of the deviation is $\Sigma(a_i - \bar{a})(s_i - \bar{s}) = 196$

Step 4. Calculate the slope of the line of regression of age on spatial test score:

$$m = \frac{\Sigma(a_i - \bar{a})(s_i - \bar{s})}{\Sigma(a_i - \bar{a})^2}$$

$$= \frac{196}{82.5}$$

$$= 2.376$$

This is the slope of the regression line.

2. a. Since there are five options per question, the probability of anyone selecting the correct answer by pure random guess is $1/5 = .2$

b. Our focus is on the 5 or more additional points that Anjie must earn in order to get an A. Anjie thinks that she has already earned 85 points, she needs only to earn 5 more points in order to secure an A. In reality, she needs *at least 5 points*, which means that she needs 5 or more points (to a maximum of 10). So we are not looking for the probability of her earning exactly 5 more points, but of earning 6, 7, 8, 9 or 10 points.

Let p be the probability of selecting the correct answer by a purely random process. The probability of selecting k correct answers out of n questions is given by the expression

$$\binom{n}{k} p^k (1 - p)^{n-k}$$

In the current task, the probability of a correct guess on one item is $p = .2$ and the number of questions is $n = 10$. When $k = 5$, we obtain

$$\binom{10}{5} .2^5 (1 - .2)^{10-5} = 252 \times .2^5 \times .8^5 = .0264241$$

We need the probability that Anjie guesses correctly 5 times *or* 6 times *or* 7 times, and so on, to 10 times. The probability that Anjie would get at least 5 correct guesses is the *sum* of the probabilities of getting 5, 6, 7, 8, 9 and 10. For 6 correct guesses, the probability is

$$\binom{10}{6} .2^6 (1 - .2)^{10-6} = 210 \times .2^6 \times .8^4 = .0055050$$

and for 7 correct guesses, the probability is

$$\binom{10}{7} .2^7 (1 - .2)^{10-7} = 120 \times .2^7 \times .8^3 = .0007864$$

The probability of 8 correct guesses is

$$\binom{10}{8} .2^8 (1 - .2)^{10-8} = 45 \times .2^8 \times .8^2 = .0000737$$

If we wish to express the answer correctly to four decimal places, we can stop here. [As we can see, the fractions are rapidly getting smaller and the probabilities of 9 and 10 correct guesses would contribute nothing useful in the final answer.]

The probability that Anjie will select at least five correct answers is

$$.0264241 + .0055050 + .0007864 + .0000737 = .0327.$$

This is the probability that she will earn an A grade if she only guesses randomly on the multiple-choice test.

3. The following simple calculation would be enough:

1 Manager:	$95,000 \times 1	=	$95,000
1 Senior Analyst:	$85,000 \times 1	=	$85,000
4 Programmers:	$30,000 \times 4	=	$120,000
5 Salespeople:	$21,000 \times 5	=	$105,000
14 Others:	$18,000 \times 14	=	$252,000
Total Salary:			$657,000
Number of Workers:	25		
Mean Salary:	$657,000 \div 25	=	$26,280
Modal Salary:			$18,000

A simple addition shows that the manager and the senior analyst together earn $180,000, that is, as much as 10 "other" workers combined. Therefore, the salaries of the manager and the senior analyst pushed the "average" salary excessively higher ($26,280). This is the average that the company's attorney would be glad to quote.

We can see that the modal salary is $18,000. Let us ignore the possibility that people who are more highly educated and, consequently, earn higher salaries, tend to have fewer children. Then we can assume that the family sizes of the workers and, hence, their responsibilities, are approximately the same, regardless of rank. Therefore the union representative would argue that the majority of the workers earn little more than minimum wages. That is, the union representative would quote the modal salary to support his/her argument that the company is paying unduly low salaries.

4.   The z value associated with the difference, $75 - 70$ is

$$z = \frac{75 - 70}{\sqrt{100}} = .5.$$

From the tables, we find that the probability associated with $z = .5$ is .3085. This is the probability that Judy will pass the test.

5.   Since the mean rating on the 15 essays was 81, the sum of the ratings must be $81 \times 15 = 1215$. 1 essay (Ann's) was missing, so the new mean rating was based on the remaining 14 essays and the sum of the ratings must be $83 \times 14 = 1162$. The missing rating must be $1215 - 1162 = 53$. This is Ann's essay rating.

Section II

Part 2

1. a.   The number of scores in each subgroup has been entered in the appropriate location in Table 2.

    b.   The range of scores in each subgroup has been entered in the appropriate cell in the table.

Table 1: Philosophy Test Scores by Department and Gender

		Social Sciences		Science & Technology	
	Age range	Female students	Male students	Female students	Male students
17 to 25 yrs	Number	46	32	28	42
	Range	83 to 94 = 12	80 to 88 = 9	75 to 84 = 10	77 to 86 = 10
26 years and over	Number	41	21	13	27
	Range	81 to 89 = 9	86 to 96 = 11	84 to 91 = 8	85 to 96 = 12

    c.   It may be observed, from the above table, that the range of scores in the subgroups varies, if only slightly. This suggests that we take a sample from each subgroup. Since the numbers of scores in the cells are unequal, we need to take *proportional random samples*. Such a sample would enhance the chance of fair representation for each subgroup.

Step 1. Determine how many scores to select from each subgroup: The total number of scores is 250, and we want to select 25. This means 1 out of every cluster of 10. There are mathematical methods for determining the number of scores to select from each subgroup, but we can easily apply an intuitive method. Observe that the numbers in the cells are close to multiples of 10. For example, there are 46 scores from the female students between 17 and 25 years old. This is close to $10 \times 5 = 50$. Let us tentatively decide on a sub-sample of 5 (1 out of every 10) from this group. Similarly, we decide on a sub-sample of 3 (approximately 1 out of every 10) from the 32 male students who are 17 to 25 years old. By applying this procedure in each subgroup, we see that we can take a sub-sample of 1 from the above-25-year-old female students in the Science & Technology Department and a sub-sample of 3 from the above-25-year-old male students in the same department. These numbers are listed in the appropriate cells in Table 2. Observe that the sum of the sub-samples is exactly 25.

Table 2: Sizes of sub-samples from various subgroups

		Social Sciences		Science & Technology	
	Age range	Female students	Male students	Female students	Male students
17 to 25 yrs	Sub-sample	5	3	3	4
26 years and over	Sub-sample	4	2	1	3

Step 2. Divide each subgroup into clusters of approximately equal size, say, 10: Let us move from left to right, from top row downwards (see Table 3). We split the top-left block (female students from 17 to 25 years of age) into clusters of approximately nine. (We want a sub-sample of 5 from 46 scores.) Counting from left to right in the top row, we mark off the first cluster of 9, between 91 and 91, as shown with the slash (/). Proceeding this way, we find that the last group contains 10 instead of 9 scores. [This should not be a problem.] Using the same procedure, we divide up the remaining blocks into clusters, as shown by the slashes. Let us apply systematic random sampling.

Step 3. Select the relevant number of scores from each cluster: There are several ways to select the scores. For example, we can use pure random sampling or systematic random sampling. Let us apply systematic random sampling. Let us draw a number randomly between 1 and 9 in order to determine the position of the score to select from each cluster in the first block (female students from 17 to 25 years of age). The number drawn by this method is 4. So we choose the 4th score in each cluster in this block. The selected scores are underlined. This procedure is repeated for the next subgroup. Here the 5th score in each cluster is selected. The 25 scores so selected from the whole table are underlined.

Table 3: Philosophy Test Scores by Department and Gender: Sample Selection

	Social Sciences		Science & Technology	
Age range	**Female students**	**Male students**	**Female students**	**Male students**
17 to 25 years	92 91 89 <u>94</u> 91 89 92 83 91/91 88 85 <u>91</u> 84 87 90 86 90/87 88 93 <u>92</u> 89 94 91 89 93/83 91 90 <u>88</u> 84 91 84 87 90/86 90 87 <u>87</u> 93 91 90 89 93 92	82 81 88 83 <u>81</u> 88 82 84 81 80 87/80 85 80 82 <u>84</u> 81 84 82 82 87 80/87 85 81 87 <u>86</u> 80 81 87 87 85	76 76 <u>83</u> 77 75 84 76 78 75/75 83 <u>80</u> 75 79 82 75 81 84/82 82 <u>77</u> 76 83 78 76 84 77 79	87 86 83 <u>89</u> 86 83 87 90 85 85/ 81 77 85 <u>77</u> 80 84 79 84 80 81/ 89 85 85 <u>84</u> 80 86 84 81 85 88/ 83 83 79 <u>90</u> 83 90 78 82 77 82 78 79
26 years and over	81 <u>89</u> 87 82 89 87 81 83 89 89/ 86 <u>84</u> 89 84 86 88 85 88 86 86/ 82 <u>83</u> 82 89 84 82 89 83 85 82/ 82 <u>88</u> 86 82 86 88 81 87 81 88 88	92 91 88 93 <u>91</u> 89 92 94 90 90/87 96 91 96 <u>87</u> 90 86 90 86 87 93	87 86 84 88 86 84 <u>87</u> 89 86 85 82 91 86	89 88 85 <u>90</u> 88 86 89 91 87/87 96 93 <u>87</u> 93 89 92 88 92/89 90 87 <u>86</u> 95 88 85 95 87

Step 4. Compute the necessary statistics (sample mean and an estimate of the population standard deviation): First, tabulate the data, as shown in the column headed "Original scores (X)" in Table 4. The mean is shown as $2155/25 = 86.2$ at the bottom of this first column. Next, compute the deviation of each score from the mean. The details and results are shown in the column headed "Deviation from mean $(X - \overline{X})$." Then, square each deviation and enter the results in the column headed "Squared deviation $(X - \overline{X})^2$." The sum of these deviations is 464.00. The number of scores in the sample is 25, and the appropriate number of degrees of freedom is 24. The population standard deviation, estimated from this sample, is

$$s = \sqrt{\frac{464}{25 \times 24}} = 0.879$$

Step 5. Based on the statistics just obtained, advise the philosophy professor as to the reliability of the mean of 85.65 which he previously obtained. This can be done in at least two ways. First we can test to see whether the provisional mean he obtained is significantly different from that we obtained by our "more sophisticated" method.

Table 4: Computation of Population Std

Original score (X)	Deviation from mean $(X - \overline{X})$	Squared deviation $(X - \overline{X})^2$
94	$94 - 86.52 = 7.8$	$7.8^2 = 60.84$
91	$91 - 86.52 = 4.8$	$4.8^2 = 23.04$
92	$92 - 86.52 = 5.8$	$5.8^2 = 33.64$
88	$88 - 86.52 = 1.8$	$1.8^2 = 3.24$
87	$87 - 86.52 = 0.8$	$0.8^2 = 0.64$
81	$81 - 86.52 = -5.2$	$5.2^2 = 27.04$
84	$84 - 86.52 = -2.2$	$2.2^2 = 4.84$
86	$86 - 86.52 = -0.2$	$0.2^2 = 0.04$
83	$83 - 86.52 = -3.2$	$3.2^2 = 10.24$
80	$80 - 86.52 = -6.2$	$6.2^2 = 38.44$
77	$77 - 86.52 = -9.2$	$9.2^2 = 84.64$
89	$89 - 86.52 = 2.8$	$2.8^2 = 7.84$
77	$77 - 86.52 = -9.2$	$9.2^2 = 84.64$
84	$84 - 86.52 = -2.2$	$2.2^2 = 4.84$
90	$90 - 86.52 = 3.8$	$3.8^2 = 14.44$
89	$89 - 86.52 = 2.8$	$2.8^2 = 7.84$
84	$84 - 86.52 = -2.2$	$2.2^2 = 4.84$
83	$83 - 86.52 = -3.2$	$3.2^2 = 10.24$
88	$88 - 86.52 = 1.8$	$1.8^2 = 3.24$
91	$91 - 86.52 = 4.8$	$4.8^2 = 23.04$
87	$87 - 86.52 = 0.8$	$0.8^2 = 0.64$
87	$87 - 86.52 = 0.8$	$0.8^2 = 0.64$
90	$90 - 86.52 = 3.8$	$3.8^2 = 14.44$
87	$87 - 86.52 = 0.8$	$0.8^2 = 0.64$
86	$86 - 86.52 = -0.2$	$0.2^2 = 0.04$
2155/25 = 86.2	0.0	464.00

To test for statistical significance, we proceed as follows. We have already computed the estimated population standard deviation, namely $s = 0.879$. The t value for this value, for $df = 24$, is

$$t = \frac{86.2 - 85.65}{0.879} = 0.626$$

On referring to the t-distribution table, we notice that this value is far less than the tabled value of $\alpha = 2.064$ at the 95% level of confidence. This shows that the provisional mean obtained by the professor is not statistically different from the one we obtained.

Alternatively, we can establish a confidence interval for the population mean, based on the mean obtained by our proportional sample. Let us write μ for the population mean. We have already seen that, for 24 degrees of freedom, $\alpha = 2.064$ and the estimated population standard deviation is $s = 0.879$. So the population mean must lie between

$$86.2 - (2.064 \times 0.879) \text{ and } 86.2 + (2.064 \times 0.879)$$

That is,

$$86.2 - 1.814 < m < 86.2 + 1.814$$

or

$$84.4 < m < 88.0$$

This means that, if we took random samples (25, a large number of times) from the students scores, the sample means would fall between 84.4 and 88.0 about 95% of the times. Since the professor's provisional mean, 85.65, lies well within these limits, we conclude that his crude sample was reasonably representative of the entire set of scores.

PRACTICE
TEST 4

AP EXAMINATION IN STATISTICS

Test 4

Section I

TIME: 90 Minutes
35 Multiple-Choice Questions

(Answer sheets appear in the back of this book.)

DIRECTIONS: For each question or incomplete statement in this section, select the best answer from among the five choices and fill in the corresponding oval on the answer sheet.

---

1. The Department of Continuing Education in a large community college is considering expanding its program offerings for both day and evening students in its five campuses. Five research assistants, Alma, Bert, Carl, Dawn and Earl, are instructed to administer a questionnaire to a representative sample of students in order to predict the popularity of weekend courses. Which of the following samples would you consider most acceptable for this purpose?

   (A = Alma, B = Bert, C = Carl, D = Dawn and E = Earl.)

   (A) Selects a random sample drawn from each of the five campuses

   (B) Selects a representative sample of students from the main campus

   (C) Selects a stratified random sample of full-time, day students from all five campuses

   (D) Selects a large sample of students who were trapped by a rain storm one evening

   (E) Selects a large sample stratified by race and gender.

Use this information to answer questions 2 and 3.

A test consists of an open-ended section and a 10-item multiple-choice section. Each multiple-choice question is worth one point. The minimum score for a B grade is 20. You have already secured 14 points on the open-ended section, but are totally unprepared for the multiple-choice questions. So you must guess randomly among the options.

2. If there are five choices per question in the multiple-choice section, what is the probability that you obtain a B grade on the test?

    (A) .9936   (D) .0055

    (B) .2   (E) .0064

    (C) .1074

3. If there are four choices per item in the multiple-choice section, what is the probability that you obtain a B grade on the test?

    (A) .0162   (D) .25

    (B) .0197   (E) .9803

    (C) .0563

4. A class test consisted of 25 multiple-choice questions. In order to express all scores on a 100-point scale, the teacher multiplied each student's score by 4. The variance of the original scores was 81. The variance of the new scores would be

    (A) 8100.   (D) 85.

    (B) 1296.   (E) 81.

    (C) 324.

5. A computer is programmed to generate random numbers from 1 to 1000, inclusive. The first number that it generated was a perfect cube. What is the probability that this number is also a perfect square?

    (A) 0.02   (D) 0.2

    (B) 0.01   (E) 0.3

    (C) 0.000002

6. Which of the following is *not* a compelling reason for using a sample survey instead of a census?

   (A) Time required to conduct the study

   (B) The cost of conducting the study

   (C) The size of the population under consideration

   (D) The homogeneity of the elements (subjects)

   (E) Whether human subjects or other entities are involved

7. The state board of education wishes to study the attitudes of parents to a newly introduced experimental curriculum component in the elementary school in urban, suburban and rural communities whose residents are of different cultural backgrounds. Which of the following sampling schemes is likely to yield the most reliable measure of the parents' attitudes?

   (A) Stratified random sample

   (B) Captive sample

   (C) Pure random sample

   (D) Systematic random sample

   (E) Volunteer sample

8. Which of the following features apply to *both* experimental studies and observational studies when human subjects are involved?

   I.   one or more specific hypotheses are stated before the data are collected
   II. some subjects are denied treatment, given phony treatments, given different treatments or given different levels of the same treatment
   III. subjects are selected on the basis of the presence, absence or level of one or more specific characteristics—the independent variable, which the researcher must not manipulate
   IV. the results are analyzed carefully and according to strict statistical principles

   (A) I and II only   (D) I and IV only

   (B) II and III only   (E) I, II, III, and IV

   (C) III and IV only

9. Assuming that the following idealized graphs represent samples of equal sizes taken from the same population, which of them shows the greatest variability?

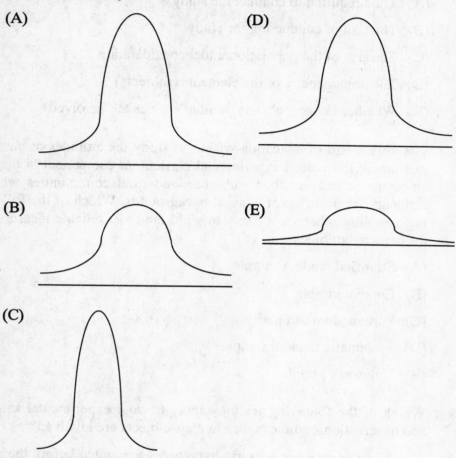

(A)

(D)

(B)

(E)

(C)

10. Five hundred applicants took a college entrance examination. You have 10 minutes to present a summary of the applicants' test performance. The computer has suddenly broken down. You must estimate the mean score of the candidates from a random sample of 10, equipped with only a pocket calculator. Here are the test scores of the ten candidates you selected:

20 14 29 26 10 34 20 30 17 20.

Compute the 95% confidence interval for the mean score of the 500 applicants.

(A) 17.6 to 23.4   (D) 7.587 to 22

(B) 17.6 to 22   (E) none of these

(C) 22 to 23.4

11. A researcher obtained multiple measures from each subject in an experiment to study the effects of practice on spelling test performance. After blocking and inspecting the data, she concluded that it did not matter whether the mean, median or modal score was taken as the average for individual blocks. This suggests that

(A) the data are evenly dispersed within blocks.

(B) the distribution appears to be skewed.

(C) this is not a serious study.

(D) the number of data points is the same for each block.

(E) all of the above statements are true.

12. A study of a large sample of students reveals that the correlation between mathematics test scores and ratings on figure skating was −0.89. Which of the following interpretations is *not* warranted from this study?

(A) Mathematical aptitude increases figure-skating skills.

(B) Figure-skating ability suppresses mathematical aptitude.

(C) A common factor increases mathematical aptitude while reducing figure-skating ability.

(D) There is no relationship between mathematical aptitude and figure-skating ability.

(E) A common factor affects mathematical aptitude and figure-skating ability similarly.

13. The linear regression model assumes that the variances of the error terms are constant. This means that the residuals should

(A) be closely clustered around the mean.

(B) be evenly distributed around the mean.

(C) be normally distributed around the mean.

(D) have a flat distribution.

(E) be similarly distributed around, below and above the mean.

Use the graphs below to answer questions 14 and 15.

(1)

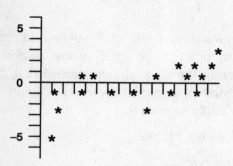

(2)

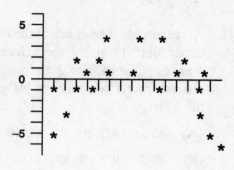

(3)

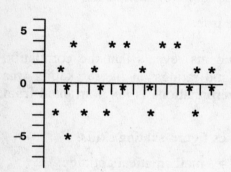

(4)

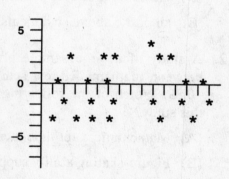

14. Which graphs suggest approximately linear relationships between the dependent and the independent variable?

    (A) 1 and 2   (D) 1 and 4

    (B) 2 and 3   (E) 2 and 4

    (C) 3 and 4

15. Which graph(s) suggest(s) some transformation of the original data before regression analysis?

    (A) 1 only   (D) 3 and 4

    (B) 2 only   (E) 1 and 2

    (C) 2 and 4

Use this information for questions 16 to 18.

The following cumulative frequency polygon shows the distribution of the ages of 105 workers in a factory.

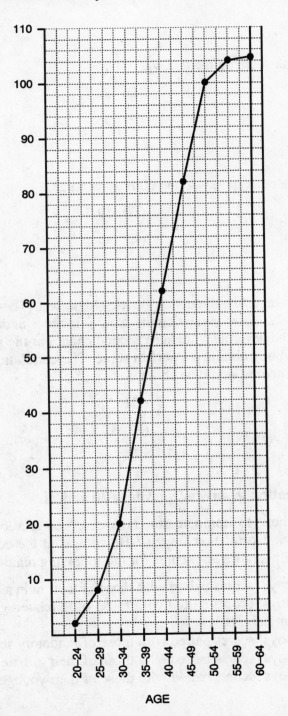

AGE

16. What score marks the 20th percentile?

    (A) 20   (D) 21%

    (B) 21   (E) 32

    (C) 20%

17. The median score on the test was

    (A) 35.   (D) 52.5.

    (B) 39.5.   (E) 55.

    (C) 42.

18. What score corresponds to the 60th percentile?

    (A) 42   (D) 59.5

    (B) 64.5   (E) 36

    (C) 62

19. Mr. Lowe gave his students a "trick" logic test. The scores ranged from 35 to 72. After reviewing the basic principles underlying the test questions, he gave the students a second chance at the same test. This time, everybody obtained a perfect score. The correlation between the two sets of scores would be about

    (A) 0.   (D) .78.

    (B) 0.34.   (E) 1.

    (C) .59.

Use this information to answer questions 20 and 21.

After learning how to compute the rank-order correlation coefficient, Steve went into a "correlation frenzy." He computed the correlations between sets of mathematics test scores for the following male-female pairs.

    I.   Boys' scores paired with those of their twin sisters
    II. Boys' scores paired with those of unrelated girls of match-
         ing heights
    III. Boys' scores paired with those of randomly selected girls
    IV. Boys' scores paired with those of their girlfriends
    V.   Boys' scores paired with those of their younger sisters

Assume that the samples were of the same size.

20. If all the children who participated in the test were aged between 15 and 16 years, which sample would yield the highest correlation coefficient?

(A) I   (D) IV

(B) II   (E) V

(C) III

21. If the children who were tested in each group ranged in age from 13 to 18 years, which sample would probably yield the lowest correlation coefficient?

(A) I   (D) IV

(B) II   (E) V

(C) III

22. The following table depicts the amount of snow that fell in five cities in the winter of 1995.

Amount of Snowfall in Five Cities

City	1	2	3	4	5
Snowfall (inches)	45	63	55	40	58

Which of the following graphs appropriately represent the data?

(I)   (II)

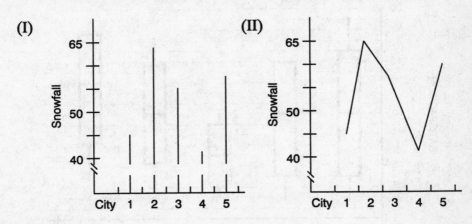

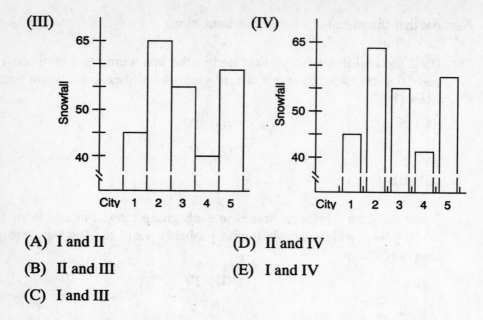

(A) I and II   (D) II and IV

(B) II and III   (E) I and IV

(C) I and III

Use this information to answer questions 23 and 24.

A social scientist set out to study the general opinion of the local community on the question of the separation of state and church. The interview question was simply, "To what extent are you satisfied with the government's handling of the issue?" Subjects were asked to rate the extent of their satisfaction on a scale of 1 to 20. Five samples of equal size were drawn as follows: a church, a shopping mall, a restaurant, an amusement park and a mixed sample consisting of equal numbers of subjects drawn from several churches, shopping malls, restaurants and amusement parks. Data obtained from the five samples are depicted in the following boxplot.

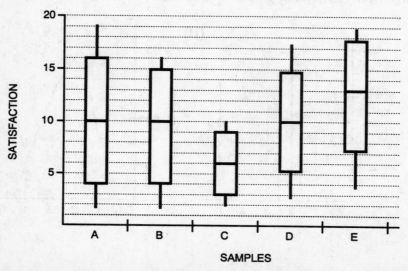

23. Which "box" most probably represents data from the sample from one church?

(A) A   (D) D

(B) B   (E) E

(C) C

24. Which "box" most probably represents data from the sample consisting of mixed groups?

(A) A   (D) D

(B) B   (E) E

(C) C

25. A teacher wishes to study the relationship between verbal fluency and spatial aptitude. As a crude measure of spatial aptitude, he records the time each of his students takes to solve a jigsaw puzzle. To measure verbal fluency, he shows a movie and asks the students to describe what they saw in the picture. He then counts the number of words in each student's essay. He finds that the coefficient of correlation between time to solve the puzzle and length of essay was 0.82. Based on this correlation coefficient and assuming that the measures themselves are valid indicators, which of the following conclusions is the most reasonable?

(A) The more verbally fluent a student is, the greater his/her verbal aptitude.

(B) The less verbally fluent a student is, the greater his/her spatial aptitude.

(C) There is no significant relationship between verbal fluency and spatial aptitude.

(D) The less verbally fluent a student is, the lower his/her spatial aptitude.

(E) No reasonable conclusion can be drawn from the data.

26. Which of the following pairs does *not* include a measure of central tendency?

   I.   Mean
   II. Median

III. Mode

IV. Range

V. Inter-quartile range

(A) I and II (D) III and IV

(B) II and III (E) II and V

(C) IV and V

27. A teacher wishes to study the effects of administering mathematics, science and history tests in different orders, with a five-minute break between tests. He assembles three groups of students in different rooms—Group 1, Group 2 and Group 3. Which of the following arrangements would be a faulty design for the study?

(I)

	First	Second	Third
Mathematics	Group 3	Group 2	Group 1
Science	Group 1	Group 3	Group 2
History	Group 2	Group 1	Group 3

(II)

	First	Second	Third
Mathematics	Group 1	Group 2	Group 3
Science	Group 3	Group 1	Group 2
History	Group 2	Group 3	Group 1

(III)

	First	Second	Third
Mathematics	Group 1	Group 2	Group 2
Science	Group 3	Group 2	Group 1
History	Group 2	Group 1	Group 3

(IV)

	First	Second	Third
Mathematics	Group 3	Group 2	Group 1
Science	Group 1	Group 3	Group 2
History	Group 2	Group 1	Group 3

(V)

	First	Second	Third
Mathematics	Group 2	Group 1	Group 3
Science	Group 1	Group 3	Group 2
History	Group 3	Group 2	Group 1

(A) I   (D) IV

(B) II   (E) V

(C) III

28. The scatterplot shows the relationship between scores on biology and
history tests, obtained from 30 students. Assuming that this sample is
representative of a parent population, which of the following conclusions is warranted by the scatterplot?

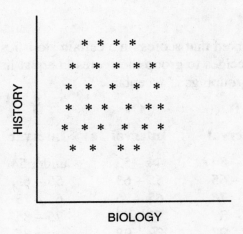

(A) Biology test scores cannot be predicted from history test scores.

(B) High scores on a biology test are associated with low scores on a
history test.

(C) Low scores on a biology test are associated with high scores on
a history test.

(D) High scores on a biology test are associated with high scores on
a history test.

(E) Low scores on a biology test are associated with low scores on a
history test.

29. The table shows the number of people from different age ranges
enrolled in day and evening programs in a small community college.
Assuming that there were no relationship between age and choice
between day and evening classes, how many people over 30 years of
age should be enrolled in evening programs?

	Evening Program	Day Program	Total
Under 25 years	400	850	1250
25 to 30 years	475	750	1225
31 years & over	560	300	860
Total	**1435**	**1900**	**3335**

(A) 633

(B) 490

(C) 400

(D) 370

(E) 300

30. A teacher observed that scores on a certain statistics test ranged from 44 to 98. He decides to group the scores in equal intervals. Which of the following groupings is acceptable?

A	B	C	D	E
Interval	**Interval**	**Interval**	**Interval**	**Interval**
44 – 53	44 – 54	44 – 53	under 54	under 55
53 – 62	55 – 65	55 – 63	55 – 65	55 – 65
62 – 71	66 – 76	65 – 75	65 – 75	66 – 75
70 – 79	77 – 87	77 – 87	75 – 85	76 – 85
79 – 98	88 – 98	88 – 98	over 85	86 and over

(A) A

(B) B

(C) C

(D) D

(E) E

Use this information to answer questions 31 to 34.

The following histogram shows the distribution of admissions test scores obtained by applicants to a junior college.

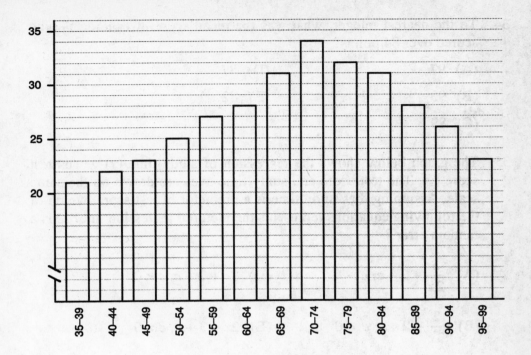

31. How many candidates scored 80 points or higher?

    (A) 27   (D) 77

    (B) 31   (E) 108

    (C) 59

32. How many candidates scored less than 55 points?

    (A) 118   (D) 27

    (B) 91   (E) 25

    (C) 63

33. To the nearest integer, what was the mean score of candidates who scored over 64 points but less than 80 points?

    (A) 67   (D) 74

    (B) 70   (E) 77

    (C) 72

34. To the nearest integer, what was the mean score of candidates who scored over 84 points?

(A) 97

(D) 87

(B) 93

(E) 82

(C) 89

35. The graph below shows the regression of study time (x) versus test score (y). The test-score and study-time axes are drawn on the same scale. Assuming that study time is a predictor of test score, which of the following equations represents the pictured regression line? [e is a random error.]

(A) $\dfrac{3}{2x} + 2 + e; e = 0$

(D) $3x + 2 + e; e < 0$

(B) $\dfrac{2}{3x} + 2 + e; e = 0$

(E) $2x + 3 + e; e > 0$

(C) $\dfrac{3}{2x} + 2 + e; e > 0$

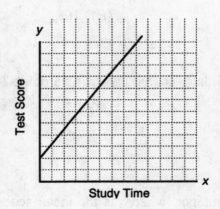

Section II

TIME: 90 Minutes
6 Free-Response Questions

DIRECTIONS: Show all your work. Grading will be based on both the methods used and the accuracy of the final answers. Please make sure that all procedures are clearly shown.

Part 1: Open-Ended

1. A cobbler near a college campus plans to open a shoe store to serve the students. He has room for 2,000 pairs of (equal numbers for men's and women's) shoes. He wishes to figure out how many pairs to buy in a given size and asks for your help. You don't have the time or the resources to do an elaborate survey. However, his records show that the first 50 pairs of shoes he repaired or polished for men in one week were in the following sizes:

    7, 8, 10, 9, 10, 12, 8, 11, 14, 8, 6, 9, 10, 12, 9, 10, 9, 8, 7, 6, 10, 11, 10, 9, 8, 10, 13, 8, 7, 9, 10, 9, 10, 8, 10, 11, 9, 12, 9, 10, 10, 13, 9, 8, 10, 11, 9, 10, 7, 14

    Based on these numbers, how many pairs of men's shoes would you advise him to buy in each size to make up a trial stock of 1,000 pairs?

2. During her first two years at college, Joan took 12 tests in computer-related courses. Her mean score on these 12 tests was 86. She was allowed to drop any two of her scores and when she did, her average score rose to 92. If her score on one of the two tests she dropped was 64, what was her score on the other?

3. Column (1) of the table below shows the ethnic composition of a small town and column (2) shows the ethnic composition of students enrolled in one private school in the same town. The principal of the school claims that the school's admission policy and criteria guarantee an enrollment that reflects the ethnic composition of the entire community.

Composition of Community and Private School Enrollment

	Entire Community	School Enrollment		
	(1)	(2) Actual	(3) Predicted	(4) Difference
European	25,324	264	_____	_____
African	15,698	148	_____	_____
Hispanic	14,852	125	_____	_____
Asian	9,587	86	_____	_____
Others	4,892	44	_____	_____
Total	70,353	667	_____	

a. If the student population in this school is representative of the ethnic composition of the community, how many students of each ethnic background should be in the school? Round the figures to three decimal places and enter them in column (3).

b. Find the difference between the actual and the predicted enrollment for each ethnic group. Enter the results in column (4). Calculate the chi-squared statistic for goodness-of-fit based on the differences between predicted and actual figures, for 4 degrees of freedom.

c. Test the claim of proportional representation at the 5% level.

4. A computer science teacher defines a passing score in his class as a score of 75 or higher; scores below 75 are failing scores. The following scores were obtained by a group of boys and girls on a computer science test.

Boys: 85 90 75 68 74 82 73 81 69 87 70 91
Girls: 81 67 74 80 75 71 85 79 74 80 88 82

a. Calculate the proportion of boys passing the test; call this p_b. Calculate the proportion of girls passing the test; call this p_g.

b. Test for significance the difference between the proportions of boys and girls who passed the test. Use the formula

$$t = \frac{P_g - P_b}{\sqrt{\dfrac{P_g(1 - P_g)}{n_g} + \dfrac{P_b(1 - P_b)}{n_b}}}$$

where n_b is the total number of boys and n_g the total number of girls.

c. Is the observed difference between the two proportions significant at the 5% level?

5. The first row of figures below depicts the scores obtained by 10 students on an admissions test taken at the beginning of the semester. The second row depicts the corresponding grade point averages (G.P.A.) for the same students at the end of the semester.

Student	1	2	3	4	5	6	7	8	9	10
Admission	18	34	23	25	34	41	37	16	24	24
G.P.A.	3.1	3.9	3.6	2.7	3.7	3.8	3.6	2.6	3.6	2.4

a. Compute the coefficient of correlation between the two measures, using the formula

$$r = \frac{\Sigma\left[(X - \bar{X})(Y - \bar{Y})\right]}{\sqrt{(X - \bar{X})^2 (Y - \bar{Y})^2}}$$

where X = admissions test score; $\bar{X}$ = students mean admissions test score; Y = individual G.P.A. and $\bar{Y}$ = students mean G.P.A.

b. Without subjecting the obtained coefficient to further statistical test, would you guess that the relationship between admissions test score and first-semester G.P.A. is direct or inverse? Explain your answer.

Part 2: Investigative Task

1. Mr. McKenzie plants pineapples on a hillside. In order to minimize erosion, he carves the hillside into ten cascading flat strips, like seats in a stadium. He has just picked pineapples from the various strips and the weights (in ounces) are shown in the table.

    If Mr. McKenzie invests money to uproot trees below strip 10, he can plant more pineapples. In order to determine the cost-effectiveness of such an investment, however, he must know what kind of yield to expect from pineapples planted below strip 10. He has only 30 minutes to make up his mind and contracts you to predict the yield for at least the 11th strip. You have only a basic calculator to work with.

    a. Select a sample of four pineapple weights from each strip. Compute the mean of these four weights and use it as the unit of measure for the particular strip. Then develop the regression equation of strip position versus yield.

    b. Calculate the predicted mean yield for the 11th strip.

    c. State any necessary precaution regarding the reliability of the prediction in part (b).

    Circle the four weights that you have selected in each strip. Show all necessary computational details.

Strip 1	14	13	19	13	11	19	12	14	10	10
	18	15	10	15	17	10	16	10	17	18
	13	10	10	19	12	12	16	10	15	16
	18	10	11	14	18	18	10	12	11	17
Strip 2	23	13	23	15	13	23	14	17	13	12
	22	18	13	18	21	12	20	12	21	21
	15	13	12	23	15	14	19	13	18	20
	19	21	13	17	22	22	12	14	13	20
Strip 3	25	24	21	27	24	22	25	14	27	27
	24	20	27	19	23	27	22	26	23	24
	17	27	16	15	20	19	25	17	24	25
	24	27	15	19	24	25	27	16	15	22

Strip 4	26	29	26	16	29	26	30	18	28	28
	24	16	25	16	19	24	18	23	19	20
	28	25	24	22	28	27	18	24	25	26
	25	29	30	18	25	25	28	31	30	23
Strip 5	18	35	31	20	34	18	23	26	20	20
	34	29	21	28	33	20	31	19	32	20
	29	25	24	22	29	28	18	25	34	18
	34	25	31	18	26	26	29	33	31	23
Strip 6	31	29	25	33	29	26	31	35	28	33
	29	23	34	22	27	33	26	32	27	28
	38	34	33	30	38	36	30	39	28	31
	29	34	35	20	29	29	33	37	35	26
Strip 7	23	43	39	25	43	39	23	28	42	42
	37	31	42	30	35	41	33	41	41	42
	31	26	25	23	30	29	39	26	36	39
	37	42	22	28	37	43	25	30	27	40
Strip 8	41	39	34	44	39	35	41	46	38	38
	38	32	45	31	37	43	35	43	36	38
	26	45	44	41	25	24	34	27	38	41
	39	45	46	29	39	39	44	24	46	35
Strip 9	43	40	35	45	40	36	43	48	39	39
	33	26	39	50	31	38	29	37	30	32
	45	39	38	35	44	43	35	46	32	35
	33	39	41	48	33	33	38	43	41	29
Strip 10	38	36	30	41	35	31	38	37	28	28
	49	41	28	40	47	55	45	54	46	49
	34	28	55	51	33	32	44	28	41	44
	42	48	50	30	42	42	47	53	50	38

AP STATISTICS

Test 4

ANSWER KEY

Section I

1.	(A)	10.	(A)	19.	(A)	28.	(A)
2.	(E)	11.	(A)	20.	(A)	29.	(D)
3.	(B)	12.	(C)	21.	(C)	30.	(B)
4.	(B)	13.	(E)	22.	(E)	31.	(E)
5.	(E)	14.	(C)	23.	(C)	32.	(B)
6.	(E)	15.	(E)	24.	(A)	33.	(C)
7.	(A)	16.	(E)	25.	(B)	34.	(B)
8.	(D)	17.	(B)	26.	(C)	35.	(A)
9.	(E)	18.	(A)	27.	(C)		

DETAILED EXPLANATIONS OF ANSWERS

Test 4

Section I

1.   **(A)**   There is no indication in any of the samples of the actual sample size, so we can ignore this factor in evaluating the choices. It is not clear how the "random sample" in choice (A) was drawn. For now, let us skip this choice. We can expect the five campuses to be situated in geographical locations with at least slightly different demographics. So a representative sample from the main campus may not necessarily be representative of all five campuses. Hence we eliminate choice (B).

We can also expect differences in important factors between full-time, day students and part-time, evening students. Hence a stratified random sample from full-time, day students may not necessarily be representative of part-time, evening students. On this basis, we can eliminate choice (C). The sample in choice (D) may be considered a captive sample, which may not be representative of the student population. For example, this sample may consist of a disproportionate number of part-time, evening students who did not drive that day. So we can eliminate choice (D).

A "large sample stratified by race and gender" need not be representative of the entire student body. We cannot assume that this sample is not biased in favor of full-time, day students or part-time, evening students, or, for that matter, against some campuses. In the absence of further information, we can select choice (A) as the most acceptable sample.

2.   **(E)**   Since you are already confident that you have secured 14 points, you need 6 additional points in order to earn a B. Actually, you need *at least 6 points*, which means that you need 6 or more points (to a maximum of 10). That is, you are not looking for the probability of earning exactly 6 more points, but of earning 6, 7, 8, 9 or 10 points.

When there are i options per question, the probability of selecting the correct answer by a purely random method is $p = 1/i$. Let P be the probability of selecting the correct answer by a purely random process when there are i options per question. The probability of selecting k correct answers out of n questions is given by the expression

$$P(k) = \binom{n}{k} p^k (1-p)^{n-k}$$

In question two, $i = 5$; $p = 1/5 = .2$ and $n = 10$. When k = 6, we obtain

$$P(6) = \binom{10}{6}.2^6(1-.2)^{10-6} = 210 \times .2^6 \times .8^4 = .0055050$$

For seven correct guesses, the probability is

$$P(7) = \binom{10}{7}.2^7(1-.2)^{10-7} = 120 \times .2^7 \times .8^3 = .0007864$$

The probability of eight correct guesses is

$$P(8) = \binom{10}{8}.2^8(1-.2)^{10-8} = 45 \times .2^8 \times .8^2 = .0000737$$

You wish to express the answer correct to 4 decimal places, so you can stop here because the fractions are rapidly getting smaller and the probabilities of 9 and 10 correct guesses would hardly contribute significantly to the final answer.

The probability that you would get at least 6 correct guesses is the *sum* of the probabilities of getting 6, 7, 8, 9 and 10. Using the figures already obtained, we see that this probability is

$$.0055050 + .0007864 + .0000737 \approx .0064.$$

This is the probability that you will earn a B grade if I only guess randomly on the multiple-choice section of the test.

3. **(B)** You are confident you scored 14 points and need 6 more points in order to earn a B. Actually, you need *at least 6 points*, which means that you need 6, 7, 8, 9 or 10 more points. [You are not looking for the probability of earning exactly 6 more points.] The probability that I would get at least 6 correct guesses is the *sum* of the probabilities of getting 6, 7, 8, 9 and 10.

When there are i options per question, the probability of selecting the correct answer by a purely random method is $p = 1/i$. Let P be the probability of selecting the correct answer by a purely random process when there are i options per question. The probability of selecting k correct answers out of n questions is

$$P(k) = \binom{n}{k} p^k (1 - p)^{n-k}$$

In this question, $i = 4$; $p = 1/4 = .25$ and $n = 10$. When $k = 6$,

$$P(6) = \binom{10}{6} .25^6 (1 - .25)^{10-6} = 210 \times .25^6 \times .75^4 = .0162220$$

For seven correct guesses, the probability is

$$P(7) = \binom{10}{7} .25^7 (1 - .25)^{10-7} = 120 \times .25^7 \times .75^3 = .0030899$$

The probability of eight correct guesses is

$$P(8) = \binom{10}{8} .25^8 (1 - .25)^{10-8} = 45 \times .25^8 \times .75^2 = .0003862$$

The probability of nine correct guesses is

$$P(9) = \binom{10}{9} .25^9 (1 - .25)^{10-9} = 10 \times .25^9 \times .75^1 = .0000286$$

You wish to express the answer correct to 4 decimal places, so you can stop here because the fractions are rapidly getting smaller, and the probability of 10 correct guesses would probably contribute nothing useful in the final answer.

The probability that you will select at least 6 correct answers by a random process is

$$.0162220 + .0030899 + .0003862 + .0000286 \cong .0197.$$

This is the probability that you will earn a B grade if you only guess randomly on the multiple-choice part of the test.

4. **(B)** The variance of the new scores would be

$$81 \times 42 = 81 \times 16 = 1296$$

For any positive numbers x and y, $(yx)^2 = y^2x^2$. An application of this fact is as follows. Let $x_1, x_2, x_3, ..., x_n$ be the original scores. Then the variance of this set is

$$\text{var}(x) = \frac{\left[x_1^2 + x_2^2 + x_3^2 + ... + x_n^2 \right]}{n}$$

[Let us ignore the usual correction factor.]

Now, if each original score is multiplied by a factor of y and then squared, the new variance becomes

$$\text{var}(yx) = \frac{\left[(yx_1)^2 + (yx_2)^2 + (yx_3)^2 + ... + (yx_n)^2 \right]}{n}$$

[Still ignoring the correction factor.]

$$= \frac{\left[y^2x_1^2 + y^2x_2^2 + y^2x_3^2 + ... + y^2x_n^2 \right]}{n}$$

$$= y^2\left[x_1^2 + x_2^2 + x_3^2 + ... + x_n^2 \right]$$

$$= y^2\,\text{var}(x)$$

This shows that, if each original score x is multiplied by a factor y, the variance of x is raised by a factor of y^2. In question four, the variance of the original is 81 and the multiplying factor is 4^2. So the variance of the new scores would be $81 \times 16 = 1296$.

5. **(E)** There are 1000 numbers from 1 to 1000 inclusive of which exactly 10 are perfect cubes, namely 1, 8, 27, 64, 125, 216, 343, 512, 729, and 1000. The probability of picking a perfect cube is

$$P(C) = \frac{10}{1000} = 0.01.$$

Between 1 and 1000, inclusive, there are only three perfect cubes that are also perfect squares: 1, 64 and 729. So the probability of picking a cube that is also a perfect square is $P(S \cap C) = 3/1000 = .003$. If the first number picked is a perfect cube, the probability that it is also a perfect square is

$$P(S|C) = \frac{P(S \cap C)}{P(C)} = \frac{.003}{.01} = .3$$

6.   **(E)**   Whether human subjects or other entities are involved, the determining factors are the time required to conduct a study, the financial cost, and the size of the population under consideration. If the elements are homogeneous, then a sample of one would do, considering the above factors. So homogeneity/heterogeneity is also an important consideration.

7.   **(A)**   A stratified random sample best enhances the chance of including significant factors, such as cultural background, gender, and needs in the various communities of different sizes. A captive sample (B), such as people who happen to be attending a seminar, may have something in common that does not represent the opinion of the general population. A volunteer group (E) may represent only people who have very strong opinions (one way or another). A   pure random sample (C) does not guarantee fair representation of the various communities. A systematic random sample is feasible mostly when a complete list of all potential participants is available in a convenient format, such as a comprehensive alphabetical listing.

8.   **(D)**   Rendering or denial of treatment (II) applies only to experimental studies, while non-manipulation (III) applies only to an observational (or other) studies. On the other hand, specific hypotheses must be stated before data are collected (I) and the results must be carefully analyzed according to statistical principles (IV), regardless of the format of the study.

9.   **(E)**   For a given sample size (assuming a common unit of measure), the more widely spread the measures, the more the graph would sprawl out.

10.   **(A)**   The first step is to estimate the population mean, $\overline{X}$, and standard deviation, s, from the sample; a summary of the computation is presented in the table below. The number of scores in the sample is $n = 10$; the sum of the scores is 220 and the mean (at the bottom of the first

column) is $\overline{X} = 220/10 = 22$. The sum of squared deviations (bottom of the last column) is $\Sigma(X - \overline{X})^2 = 518$. So the standard deviation is

$$s = \sqrt{\frac{\Sigma(X - \overline{X})^2}{n - 1}} = \sqrt{\frac{518}{9}} = 7.587$$

X	$(X - \overline{X})$	$(X - \overline{X})^2$
20	$20 - 22 = -2$	$(-2)^2 = 4$
14	-8	64
29	7	49
26	4	16
10	-12	144
34	12	144
20	-2	4
30	8	64
17	-5	25
20	-2	4
220	0	518

The second step is to compute the confidence interval; For 9 degrees of freedom, the t value associated with the 95% confidence limit is 1.833. The lower limit of the population mean, μ, is

$$\overline{X} - \frac{s * \alpha}{n} = \frac{7.587 * 1.833}{\sqrt{10}} = 22 - 4.398 = 17.6$$

The lower limit of the population mean, μ, is

$$\overline{X} + \frac{s * \alpha}{n} = \frac{7.587 * 1.833}{\sqrt{10}} = 22 + 4.398 = 26.4$$

So μ lies between 17.6 and 23.4.

11. **(A)** If the data were skewed (B), the mean might not be appropriate. There is no justification for assuming that the study was not a serious one, so we reject choice (C). The number of data points (D) is irrelevant. Since at least one of the options is false, "all of the above ..." would be a contradictory choice.

12. **(C)** The correlation coefficient by itself is no evidence of a causal relationship, as suggested by choices (A) and (B). A correlation coefficient of $-.89$ is a strong indication of strong relationship between any two variables, so (D) must be rejected. The key word that throws out choice (E) is "similarly." If this factor affected the two variables similarly, the correlation coefficient should have been positive.

13. **(E)** "Constant variance" simply means having approximately the same variance along the entire range.

14. **(C)** Plot 1 suggests an increasing sinusoidal curve, while plot 2 suggests a power function. On the other hand, most of the dots in plots 3 and 4 can be enclosed with a pair of horizontal parallel lines.

15. **(E)** The general outlines of the points in 1 and 2 suggest curvilinear rather than rectilinear forms, as shown in the heavy dotted lines below.

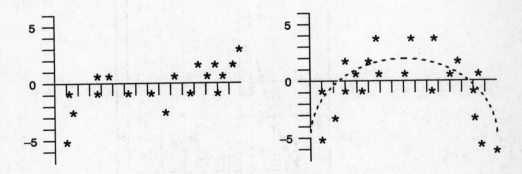

16. **(E)** 20% of 105 is 21. Careful examination of the vertical scale of the graph shows that each space represents 2. So 21 must be located on the vertical axis between the 20 mark and the next higher horizontal line, as shown on the graph. This line intersects the graph and the dotted vertical line leading from the middle of the 30–34 interval. The middle score in this interval is $(34 + 30)/2 = 32$. This is the score that corresponds with the 20th percentile.

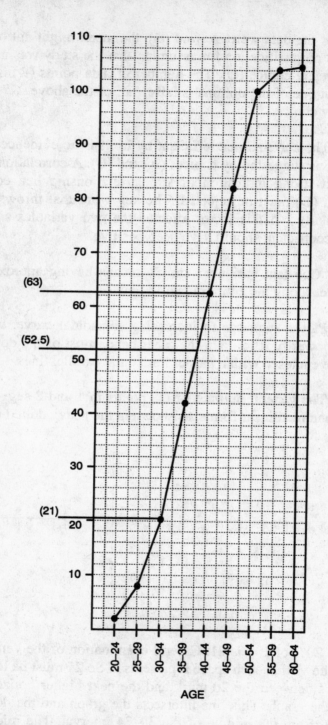

AGE

17. **(B)** The median marks the score point dividing the top 50% of the group from the bottom 50%. 50% of 105 is 52.5. Moving along the vertical axis, we find that 52.5 is located 1/4 of the way up between the 52 and

54 marks. A horizontal line (shown in the graph on the previous page) leading from this point intersects the graph approximately halfway between the 35–39 and the 40–44 intervals on the horizontal axis. We know intuitively that this point is $(39 + 40)/2 = 39.5$. This is the median score.

18. **(A)**   The 60th percentile corresponds to 60% of the sample, and 60% of 105 is 63. Since the vertical axis is on a scale of 1 to 2, 63 is located halfway between the 2nd and the 3rd horizontal (dotted) lines above the 60 mark. A horizontal line through this point intersects the graph directly above the 40–44 score interval. The midpoint of this interval is $(40 + 44)/2 = 42$, and this is the score marking the 60th percentile.

19. **(A)**   We do not know exactly what constituted a "perfect score," although common sense tells us that it must be over 72 in this case. The exact number does not matter. The important thing is that the scores on the repeat test were *all equal*. This means that the variance of this set of scores is 0. The implication is that the correlation between this set and anything else must be exactly zero.

20. **(A)**   Within the narrow age range of 15 to 16 years, age should not be an important factor and, therefore, neither should height be (choice B). So we eliminate choice (B). If boys are paired with randomly selected girls, their scores would be independent of each other, hence we reject choice (C). Mathematical ability is *not generally* an important factor in selecting a boy or girl friend, hence the paired scores would hardly be highly correlated. Siblings' scores might be more highly correlated than scores of unrelated persons. However, the correlation between twin siblings' scores are generally higher than those of other pairs of siblings. Hence we choose choice (A) over choice (E).

21. **(C)**   For the wide range of 13 to 18 years, age should be an important factor in determining performance on a mathematics test. However, if boys are paired with randomly selected girls, the influence of age would potentially become minimal. Hence we choose choice (C).

   If boys are paired with girls of matching heights, there would be an interaction between age and height. So a measurable (if moderate) correlation can be expected between their scores. Hence we reject choice (B). Similarly, age would be an important factor in male-female friendships. Hence we reject choice (D). A high correlation between scores of sibling pair, choices (A) and (D), is very obvious.

22. **(E)** The variable, "city" or location, in this context, is not a continuum. So the amounts of snowfall in the various cities cannot be represented by a continuous function. The data should only be represented by separate spikes (as in (I)) or bars (as in (IV)). The graphs in (II) and (III) are appropriate only for continuous data, not in categorical data.

23. **(C)** A greater agreement (positive or negative) would be expected within the church than from any of the other groups. So responses from a congregation should have a narrower spread than those of the other groups. (Box C shows the narrowest spread).

24. **(A)** The more varied the locations from which the samples are drawn, the greater the differences in opinion. In other words, the wider the spread of the responses. Box A shows the widest spread.

25. **(B)** The correlation of .82 in this context suggests that the more time a student spends on the puzzle, the higher his/her score on the verbal fluency test. Choice (A) contradicts this interpretation and must be rejected. Although no report of a statistical test was presented here, a correlation of .82 cannot just be brushed aside, hence we reject choices (C) and (E). Choice (D) is simply an alternative statement of choice (A), and must similarly be rejected.

26. **(C)** Range (IV) and inter-quartile range (V) tell us little about central tendency. Hence we choose choice (C).

27. **(C)** The simplest way to identify the faulty design in this particular case is to find the sums of the numerals used as group labels: 1, 2 and 3. Within a design, the sums should be constant across rows and down columns. In this case the constant sum is $1 + 2 + 3 = 6$. We find a violation in design C.

28. **(A)** The scatterplot does not suggest any linear or curvilinear relationship.

29. **(D)** The expected frequency, to the nearest integer, can be computed from the expression $(1435 \times 860)/3335 = 370$.

30. **(B)** The intervals in (A) and (D) overlap. There are gaps between the intervals in (C). The widths of the intervals in (E) are inconsistent. So these choices must be rejected.

Under certain circumstances, for example, for severely skewed or open-ended distributions, wider intervals may be allowed at the top and bottom. However, this does not appear to be one of those circumstances. Besides, we have a choice that has equal, non-overlapping intervals (B).

31. **(E)**   Reading off the heights of the bars in the intervals 80–84 to 95–99, we find that the total number of students who scored 80 points or higher is $31 + 28 + 26 + 23 = 108$.

32. **(B)**   Students who scored less than 55 points are those whose scores lie between 35 and 54, inclusive. Reading off the heights of the relevant bars, we have $21 + 22 + 23 + 25 = 91$.

33. **(C)**   The candidates who scored over 64 but less than 80 are those whose scores lie between 65 and 79 inclusive, that is, the intervals: 65–69, 70–74 and 75–79. The mid-points of these intervals are $(65 + 69)/2 = 67$; $(70 + 74)/2 = 72$ and $(75 + 79)/2 = 77$. The frequencies for these intervals are 31, 34 and 32. So the sum of scores from these cohorts is

$$\frac{(67 \times 31 + 72 \times 34 + 77 \times 32)}{(31 + 34 + 32)} = 72.05 \approx 72$$

34. **(B)**   The students who scored over 84 points are the ones whose scores lie in the intervals 85–89, 90–94 and 95–99. The mid-points of these intervals are, respectively, $(85 + 89)/2 = 87$; $(90 + 94)/2 = 92$ and $(95 + 99)/2 = 97$. Reading off the corresponding bars, we find that the corresponding frequencies are 28, 26 and 23. So their mean score would be

$$\frac{(87 \times 29 + 92 \times 26 + 97 \times 23)}{(28 + 26 + 23)} = 92.81 \approx 93$$

35. **(A)**   By completing a right triangle with a hypotenuse on the graph, we find that the slope of the line is 3/2, with a vertical intercept of 2. This is shown only in the equations in (A) and (C). Given that study time is a perfect predictor of test performance, we expect the error to be 0. Only choice (A) meets these criteria.

[The length of the base of the triangle is 4 units; the height measures 6 units; so the slope of the hypotenuse is 6/4 = 3/2. This is just one of the potentially infinite triangles that could have been constructed for the purpose of visually deriving the measure of the slope of the graph.]

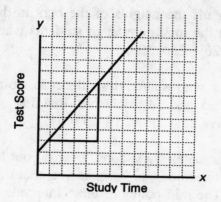

Section II

Part 1

1.   In the absence of further information about the male student population, we must assume that those who carried their shoes in for repairs or polishing represent a cross-section of these students, with reference to their shoe sizes. This allows us to assume further that it is safe to stock shoes in sizes in the same proportion as those repaired or polished.

Careful observation of the figures shows that the smallest shoe size in the sample is 6 and the largest is 14. So the range is only $(14 - 6 + 1) = 9$, and there is no need to group the data. We can tabulate the data as in columns (1) and (2) of the table below.

Size (1)	Frequency (2)	Proportion (3)	# of Pairs/1000 (4)
6	2	2/50 = 0.04	0.04 × 1000 = 40
7	4	4/50 = 0.08	0.08 × 1000 = 80
8	8	8/50 = 0.16	0.16 × 1000 = 160
9	11	11/50 = 0.22	0.22 × 1000 = 220
10	14	14/50 = 0.28	0.28 × 1000 = 280
11	4	4/50 = 0.08	0.08 × 1000 = 80
12	3	3/50 = 0.06	0.06 × 1000 = 60
13	2	2/50 = 0.04	0.04 × 1000 = 40
14	2	2/50 = 0.04	0.04 × 1000 = 40
Total	50	1.00	1000

In the sample of 50, there are two pairs of size 6 shoes. There are several ways to find out how many pairs of size 6 shoes the cobbler needs to make up the 1000 pairs. One way is to find out what fraction of 50 the two pairs represent. This is simply $2/50 = 0.04$. This result is entered in the first row of the table, under column (3). Next, we calculate 0.04 of 1000, namely, $0.04 \times 1000 = 40$. Thus the cobbler should be advised to buy 40 pairs of size 6 shoes for men. This is entered in the last cell in the first row, under column (4). Following a similar procedure, we can determine how many pairs of shoes in each of the remaining shoe sizes the cobbler must buy.

An alternative procedure would be to set up a series of proportions. For example, to determine how many pairs of size 6 shoes the cobbler may be advised to buy, we can think:

2 is to 50 as y is to 1000

or, more conveniently:

$$2{:}50 = y{:}1000$$

This leads to the simple equation:

$$50y = 2 \times 1000$$
$$\text{and yields } y = 40$$

Following this procedure, we can arrive at the same figures as were obtained in the tabular arrangement.

2. Since Joan's average score on 12 tests is 86, her total score on the 12 tests must be $86 \times 12 = 1032$. After dropping two tests, her new mean score would have to be based on the remaining $12 - 2 = 10$ scores. Her total score on these remaining 10 tests must be $92 \times 10 = 920$.

The sum of the two scores that Joan dropped must be $1032 - 920 = 112$. Since one of the scores she dropped is known to be 64, the missing score must be $112 - 64 = 48$.

3. a. In order to figure out what proportion of the students of European parentage should enroll at the school, we need to know the proportion of the entire population the Europeans represent. The total population is 70,353, of which 25,324 are Europeans. So Europeans represent

$$\frac{25324}{70353} = .360$$

(to three decimal places) of the population. This should be reflected in the enrollment figure for European children. The total school enrollment is 667. So .360 of this number should be of European descent. Hence the expected number of students of European origin should be $667 \times .360 = 240.120$. This figure has been entered in the table. The expected numbers for students of other ethnic origins are calculated in the same manner.

Composition of Community and Private School Enrollment

	Entire Community	School Enrollment			
	(1)	(2)	(3)	(4)	(5)
		Actual (O)	Predicted (E)	Difference (E − O)	$\dfrac{(E-O)^2}{E}$
European	25,324	264	240.120	23.880	2.375
African	15,698	148	148.741	0.741	0.004
Hispanic	14,852	125	140.737	15.737	1.760
Asian	9,587	86	90.712	4.712	0.245
Others	4,892	44	46.690	2.690	0.155
Total	70,353	667	667		4.539

b.   The differences between actual and expected enrollment figures are entered in column (4) of the table. In order to compute the chi-square components from these differences, we must square each difference and divide the result by the expected values. For example, the chi-square component from the difference between the actual and the expected numbers of European children enrolled at the school is

$$X^2 = \frac{(23.880)^2}{240.120} = 2.375$$

c.   This figure has been entered in column (5). The rest of the values in column (5) are computed by the same procedure. The sum of these figures is $X^2 = 4.539$. For $5 - 1 = 4$ degrees of freedom, this value is less than the tabled value of 5.49. So the school's claim of proportional representation is a fair one.

4.   a.   Seven boys passed the test (scored above 74), so the proportion of boys passing is $7/12 = .583$. Eight girls passed the test, so the proportion of girls passing is $8/12 = .667$.

b.   The *t* value associated with the difference between the proportions of girls and boys passing the test is obtained by substituting the relevant figures in the formula

$$t = \frac{p_g - p_b}{\sqrt{\dfrac{p_g(1 - p_g)}{n_g} + \dfrac{p_b(1 - p_b)}{n_b}}} = \frac{.667 - .583}{\sqrt{\dfrac{.667(1 - .667)}{12} + \dfrac{.583(1 - .583)}{12}}} = 0.42$$

c.   Even without looking at the table, we know that this value is not significant at the 5% level.

5.   A systematic way of carrying out the computation is to set it up in tabular form. We shall need five columns and 13 rows (one for each student).

a.   *Step 1.* Compute the mean score on the admissions test; the original admissions test scores are listed under the column headed X. The mean of these scores is $280/10 = 28$.

Step 2. Calculate the deviation of each admissions test score from the mean: The deviations are listed under the column headed $(X - \bar{X})$.

Student	X	$(X - \bar{X})$	$(X - \bar{X})^2$	Y	$(Y - \bar{Y})$	$(Y - \bar{Y})^2$	$(X - \bar{Y})(Y - \bar{Y})$
1	18	$28 - 18 = -10$	$(-10)^2 = 100$	3.1	$3.1 - 3.3 = -0.2$	$(-0.2)^2 = 0.04$	$(-10)(-0.20) = 2.0$
2	34	6	36	3.9	0.6	0.36	3.6
3	23	-5	25	3.6	0.3	0.09	-1.5
4	25	-3	9	2.7	-0.6	0.36	1.8
5	34	6	36	3.7	0.4	0.16	2.4
6	41	13	169	3.8	0.5	0.25	6.5
7	37	9	81	3.6	0.3	0.09	2.7
8	16	-12	144	2.6	-0.7	0.49	8.4
9	24	-4	16	3.6	0.3	0.09	-1.2
10	28	0	0	2.4	-0.9	0.81	0.0
Sum	280	0	616	33.0	0.0	2.74	24.7
Mean	28	—	—	3.3	—	—	—

Step 3. Square each of these deviations; enter the squares under the column headed $(X - \bar{X})^2$. Add these squared deviations. The obtained sum of squares is 6.6.

Steps 4 – 6. Compute the sum of squares for the G.P.A., following steps 1 to 3 above and using the G.P.A. figures. The sum of squares for the G.P.A. is 2.74.

Step 7. Calculate the cross-products of the corresponding deviations: The cross-products are entered in the final column of the table, headed $(X - \overline{Y})(Y - \overline{Y})$. The sum of these cross-products is 24.7.

Step 8. Insert the sums of squares and the cross-products in the formula for r:

$$r = \frac{\Sigma\left[(X - \overline{X})(Y - \overline{Y})\right]}{\sqrt{(X - \overline{X})^2 (Y - \overline{Y})^2}} = \frac{24.7}{\sqrt{(616)(2.74)}} = 0.6.$$

b.   Although .6 is clearly positive, a sample of 10 is relatively small and further evidence would be needed in order to determine more definitively whether the relationship between admissions test scores and G.P.A. is direct or inverse.

Section II

Part 2

1. a.   There are several ways to select a sample of four from each subset. For example, you may select one from each of the four rows in a strip by spinning a wheel with ten compartments numbered 1 to 10. In the sample solution that follows, we have used a computer to select the four weights from each strip. The weights selected from each strip have been listed in the following table.

Strip	Selected Weights	Mean Weight
1	14 17 18 19	17
2	23 21 19 12	18.75
3	16 27 15 27	21.25
4	25 29 28 25	26.75
5	29 20 28 23	25
6	36 26 33 31	31.5
7	39 42 43 42	41.5
8	46 41 45 44	44
9	37 41 48 38	41
10	44 36 28 30	34.5

The term *predict* suggests that we need to do a regression analysis. For convenience, we set the data in tabular form. The mean weights for the individual strips have been entered in the next table, under the column headed Y. Some of the computational details are shown in that table. X denotes strip and Y denotes yield.

From the last but one row of that table, we see that

1)   strip mean is

$$\bar{X} = 5.5$$

2) overall mean weight is

$$\bar{Y} = 30.13$$

3) sum of squared deviations for strip is

$$\Sigma\left(X - \bar{X}^2\right) = 82.50$$

4) sum of cross-products of deviations is

$$\Sigma\left[\left(X - \bar{X}\right)\left(Y - \bar{Y}\right)\right] = 238.875$$

Using these values, we find that the slope of the regression line is

$$\hat{m} = \frac{\Sigma\left[\left(X - \bar{X}\right)\left(Y - \bar{Y}\right)\right]}{\Sigma\left(X - \bar{X}\right)^2} = \frac{238.875}{82.5} = 2.895$$

the intercept is

$$\hat{b} = \bar{Y} - \hat{m}\bar{X} = 30.13 - (2.895 \times 5.5) = 14.208$$

and the equation of the regression line is

$$Y_{\text{predicted}} = \hat{m}X + \hat{b}$$

b.   By replacing $\hat{m}$, $\hat{b}$ and X with the relevant values, we obtain a predicted mean pineapple weight for the 11th strip:

$$Y_{\text{predicted}} = \hat{m}X + \hat{b} = (2.895 \times 11) + 14.208 = 46.05$$

So the mean weight of pineapples from the 11th strip would be about 46 ounces.

c.   The regression equation was based on a sample of yields from up to the 10th strip. There is danger in extrapolating beyond the range of observed values. So Mr. McKenzie should be aware that the predicted mean weight of 46 ounces may not be reliable. [The prediction interval could be calculated, but it was not asked for.]

Strip Position			Pineapple Weight		
X	$(X - \bar{X})$	$(X - \bar{X})^2$	Y	$(Y - \bar{Y})$	$(X - \bar{X})(Y - \bar{Y})$
1	$1 - 5.5 = -4.5$	$(-4.5)^2 = 20.25$	17.00	$17 - 30.13 = -13.13$	$(-4.5)(-13.13) = 59.085$
2	-3.5	12.25	18.75	-11.38	39.830
3	-2.5	6.25	21.25	-8.88	22.200
4	-1.5	2.25	26.75	-3.38	5.070
5	-0.5	0.25	25.00	-5.13	2.565
6	0.5	0.25	31.50	1.37	0.685
7	1.5	2.25	41.50	11.37	17.055
8	2.5	6.25	44.00	13.87	34.675
9	3.5	12.25	41.00	10.87	38.045
10	4.5	20.25	34.5	4.37	19.665
55	0.0	82.50	301.25	0.0	238.875

$55/10 = 5.5$ $301.25/10 = 30.13$

PRACTICE
TEST 5

AP EXAMINATION IN STATISTICS

Test 5

Section I

TIME: 90 Minutes
35 Multiple-Choice Questions

(Answer sheets appear in the back of this book.)

DIRECTIONS: For each question or incomplete statement in this section, select the best answer from among the five choices and fill in the corresponding oval on the answer sheet.

---

1. A sample of 150 people are checked to determine their blood type. The results show that 60 have Type O, 40 have Type A, 30 have Type B, and the remaining individuals have Type AB. If one person is randomly selected, what is the probability that this person has either type A or type AB blood?

   (A) $\dfrac{8}{225}$ (D) $\dfrac{3}{5}$

   (B) $\dfrac{2}{25}$ (E) $\dfrac{13}{15}$

   (C) $\dfrac{2}{5}$

2. At a party of 10 men and 20 women, four of the men and 10 of the women are smokers. If two men and two women are randomly selected, what is the probability that all four of these people are smokers? (Approximately)

(A) .312   (D) .032

(B) .133   (E) .020

(C) .040

3. On a charter flight, the mean weight of all the children aboard the plane is 70 pounds, and their total weight is 1050 pounds. The mean weight of all men is 160 pounds, and their total weight is 1920 pounds. The 18 women on the flight have a total weight of 2070 pounds. What is the mean weight of all the people on this flight?

(A) 121 lbs.   (D) 110 lbs.

(B) 115 lbs.   (E) 105 lbs.

(C) 112 lbs.

4. A woman has three pairs of stockings similar in color. If she decides to pair the six stockings in a random fashion, what is the probability that each stocking has been properly matched?

(A) $\dfrac{1}{15}$ (D) $\dfrac{1}{3}$

(B) $\dfrac{1}{9}$ (E) $\dfrac{1}{2}$

(C) $\dfrac{1}{6}$

5. A population of data consists only of the numbers 4, 6, 8, 10, and 12. There are seven 4's, four 6's, and eight 8's. If this population's modes are 8 and 10, what is the maximum allowable number of data?

(A) 40   (D) 27

(B) 34   (E) 16

(C) 28

6. In a normal distribution of data, the mean is 30, and the standard deviation is 4. Among the following, which raw score has the lowest frequency?

(A) 25   (D) 32

(B) 23   (E) 34

(C) 38

7. In a standardized normal distribution, the mean = _____ and the standard deviation = _____.

(A) 1, −1   (D) 1, 1

(B) −1, 0   (E) 0, 1

(C) 0, 0

8. An extremely large population has a mean of 16 and a standard deviation of 8. Consider all possible samples of size 100. What would be the value of the standard deviation of the 100 sample means?

(A) .80   (D) .16

(B) .50   (E) .08

(C) .24

9. Lamps used to light streets have a mean lifetime of 350 days and a standard deviation of 30 days. Assuming that the lifetimes of these lamps represent a normal distribution, what percent of these lamps will last less than 305 days? (Assume that the lifetimes represent a continuous random variable.) Answer will be approximate.

(A) 4.5%   (D) 10.5%

(B) 6.5%   (E) 12.5%

(C) 8.5%

10. An aptitude test was given to 150 applicants, and the resulting scores were put into grouped data form. The first interval consisted of scores ranging from 10 through 19; the second interval contained scores of 20 through 29, etc. The last interval contained scores of 90 through 99. If 47 scores are less than 50, and 42 scores lie in the interval with scores from 50 through 59, what is the best estimate of the median score?

(A) 53.4   (D) 56.2

(B) 54.7   (E) 57.3

(C) 55.5

11. In a group of 32 car batteries, the lifetimes are found to have a mean of four years and a standard deviation of 1.5 years, using Chebyshev's theorem. What is the maximum number of batteries which will last longer than 10 years?

   (A) 2

   (B) 4

   (C) 5

   (D) 7

   (E) 8

12. Given a normal distribution (of continuous data) in which the mean is 150 and the standard deviation is 12, which score separates the lower 4% from the upper 96%?

   (A) 124

   (B) 126

   (C) 129

   (D) 131

   (E) 134

13. A sample of six data is arranged in ascending order. The lowest value is 8 and the range of the data is 10. Which one of the following statements *must* be true?

   (A) The median equals the third number.

   (B) The mode is the value of the sixth number.

   (C) The mean is greater than 10.

   (D) The mode is 10.

   (E) The median equals the mean of the third and fourth numbers.

14. In Jennifer's history class, the professor bases the course grade on one quiz, one midterm, and one final exam. The quiz counts 20%, the midterm counts 35%, and the final exam counts 45%. If her quiz grade was 90 and her midterm grade was 70, approximately what grade will she need on the final exam in order to receive a course grade of 80?

   (A) 77

   (B) 79

   (C) 81

   (D) 83

   (E) 85

15. There are two finalists in a golf tournament, with the winner getting $40,000 and the runner-up getting $15,000. If the mathematical expectation of the better player is $32,500, what is his probability of winning?

    (A) .55   (D) .70

    (B) .60   (E) .75

    (C) .65

16. Given a binomial distribution in which the probability of success is .88 and the number of trials is 20, what is the approximate probability of getting at least 19 successes?

    (A) .37   (D) .25

    (B) .33   (E) .21

    (C) .29

17. A doctor knows that 15% of all her patients are late for their appointments. Given five randomly selected patients, what is the approximate probability that exactly three of them are late for their appointments?

    (A) .004   (D) .114

    (B) .024   (E) .154

    (C) .064

18. Given events A, B where Prob (A) = .25, Prob (B) = .30; let Prob (A/B) mean the probability of event A given that event B has occurred. If Prob (A/B) = .40, what is the value of Prob (B/A)?

    (A) .45   (D) .62

    (B) .48   (E) .67

    (C) .54

19. Using thze Poisson distribution and assuming a bank averages seven bad checks per day, what is the approximate probability that the bank receives 5 bad checks on a given day?

    (A) .180   (D) .126

    (B) .162   (E) .108

    (C) .144

20. In a certain frequency table of grouped data, the class marks for the first three classes are 7.5, 8.2, and 8.9, respectively. Assuming all classes have the same width and given that the lower limit for the first class is 7.2, what is the lower boundary for the third class?

    (A) 8.45   (D) 8.6

    (B) 8.5   (E) 8.65

    (C) 8.55

21. In a music class of five students, each student listens to the same four songs. Each student then selects his or her favorite song without consulting the other students. What is the probability (approximate) that all five students select the same song?

    (A) .0003   (D) .0025

    (B) .0010   (E) .0039

    (C) .0016

22. Given any two positive standard z-scores of a standard normal distribution, which of the following statements must be true?

    (A) The percent of data between these scores is less than 50.

    (B) The percent of data greater than the larger score is more than 20.

    (C) The percent of data less than the smaller score is less than 20.

    (D) The percent of data between the scores is more than 20.

    (E) The percent of data less than the smaller score equals the percent of data greater than the larger score.

23. For which of the following samples is the coefficient of variation the smallest?

    (A) $s = 2$ and $\bar{x} = 12$ (D) $s = 5$ and $\bar{x} = 29$

    (B) $s = 3$ and $\bar{x} = 15$ (E) $s = 6$ and $\bar{x} = 38$

    (C) $s = 4$ and $\bar{x} = 17$

24. Given events A,B are independent and Prob $(A) = 1/3$, which of the following conditions could exist?

(A) Prob $(B) = \dfrac{4}{5}$ and Prob $(A$ and $B) = \dfrac{2}{15}$

(B) Prob $(B) = \dfrac{1}{2}$ and Prob $\left(\dfrac{B}{A}\right) = \dfrac{1}{6}$

(C) Prob $(B) = \dfrac{2}{3}$ and Prob $(A$ or $B) = \dfrac{2}{9}$

(D) Prob $(B) = \dfrac{1}{4}$ and Prob $(A$ and $B) = \dfrac{1}{12}$

(E) Prob $(B) = \dfrac{1}{5}$ and Prob $\left(\dfrac{A}{B}\right) = \dfrac{8}{15}$

25. A license plate consists of two letters of the alphabet, followed by three odd integers. A letter may be repeated, but the three digits must be different. How many different license plates are there?

(A) 39,000

(B) 40,560

(C) 52,440

(D) 81,250

(E) 84,500

26. Given an extremely large size for a population, suppose a sample of this population has 144 data, with a mean of 18 and a standard deviation of 6. With what percent confidence (approximately) can it be stated that the actual mean of the population lies between 17.5 and 18.5?

(A) 83

(B) 78

(C) 73

(D) 68

(E) 63

27. If a distribution of data has no mode, which of the following conditions must exist?

(A) Each piece of data must be positive.

(B) The number of positive data equals the number of negative data.

(C) Each piece of data has the same frequency.

(D) The mean must be zero.

(E) The variance is 1.

28. A delivery company has 20 trucks, three of which have faulty brakes. If three of the 20 trucks are randomly selected, what is the approximate probability that the first two trucks have good brakes, and the third truck has faulty brakes?

(A) .12

(B) .15

(C) .18

(D) .21

(E) .24

29. In a sample of data, the 20th percentile is 30, the 50th percentile is 40, the 70th percentile is 48, and the mean is 35. Which of the following would convert to a positive z-score and have an original value lower than the median?

(A) 32

(B) 36

(C) 40

(D) 44

(E) 48

30. Next weekend, you are expecting a visit from Bonnie and Clyde. The probability that Bonnie will show up is .4, whereas the probability that Clyde will show up is .8. What is the probability that at least one of them will visit you next weekend?

(A) .32

(B) .40

(C) .52

(D) .76

(E) .88

31. At a party, there are five husband-wife couples. If each wife gives a gift to everyone at the party except her own husband, how many gifts are given?

(A) 40

(B) 36

(C) 30

(D) 24

(E) 20

32. Assuming an ordinary six-sided die is unbiased, what are the approximate odds against getting a "2" twice when tossing this die nine times?

(A) .28 to 1   (D) .39 to 1

(B) 2.57 to 1   (E) 6 to 1

(C) .72 to 1

33. How many different permutations are possible using all the letters in the word "INDIVIDUAL?"

(A) 100,600   (D) 3,628,800

(B) 302,400   (E) 5,443,200

(C) 529,200

34. In a sample of five pieces of data, the standard z-scores for three of the data are -1.1, $-.3$, and $.2$. If the remaining two pieces of data have the same z scores, what is the value of the z scores?

(A) .6   (D) 1.5

(B) .9   (E) 1.8

(C) 1.2

35. A distribution of data is positively skewed. This implies which one of the following?

(A) The median is less than the mode.

(B) The mean, median, and mode are all positive values.

(C) The mean is the average of the median and mode.

(D) The mean is greater than the median.

(E) The mode is less than the mean.

Section II

TIME: 90 Minutes
6 Free-Response Questions

DIRECTIONS: Show all your work. Grading will be based on both the methods used and the accuracy of the final answers. Please make sure that all procedures are clearly shown.

Part 1: Open-Ended

1.   A dietitian wants to be 97% sure of estimating correctly the mean number of calories consumed each day by a large group of employees in her company. If she wants her estimate to be within 40 calories and she can safely assume the population standard deviation, σ, is 240 calories, what is the minimum size sample required?

2.   A man wishes to own a shoe store, and he would like to predict his profit in dollars based on the size of the store. Let X = store size, measured in hundreds of square feet, and Y = profit, measured in thousands of dollars. Suppose his sample consists of three stores, where X = 10, 15, 20 and Y = 8, 11, 16, respectively. What is the equation of the least-squares line to fit these data?

3.   We want to test the null hypothesis that a certain diamond is selling around the country for an average price of $523 against the alternative hypothesis that the diamond is *not* selling for the average price. We take a random sample of 100 jewelry stores and decide to reject the null hypothesis if our sample average is less than $515 or more than $531. We can assume that our standard deviation is $42.

   a.   What is the probability of a Type I error?

   b.   What is the probability of a Type II error if in reality the average price of the diamond is $532?

4.   A car rental company, because of continual problems, suspects the claim of the auto manufacturer that the transmissions on their cars has an average lifetime of at least 50,000 miles. Checking on this

claim, the car-rental company determines that 50 cars chosen at random have transmissions that last an average of 48,900 miles, with a standard deviation of 3,175 miles. Does the car-rental company accept the manufacturer's claim if the probability of a Type I error is to be at most 0.01? Give each of the following:

a.   the null hypothesis.

b.   the alternative hypothesis.

c.   the conditions under which the null is rejected.

d.   the results and the conclusion.

5.   It has been shown that a certain a certain medication alleviates arthritis symptoms in 26% of all cases.

a.   On the average, how many out of the next 40 people given the medication will be helped?

b.   What is the standard deviation for this situation?

c.   What is the probability that exactly 10 out of the next 40 will be helped?

d.   What is the probability that at most 10 out of the next 40 will be helped?

Part 2: Investigative Task

1. Groups of 10 students were randomly assigned to two teachers, Mr. Xavier with 5 years of teaching experience, and Mr. Yates with over 15 years of teaching experience. The two teachers taught their respective groups the same subject for the same length of time. At the end of the session, the students took a common test. Here are their test scores.

    Mr. Xavier: 84 87 77 69 75 83 77 82 70 88
    Mr. Yates: 80 67 77 80 75 71 88 79 74 81

    a. Compute the mean and standard deviation for each subgroup. Denote the mean score of Mr. Yates's group by $\bar{Y}$ and the standard deviation of this set by σ_y; denote the mean score of Mr. Xavier's group by $\bar{X}$ and the standard deviation of this set by σ_x;

    b. At the 95% level of confidence, test the hypothesis that the more experienced teacher (Mr. Xavier) is more effective than the less experienced teacher (Mr. Yates). You may use the formula

    $$t = \frac{\bar{X} - \bar{Y}}{\sqrt{\dfrac{\sigma_x + \sigma_y}{n}}}$$

    where n is the number of students in each group.

AP STATISTICS

Test 5

ANSWER KEY

Section I

1.	(C)	10.	(D)	19.	(D)	28.	(A)
2.	(D)	11.	(A)	20.	(C)	29.	(B)
3.	(C)	12.	(C)	21.	(E)	30.	(E)
4.	(A)	13.	(E)	22.	(A)	31.	(A)
5.	(B)	14.	(D)	23.	(E)	32.	(B)
6.	(C)	15.	(D)	24.	(D)	33.	(B)
7.	(E)	16.	(C)	25.	(B)	34.	(A)
8.	(A)	17.	(B)	26.	(D)	35.	(D)
9.	(B)	18.	(B)	27.	(C)		

DETAILED EXPLANATIONS
OF ANSWERS

Test 5

Section I

1. **(C)**   First you must determine how many of the 150 people studied has Type AB blood:

$$150 - 60 - 40 - 30 = 20$$

Twenty people in the sample have Type AB blood. We know 40 people have Type A blood. Then

$$\text{Prob (A or AB)} = \frac{(40 + 20)}{150} = \frac{2}{5}$$

2. **(D)**   The order in which the two men and two women are chosen is immaterial. Assuming we are determining the probability that the first two people are men, the probability for two men, then two women is

$$\left(\frac{4}{10}\right)\left(\frac{3}{9}\right)\left(\frac{10}{20}\right)\left(\frac{9}{19}\right) \approx .032$$

3. **(C)**   First, divide the total weight of the children on the flight by the mean weight of all the children to determine how many children are on the flight.

$$\frac{1050}{70} = 15 \text{ children}$$

Next, divide the total weight of the men on the flight by the mean weight of the men to determine how many men are on the flight.

$$\frac{1920}{160} = 12 \text{ men}$$

Finally, divide the total weight of every passenger on the charter flight by the total amount of passengers on the plane to determine the mean weight of all the people on the flight.

$$\frac{(1050 + 1920 + 2070)}{(15 + 12 + 18)} = 112 \text{ pounds}$$

4.　**(A)**　Select any stocking. The probability that the next stocking selected is a match is 1/5. Now select a third stocking from the remaining four stockings. The probability that the fourth stocking will match the third one is 1/3. At this point, if both pairs have matched, the last two stockings must match. Finally, the required probability is

$$\left(\frac{1}{5}\right)\left(\frac{1}{3}\right) = \frac{1}{15}.$$

5.　**(B)**　Since 8 and 10 are both modes, there are eight 10's. The maximum number of 12's would then be seven. Then the maximum number of data is

$$7 + 4 + 8 + 8 + 7 = 34.$$

6.　**(C)**　In a normal distribution, the further away from the mean a raw score lies, the lower its frequency. Therefore, a raw score of 38 has the lowest frequency.

7.　**(E)**　Whenever any normal distribution has been standardized, each raw score will change to a standard z-score. The mean will be 0 and the standard deviation will be 1.

8.　**(A)**　The standard deviation of sample means taken from an extremely large population is

$$\frac{\sigma}{\sqrt{n}} = \frac{8}{\sqrt{100}} = .80$$

The value of the mean is not used.

9.　**(B)**　Using 304.5, since the lifetimes are a continuous set of variables, change 304.5 to a standard score with the computation

$$(304.5 - 350) \div 30 \approx -1.52.$$

Using the table of normal distribution (standard),

$$\text{Prob. } (z < -1.52) \approx .065 \text{ or } 6.5\%.$$

10. **(D)** $\dfrac{150}{2} - 75,$

so we must approximate the 75th score. Since 47 scores lie below 50, we need to count $75 - 47 = 28$ scores in the interval containing scores of 50 thru 59. Each interval has a width of 10 and the lower boundary of the interval containing 50 through 59 is 49.5. The median is approximated by

$$49.5 + \left(\frac{28}{42}\right)(10) \approx 56.2.$$

11. **(A)** $\dfrac{(10-4)}{1.5} = 4$ standard deviations.

By Chebyshev's theorem, at most

$$\frac{1}{4^2} = \frac{1}{16}$$

of the data lies beyond 4 standard deviations from the mean. Then

$$\left(\frac{1}{16}\right)(32) = 2.$$

12. **(C)** The standard z-score which separates the lower 4% from the remaining data of a normal distribution is -1.75. The corresponding raw score is

$$150 + (-1.75)(12) = 129.$$

13. **(E)** Given any six data, the median must be the mean of the third and fourth numbers, when arranged in ascending order.

14. **(D)** Let x = Jennifer's final exam score. Then

$$(90)(.20) + (70)(.35) + .45x = 80.$$
$$x \approx 83$$

15. **(D)**   Let p = probability of better player winning. Then

$$\$40,000\,p + \$15,000\,(1-p) = \$32,500.$$
$$p = .70.$$

16. **(C)** $_nC_R$ means combinations of n items taken R at a time. The probability of at least 19 successes out of 20 trials is

$$(_{20}C_{19})\,(.88)^{19}\,(.12)^1 + (_{20}C_{20})\,(.88)^{20}\,(.12)^0 \approx .2115 + .0775 \approx .29.$$

17. **(B)** $_nC_R$ means combinations of n items taken R at a time. The probability of exactly three late appointments is $(_5C_3)\,(.15)^3\,(.85)^2 \approx .024$.

18. **(B)**   Since Prob $(A \cap B)$ = Prob (A). Prob $(B\,|\,A)$ = Prob $(B) \cdot$ Prob $(A\,|\,B)$, $(.25) \cdot$ (Prob $(B\,|\,A)) = (.30)(.40)$. Solving, Prob $(B\,|\,A) = .48$.

19. **(D)**   The required probability is given by

$$\frac{\lambda^x e^{-\lambda}}{x!},$$

where λ is the expected number of "successes", and x is the actual number of "successes." In this example, the probability is

$$\frac{7^5 e^{-7}}{5!} \approx .126$$

20. **(C)**   The limits for the first, second, and third classes are:

7.2 and 7.8, 7.9 and 8.5, 8.6 and 9.2, respectively.

The lower boundary of the third class

$$\frac{(8.5 + 8.6)}{2} = 8.55$$

21. **(E)**   The first student's selection is immaterial. The probability that the next four students will each pick the same song as the first one is

$$(.25)^4 \approx .0039.$$

22. **(A)**   For any two positive z-scores, the percent of data between them must be less than 50.

23. **(E)**   The coefficient of variation is

$$\frac{s}{\bar{x}} \cdot 100$$

In choice (E),

$$\left(\frac{6}{38}\right)(100) \approx 15.8$$

which is lower than the other selections.

24. **(D)**   If A,B are independent, Prob $(A$ and $B) = $ (Prob A) (Prob B). Also, Prob $(A/B) = $ Prob (A), Prob $(B/A) = $ Prob (B).

25. **(B)**   The number of different license plates is

$$(26)\,(26)\,(5)\,(4)\,(3) = 40{,}560.$$

26. **(D)**   Using

$\mu = $ mean of the population,
$\bar{x} = $ mean of the sample,
$s = $ sample standard deviation,
$n = $ size of the sample and
$z = $ standard score of a normal distribution,

the confidence interval is given by:

$$\bar{x} - \frac{zs}{\sqrt{n}} < \mu < \bar{x} + \frac{zs}{\sqrt{n}}$$

Since the confidence interval's length is 1 (18.5 – 17.5),

$$\frac{zs}{\sqrt{n}} = .5$$

Then

$$\frac{6z}{\sqrt{144}} = .5$$

so $z = 1$. Finally, the Prob $(-1 < z < 1) \approx .68 = 68\%$ confidence.

27. **(C)**   If each piece of data has the same frequency, there is no mode.

28. **(A)** The required probability is

$$\left(\frac{17}{20}\right)\left(\frac{16}{19}\right)\left(\frac{3}{18}\right) \approx .12$$

29. **(B)** A positive z score indicates a value above the mean, and since the median is the 50th percentile (40), the value sought lies between 35 and 40.

30. **(E)** The probability that at least one will visit = 1 – the probability that neither will visit = $1 - (.6)(.2) = .88$.

31. **(A)** Each wife gives a gift to eight other people. Since there are five wives, (8)(5), 40 gifts are given.

32. **(B)** Since the probability of getting "2" twice is .28, the probability of not getting "2" twice is .72. The odds against getting "2" twice is

$$\frac{72}{.28} \approx 2.57 \text{ to } 1.$$

33. **(B)** Since there are ten letters, with three I's and two D's, the number of permutations is

$$\frac{10!}{(3! \cdot 2!)} = 302,400$$

34. **(A)** Let x = value of each z score. The sum of all z scores of any sample must be zero. Then $-1.1 - .3 + .2 + 2x = 0$. Solving, $x = .6$.

35. **(D)** For a positively skewed distribution of data, the mean must be greater than the median.

Section II

Part 1

1. The formula needed is

$$n = \left[\frac{z_{\alpha/2} \cdot \sigma}{E}\right]^2$$

where n = sample size, $z_{\alpha/2}$ is the critical z value for a level of confidence of $1 - \alpha = z_{.03/2} = z_{.015} \approx 2.17$, σ = population standard deviation, and E = actual error in calories. Then

$$n = \left[\frac{(2.17)(240)}{40}\right]^2 \approx 170$$

2. The least-squares line $y = a + bx$, where a, b are constants, is determined by solving the following equations for a, b:

$$\sum y = na + b\sum x \quad \text{and} \quad \sum xy = a\sum x + b\left(\sum x^2\right)$$

where n = number of paired data. For this example, we get:

$$35 = 3a + 45b \quad \text{and} \quad 565 = 45a + 725b$$

Solving,

$$a = -\frac{1}{3} \quad \text{and} \quad b = \frac{4}{5}$$

The required least squares line:

$$y = -\frac{1}{3} + \frac{4}{5}x$$

3. a. The normal curve representation of this situation is shown by

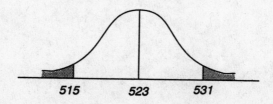

515   523   531

The shaded area represents the probability of a Type I error. Our Z-value formula is

$$Z = \frac{\bar{x} - \mu}{\dfrac{\sigma}{\sqrt{n}}}$$

$$Z = \frac{531 - 523}{\dfrac{42}{\sqrt{100}}}$$

$$Z = 1.90$$

using the normal curve table, the shaded area is $2x(.0287) \approx .057$ or <u>5.7%</u>.

b.   The normal curve representation of this situation is shown by

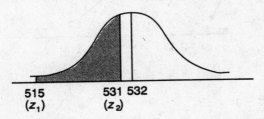

515
(z_1) 531 532
              (z_2)

The shaded area represents the probability of a Type II error. Our Z-value formula is

$$Z = \frac{\bar{x} - \mu}{\dfrac{\sigma}{\sqrt{n}}}$$

we use it twice.

$$Z_1 = \frac{515 - 532}{\dfrac{42}{\sqrt{100}}}$$

$$= -4.05$$

$$Z_1 = \frac{531 - 532}{\dfrac{42}{\sqrt{100}}}$$

$$= -0.24$$

Using the normal curve table, the shaded area is $.4052 - .0000 = .4052$ or 41%.

4.   a.   Null hypothesis is one-tailed because of the phrase "*at least* 50,000 miles."

$$H_0: \mu \geq 50{,}000$$

   b.   Alternative hypothesis is what the car-rental company believes to be true:

$$H_A: \mu < 50{,}000$$

   c.   For the one-tailed situation, at the 0.01 level, the critical Z-value is -2.33. The test is:

$$Z < -2.33$$

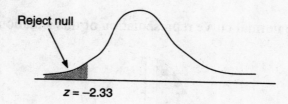

Reject null

$z = -2.33$

   d. $$Z = \dfrac{\bar{x} - \mu}{\dfrac{s}{\sqrt{n}}}$$

$$Z = \dfrac{48{,}900 - 50{,}000}{\dfrac{3{,}175}{\sqrt{50}}}$$

$$Z = -2.45$$

Because $-2.45 < -2.33$, the car rental company can reject the auto manufacturer's claim.

5.   a.   This is a binomial situation, so

$$\mu = n \cdot p \text{ and } \sigma = \sqrt{np(1-p)}$$

so

$$\mu = n \cdot p$$
$$\mu = (40)(.26)$$
$$\mu = 10.4$$

b. $\sigma = \sqrt{np(1-p)}$

$\sigma = \sqrt{(40)(.26)(.74)}$

$\sigma = 2.77$

c. The normal curve for this situation is

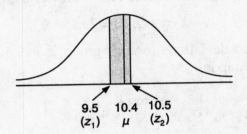

9.5   10.4   10.5
(z_1) μ (z_2)

where "exactly 10" must be altered through the continuity correction to "from 9.5 to 10.5," and we must determine the area of the shaded region under the curve. We use the z-value equation twice.

$$z = \frac{x - \mu}{\sigma}$$

(Note that we do *not* use the z-value equation for a sampling distribution.)

$$z_1 = \frac{9.5 - 10.4}{2.77}$$

$$z_1 \approx -0.32$$

$$z_2 = \frac{10.5 - 10.4}{2.77}$$

$$z_2 \approx 0.04$$

The area between these z-values is obtained from the normal curve table as .5160 − .3745 or .1415 or approximately 14%. (If your normal curve table gives areas from the mean to z, the shaded area would be given by .1255 + .0160 or .1415.)

d. "At most 10" means all values less than and including 10. From the continuity correction, this means from 10.5 down. We know that z for $x = 10.5$ is 0.04, and the area to its left is .5160 or about 52%. So the probability that at most 10 out of the next 40 people will be helped is about 52%.

Section II

Part 2

1.   a.   The making of the mean and standard deviation for each group is shown in the table. The mean score for Mr Xavier's group is

$$\overline{X} = 792/10 = 79.2.$$

The sum of squared deviations for this group is 399.6. So the standard deviation for this group is

$$\sigma_x = \sqrt{\frac{399.6}{10}} = 5.828$$

Computational Steps for Standard Deviations: X = Xavier; Y = Yates

X	$\left(X - \overline{X}\right)$	$\left(X - \overline{X}\right)^2$	Y	$\left(Y - \overline{Y}\right)$	$\left(Y - \overline{Y}\right)^2$
84	4.8	23.04	80	2.8	7.84
87	7.8	60.84	67	−10.2	104.04
77	−2.2	4.84	77	−0.2	0.04
69	−10.2	104.04	80	2.8	7.84
75	−4.2	17.64	75	−2.2	4.84
83	3.8	14.44	71	−6.2	38.44
77	−2.2	4.84	88	10.8	116.64
82	2.8	7.84	79	1.8	3.24
70	9.2	84.64	74	−3.2	10.24
88	8.8	77.44	81	3.8	14.44
792		399.6	772		307.6

The mean score for Mr. Yates's group is

$$\overline{Y} = 772/10 = 77.2.$$

The sum of squared deviations for this group is 307.6. So the standard deviation for this group is

$$\sigma_y = \sqrt{\frac{307.6}{10}} = 5.546$$

b.   The *t*-value associated with the difference between the two mean scores is

$$t = \frac{\overline{X} - \overline{Y}}{\sqrt{\dfrac{\sigma_x + \sigma_y}{n}}} = \frac{79.2 - 77.2}{\sqrt{\dfrac{5.828 + 5.546}{10}}} = 1.875$$

The total number of students in the two groups is $10 + 10 = 20$. For $20 - 2 = 18$ degrees of freedom, the tabled t value for the 95% confidence level is 1.734, which is less than the obtained value of 1.875. This suggests that, at the 95% confidence level, the more experienced teacher was more effective.

PRACTICE
TEST 6

AP EXAMINATION IN STATISTICS

Test 6

Section I

TIME: 90 Minutes
35 Multiple-Choice Questions

(Answer sheets appear in the back of this book.)

> **DIRECTIONS**: For each question or incomplete statement in this section, select the best answer from among the five choices and fill in the corresponding oval on the answer sheet.

1. For a binomial distribution, n = number of trials, p = probability of success, and q = probability of failure. For which one of the following situations would the Normal Distribution approximation *not* be considered an adequate estimation?

    (A) $n = 150, p = .95$ (D) $n = 250, p = .85$

    (B) $n = 180, p = .90$ (E) $n = 300, p = .60$

    (C) $n = 200, p = .98$

2. A suspected criminal is being tried in court, and the probability he will be found guilty if a key witness is called to testify is .90. Historically, the probability that a key witness has been called whenever a suspect is found guilty is .75. If the probability that this key witness is called to testify is .65, what is the probability that this suspected criminal will be found guilty?

    (A) .44   (D) .68

    (B) .59   (E) .78

    (C) .63

3. In a high school graduating class of 100 students, Jane was ranked 3rd, Jim was ranked 10th, and Nancy was ranked 15th. These numbers are an example of _____ level measurement.

   (A) nominal   (D) interval

   (B) ordinal   (E) proportional

   (C) ratio

4. A population of data has a mean of 24 and a standard deviation of 4. Using Chebyshev's Theorem, what is the minimum fraction of data whose value lies between 18 and 30?

   (A) $\dfrac{1}{3}$ (D) $\dfrac{7}{10}$

   (B) $\dfrac{1}{2}$ (E) $\dfrac{4}{5}$

   (C) $\dfrac{5}{9}$

5. In a sample of grouped data, the upper class limits for the three classes are 7.5, 7.9, and 8.3. If the upper boundary for the first class is 7.55, what is the class mark for the third class?

   (A) 7.35   (D) 8.15

   (B) 7.75   (E) 8.25

   (C) 7.95

6. The coefficient of variation for a sample is .40. If the standard deviation is 5, what is the value of the mean?

   (A) 12.5   (D) 4.5

   (B) 10   (E) 2

   (C) 7.5

7. A store sells only televisions, radios, and clocks. There are 15 televisions in the store which sell for $300 each. The number of radios and clocks combined is 50. If each radio sells for $100, and each clock sells for $50, and the mean cost of all the items in this store is $120, exactly how many radios are in the store?

(A) 10   (D) 28

(B) 16   (E) 34

(C) 22

For questions 8 and 9, use the following grouped data distribution concerning seniority (in years) of the people working in a machine shop.

Seniority:	0 – 4	5 – 9	10 – 14	15 – 19
Frequency:	5	7	10	8

8. What is the best approximation for the 30th percentile?

(A) 5.6   (D) 7.4

(B) 6.2   (E) 8.0

(C) 6.8

9. What is the best approximation of the median?

(A) 9   (D) 10.5

(B) 9.5   (E) 11

(C) 10

10. Given a normal approximation of *discrete* data, with a mean of 50 and a standard deviation of 6, approximately how many data have a value of 55 if the total population is 5000?

(A) 236   (D) 335

(B) 271   (E) 367

(C) 303

11. Suppose an extremely large population has a mean of 100 and a standard deviation of 8. If the sample means of all samples of size 9 were extracted, what would be the value of the standard deviation of this group of sample means?

(A) $\dfrac{9}{100}$ (D) $\dfrac{100}{9}$

(B) $\dfrac{8}{9}$ (E) $\dfrac{100}{3}$

(C) $\dfrac{8}{3}$

12. Using the Poisson distribution function, if 1.2 accidents can be expected at a certain intersection every day, what is approximately the probability that there will be two accidents at that intersection on any given day?

    (A) .34   (D) .22

    (B) .30   (E) .18

    (C) .26

13. Mark, Linda, Bill, and Joan are billing clerks in an office. Of the number of erroneous billings prepared, 40% were done by Mark, 20% were done by Bill, 10% were done by Linda, and the rest were done by Joan. Given seven random erroneous billings, what is the approximate probability that two were prepared by Mark, one by Bill, one by Linda, and three by Joan?

    (A) .036   (D) .069

    (B) .047   (E) .082

    (C) .058

14. Given a probability distribution in which the random variable X assumes only the values 0, 1, 2, 3, 4, suppose Prob $(X = 2) = .08$, Prob $(X = 3) = .12$, and Prob $(X = 4) = .22$. Which one of the following *must* be true?

    (A) Prob $(X = 0) =$ Prob $(X = 1)$

    (B) Prob $(X = 0) <$ Prob $(X = 1)$

    (C) Prob $(X = 0) +$ Prob $(X = 1) +$ Prob $(X = 2) = .66$

    (D) Prob $(X = 0) +$ Prob $(X = 4) > .50$

    (E) Prob $(X = 0) >$ Prob $(X = 1) +$ Prob $(X = 4)$

15. Which one of the following binomial experiments contains two trials per outcome?

    (A) Flipping a fair coin 3 times.

    (B) Drawing 1 card from a deck of cards.

    (C) Drawing 5 cards from a deck of cards, with replacement.

    (D) Flipping a biased coin once.

    (E) Tossing a 4-sided die twice.

16. Let $P(X) = \dfrac{X}{48}$ represent a probability function. If the random variable X assumes only 4 consecutive odd numbers, what is the largest value of $P(X)$?

(A) $\dfrac{3}{10}$

(D) $\dfrac{1}{2}$

(B) $\dfrac{5}{16}$

(E) $\dfrac{11}{20}$

(C) $\dfrac{3}{8}$

Use the following information to answer questions 17 and 18.

Assume that the tires sold by the Goodmonth Corporation are normally distributed with a mean life of 43,000 miles and a standard deviation of 2000 miles.

17. If John buys four Goodmonth tires, what is the approximate probability that all four will last longer than 42,000 miles?

(A) .07

(D) .45

(B) .12

(E) .69

(C) .23

18. If Karen buys 6 tires, approximately what is the probability that they will average less than 41,500 miles?

(A) .03

(D) .27

(B) .11

(E) .35

(C) .19

19. For a large population with the shape of a normal distribution, the standard error of the median for all samples of size 25 is 2.4. What is the approximate value of the population standard deviation?

(A) 14.4

(D) 7.2

(B) 12.0

(E) 4.8

(C) 9.6

20. The Alpha car manufacturer claims that their automobiles get at least 10 miles per gallon more than the automobiles from the Beta car manufacturer. Let μ_1 = mean miles per gallon for Alpha cars and μ_2 = mean miles per gallon for Beta cars. If hypothesis testing was conducted for the Alpha car manufacturer's claim, which of the following would be the alternative hypothesis?

(A) $\mu_1 + \mu_2 < 10$

(D) $\mu_1 - \mu_2 < 10$

(B) $\mu_1 - \mu_2 > 10$

(E) $\mu_1 - \mu_2 = 10$

(C) $\mu_1 + \mu_2 > 10$

21. The manager of a department store chain is trying to test whether the mean outstanding balance on 30-day charge accounts is the same in its two suburban branch stores. A random sample of 100 such accounts in each store was taken. In the first store, the mean outstanding balance was $65, and the standard deviation was $15. In the second store, the corresponding numbers were $70 and $18. Which of the following levels of significance would be the *lowest* for which the null hypothesis of equal outstanding balances would have to be rejected?

(A) .05

(D) .02

(B) .04

(E) .01

(C) .03

22. What is the value of the interquartile range for the following sample?

$$3, 3, 4, 6, 7, 7, 7, 8, 10, 20$$

(A) 17

(D) 7

(B) 14

(E) 4

(C) 11

23. How many different arrangements using each of the letters of the word "INSTITUTIONAL" are possible, if the first letter must be "I" or "N"?

(A) 30,624,000

(D) 39,642,000

(B) 33,264,000

(E) 42,246,000

(C) 36,426,000

24. Six students were given a standardized exam in math and English, with results shown in the chart that follows:

Student	Amy	Bob	Cathy	Don	Edna	Frank
Math Score	80	70	65	90	85	60
English Score	75	60	65	80	75	70

In testing the null hypothesis of no correlation between math scores and English scores on this exam, which of the following statements is correct?

(A) Reject the null hypothesis at the .05, .02, and .01 levels of significance.

(B) Accept the null hypothesis at the .05 level, but reject it at the .02 and .01 levels.

(C) Not enough information is given to determine any correlation between the math scores and English scores.

(D) Accept the null hypothesis at the .05 and .02 levels, but reject it at the .01 level.

(E) Accept the null hypothesis at the .05, .02, and .01 levels of significance.

25. A stratified sample of size $n = 60$ is to be taken from a population of size $N = 3600$ which consists of three strata: N_1, N_2, and N_3. For N, of size 1800, $\sigma_1 = 6$. For N_2 of size 1200, $\sigma_2 = 8$. For N_3 of size 600, $\sigma_3 = 10$. What sample size n, should be selected from N, in order to achieve optimum allocation? (Approximately)

(A) 40 (D) 25

(B) 36 (E) 18

(C) 30

26. A marketing firm is interested in studying the potential market for a new cereal. The cities of Boston, Chicago, Detroit, and Miami will be studied as potential markets. Four different kinds of packaging P_1, P_2, P_3, P_4 will be used; four kinds of advertising A, B, C, D will be used. For the following Latin Square, how should the letters A, B, C, D be placed in the third column from top to bottom?

	P_1	P_2	P_3	P_4
Boston	A	B		D
Chicago	B	C		A
Detroit	C	D		B
Miami	D	A		C

(A) ADBC   (D) CDBA

(B) DBCA   (E) CDAB

(C) ADCB

27. A multiple-choice test consists of 12 questions. The first 8 questions have choices A, B, C, D, E, whereas the remaining 4 questions have choices A, B, C. How many different ways are possible for a student to answer all 12 questions (*in millions*, approximately)?

(A) 2.1   (D) 31.6

(B) 11.3   (E) 42.5

(C) 25.0

28. For which *two* of the following are the statement and the hypotheses correctly matched? (H_0 = null hypothesis, H_1 = alternative hypothesis)

    I.   The mean age of all accountants is at least 34. H_0: $\mu \geq 34$ and H_1: $\mu < 34$.

    II.   The proportion of all adults owning credit cards is less than .70. H_0: $p \leq .70$ and H_1: $p > .70$

    III. The variance for waiting time in a bank line is more than 5 minutes. H_0: $s^2 \leq 5$ and H_1: $s^2 > 5$

    IV. The mean height, μ_1, for basketball players is greater than the mean height, μ_2, for football players. H_0: $\mu_1 = \mu_2$ and H_1: $\mu_1 \neq \mu_2$

(A) II, IV   (D) I, II

(B) III, IV   (E) II, III

(C) I, III

29. In defending his client, a lawyer must decide whether to charge a flat fee of $2000 or a contingent fee of $5000. He will receive this contingent fee only if he wins the case. If the lawyer eventually decides he

would rather take the $2000 flat fee, which of the following could represent the probability that the lawyer believes that he can win the case?

(A) .35

(B) .45

(C) .55

(D) .65

(E) .75

30. Events A, B, C, D are mutually exclusive. Prob $(A) = 2$ - Prob (B), Prob $B = 3$ - Prob (C), Prob $(C) = 4$ - Prob (D). Then Prob $(A \cup D)$ is

(A) .39.

(B) .45.

(C) .55.

(D) .61.

(E) .72.

31. In a normal distribution where the mean is 50, a raw score of 46.16 represents the 10th percentile. What raw score represents the 20th percentile? (Approximate)

(A) 44.59

(B) 47.48

(C) 50.37

(D) 53.26

(E) 56.16

32. A study was conducted among 70 people to determine whether being a homeowner is independent of opinions regarding a gun control bill. The results are shown below.

	In Favor	Opposed
Homeowner	15	13
Not A Homeowner	35	7

Which of the following would be the *lowest* level of significance for which the claim of independence would be rejected?

(A) .005

(B) .01

(C) .025

(D) .05

(E) .10

33. Which *two* of the following are probability distributions?

    I.   Prob $(X) = X^2$ for $X = .3, .4, .5$

    II.   Prob $(X) = \dfrac{1}{3} X$, for $X = 1, 2$

    III. Prob $(X) = X - 1.5$ for $X = 2, 3$

    IV. Prob $(X) = \dfrac{3}{[5 \cdot (X + 1)!]}$ For $X = 0, 1, 2$

(A) I, IV

(B) II, III

(C) III, IV

(D) I, III

(E) II, IV

34. A particular population of data is negatively skewed. If the mean is 10 and the mode is 25, what *must* be true about the value of the median?

(A) It must be less than 25.

(B) It must be less than 10.

(C) It must be greater than 10.

(D) It must be greater than 25.

(E) It must lie between 10 and 25.

35. Given events A and B, where Prob (not A) = 1/4, Prob $(A \cup B) = 7/8$, and Prob $(A \cap B) = 1/5$, what is the value of Prob (B)?

(A) $\dfrac{13}{40}$

(B) $\dfrac{3}{10}$

(C) $\dfrac{7}{25}$

(D) $\dfrac{11}{50}$

(E) $\dfrac{3}{20}$

Section II

TIME: 90 Minutes
6 Free-Response Questions

DIRECTIONS: Show all your work. Grading will be based on both the methods used and the accuracy of the final answers. Please make sure that all procedures are clearly shown.

Part 1: Open-Ended

1. In a random sample of 200 vacationers interviewed at a resort, 144 of them said they chose the resort mainly because of its location. With approximately what percent confidence can one state that the true proportion of vacationers who would choose this resort primarily for its location lies between .674 and .766?

2. The manager of a car dealership would like to use the method of least squares to predict the number of cars sold in a given week based on the number of ads he places in various newspapers. During a period of 4 weeks, he placed the following number of ads each week: 6, 10, 7, 12. The corresponding number of cars sold for each of those weeks was 15, 27, 20, 25. Using the least-squares line to fit this data, how many cars would the manager expect to sell during a week in which he placed 20 ads in the newspapers?

3. A cereal manufacturer claims that one serving of Chipper Chex provides 38% of a certain vitamin's minimum daily requirement. A consumer group, in the process of studying the nutritional value of breakfast foods, evaluates this claim for accuracy by taking a random sample of 12 servings and records an average value of 34% of the minimum daily requirement with a standard deviation of 6%. Does the consumer group accept the cereal manufacturer's claim at the 0.05 level of significance?

4. On one rainy morning, a number of students were absent from each of two adjacent classrooms. A '+' sign was marked against the name

of each student who was present and the '−' sign was marked against the names of the absentees. Here is a summary of the data.

Room A: − + − + + + − + − − + + +

Room B: + + − + + + − + + + + − + − − + −

a. Calculate the proportion of students who were absent in Room A; call this p_a.

Calculate the proportion of students who were absent in Room B; call this p_b.

b. Test for significance the difference between the proportions of students who were absent from the two classrooms. Use the formula

$$z = \frac{p_a - p_b}{\sqrt{\dfrac{p_a(1 - p_a)}{n_a} + \dfrac{p_b(1 - p_b)}{n_b}}}$$

where n_a is the total number of students in Room A and n_b is the total number of students in Room B.

c. At the 95% confidence level, does this test indicate a significant difference between the proportions of students who were absent from the two classrooms?

5. After reviewing patterns of rainfall in one city during the month of September for over 10 years, a meteorologist predicted a 50% chance of rainfall every day in September of the current year. The actual number of rainy days was 17. At the 95% level, is the meteorologist's prediction significantly different from the actual number of rainy days? You may use the formula

$$\sigma = \sqrt{\frac{p(1 - p)}{n}}$$

where p is the proportion of actual rainfall and n is the total number of days in September.

Part 2: Investigative Task

1. In order to graduate, senior students have the option of taking either a multiple-choice test or an open-ended test. The multiple-choice test has a mean of 76 and a standard deviation of 5; the open-ended test has a mean of 70 and a standard deviation of 6. The passing scores on the open-ended and multiple-choice tests are 75 and 80, respectively. Assume that Rhonda's potential score on each test is a random variate with the same mean and standard deviation as the population.

   a. Calculate the probability that Rhonda will pass the open-ended test.

   b. Calculate the probability that she will pass the multiple-choice test.

   c. Which of the two tests gives Rhonda a better chance for graduating?

AP STATISTICS

Test 6

ANSWER KEY

Section I

1.	(C)	10.	(A)	19.	(C)	28.	(C)
2.	(E)	11.	(C)	20.	(D)	29.	(A)
3.	(B)	12.	(D)	21.	(B)	30.	(D)
4.	(C)	13.	(A)	22.	(E)	31.	(B)
5.	(D)	14.	(C)	23.	(B)	32.	(B)
6.	(A)	15.	(E)	24.	(E)	33.	(E)
7.	(B)	16.	(B)	25.	(D)	34.	(C)
8.	(D)	17.	(C)	26.	(E)	35.	(A)
9.	(E)	18.	(A)	27.	(D)		

DETAILED EXPLANATIONS OF ANSWERS

Test 6

Section I

1. **(C)** In order for the Normal Distribution to be an accurate estimation for the Binomial Distribution, both $np > 5$ and $nq > 5$ must exist. In choice (C), $nq = (200)(.02) = 4$.

2. **(E)** Let Prob (G) = probability the suspect is found guilty,

Prob (W) = probability the witness is called to testify,

Prob $(G \mid W)$ = probability the suspect is found guilty, given that the witness is called to testify,

Prob $(W \mid G)$ = probability key witness has been called, given that a suspect has been found guilty.

Then,

$$\text{Prob}\,(W \mid G) = \frac{\left[\text{Prob}\,(W)\,\text{Prob}\,(G \mid W)\right]}{\text{Prob}\,(G)}$$

So

$$.75 = \frac{(.65)(.90)}{\text{Prob}\,(G)}$$

Solving,

$$\text{Prob}\,(G) = .78.$$

3. **(B)** At the ordinal level of measurement, data can be ranked but the differences between data cannot be absolutely determined in numerical value.

4. **(C)** By Chebyshev's Theorem, for any given set of data, at least

$$1 - \frac{1}{K^2}$$

of the data must lie within K standard deviations of the mean. Since

$$K = \frac{(30 - 40)}{4} = 1.5,$$

$$1 - \frac{1}{K^2} = 1 - \frac{1}{2.25},$$

which simplifies to $\frac{5}{9}$.

5. **(D)** The lower limit for the second class must be 7.6, since

$$\frac{(7.6 + 7.5)}{2} = 7.55 = \text{upper boundary for the first class.}$$

The classes, identified with class limits appear as follows:

$$7.2 - 7.5, 7.6 - 7.9, \text{ and } 8.0 - 8.3;$$

thus the class mark for the third class is

$$\frac{(8.0 + 8.3)}{2} = 8.15$$

6. **(A)** Coefficient of variation $= \dfrac{\text{standard deviation}}{\text{mean} .4} = \dfrac{5}{\text{mean}}$

Solving, mean $= 12.5$.

7. **(B)** Let x = number of radios, so $50 - x$ = number of clocks. Then

$$\frac{[(15)(300) + (x)(100) + (50 - x)(50)]}{65} = 120.$$

Solving, $x = 16$.

8. **(D)** $(.30)(30) = $ 9th score. Since 5 scores are included in the class $0 - 4$, we must add 4 scores from the 2nd class. Using the upper class boundary from the 1st class,

$$4.5 + \left(\frac{4}{7}\right)(5) \approx 7.4.$$

The 5 was used as a multiplier of $\frac{4}{7}$ since 5 is the width of each class.

9. **(E)** $\frac{30}{2} = $ 15th score.

Since 12 scores are included in the first two classes,

$$\text{median} = 9.5 + \left(\frac{3}{10}\right)(5) = 11.$$

10. **(A)** Using 54.5 and 55.5, 54.5 becomes a z-score of

$$\left(\frac{54.5 - 50}{6}\right) = .75$$

and 55.5 becomes a z- score of

$$\left(\frac{55.5 - 50}{6}\right) \approx .917.$$

The area between these two z-scores (in a Standard Normal Curve) $\approx$ 0471. Finally, we get (.0471) (5000) $\approx$ 236. Note: The continuity correction factor is being used to obtain 54.5 and 55.5.

11. **(C)** The standard deviation of the sampling distribution of means is

$$\frac{\sigma}{\sqrt{n}} = \frac{8}{\sqrt{9}} = \frac{8}{3}.$$

12. **(D)** For the Poisson distribution function,

$$f(2) = \frac{\left(1.2^2\right)\left(e^{-1.2}\right)}{2!} \approx .22$$

13. **(A)** This is an example of the multinomial distribution. The required probability is

$$\left[\frac{7!}{(2!)(1!)(1!)(3!)}\right]\cdot\left[(.4)^2(.2)^1(.1)^1(.3)^3\right]\approx .036.$$

14. **(C)** Prob $(x = 0)$ + Prob $(x = 1)$ = $1 - .08 - .12 - .22 = .58$.

Thus Prob $(x = 0)$ + Prob $(x = 1)$ + Prob $(x = 2)$ = $.58 + .08 = .66$.

15. **(E)** Assume the numbers on the die are 1, 2, 3, 4. Each outcome would appear as follows: 11, 12, 13, …. Each outcome would have two trials; ij = the number i occurs on the first trial and the number j occurs on the second trial.

16. **(B)** Let x, $x + 2$, $x + 4$, $x + 6$ represent the odd numbers. Then $x + (x + 2) + (x + 4) + (x + 6) = 48$. Solving, $x = 9$, so 9, 11, 13, 15 are the four x values. Finally,

$$P(15) = \frac{15}{48} = \frac{5}{16}.$$

17. **(C)** To find the probability that an individual tire, x, will last longer than 42,000 miles. Calculate: $Pr(X > 42000)$. Now standardize:

$$\Pr\left(\frac{X - 43000}{2000} > \frac{42000 - 43000}{2000}\right)$$

$$\Pr(z > -.50)$$
$$= 1 - \Pr(z < -.50)$$
$$= 1 - .3085$$

then Prob $(z > -.50) \approx .6915$. Finally, $(.6915)^4 \approx .23$.

18. **(A)** The standard error of estimate for the sample average is

$$\sigma\bar{x} = \frac{\sigma}{\sqrt{n}} = \frac{2000}{\sqrt{6}} \approx 816.5$$

and the mean is $\mu\bar{x} = 43000$. $\Pr(\bar{x} < 41500)$ after standardizing =

$$\Pr\left(\frac{\bar{x} - 43000}{816.5} < \frac{415000 - 43000}{816.5}\right)$$

Then we have Prob $(z < -1.84) \approx .03$.

19. **(C)**   The standard error of the median =

$$\left(\sqrt{\frac{\pi}{2}}\right)\left(\frac{\sigma}{\sqrt{n}}\right) \approx (1.2533)\left(\frac{\sigma}{\sqrt{n}}\right),$$

where σ = population standard deviation and n = sample size. Now

$$2.4 = (1.2533)\left(\frac{\sigma}{\sqrt{25}}\right)$$

Solving, $\sigma \approx 9.6$.

20. **(D)**   The null hypothesis would be $\mu_1 - \mu_2 \geq 10$, so the alternative hypothesis must be $\mu_1 - \mu_2 < 10$.

21. **(B)**   The test statistic

$$z = \frac{(65 - 70)}{\sqrt{\dfrac{15^2}{100} + \dfrac{18^2}{100}}} \approx -2.13.$$

At the .04 level of significance, the critical z-values are ± 2.05, but at the .03 level of significance. The critical z-values are ± 2.17. Since $-2.13 < -2.05$ but $-2.13 > -2.17$, .04 is the lowest allowable level.

22. **(E)**   The interquartile range = $Q_3 - Q_1$.

$$Q_3 = \text{75th percentile; So,}$$

$$(.75)\,(10) = 7.5,$$

which becomes the 8th number = 8.

$$Q_1 = \text{25th percentile, So,}$$

$$(.25)\,(10) = 2.5,$$

which becomes the 3rd number = 4.

Finally, $8 - 4 = 4$.

23. **(B)**   Using "*I*" as the first letter, there are

$$\frac{12!}{[(3!)(2!)(2!)]} = 19,958,400$$

arrangements. Using "N" as the first letter, there are

$$\frac{12!}{[(3!)(3!)]} = 13,305,600$$

arrangements. The grand total = 33,264,000.

24. **(E)**   The correlation coefficient =

$$\frac{S_{xy}}{\sqrt{(S_{xx})(S_{yy})}},$$

where

$$S_{xy} = \sum xy - \frac{1}{n}(\sum x)(\sum y),$$

$$S_{xx} = \sum x^2 - \frac{1}{n}(\sum x)^2, \text{ and}$$

$$S_{yy} = \sum y^2 - \frac{1}{n}(\sum y)^2.$$

In this example,

$$S_{xy} = 32,200 - \left(\frac{1}{6}\right)(450)\,(425) = 325$$

$$S_{xx} = 34,450 - \left(\frac{1}{6}\right)(202,500) = 700$$

$$S_{yy} = 30,375 - \left(\frac{1}{6}\right)(180,625) \approx 270.83$$

The correlation coefficient =

$$\frac{325}{\sqrt{(700)(270.83)}} \approx .7464.$$

The critical values for the correlation coefficient at the .05, .02, and .01 levels are .811, .882, and .917 respectively. Thus, the null hypothesis of no correlation is accepted at all three levels of significance. Note: A Chart of critical values of the Pearson Correlation Coefficient is required.

25. **(D)**   The formula is

$$n_1 = \frac{n \cdot N_1 \cdot \sigma_1}{\left[N_1\sigma_1 + N_2\sigma_2 + N_3\sigma_3\right]} = \frac{648,000}{26,400} \approx 25.$$

26. **(E)**   In a Latin Square, each letter must occur only once in each column and each row. The correct entries from top to bottom in the 3rd column are CDAB.

27. **(D)**   The number of different ways + $(5^8)(3^4) = 31,640,625 \approx 31.6$ million.

28. **(C)**   The "equal" sign *must* be included in H_0, so statements I and III satisfy this condition. Statement II is wrong because Ho should be $p \geq .70$ and H_1 should be $p < .70$. Statement IV is wrong because H_0 should be $\mu_1 \leq \mu_2$ and H_1 should be $\mu_1 > \mu_2$.

29. **(A)**   If p = the lawyer's belief that he can win the case, then \$5000 p = his mathematical expectation. Since he believes he would fare better with the flat \$2000 fee, $5000\ p < 2000$. This means $p < .40$. Only choice (A) satisfies this requirement.

30. **(D)**   Let x, $4x$, $12x$, $24x$ represent Prob (D), Prob (C), Prob (B), Prob (A), respectively. Then $x + 4x + 12x + 24x = 1$. Solving, $x \approx .0244$. Finally, $x + 24x = 25x = .61$.

31. **(B)**   A z-score of -1.28 corresponds to the 10th percentile of a normal distirbution. The standard deviation, σ, can be found by solving

$$-1.28 = \frac{(46.16 - 50)}{\sigma}.$$

Then $\sigma = 3$. Since a z-score of $-.84$ represents the 20th percentile, letting x = unknown raw score,

$$-.84 = \frac{(x - 50)}{3}$$

Thus, $x = 47.48$.

32. **(B)**   The expected values for 15, 35, 13, and 7 are:

$$\frac{(28)(50)}{70},$$

$$\frac{(42)(50)}{70},$$

$$\frac{(28)(20)}{70}, \text{ and}$$

$$\frac{(42)(20)}{70},$$

which become 20, 30, 8, and 12 respectively. The chi-square (χ^2) test statistic =

$$\frac{(15-20)^2}{20} + \frac{(35-30)^2}{30} + \frac{(13-8)^2}{8} + \frac{(7-12)^2}{12} \approx 7.29.$$

Since $\chi^2_{.01} = 6.635$ and $\chi^2_{.005} = 7.879$, .01 is the lowest level for rejection. Note: Since this is a 2 × 2 table of values, the chi-square statistics uses $(2-1) \times (2-1) = 1$ degree of freedom in the required calculation.

33. **(E)**   For II, Prob (1) + Prob (2) =

$$\frac{1}{3} + \frac{2}{3} = 1$$

and for IV, Prob (0) + Prob (1) + Prob (2) =

$$\frac{3}{5} + \frac{3}{10} + \frac{3}{30} = 1.$$

Item I is not a proability distribution because

$$\text{Prob (.3) + Prob (.4) + Prob (.5)} = .5.$$

Item III fails the probability distribution criterion because

$$\text{Prob (2) + Prob (3)} = 2.$$

34. **(C)**   For a negatively skewed distribution, the median must be greater than the mean.

35. **(A)**   Prob $(A \cup B)$ = Prob (A) + Prob (B) - Prob $(A \cap B)$. Thus,

$$\frac{7}{8} = \frac{3}{4} + \text{Prob}(B) - \frac{1}{5}.$$

Solving, Prob $(B) = \frac{13}{40}$.

Section II

Part 1

1. A $(1- \alpha)$ 100 percent confidence interval for the true proportion. p is given by:

$$\frac{x}{n} - x_{\alpha/2}\sqrt{\frac{\frac{x}{n}\left(1-\frac{x}{n}\right)}{n}} < p < z_{\alpha/2}\sqrt{\frac{\frac{x}{n}\left(1-\frac{x}{n}\right)}{n}}.$$

Since $x = 144$, $n = 200$, $z_{\alpha/2}$ is unknown, but

$$z_{\alpha/2}\sqrt{\frac{\frac{x}{n}\left(1-\frac{x}{n}\right)}{n}}$$

must be equivalent to

$$\frac{144}{200} - .674 \text{ or } .766 - \frac{144}{200} = .046.$$

Then

$$z_{\alpha/2}\sqrt{\frac{.72(1-.72)}{200}} = .046,$$

and this leads to $z_{\alpha/2} \approx 1.45$.

Using a Table of Normal Curves,

$$\alpha/2 \approx .5 - .4265 = .0735, \text{ so } \alpha = .147.$$

Finally, the percent confidence is given by $(1 - .147)(100) = 85.3\%$

2. The Least-Squares line $y = a + bx$, where a, b are constants, is determined by solving the following equations for a, b:

$$\Sigma y = na + b\Sigma x \text{ and } \Sigma xy = a\Sigma x + b(\Sigma x^2),$$

where n = number of paired data. For this example, $87 = 4a + 35b$ and $800 = 35a + 329b$. Solving $a \approx 6.88$ and $b \approx 1.70$. The Least-Squares line is $y = 6.88 + 1.70x$. Letting $x = 20$, $y \approx 41$ cars.

3. The null hypothesis here is that the value being examined equals 88% or $\mu = .38$. The alternative hypothesis for this two-tailed situation is that $\mu \neq .38$. Note that the situation is two-tailed because the claim of the cereal manufacturer is not that the cereal contains *at least* 88%. Also the phrase "for accuracy" implies a two-tailed situation. Here $n < 30$, so we have a t-statistic test. The degrees of freedom is one less than the size of the sample, so d.f. $= n - 1 = 12 - 1 = 11$. Looking up the critical t-value in the table yields $t = 2.201$, so we reject the null if $t < -2.201$ or $t > 2.201$.

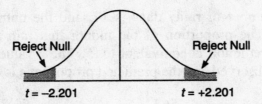

Reject Null   Reject Null

$t = -2.201$ $t = +2.201$

Calculating

$$t = \frac{\bar{x} - \mu}{\frac{s}{\sqrt{n}}}$$

$$t = \frac{.34 - .38}{\frac{.06}{\sqrt{.2}}}$$

$$t = -2.31$$

The consumer group has to reject the cereal manufacturer»s claim because $-2.31 < -2.201$.

4. a.   There are 13 students in Room A. By counting the $-$'s, we find that five of these students were absent. The proportion of the class that was absent is $5/13 = 0.385$. The minus $(-)$ signs show that six students were absent in Room B. The proportion of students who are absent in this room is $6/17 = 0.353$.

$$\frac{6}{17} = 0.353.$$

b.   The z value for the difference between the two proportions may be obtained as follows:

$$z = \frac{.385 - .353}{\sqrt{\dfrac{.385(1-.615)}{13} + \dfrac{.353(1-.647)}{15}}} = 0.182$$

c.   Even without consulting the tables, we can see that this value is not statistically significant. In other words, there is little difference between the proportions of students who were absent from the two rooms.

5.   The actual number of rainy days is 17, and the number of days in September is 30. The proportion of the month that rain fell is 17/30 = 0.567. The 50% prediction is equivalent to .5. The z value for the difference between the observed and the predicted proportions is

$$z = \frac{.567 - .5}{\sqrt{\dfrac{.567 \times .5}{30}}} = .744$$

The question was whether there was a significant difference between the predicted and the observed proportions, regardless of the direction. So we treat this as a two-tailed test. In order for the difference to be statistically significant at the 95% confidence level, the associated z value must be at least ±1.96. Since the obtained z value falls far below this figure, we conclude that the meteorologist's prediction was not significantly off.

Section II

Part 2

1.   a.   The probability that Rhonda will pass the open-ended test may be computed as follows:

The z value for a score of 75 when the population mean is 70 and standard deviation is 6 is

$$z = \frac{75 - 70}{6} = 0.8333$$

The probability associated with this z value (from the tables) is .2033.

     b.   The probability that she will pass the multiple-choice test may be computed as follows:

The z value for a score of 80 (population mean = 76 and standard deviation = 5) is

$$z = \frac{80 - 76}{5} = .8$$

The probability associated with this z value (from the tables) is .2119.

     c.   Rhonda has a slightly better chance of graduating if she takes the open-ended test than if she takes the multiple-choice test.

APPENDIX:
FORMULAS
AND TABLES

Appendix

APPENDIX: FORMULAS AND TABLES

The following is a list of formulas and tables that will be provided to students taking the AP examination. The students taking this course should concentrate on developing an understanding of the fundamental concepts of statistics and are not required to memorize formulas.

DESCRIPTIVE STATISTICS

$$\bar{x} = \frac{\sum x_i}{n}$$

$$s_x = \sqrt{\frac{1}{n-1}\sum(x_i - \bar{x})^2}$$

$$s_p = \sqrt{\frac{(n_1 - 1)s_1^2 + (n_2 - 1)s_2^2}{(n_1 - 1) + (n_2 - 1)}}$$

$$\hat{y} = b_0 + b_1 x$$

$$b_1 = \frac{\sum(x_i - \bar{x})(y_i - \bar{y})}{\sum(x_i - \bar{x})^2}$$

$$b_0 = \bar{y} - b_1 \bar{x}$$

$$r = \frac{1}{n-1}\sum\left(\frac{x_1-\bar{x}}{s_x}\right)\left(\frac{y_i-\bar{y}}{s_y}\right)$$

$$b_1 = r\frac{s_y}{s_x}$$

$$s_{b_1} = \frac{\sqrt{\dfrac{\sum(y_i-\hat{y}_i)^2}{n-2}}}{\sqrt{\sum(x_i-\bar{x})^2}}$$

PROBABILITY

$$P(A \cup B) = P(A) + P(B) - P(A \cap B)$$

$$P(A|B) = \frac{P(A \cap B)}{P(B)}$$

$$E(X) = \mu_x = \sum x_i p_i$$

$$Var(X) = \sigma_x^2 = \sum(x_i-\mu_x)^2 p_i$$

If X has a binomial distribution with parameters n and p, then:

$$P(X = k) = \binom{n}{k}p^k(1-p)^{n-k}$$

$$\mu_x = np$$

$$\sigma_x = \sqrt{np(1-p)}$$

$$\mu_{\hat{p}} = p$$

$$\sigma_{\hat{p}} = \sqrt{\frac{p(1-p)}{n}}$$

If X has a normal distribution with mean μ and standard deviation σ, then:

$$\mu_{\bar{x}} = \mu$$

$$\sigma_{\bar{x}} = \frac{\sigma}{\sqrt{n}}$$

INFERENTIAL STATISTICS

standardized test statistic: $\dfrac{\text{estimate} - \text{parameter}}{\text{standard deviation of the estimate}}$

confidence interval: estimate $\pm$ (critical value) $\cdot$ (standard deviation of the estimate)

Single Sample

statistic	standard deviation
mean	$\dfrac{\sigma}{\sqrt{n}}$
proportion	$\sqrt{\dfrac{p(1-p)}{n}}$

Two Sample

statistic	standard deviation
difference of means (unequal variances)	$\sqrt{\dfrac{\sigma_1^2}{n_1} + \dfrac{\sigma_2^2}{n_2}}$
difference of means (equal variances)	$\sigma\sqrt{\dfrac{1}{n_1} + \dfrac{1}{n_2}}$
difference of proportions (unequal variances)	$\sqrt{\dfrac{p_1(1-p_1)}{n_1} + \dfrac{p_2(1-p_2)}{n_2}}$
difference of proportions (equal variances)	$\sqrt{p(1-p)}\sqrt{\dfrac{1}{n_1} + \dfrac{1}{n_2}}$

TABLES

TABLE 1: STANDARD NORMAL PROBABILITIES

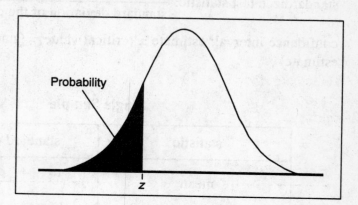

Table entry for z is the probability lying below z.

Probability

z	.00	.01	.02	.03	.04	.05	.06	.07	.08	.09
-3.4	.0003	.0003	.0003	.0003	.0003	.0003	.0003	.0003	.0003	.0002
-3.3	.0005	.0005	.0005	.0004	.0004	.0004	.0004	.0004	.0004	.0003
-3.2	.0007	.0007	.0006	.0006	.0006	.0006	.0006	.0005	.0005	.0005
-3.1	.0010	.0009	.0009	.0009	.0008	.0008	.0008	.0008	.0007	.0007
-3.0	.0013	.0013	.0013	.0012	.0012	.0011	.0011	.0011	.0010	.0010
-2.9	.0019	.0018	.0018	.0017	.0016	.0016	.0015	.0015	.0014	.0014
-2.8	.0026	.0025	.0024	.0023	.0023	.0022	.0021	.0021	.0020	.0019
-2.7	.0035	.0034	.0033	.0032	.0031	.0030	.0029	.0028	.0027	.0026
-2.6	.0047	.0045	.0044	.0043	.0041	.0040	.0039	.0038	.0037	.0036
-2.5	.0062	.0060	.0059	.0057	.0055	.0054	.0052	.0051	.0049	.0048
-2.4	.0082	.0080	.0078	.0075	.0073	.0071	.0069	.0068	.0066	.0064
-2.3	.0107	.0104	.0102	.0099	.0096	.0094	.0091	.0089	.0087	.0084
-2.2	.0139	.0136	.0132	.0129	.0125	.0122	.0119	.0116	.0113	.0110
-2.1	.0179	.0174	.0170	.0166	.0162	.0158	.0154	.0150	.0146	.0143
-2.0	.0228	.0222	.0217	.0212	.0207	.0202	.0197	.0192	.0188	.0183
-1.9	.0287	.0281	.0274	.0268	.0262	.0256	.0250	.0244	.0239	.0233
-1.8	.0359	.0351	.0344	.0336	.0329	.0322	.0314	.0307	.0301	.0294
-1.7	.0446	.0436	.0427	.0418	.0409	.0401	.0392	.0384	.0375	.0367
-1.6	.0548	.0537	.0526	.0516	.0505	.0495	.0485	.0475	.0465	.0455
-1.5	.0668	.0655	.0643	.0630	.0618	.0606	.0594	.0582	.0571	.0559
-1.4	.0808	.0793	.0778	.0764	.0749	.0735	.0721	.0708	.0694	.0681
-1.3	.0968	.0951	.0934	.0918	.0901	.0885	.0869	.0853	.0838	.0823
-1.2	.1151	.1131	.1112	.1093	.1075	.1056	.1038	.1020	.1003	.0985
-1.1	.1357	.1335	.1314	.1292	.1271	.1251	.1230	.1210	.1190	.1170
-1.0	.1587	.1562	.1539	.1515	.1492	.1469	.1446	.1423	.1401	.1379
-0.9	.1841	.1814	.1788	.1762	.1736	.1711	.1685	.1660	.1635	.1611
-0.8	.2119	.2090	.2061	.2033	.2005	.1977	.1949	.1922	.1894	.1867
-0.7	.2420	.2389	.2358	.2327	.2296	.2266	.2236	.2206	.2177	.2148
-0.6	.2743	.2709	.2676	.2643	.2611	.2578	.2546	.2514	.2483	.2451
-0.5	.3085	.3050	.3015	.2981	.2946	.2912	.2877	.2843	.2810	.2776
-0.4	.3446	.3409	.3372	.3336	.3300	.3264	.3228	.3192	.3156	.3121
-0.3	.3821	.3783	.3745	.3707	.3669	.3632	.3594	.3557	.3520	.3483
-0.2	.4207	.4168	.4129	.4090	.4052	.4013	.3974	.3936	.3897	.3859
-0.1	.4602	.4562	.4522	.4483	.4443	.4404	.4364	.4325	.4286	.4247
-0.0	.5000	.4960	.4920	.4880	.4840	.4801	.4761	.4721	.4681	.4641

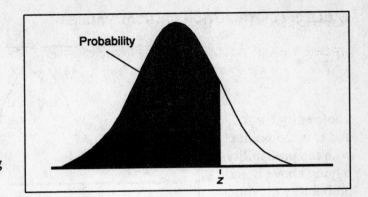

Table entry for *z* is
the probability lying
below *z*.

Table A *(Continued)*

z	.00	.01	.02	.03	.04	.05	.06	.07	.08	.09
0.0	.5000	.5040	.5080	.5120	.5160	.5199	.5239	.5279	.5319	.5359
0.1	.5398	.5438	.5478	.5517	.5557	.5596	.5636	.5675	.5714	.5753
0.2	.5793	.5832	.5871	.5910	.5948	.5987	.6026	.6064	.6103	.6141
0.3	.6179	.6217	.6255	.6293	.6331	.6368	.6406	.6443	.6480	.6517
0.4	.6554	.6591	.6628	.6664	.6700	.6736	.6772	.6808	.6844	.6879
0.5	.6915	.6950	.6985	.7019	.7054	.7088	.71.23	.7157	.7190	.7224
0.6	.7257	.7291	.7824	.7857	.7889	.7422	.7454	.7486	.7517	.7549
0.7	.7580	.7611	.7642	.7673	.7704	.7734	.7764	.7794	.7823	.7852
0.8	.7881	.7910	.7939	.7967	.7995	.8023	.8051	.8078	.8106	.8133
0.9	.8159	.8186	.8212	.8238	.8264	.8289	.8315	.8340	.8365	.8389
1.0	.8413	.8438	.8461	.8485	.8508	.8531	.8554	.8577	.8599	.8621
1.1	.8643	.8665	.8686	.8708	.8729	.8749	.8770	.8790	.8810	.8830
1.2	.8849	.8869	.8888	.8907	.8925	.8944	.8962	.8980	.8997	.9015
1.3	.9032	.9049	.9066	.9082	.9099	.9115	.9131	.9147	.9162	.9177
1.4	.9192	.9207	.9222	.9236	.9251	.9265	.9279	.9292	.9306	.9319
1.5	.9382	.9345	.9357	.9370	.9382	.9394	.9406	.9418	.9429	.9441
1.6	.9452	.9463	.9474	.9484	.9495	.9505	.9515	.9525	.9535	.9545
1.7	.9554	.9564	.9573	.9582	.9591	.9599	.9608	.961.6	.9625	.9633
1.8	.9641	.9649	.9656	.9664	.9671	.9678	.9686	.9693	.9699	.9706
1.9	.9713	.9719	.9726	.9732	.9738	.9744	.9750	.9756	.9761	.9767
2.0	.9772	.9778	.9783	.9788	.9793	.9798	.9803	.9808	.9812	.9817
2.1	.9821	.9826	.9830	.9834	.9838	.9842	.9846	.9850	.9854	.9857
2.2	.9861	.9864	.9868	.9871	.9875	.9878	.9881	.9884	.9887	.9890
2.3	.9893	.9896	.9898	.9901	.9904	.9906	.9909	.9911	.9913	.9916
2.4	.9918	.9920	.9922	.9925	.9927	.9929	.9931	.9932	.9934	.9936
2.5	.9988	.9940	.9941	.9943	.9945	.9946	.9948	.9949	.9951	.9952
2.6	.9953	.9955	.9956	.9957	.9959	.9960	.9961	.9962	.9963	.9964
2.7	.9965	.9966	.9967	.9968	.9969	.9970	.9971	.9972	.9973	.9974
2.8	.9974	.9975	.9976	.9977	.9977	.9978	.9979	.9979	.9980	.9981
2.9	.9981	.9982	.9982	.9983	.9984	.9984	.9985	.9985	.9986	.9986
3.0	.9987	.9987	.9987	.9988	.9988	.9989	.9989	.9989	.9990	.9990
3.1	.9990	.9991.	.9991	.9991	.9992	.9992	.9992	.9992	.9993	.9993
3.2	.9993	.9993	.9994	.9994	.9994	.9994	.9994	.9995	.9995	.9995
3.3	.9995	.9995	.9995	.9996	.9996	.9996	.9996	.9996	.9996	.9997
3.4	.9997	.9997	.9997	.9997	.9997	.9997	.9997	.9997	.9997	.9998

TABLE 2: *t*-DISTRIBUTION CRITICAL VALUES

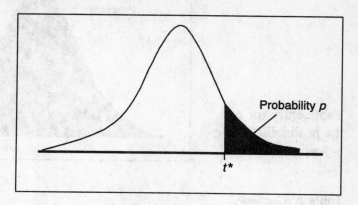

Table entry for p and C is the point t^* with the probability p lying above it and probability C lying between $-t^*$ and t^*.

Probability p

t^*

df	Tail probability p											
	.25	.20	.15	.10	.05	.025	.02	.01	.005	.0025	.001	.0005
1	1.000	1.376	1.963	3.078	6.314	12.71	15.89	31.82	63.66	127.3	318.3	636.6
2	.816	1.061	1.386	1.886	2.920	4.303	4.849	6.965	9.925	14.09	22.33	31.60
3	.765	.978	1.250	1.638	2.353	3.182	3.482	4.541	5.841	7.453	10.21	12.92
4	.741	.941	1.190	1.533	2.132	2.776	2.999	3.747	4.604	5.598	7.173	8.610
5	.727	.920	1.156	1.476	2.015	2.571	2.757	3.365	4.032	4.773	5.893	6.869
6	.718.	906	1.134	1.440	1.943	2.447	2.612	3.143	3.707	4.317	5.208	5.959
7	.711	.896	1.119	1.415	1.895	2.365	2.517	2.998	3.499	4.029	4.785	5.408
8	.706	.889	1.108	1.397	1.860	2.306	2.449	2.896	3.355	3.833	4.501	5.041
9	.703	.883	1.100	1.383	1.833	2.262	2.398	2.821	3.250	3.690	4.297	4.781
10	.700	.879	1.093	1.372	1.812	2.228	2.359	2.764	3.169	3.581	4.144	4.587
11	.697	.876	1.088	1.363	1.796	2.201	2.328	2.718	3.106	3.497	4.025	4.437
12	.695	.873	1.083	1.356	1.782	2.179	2.303	2.681	3.055	3.428	3.930	4.318
13	.694	.870	1.079	1.350	1.771	2.160	2.282	2.650	3.012	3.372	3.852	4.221
14	.692	.868	1.076	1.345	1.761	2.145	2.264	2.624	2.977	3.326	3.787	4.140
15	.691	.866	1.074	1.341	1.753	2.131	2.249	2.602	2.947	3.286	3.733	4.073
16	.690	.865	1.071	1.337	1.746	2.120	2.235	2.583	2.921	3.252	3.686	4.015
17	.689	.863	1.069	1.333	1.740	2.110	2.224	2.567	2.898	3.222	3.646	3.965
18	.688	.862	1.067	1.330	1.734	2.101	2.214	2.552	2.878	3.197	3.611	3.922
19	.688	.861	1.066	1.328	1.729	2.093	2.205	2.539	2.861	3.174	3.579	3.883
20	.687	.860	1.064	1.325	1.725	2.086	2.197	2.528	2.845	3.153	3.552	3.850
21	.686	.859	1.063	1.323	1.721	2.080	2.189	2.518	2.831	3.135	3.527	3.819
22	.686	.858	1.061	1.321	1.717	2.074	2.183	2.508	2.819	3.119	3.505	3.792
23	.685	.858	1.060	1.319	1.714	2.069	2.177	2.500	2.807	3.104	3.485	3.768
24	.685	.857	1.059	1.318	1.711	2.064	2.172	2.492	2.797	3.091	3.467	3.745
25	.684	.856	1.058	1.316	1.708	2.060	2.167	2.485	2.787	3.078	3.450	3.725
26	.684	.856	1.058	1.315	1.706	2.056	2.162	2.479	2.779	3.067	3.435	3.707
27	.684	.855	1.057	1.314	1.703	2.052	2.158	2.473	2.771	3.057	3.421	3.690
28	.683	.855	1.056	1.313	1.701	2.048	2.154	2.467	2.763	3.047	3.408	3.674
29	.683	.854	1.055	1.311	1.699	2.045	2.150	2.462	2.756	3.038	3.396	3.659
30	.683	.854	1.055	1.310	1.697	2.042	2.147	2.457	2.750	3.030	3.385	3.646
40	.681	.851	1.050	1.303	1.684	2.021	2.123	2.423	2.704	2.971	3.307	3.551
50	.679	.849	1.047	1.299	1.676	2.009	2.109	2.403	2.678	2.937	3.261	3.496
60	.679	.848	1.045	1.296	1.671	2.000	2.099	2.390	2.660	2.915	3.232	3.460
80	.678	.846	1.043	1.292	1.664	1.990	2.088	2.374	2.639	2.887	3.195	3.416
100	.677	.845	1.042	1.290	1.660	1.984	2.081	2.364	2.626	2.871	3.174	3.390
1000	.675	.842	1.037	1.282	1.646	1.962	2.056	2.330	2.581	2.813	3.098	3.300
∝	674.	841	1.036	1.282	1.645	1.960	2.054	2.326	2.576	2.807	3.091	3.291
	50%	60%	70%	80%	90%	95%	96%	98%	99%	99.5%	99.8%	99.9%

Confidence level C

TABLE 3: X² CRITICAL VALUES

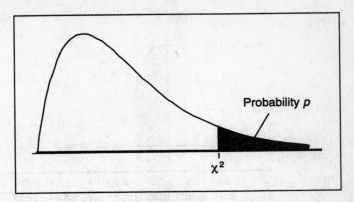

Table entry for p is the point (c^2) with probability p lying above it.

					Tail probability p						
df	.25	.20	.15	.10	.05	.025	.02	.01	.005	.0025	.001
1	1.32	1.64	2.07	2.71	3.84	5.02	5.41	6.63	7.88	9.14	10.83
2	2.77	3.22	3.79	4.61	5.99	7.38	7.82	9.21	10.60	11.98	13.82
3	4.11	4.64	5.32	6.25	7.81	9.35	9.84	11.34	12.84	14.32	16.27
4	5.39	5.99	6.74	7.78	9.49	11.14	11.67	13.28	14.86	16.42	18.47
5	6.63	7.29	8.12	9.24	11.07	12.83	13.39	15.09	16.75	18.39	20.51
6	7.84	8.56	9.45	10.64	12.59	14.45	15.03	16.81	18.55	20.25	22.46
?	9.04	9.80	10.75	12.02	14.07	16.01	16.62	18.48	20.28	22.04	24.32
8	10.22	11.08	12.03	18.86	15.51	17.53	18.17	20.09	21.95	23.77	26.12
9	11.39	12.24	18.29	14.68	16.92	19.02	19.68	21.67	23.59	25.46	27.88
10	12.55	18.44	14.58	15.99	18.31	20.48	21.16	28.21	25.19	27.11	29.59
11	13.70	14.63	15.77	17.28	19.68	21.92	22.62	24.72	26.76	28.73	31.26
12	14.85	15.81	16.99	18.55	21.03	23.34	24.05	26.22	28.30	30.32	32.91
13	15.98	16.98	18.20	19.81	22.36	24.74	25.47	27.69	29.82	31.88	34.53
14	17.12	18.15	19.41	21.06	23.68	26.12	26.87	29.14	31.32	33.43	36.12
15	18.25	19.31	20.60	22.31	25.00	27.49	28.26	30.58	32.80	34.95	37.70
16	19.37	20.47	21.79	23.54	26.80	28.85	29.63	32.00	34.27	36.46	39.25
17	20.49	21.61	22.98	24.77	27.59	80.19	:31.00	33.41	35.72	37.95	40.79
18	21.60	22.76	24.16	25.99	28.87	81.53	32.35	34.81	37.16	39.42	42.31
19	22.72	23.90	25.38	27.20	30.14	82.85	33.69	36.19	38.58	40.88	43.82
20	23.88	25.04	26.50	28.41	31.41	84.17	35.02	37.57	40.00	42.34	45.31
21	24.93	26.17	27.66	29.62	32.67	35.48	36.34	38.93	41.40	43.78	46.80
22	26.04	27.30	28.82	30.81	33.92	36.78	37.66	40.29	42.80	45.20	48.27
23	27.14	28.48	29.98	32.01	35.17	38.08	38.97	41.64	44.18	46.62	49.73
24	28.24	29.55	31.13	33.20	36.42	39.36	40.27	42.98	45.56	48.03	51.18
25	29.34	30.68	32.28	34.38	37.65	40.65	41.57	44.31	46.93	49.44	52.62
26	80.48	81.79	88.48	35.56	38.89	41.92	42.86	45.64	48.29	50.83	54.05
27	31.53	82.91	84.57	36.74	40.11	48.19	44.14	46.96	49.64	52.22	55.48
28	82.62	84.08	85.71	87.92	41.84	44.46	45.42	48.28	50.99	53.59	56.89
29	88.71	85.14	86.85	89.09	42.56	45.72	46.69	49.59	52.34	54.97	58.30
30	84.80	86.25	87.99	40.26	43.77	46.98	47.96	50.89	53.67	56.33	59.70
40	45.62	47.27	49.24	51.81	55.76	59.34	60.44	63.69	66.77	69.70	73.40
50	56.83	58.16	60.85	63.17	67.50	71.42	72.61	76.15	79.49	82.66	86.66
60	66.98	68.97	71.34	74.40	79.08	83.30	84.58	88.38	91.95	95.34	99.61
80	88.13	90.41	93.11	96.58	101.9	106.6	108.1	112.3	116.3	120.1	124.8
100	109.1	111.7	114.7	118.5	124.3	129.6	131.1	135.8	140.2	144.3	149.4

TABLE 4: Area Under the Curve for the Standard Normal Distribution

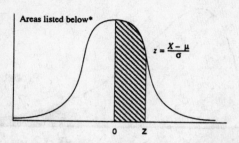

Areas listed below*

$$z = \frac{X - \mu}{\sigma}$$

Z	.00	.01	.02	.03	.04	.05	.06	.07	.08	.09
0.0	.0000	.0040	.0080	.0120	.0160	.0199	.0239	.0279	.0319	.0359
0.1	.0398	.0438	.0478	.0517	.0557	.0596	.0636	.0675	.0714	.0753
0.2	.0793	.0832	.0871	.0910	.0948	.0987	.1026	.1064	.1103	.1141
0.3	.1179	.1217	.1255	.1293	.1331	.1368	.1406	.1443	.1480	.1517
0.4	.1554	.1591	.1628	.1664	.1700	.1736	.1772	.1808	.1844	.1879
0.5	.1915	.1950	.1985	.2019	.2054	.2088	.2123	.2157	.2190	.2224
0.6	.2257	.2291	.2324	.2357	.2389	.2422	.2454	.2486	.2518	.2549
0.7	.2580	.2612	.2642	.2673	.2704	.2734	.2764	.2794	.2823	.2852
0.8	.2881	.2910	.2939	.2967	.2995	.3023	.3051	.3078	.3106	.3133
0.9	.3159	.3186	.3212	.3238	.3264	.3289	.3315	.3340	.3365	.3389
1.0	.3413	.3438	.3461	.3485	.3508	.3531	.3554	.3577	.3599	.3621
1.1	.3643	.3665	.3686	.3708	.3729	.3749	.3770	.3790	.3810	.3830
1.2	.3849	.3869	.3888	.3907	.3925	.3944	.3962	.3980	.3997	.4014
1.3	.4032	.4049	.4066	.4082	.4099	.4115	.4131	.4147	.4162	.4177
1.4	.4192	.4207	.4222	.4236	.4251	.4265	.4279	.4292	.4306	.4319
1.5	.4332	.4345	.4357	.4370	.4382	.4394	.4406	.4418	.4429	.4441
1.6	.4452	.4463	.4474	.4484	.4495	.4505	.4515	.4525	.4535	.4545
1.7	.4554	.4564	.4573	.4582	.4591	.4599	.4608	.4616	.4625	.4633
1.8	.4641	.4649	.4656	.4664	.4671	.4678	.4686	.4693	.4699	.4706
1.9	.4713	.4719	.4726	.4732	.4738	.4744	.4750	.4756	.4761	.4767
2.0	.4772	.4778	.4783	.4788	.4793	.4798	.4803	.4808	.4812	.4817
2.1	.4821	.4826	.4830	.4834	.4838	.4842	.4846	.4850	.4854	.4857
2.2	.4861	.4864	.4868	.4871	.4875	.4878	.4881	.4884	.4887	.4890
2.3	.4893	.4896	.4898	.4901	.4904	.4906	.4909	.4911	.4913	.4916
2.4	.4918	.4920	.4922	.4925	.4927	.4929	.4931	.4932	.4934	.4936
2.5	.4938	.4940	.4941	.4943	.4945	.4946	.4948	.4949	.4951	.4952
2.6	.4953	.4955	.4956	.4957	.4959	.4960	.4961	.4962	.4963	.4964
2.7	.4965	.4966	.4967	.4968	.4969	.4970	.4971	.4972	.4973	.4974
2.8	.4974	.4975	.4976	.4977	.4977	.4978	.4979	.4979	.4980	.4981
2.9	.4981	.4982	.4983	.4983	.4984	.4984	.4985	.4985	.4986	.4986
3.0	.4987									
3.5	.4997									
4.0	.4999									

TABLE 5: Area Under the Curve for the Student's t-Distribution

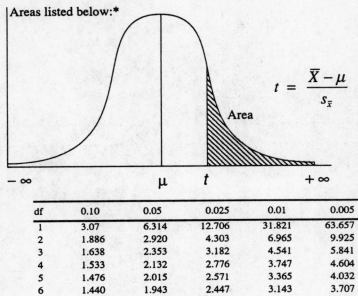

Areas listed below:*

$$t = \frac{\overline{X} - \mu}{s_{\overline{x}}}$$

Area

$-\infty$ μ t $+\infty$

df	0.10	0.05	0.025	0.01	0.005
1	3.07	6.314	12.706	31.821	63.657
2	1.886	2.920	4.303	6.965	9.925
3	1.638	2.353	3.182	4.541	5.841
4	1.533	2.132	2.776	3.747	4.604
5	1.476	2.015	2.571	3.365	4.032
6	1.440	1.943	2.447	3.143	3.707
7	1.415	1.895	2.365	2.998	3.499
8	1.397	1.860	2.306	2.896	3.355
9	1.383	1.833	2.262	2.821	3.250
10	1.372	1.812	2.228	2.764	3.169
11	1.363	1.796	2.201	2.718	3.106
12	1.356	1.782	2.179	2.681	3.055
13	1.350	1.771	2.160	2.650	3.012
14	1.345	1.761	2.145	2.624	2.977
15	1.341	1.753	2.131	2.602	2.947
16	1.337	1.746	2.120	2.583	2.921
17	1.333	1.740	2.110	2.567	2.898
18	1.330	1.734	2.101	2.552	2.878
19	1.328	1.729	2.093	2.539	2.861
20	1.325	1.725	2.086	2.528	2.845
21	1.323	1.721	2.080	2.518	2.831
22	1.321	1.717	2.074	2.508	2.819
23	1.319	1.714	2.069	2.500	2.807
24	1.318	1.711	2.064	2.492	2.797
25	1.316	1.708	2.060	2.485	2.787
26	1.315	1.706	2.056	2.479	2.779
27	1.314	1.703	2.052	2.473	2.771
28	1.313	1.701	2.048	2.467	2.763
29	1.311	1.699	2.045	2.462	2.756
30	1.310	1.697	2.042	2.457	2.750
40	1.303	1.684	2.021	2.423	2.704
60	1.296	1.671	2.000	2.390	2.660
120	1.289	1.658	1.980	2.358	2.617
∞	1.282	1.645	1.960	2.326	2.576

ANSWER SHEETS

AP Statistics
Practice Test 1

1. Ⓐ Ⓑ Ⓒ Ⓓ Ⓔ   13. Ⓐ Ⓑ Ⓒ Ⓓ Ⓔ   25. Ⓐ Ⓑ Ⓒ Ⓓ Ⓔ
2. Ⓐ Ⓑ Ⓒ Ⓓ Ⓔ   14. Ⓐ Ⓑ Ⓒ Ⓓ Ⓔ   26. Ⓐ Ⓑ Ⓒ Ⓓ Ⓔ
3. Ⓐ Ⓑ Ⓒ Ⓓ Ⓔ   15. Ⓐ Ⓑ Ⓒ Ⓓ Ⓔ   27. Ⓐ Ⓑ Ⓒ Ⓓ Ⓔ
4. Ⓐ Ⓑ Ⓒ Ⓓ Ⓔ   16. Ⓐ Ⓑ Ⓒ Ⓓ Ⓔ   28. Ⓐ Ⓑ Ⓒ Ⓓ Ⓔ
5. Ⓐ Ⓑ Ⓒ Ⓓ Ⓔ   17. Ⓐ Ⓑ Ⓒ Ⓓ Ⓔ   29. Ⓐ Ⓑ Ⓒ Ⓓ Ⓔ
6. Ⓐ Ⓑ Ⓒ Ⓓ Ⓔ   18. Ⓐ Ⓑ Ⓒ Ⓓ Ⓔ   30. Ⓐ Ⓑ Ⓒ Ⓓ Ⓔ
7. Ⓐ Ⓑ Ⓒ Ⓓ Ⓔ   19. Ⓐ Ⓑ Ⓒ Ⓓ Ⓔ   31. Ⓐ Ⓑ Ⓒ Ⓓ Ⓔ
8. Ⓐ Ⓑ Ⓒ Ⓓ Ⓔ   20. Ⓐ Ⓑ Ⓒ Ⓓ Ⓔ   32. Ⓐ Ⓑ Ⓒ Ⓓ Ⓔ
9. Ⓐ Ⓑ Ⓒ Ⓓ Ⓔ   21. Ⓐ Ⓑ Ⓒ Ⓓ Ⓔ   33. Ⓐ Ⓑ Ⓒ Ⓓ Ⓔ
10. Ⓐ Ⓑ Ⓒ Ⓓ Ⓔ   22. Ⓐ Ⓑ Ⓒ Ⓓ Ⓔ   34. Ⓐ Ⓑ Ⓒ Ⓓ Ⓔ
11. Ⓐ Ⓑ Ⓒ Ⓓ Ⓔ   23. Ⓐ Ⓑ Ⓒ Ⓓ Ⓔ   35. Ⓐ Ⓑ Ⓒ Ⓓ Ⓔ
12. Ⓐ Ⓑ Ⓒ Ⓓ Ⓔ   24. Ⓐ Ⓑ Ⓒ Ⓓ Ⓔ

Use this page on which to write your free-response questions.
If additional pages are needed, use your own lined paper.

AP Statistics
Practice Test 2

1. Ⓐ Ⓑ Ⓒ Ⓓ Ⓔ
2. Ⓐ Ⓑ Ⓒ Ⓓ Ⓔ
3. Ⓐ Ⓑ Ⓒ Ⓓ Ⓔ
4. Ⓐ Ⓑ Ⓒ Ⓓ Ⓔ
5. Ⓐ Ⓑ Ⓒ Ⓓ Ⓔ
6. Ⓐ Ⓑ Ⓒ Ⓓ Ⓔ
7. Ⓐ Ⓑ Ⓒ Ⓓ Ⓔ
8. Ⓐ Ⓑ Ⓒ Ⓓ Ⓔ
9. Ⓐ Ⓑ Ⓒ Ⓓ Ⓔ
10. Ⓐ Ⓑ Ⓒ Ⓓ Ⓔ
11. Ⓐ Ⓑ Ⓒ Ⓓ Ⓔ
12. Ⓐ Ⓑ Ⓒ Ⓓ Ⓔ

13. Ⓐ Ⓑ Ⓒ Ⓓ Ⓔ
14. Ⓐ Ⓑ Ⓒ Ⓓ Ⓔ
15. Ⓐ Ⓑ Ⓒ Ⓓ Ⓔ
16. Ⓐ Ⓑ Ⓒ Ⓓ Ⓔ
17. Ⓐ Ⓑ Ⓒ Ⓓ Ⓔ
18. Ⓐ Ⓑ Ⓒ Ⓓ Ⓔ
19. Ⓐ Ⓑ Ⓒ Ⓓ Ⓔ
20. Ⓐ Ⓑ Ⓒ Ⓓ Ⓔ
21. Ⓐ Ⓑ Ⓒ Ⓓ Ⓔ
22. Ⓐ Ⓑ Ⓒ Ⓓ Ⓔ
23. Ⓐ Ⓑ Ⓒ Ⓓ Ⓔ
24. Ⓐ Ⓑ Ⓒ Ⓓ Ⓔ

25. Ⓐ Ⓑ Ⓒ Ⓓ Ⓔ
26. Ⓐ Ⓑ Ⓒ Ⓓ Ⓔ
27. Ⓐ Ⓑ Ⓒ Ⓓ Ⓔ
28. Ⓐ Ⓑ Ⓒ Ⓓ Ⓔ
29. Ⓐ Ⓑ Ⓒ Ⓓ Ⓔ
30. Ⓐ Ⓑ Ⓒ Ⓓ Ⓔ
31. Ⓐ Ⓑ Ⓒ Ⓓ Ⓔ
32. Ⓐ Ⓑ Ⓒ Ⓓ Ⓔ
33. Ⓐ Ⓑ Ⓒ Ⓓ Ⓔ
34. Ⓐ Ⓑ Ⓒ Ⓓ Ⓔ
35. Ⓐ Ⓑ Ⓒ Ⓓ Ⓔ

Use this page on which to write your free-response questions.
If additional pages are needed, use your own lined paper.

AP Statistics
Practice Test 3

1. Ⓐ Ⓑ Ⓒ Ⓓ Ⓔ
2. Ⓐ Ⓑ Ⓒ Ⓓ Ⓔ
3. Ⓐ Ⓑ Ⓒ Ⓓ Ⓔ
4. Ⓐ Ⓑ Ⓒ Ⓓ Ⓔ
5. Ⓐ Ⓑ Ⓒ Ⓓ Ⓔ
6. Ⓐ Ⓑ Ⓒ Ⓓ Ⓔ
7. Ⓐ Ⓑ Ⓒ Ⓓ Ⓔ
8. Ⓐ Ⓑ Ⓒ Ⓓ Ⓔ
9. Ⓐ Ⓑ Ⓒ Ⓓ Ⓔ
10. Ⓐ Ⓑ Ⓒ Ⓓ Ⓔ
11. Ⓐ Ⓑ Ⓒ Ⓓ Ⓔ
12. Ⓐ Ⓑ Ⓒ Ⓓ Ⓔ

13. Ⓐ Ⓑ Ⓒ Ⓓ Ⓔ
14. Ⓐ Ⓑ Ⓒ Ⓓ Ⓔ
15. Ⓐ Ⓑ Ⓒ Ⓓ Ⓔ
16. Ⓐ Ⓑ Ⓒ Ⓓ Ⓔ
17. Ⓐ Ⓑ Ⓒ Ⓓ Ⓔ
18. Ⓐ Ⓑ Ⓒ Ⓓ Ⓔ
19. Ⓐ Ⓑ Ⓒ Ⓓ Ⓔ
20. Ⓐ Ⓑ Ⓒ Ⓓ Ⓔ
21. Ⓐ Ⓑ Ⓒ Ⓓ Ⓔ
22. Ⓐ Ⓑ Ⓒ Ⓓ Ⓔ
23. Ⓐ Ⓑ Ⓒ Ⓓ Ⓔ
24. Ⓐ Ⓑ Ⓒ Ⓓ Ⓔ

25. Ⓐ Ⓑ Ⓒ Ⓓ Ⓔ
26. Ⓐ Ⓑ Ⓒ Ⓓ Ⓔ
27. Ⓐ Ⓑ Ⓒ Ⓓ Ⓔ
28. Ⓐ Ⓑ Ⓒ Ⓓ Ⓔ
29. Ⓐ Ⓑ Ⓒ Ⓓ Ⓔ
30. Ⓐ Ⓑ Ⓒ Ⓓ Ⓔ
31. Ⓐ Ⓑ Ⓒ Ⓓ Ⓔ
32. Ⓐ Ⓑ Ⓒ Ⓓ Ⓔ
33. Ⓐ Ⓑ Ⓒ Ⓓ Ⓔ
34. Ⓐ Ⓑ Ⓒ Ⓓ Ⓔ
35. Ⓐ Ⓑ Ⓒ Ⓓ Ⓔ

Use this page on which to write your free-response questions.
If additional pages are needed, use your own lined paper.

AP Statistics
Practice Test 4

1. (A) (B) (C) (D) (E)
2. (A) (B) (C) (D) (E)
3. (A) (B) (C) (D) (E)
4. (A) (B) (C) (D) (E)
5. (A) (B) (C) (D) (E)
6. (A) (B) (C) (D) (E)
7. (A) (B) (C) (D) (E)
8. (A) (B) (C) (D) (E)
9. (A) (B) (C) (D) (E)
10. (A) (B) (C) (D) (E)
11. (A) (B) (C) (D) (E)
12. (A) (B) (C) (D) (E)

13. (A) (B) (C) (D) (E)
14. (A) (B) (C) (D) (E)
15. (A) (B) (C) (D) (E)
16. (A) (B) (C) (D) (E)
17. (A) (B) (C) (D) (E)
18. (A) (B) (C) (D) (E)
19. (A) (B) (C) (D) (E)
20. (A) (B) (C) (D) (E)
21. (A) (B) (C) (D) (E)
22. (A) (B) (C) (D) (E)
23. (A) (B) (C) (D) (E)
24. (A) (B) (C) (D) (E)

25. (A) (B) (C) (D) (E)
26. (A) (B) (C) (D) (E)
27. (A) (B) (C) (D) (E)
28. (A) (B) (C) (D) (E)
29. (A) (B) (C) (D) (E)
30. (A) (B) (C) (D) (E)
31. (A) (B) (C) (D) (E)
32. (A) (B) (C) (D) (E)
33. (A) (B) (C) (D) (E)
34. (A) (B) (C) (D) (E)
35. (A) (B) (C) (D) (E)

Use this page on which to write your free-response questions.
If additional pages are needed, use your own lined paper.

AP Statistics
Practice Test 5

1. (A) (B) (C) (D) (E)
2. (A) (B) (C) (D) (E)
3. (A) (B) (C) (D) (E)
4. (A) (B) (C) (D) (E)
5. (A) (B) (C) (D) (E)
6. (A) (B) (C) (D) (E)
7. (A) (B) (C) (D) (E)
8. (A) (B) (C) (D) (E)
9. (A) (B) (C) (D) (E)
10. (A) (B) (C) (D) (E)
11. (A) (B) (C) (D) (E)
12. (A) (B) (C) (D) (E)

13. (A) (B) (C) (D) (E)
14. (A) (B) (C) (D) (E)
15. (A) (B) (C) (D) (E)
16. (A) (B) (C) (D) (E)
17. (A) (B) (C) (D) (E)
18. (A) (B) (C) (D) (E)
19. (A) (B) (C) (D) (E)
20. (A) (B) (C) (D) (E)
21. (A) (B) (C) (D) (E)
22. (A) (B) (C) (D) (E)
23. (A) (B) (C) (D) (E)
24. (A) (B) (C) (D) (E)

25. (A) (B) (C) (D) (E)
26. (A) (B) (C) (D) (E)
27. (A) (B) (C) (D) (E)
28. (A) (B) (C) (D) (E)
29. (A) (B) (C) (D) (E)
30. (A) (B) (C) (D) (E)
31. (A) (B) (C) (D) (E)
32. (A) (B) (C) (D) (E)
33. (A) (B) (C) (D) (E)
34. (A) (B) (C) (D) (E)
35. (A) (B) (C) (D) (E)

Use this page on which to write your free-response questions.
If additional pages are needed, use your own lined paper.

AP Statistics
Practice Test 6

1. Ⓐ Ⓑ Ⓒ Ⓓ Ⓔ
2. Ⓐ Ⓑ Ⓒ Ⓓ Ⓔ
3. Ⓐ Ⓑ Ⓒ Ⓓ Ⓔ
4. Ⓐ Ⓑ Ⓒ Ⓓ Ⓔ
5. Ⓐ Ⓑ Ⓒ Ⓓ Ⓔ
6. Ⓐ Ⓑ Ⓒ Ⓓ Ⓔ
7. Ⓐ Ⓑ Ⓒ Ⓓ Ⓔ
8. Ⓐ Ⓑ Ⓒ Ⓓ Ⓔ
9. Ⓐ Ⓑ Ⓒ Ⓓ Ⓔ
10. Ⓐ Ⓑ Ⓒ Ⓓ Ⓔ
11. Ⓐ Ⓑ Ⓒ Ⓓ Ⓔ
12. Ⓐ Ⓑ Ⓒ Ⓓ Ⓔ

13. Ⓐ Ⓑ Ⓒ Ⓓ Ⓔ
14. Ⓐ Ⓑ Ⓒ Ⓓ Ⓔ
15. Ⓐ Ⓑ Ⓒ Ⓓ Ⓔ
16. Ⓐ Ⓑ Ⓒ Ⓓ Ⓔ
17. Ⓐ Ⓑ Ⓒ Ⓓ Ⓔ
18. Ⓐ Ⓑ Ⓒ Ⓓ Ⓔ
19. Ⓐ Ⓑ Ⓒ Ⓓ Ⓔ
20. Ⓐ Ⓑ Ⓒ Ⓓ Ⓔ
21. Ⓐ Ⓑ Ⓒ Ⓓ Ⓔ
22. Ⓐ Ⓑ Ⓒ Ⓓ Ⓔ
23. Ⓐ Ⓑ Ⓒ Ⓓ Ⓔ
24. Ⓐ Ⓑ Ⓒ Ⓓ Ⓔ

25. Ⓐ Ⓑ Ⓒ Ⓓ Ⓔ
26. Ⓐ Ⓑ Ⓒ Ⓓ Ⓔ
27. Ⓐ Ⓑ Ⓒ Ⓓ Ⓔ
28. Ⓐ Ⓑ Ⓒ Ⓓ Ⓔ
29. Ⓐ Ⓑ Ⓒ Ⓓ Ⓔ
30. Ⓐ Ⓑ Ⓒ Ⓓ Ⓔ
31. Ⓐ Ⓑ Ⓒ Ⓓ Ⓔ
32. Ⓐ Ⓑ Ⓒ Ⓓ Ⓔ
33. Ⓐ Ⓑ Ⓒ Ⓓ Ⓔ
34. Ⓐ Ⓑ Ⓒ Ⓓ Ⓔ
35. Ⓐ Ⓑ Ⓒ Ⓓ Ⓔ

Use this page on which to write your free-response questions.
If additional pages are needed, use your own lined paper.

REA's Test Preps
The Best in Test Preparation

- REA "Test Preps" are **far more** comprehensive than any other test preparation series
- Each book contains up to **eight** full-length practice exams based on the most recent exams
- **Every** type of question likely to be given on the exams is included
- Answers are accompanied by **full** and **detailed** explanations

REA has published over 60 Test Preparation volumes in several series. They include:

Advanced Placement Exams (APs)
Biology
Calculus AB & Calculus BC
Chemistry
Computer Science
English Language & Composition
English Literature & Composition
European History
Government & Politics
Physics
Psychology
Statistics
Spanish Language
United States History

College-Level Examination Program (CLEP)
American History I
Analysis & Interpretation of Literature
College Algebra
Freshman College Composition
General Examinations
General Examinations Review
Human Growth and Development
Introductory Sociology
Principles of Marketing
Spanish

SAT II: Subject Tests
American History
Biology
Chemistry
English Language Proficiency Test
French

SAT II: Subject Tests (continued)
German
Literature
Mathematics Level IC, IIC
Physics
Spanish
Writing

Graduate Record Exams (GREs)
Biology
Chemistry
Computer Science
Economics
Engineering
General
History
Literature in English
Mathematics
Physics
Political Science
Psychology
Sociology

ACT - American College Testing Assessment

ASVAB - Armed Services Vocational Aptitude Battery

CBEST - California Basic Educational Skills Test

CDL - Commercial Driver's License Exam

CLAST - College Level Academic Skills Test

ELM - Entry Level Mathematics

ExCET - Exam for Certification of Educators in Texas

FE (EIT) - Fundamentals of Engineering Exam

FE Review - Fundamentals of Engineering Review

GED - High School Equivalency Diploma Exam (US & Canadian editions)

GMAT - Graduate Management Admission Test

LSAT - Law School Admission Test

MAT - Miller Analogies Test

MCAT - Medical College Admission Test

MSAT - Multiple Subjects Assessment for Teachers

NJ HSPT- New Jersey High School Proficiency Test

PPST - Pre-Professional Skills Tests

PRAXIS II/NTE - Core Battery

PSAT - Preliminary Scholastic Assessment Test

SAT I - Reasoning Test

SAT I - Quick Study & Review

TASP - Texas Academic Skills Program

TOEFL - Test of English as a Foreign Language

RESEARCH & EDUCATION ASSOCIATION
61 Ethel Road W. • Piscataway, New Jersey 08854
Phone: (908) 819-8880

Please send me more information about your Test Prep Books

Name _____

Address _____

City _____ State _____ Zip _____